Malcolm X

Studies in Critical Social Sciences Book Series

Haymarket Books is proud to be working with Brill Academic Publishers (www.brill.nl) to republish the *Studies in Critical Social Sciences* book series in paperback editions. This peer-reviewed book series offers insights into our current reality by exploring the content and consequences of power relationships under capitalism, and by considering the spaces of opposition and resistance to these changes that have been defining our new age. Our full catalog of *SCSS* volumes can be viewed at https://www.haymarketbooks.org/series_collections/4-studies-in-critical-social-sciences.

Series Editor
David Fasenfest, Wayne State University

Editorial Board
Eduardo Bonilla-Silva (Duke University)
Chris Chase-Dunn (University of California–Riverside)
William Carroll (University of Victoria)
Raewyn Connell (University of Sydney)
Kimberlé W. Crenshaw (University of California–LA, and Columbia University)
Heidi Gottfried (Wayne State University)
Karin Gottschall (University of Bremen)
Mary Romero (Arizona State University)
Alfredo Saad Filho (University of London)
Chizuko Ueno (University of Tokyo)
Sylvia Walby (Lancaster University)

MALCOLM X

From Political Eschatology to Religious Revolutionary

Edited by
DUSTIN J. BYRD
SEYED JAVAD MIRI

Haymarket Books
Chicago, IL

First published in 2016 by Brill Academic Publishers, The Netherlands.
© 2016 Koninklijke Brill NV, Leiden, The Netherlands

Published in paperback in 2017 by
Haymarket Books
P.O. Box 180165
Chicago, IL 60618
773-583-7884
www.haymarketbooks.org

ISBN: 978-1-60846-808-9

Trade distribution:
In the U.S. through Consortium Book Sales, www.cbsd.com
In the UK, Turnaround Publisher Services, www.turnaround-uk.com
In Canada, Publishers Group Canada, www.pgcbooks.ca
All other countries, Ingram Publisher Services International, ips_intlsales@ingramcontent.com

Cover design by Jamie Kerry of Belle Étoile Studios and Ragina Johnson.

This book was published with the generous support of Lannan Foundation and the Wallace Action Fund.

Entered into digital printing, January 2018.

Library of Congress Cataloging-in-Publication Data is available.

The year 2015 marked 50 years after the tragic and unjust assassination of Malcolm X, El-hajj Malik El-Shabazz. Although the man has departed, the vision of a just society that he embraced while on pilgrimage to Mecca remains a potent symbol for what is still possible. This book is dedicated to the memory of his life, the memory of his work, and to those who continue to strive for such a just and equal society.

∴

Contents

List of Contributors   IX

1   Introduction   1
    Dustin J. Byrd and Seyed Javad Miri

2   Malcolm X as Religious Peripatetic   5
    William David Hart

3   On the Dialectical Evolution of Malcolm X's Anti-Capitalist Critique:
    Interrogating His Political Philosophy of Black Nationalism   37
    John H. McClendon III and Stephen C. Ferguson II

4   Malcolm X and Revolutionary Religion: Christianity, Islam and their
    Emancipatory Potentials   91
    Dustin J. Byrd

5   Malcolm X and the Meccan Epistle   131
    Seyed Javad Miri

6   Malcolm X – A Martyr of Freedom   141
    Rudolf J. Siebert

7   "The Enemy of My Enemy": Malcolm X and the Legacy of John
    Brown   179
    Louis A. DeCaro, Jr.

8   Malcolm X, Alatas and Critical Theory   195
    Syed Farid Alatas

9   Malcolm X: Message to Humanity   211
    John Andrew Morrow

10 Malik al-Shabazz's Practice of Self-Liberation 227
   Emin Poljarevic

11 From Malcolm X to Generation Y: The African American Muslim Community after 1965 252
   Bethany Beyyette

12 From Hell to Heaven: The Malcolm X Narrative of Muslim Artists
   The Meaning of his Life in Relation to the Doctrine of Predestination for British and American Performing Artists in the 21st Century 273
   Yolanda van Tilborgh

13 Rationalization of Malcolm X's Religious Understandings, Political Perspectives and Organizational Objectives 321
   Nuri Tinaz

Index 367

List of Contributors

Syed Farid Alatas
is Associate Professor of Sociology at the National University of Singapore. He obtained his Ph.D. in Sociology from the Johns Hopkins University and lectured at the University of Malaya in the Department of Southeast Asian Studies prior to his appointment at Singapore. His earlier books include Alternative Discourse in Asian Social Science: Responses to Eurocentrism (Sage, 2006) and An Islamic Perspective on the Commitment to Inter-Religious Dialogue, (Institute of Advanced Islamic Studies Malaysia, 2008). He has also edited Asian Inter-Faith Dialogue: Perspectives on Religion, Education and Social Cohesion (RIMA and the World Bank, 2003) and Asian Anthropology, with Jan van Bremen and Eyal Ben-Ari (Routledge, 2005). As part of his interest in creating alternative social sciences, he has recently published two books on Ibn Khaldun: Ibn Khaldun (Oxford University Press, 2013) and Applying Ibn Khaldun: The Recovery of a Lost Tradition in Sociology (Routledge, 2014). He is currently preparing a book manuscript for publication on the social theology of Bediuzzaman Said Nursi and is co-authoring another book on alternative social theory (with Vineeta Sinha).

Dustin J. Byrd
is currently Assistant Professor of Humanities at Olivet College in Olivet, Michigan, where he teaches religion, philosophy, western history and Arabic. He studied Comparative Religion, at Western Michigan University, where he concentrated on the Critical Theory, Islam, Christian-Muslim Relations and philosophy of religion. He later obtained his Ph.D. from Michigan State University in continental philosophy, specializing in the Critical Theory of Religion. He is especially interested in the work of the Frankfurt School and its application to Islam and the Muslim world. He has recently published his book *A Critique of Ayn Rand's Philosophy of Religion: The Gospel According to John Galt*, with Lexington Books (2015), in addition to his first book *Ayatollah Khomeini and the Anatomy of the Islamic Revolution in Iran: Towards a Theory of Prophetic Charisma* (2011), published by University Press of America. He is currently writing a book on Islam in the post-Secular society.

Bethany Beyyette
is Collegiate Assistant Professor at University of Maryland University College-Europe. She is presently at the forefront of academic research associated with non-Arab American Islamic identities. Her research focuses on the experiences

of American converts to Islam and their descendants, studying the ways ethnically different American Muslims conceptualize, enact, and negotiate Islamic practices and roles in contrast to traditionalist interpretations of individual (e.g., speech, greetings, dress, etc.) and group (e.g., membership roles and expectations) practices. Bethany is currently working to expand her research on Muslim identities into Germany, focusing on interrelations between co-religionists of different racial backgrounds.

Louis A. DeCaro Jr.
is associate professor of church history at Alliance Theological Seminary in New York City. He holds a Ph.D. from New York University, and has written a number of books and articles on the African American Muslim leader, Malcolm X. However, since the late 1990s, he has been an enthusiastic student of the life and letters of John Brown the abolitionist. His first two biographical works on Brown are "Fire from the Midst of You": A Religious Life of John Brown (NYU Press, 2002), and John Brown – the Cost of Freedom (International Publishers, 2007), the latter including twenty documents from Brown's hand, some of which have never been published. His latest are Freedom's Dawn: The Last Days of John Brown in Virginia, and an accompanying collection, John Brown Speaks: Letters and Statements from (Rowman & Littlefield Publishers). Lou has also contributed to a number of publications, including The Afterlife of John Brown (Palgrave Macmillan, 2005), and a forthcoming collection, The Fluid Frontier: Slavery, Resistance and the Underground Railroad Along the Detroit River. In 2007, he stood on behalf of John Brown's induction into the National Abolition Hall of Fame in Peterboro, N.Y., and has spoken in a variety of John Brown programs in the United States and Canada. In 2009, Lou was a keynote speaker at events in Philadelphia, Pennsylvania, New Haven, Connecticut, and Lake Placid, New York in conjunction with the John Brown/Harper's Ferry Raid Sesquicentennial. His blog, "John Brown the Abolitionist," has been published since late 2005. Visit it at http://abolitionist-john-brown.blogspot.com

Stephen C. Ferguson II
is an associate professor at North Carolina A & T State University. He holds a Bachelors degree in History and Philosophy with a minor in Black Studies from the University of Missouri-Columbia and the MA and doctorate in Philosophy from the University of Kansas. Ferguson's areas of expertise include Africana philosophy, philosophy of sports and social-political philosophy. He has served as the co-editor of the *Oxford Handbook on World Philosophy* (Oxford January 2011). He is author of *Philosophy of African American Studies: Nothing Left*

of Blackness (Palgrave, 2015) and *Beyond The White Shadow: Philosophy, Sports and the African American Experience*, which he co-authored with John McClendon. He has published in *Socialism & Democracy, Cultural Logic, The Black Scholar* among others.

William David Hart

(Ph.D., Princeton University, 1994) is professor of religious studies at Macalester College. A "critical theorist of religion," interested in the construction of religion and its ethical-political uses, Hart is the author of *Edward Said and the Religious Effects of Culture* (Cambridge, 2000), Black Religion: *Malcolm X, Julius Lester, and Jan Willis* (Palgrave, 2008), and *Afro-Eccentricity: Beyond the Standard Narrative of Black Religion* (2011).

John H. McClendon III

is a professor in the Department of Philosophy at Michigan State University. He is the author of *C.L.R. James's Notes on Dialectics: Left-Hegelianism or Marxism-Leninism* (Lexington Books, 2005) and *Beyond the White Shadow: Philosophy, Sports, and the African-American Experience*, which he co-authored with Dr. Stephen C Ferguson II (Kendall Hunt, 2012). He is Co-editor of the *American Philosophical Association Newsletter on Philosophy of the Black Experience*, a Consulting Editor of the *Journal of the American Philosophical Association*, Advisory Board Member of *Blackpast.Org*, serves on the Editorial Advisory Board of the journal, *Cultural Logic* and the Editorial Board of the *Journal on African Philosophy*.

Seyed Javad Miri

is an Irano-Swedish professor of sociology and history of religions at the Institute of Humanities and Cultural Studies in Tehran, Iran. He has written over 40 books in English, Russian, Swedish and Persian. His recent books are *Reimagining Malcolm X: Street Thinker versus Homo Academicus* published by University Press of America. Professor Miri has taught and lived in more than 74 countries at various universities such as Chita State University in Siberia, Russia and Harbin University in China.

John Andrew Morrow

is an intellectual adventurer who focuses on Hispanic, Native, and Islamic Studies. He is the author, editor, and translator of over a dozen books, including *The Covenants of the Prophet Muhammad with the Christians of the World, Religion and Revolution: Spiritual and Political Islam in Ernesto Cardenal*, and *The Encyclopedia of Islamic Herbal Medicine*, among others. He has published many articles on Malcolm X in cultural magazines, peer-reviewed journals, and scholarly books. He has worked for many major universities, including the University of Virginia's Semester at Sea program, and is currently a Full Professor of Foreign Languages at Ivy Tech-Northeast.

Emin Poljarevic
a Visiting Scholar at the Department of Politics and International Relations, University of Edinburgh with a Ph.D. from the European University Institute in Florence, Italy. He is a political sociologist with a special interest in studying Islamist social mobilization and social motivations of Muslim activists in Middle East and North Africa. His publications range from articles on social impact of Islamism, especially Salafism, and Muslim social activism to texts related to the impact of social agency in mobilization processes and identity (re)formation among ethnic and religious minorities.

Rudolf J. Siebert
was born in Frankfurt a.m., Germany. He has studied history, philology, philosophy, psychology, sociology and theology at the University of Frankfurt, the University of Mainz, the University of Munster and the Catholic University of America, Washington D.C. Siebert created and is a specialist in the Critical Theory of Religion, or Dialectical Religiology. He has taught, lectured and published widely in Western and Eastern Europe, the United States, Canada and Japan. He is currently Professor of religion and society and the director of the Center for Humanistic Future Studies at Western Michigan University, and director of the international course on the "Future of Religion" in the Inter-University Centre, Dubrovnik, Croatia, and the director of the international course of "Religion and Civil Society" in Yalta, Crimea, Russia. He recently published the three-volume *Manifesto of the Critical Theory of Society and Religion: The Wholly Other, Liberation, Happiness and the Rescue of the Hopeless*, with Brill Publishers, 2010.

Nuri Tinaz
holds a Ph.D. in sociology from the University of Warwick, UK, where he worked over two years as a post-doctoral The Leverhulme Research Fellow. He later worked as an affiliated lecturer at Department of Sociology, Faculty of Social and Political Sciences, University of Cambridge, 2002–2005. He participated in Routledge book project on Islam (Islam and its Critical Concepts, 4. Vols) with Professor Bryan S. Turner at Cambridge University, 2001–2002. He moved to Turkey in 2005 to take up a Research Fellowship post at Centre for Islamic Studies (ISAM) in Istanbul, Turkey, 2005–2011. In 2008, he won the

Fulbright Scholarship and taught at Utah State University and gave courses and seminar series at several universities on Islam and Muslims in the USA. Later, he worked at International Balkan University, Skopje, Macedonia, 2009-2011. He is currently working as Associate Professor of Sociology at Department of Sociology, Marmara University. He is a chief academic adviser of Centre for Values Education, the Ensar Foundation, on its academic programs – seminars, workshops, conferences and seminary courses. His interests cover in the areas of sociology of religion, ethnicity and migration, and social, ethnic, nationalist and religious movements, and New Religious Movements (NRMs) and Islamic movements and communities in the West both the USA and EU, religious communities in Turkey, Islamophobia, media and religion, portrayal and coverage of Islam and Muslim in Media, Muslim Use of media & internet, digital and social media.

He is currently working to turn his thesis into a book: *The Journey of African Americans to Islam; a Sociological Analysis (the Nation of Islam) in US*, to be published by American University Press.

Yolanda Van Tilborgh
who graduated cum laude at the University of Amsterdam in Cultural Sociology, has been working on her dissertation *Singing or Sinning* since 2009, exploring the transnational field of Muslim performing artists in hip-hop, spoken word, comedy, theatre and contemporary art in the United States and the United Kingdom. Partly funded by the NWO, the Netherlands Organization for Scientific Research, this study on if and how Muslim performing artists with different ethnic and religious backgrounds synthesize their ideals toward art and Islam in their careers as authentic Muslims and distinct artists has respectively taken place at Radboud University Nijmegen (Religious Studies) and the University of Amsterdam (Cultural Sociology). Besides writing on the much-discussed relation between culture and Islam, Van Tilborgh is author of *Wij zijn Nederland, moslima's over Ayaan Hirsi Ali* (*We are the Netherlands, Muslimas on Ayaan Hirsi Ali*), which analyzes the debate on Islam in the Dutch media in comparison to discursive strategies used by various Muslim women to cope with public criticism of Islam by Ayaan Hirsi Ali after the turn of the century.

CHAPTER 1

Introduction

Dustin J. Byrd and Seyed Javad Miri

Malcolm X relates in his autobiography the frustration he felt when traveling to various parts of the Muslim world. While there, he was often asked about why the 'Muslims' in America believed such erroneous claims taught by Elijah Muhammad, especially 'Yacub's History' and the idea that Muslims do not believe in an afterlife. Malcolm's response was acerbic, "I reminded them," he wrote, "that it was their fault, since they themselves hadn't done enough to make real Islam known in the West. Their silence left a vacuum into which any religious faker could step and mislead our people" (Malcolm X, 1992: 194). The problem for the contemporary is no longer whether or not Elijah Muhammad or the Nation of Islam are teaching erroneous doctrine, but whether Malcolm X is remembered, studied and is his teaching fulfilled. We are facing a younger generation that has very little exposure to Malcolm X, let alone the liberational thought he contributed to. The *zeitgeist* of individualistic entertainment, which allows no space for critical philosophy and radical praxis on any meaningful level, threatens to dissolve Malcolm's work into 'interesting history,' which excludes him from contemporary relevance. The task therefore is similar to the one that Malcolm highlighted in his autobiography; it is the responsibility for scholars, activists and followers of Malcolm X, regardless of whether they are Muslim or not, to bring his thought to the next generation, so that it is not forgotten, and the radical vision of equality and justice he pursued in life survives his death. Because the social, economic and political conditions of modern society call for a Malcolm X, he must be taught.

Yet whenever scholars, activists and revolutionaries turn their attention to the study of Malcolm X, they find themselves intractably caught between two equally impelling imperatives. The first is that Malcolm X and the meaning of his thought and praxis should never be forgotten. For many, forgetting him is simply unthinkable, as Malcolm X continues to be a foundational influence within their intellectual, spiritual and political lives, and is therefore no more forgettable than one's own name. However, as impossible as it may seem to some, Ilyasah Shabazz, the third daughter of Malcolm X, has sounded the alarm. After watching the second inauguration of President Barack Obama, she began to wonder if her father was "being written out of history" (Bartlett, 2015). In our post-9/11 society, where the popular image of Muslims is unjustly fused with the image of airliners crashing into skyscrapers, the mass murder of Christians and Yazidis in the Middle East, as well as the barbaric beheadings of civilians by ISIS in the aftermath of Bush's war in Iraq, Malcolm X, the Muslim revolutionary activist, has receded behind the dominant hatred and/or fear of Muslims in contemporary society. Additionally, it has become an all-too frequent mantra of the latest generation that 'racism no longer exists' in America and therefore what Malcolm X had to say about race and religion is too passé to take seriously. Furthermore, it is difficult for many Americans to admit that one of their greatest minds, who bravely faced the viciousness of American bigotry, left Christianity and embraced Islam, the religion of the 'terrorists.' Even President Obama, who wrote about the lasting affects Malcolm's "blunt poetry" had upon his own life, felt compelled to display a bust of Dr. Martin Luther King Jr. as opposed to Malcolm X in the oval office (Bartlett, 2015; Obama, 1995: 131). Malcolm X was simply not acceptable in the most powerful halls of Washington D.C., but nor did he ever want to be. It seems to many, including Malcolm's own daughter, that history is unjustly leaving her father behind. In light of this possibility, our imperative has become thus: to never forget Malcolm X and what he fought and died for and to continue to work on behalf of his vision for a more peaceful and just society.

Although it is difficult to understand the motives of those who would untether Malcolm X from history and allow him to drift into the vacuousness of the forgotten, there are others who are merely afraid we speak too much of Malcolm X. Although their love for him goes unquestioned, they believe that too much talking about him diminishes his significance, placates his fire and dilutes his prophetic nature. In a 2000 conversation with Ossie Davis, who delivered the eulogy at Malcolm's funeral, the famous actor and dear friend of Malcolm said that "if you talk too much about somebody, you will ultimately destroy their meaning" (Davis, 2000: 14). The fear is that if Malcolm becomes too "commonplace," if we become too accustomed to him being with us and in our lives, then the uncomfortable truths he so forcefully spoke will lose their critical potency, and his bitter truth-telling will no longer disturb our complacent sensibilities. If spoken of too often, Malcolm becomes irrelevant to our contemporary times, being quietly absorbed into popular "culture"; "culture" being what the philosopher Slavoj Žižek often describes as "what we do but no longer take seriously." Therefore, the second imperative we face in our studies of Malcolm X is to resist what Davis warned us about; to lose Malcolm through our own linguistic domestication and academic pacification of him; to make him into a powerless historical artifact; to petrify him within his own times; or to mistakenly focus an inordinate amount of time of "historical speculation" over issues that simply are not essential to understanding the his religio-political mission. Although it is easy to do so, we cannot smother Malcolm X with our gratitude and love for him.

Therefore, we must persevere in taking Malcolm X seriously, to expand upon his thought, to return to him when the antagonisms of racism, class divisions, and Islamophobia infect our body-politic, and to continually rejuvenate the spirit of resistance that he embodied. To not study Malcolm X, or to not talk about his life and thought is to rob the world of one of its most powerful and prophetic voices, precisely at a time when it's in desperate need for such critical voices. Additionally, to allow him to be written out of history is to abandon the very world which Malcolm fought to bring into existence. The vision of a world reconciled, where the antagonisms of race, class, gender, etc., no longer animate our society, stands on the backs of men and women like Malcolm X, who never wilted in the face of entrenched opposition. The scholars represented in this book wish not only to remember Malcolm X, but to augment his memory by continuing to develop his critique of a brutal and unjust world; to advance on the battlefield against the antagonistic society which expresses itself in racial superiority, greed, and hatred for the other, and to abate, arrest and negate the world that abuses, rapes and discards those it finds unworthy of moral consideration. In other words, it is imperative to study Malcolm X and other voices of resistance now more than ever, as the conditions that created the need for such voices continues to advance. The "globalization of indifference" and the "economy that kills," which the Latin American Pope Francis often speaks of, creates ever-more victims in the name of prosperity and progress (Pope Francis, 2013). Unfortunately, the same brutal logic of domination animates the struggle for justice in the global south today just as it did – and still does – in the United States during Malcolm's life; the reality of which he came to realize as he traveled abroad in the last years of his life. Such a situation cannot go unopposed, and thus our return to and invocation of Malcolm X.

The scholars represented in this volume come from various backgrounds. Some are sociologists and historians, while others are theologians and philosophers; they live and work in North America, Europe, the Middle East and South East Asia, and teach at some of the finest institutions of higher learning. Together they give us some of the most compelling reasons why Malcolm X is relevant to our world today; why he *must* be studied, spoke of, debated and advanced, and why his religious faith, coupled with his prophetic way-of-being in the world, shed a new light on what the religion of Islam is capable of when its *humanistic* spirit is brought to the forefront of its praxis. Malcolm X is the finest example of both Islam and the African-American community. Unencumbered by fanatic dogmatism, fundamentalism and tribalism, Islam is capable of motivating humanity to strive for a more just and peaceful world, just as Prophet Muhammad had done in Arabia, while African-American resistance to American dehumanization and unmitigated violence (both psychological and physical), and its ability to rise above the ugliness of white supremacy, congealed in the ferocity of Malcolm's words and deeds. Embodied in one man, we find the prophetic spirit of both Islam and those who were martyred for African-American emancipation and freedom.

We think Malcolm X is not only important as a historical figure who could inspire generations to come but his intellectual significance is an issue which we should also reflect upon in a profound fashion. Mere historical accounts of Malcolm X that are prevalent in academia tend to ignore the theoretical importance of his work. We think it is important to realize that post-racial theories without his contributions would be deeply incomplete. In other words, if we are serious about overcoming the 'cancer of racism' or the fundamentals of unjust system of capitalism in the world, we need to turn to Malcolm X in conjunction with others, such as Ali Shariati and Frantz Fanon, as they provide us with alternative theoretical trajectories. Of course, this is not a call to adore Malcolm X but rather it is an attempt to revitalize the possibilities of a Malcolmian perspective in the context of critical social theory. To state it differently, we reject the idea that Malcolm X is passé; rather his corpus of thought illuminates alternative possibilities which may appear in the future of humanity if we are serious about curing the 'social cancers' which have afflicted the soul of humankind.

Bibliography

Bartlett, Karen. "Why Malcolm X is Getting Written Out of History." *Newsweek*. February 20, 2015. http://www.newsweek.com/2015/02/27/i-worry-my-father-being-written-out-history-307941.html.

Davis, Ossie. "A Conservation with Ossie Davis." *Souls* 2, no. 3 (2000): 14–16.

Pope Francis. *Evangelii Gaudium*. Washington D.C.: United States Conference of Catholic Bishops, 2013.

Malcolm X. *The Autobiography of Malcolm X as told to Alex Haley*. New York: First Ballantine Books, 1992.

CHAPTER 2

Malcolm X as Religious Peripatetic

William David Hart

Malcolm X was a religious peripatetic. He traveled within and among religious traditions; he wondered as he wandered. The metaphors of wandering and wondering may be a good way of getting our arms around his religious itinerary. He donned these traditions like garments. Some he wore loosely, others tightly; their relative fit, often a retrospective affair governed by his present commitments, sympathies, and antipathies. The autobiographical X and, perhaps, the biographical one as well, staged an intra-religious war among various iterations of himself: Baptist, Adventist, Pentecostal, atheist, Nationalist Islam, Sunni Islam, and post-dogmatic, ecumenical advocate of black unity rooted in the Garveyite spiritual commonwealth. Using the metaphors of 'wandering' and 'wondering' and the concept of religious peripatetic, I will explore various perspectives on Malcolm X's itinerary: the religion as a hustle thesis; the religion as mask thesis; declension and ascension narratives; the inter-religious polemic that accompanied his embrace of Islam, and the intra-religious polemic that characterized his retrospective view of Nationalist Islam. I shall argue that Malcolm's Nation of Islam phase represented a frontal challenge to the assumptions that define the Christendom-derived modern category of religion.

Malcolm's Childhood Religious World

Malcolm X does not provide much information about his childhood religiosity. His account is essentially restricted to spare observations in the first two chapters of the *Autobiography*. So I will take the liberty of quoting these passages at length. Regarding early childhood images of his father that he still remembered, he remarks:

> One [image] was his role as a Baptist preacher. He never pastored in any regular church of his own; he was always a "visiting preacher." I remember especially his favorite sermon: "That little *black* train is a-comin' ... and you better get all your business right!" I guess this also fit his association with the back-to-Africa movement, with Marcus Garvey's "Black Train Homeward." My brother Philbert, the one just older than me, loved

church, but it confused and amazed me. I would sit goggle-eyed at my father jumping and shouting as he preached, with the congregation jumping and shouting behind him, their souls and bodies devoted to singing and praying. Even at that young age, I just couldn't believe in the Christian concept of Jesus as someone divine.

MALCOLM X, 1965: 7

Regarding his mother's attraction to Seventh-day Adventism, he remarks:

It is my belief that what mostly influenced her was that they had even more diet restrictions than she always had taught and practiced with us. Like us, they were against eating rabbit and pork; they followed the Mosaic dietary laws. They ate nothing of the flesh without a split hoof, or that didn't chew a cud. We began to go with my mother to the Adventist meeting further out in the country. For us children, I know that the main attraction was the good food they served. But we listened too. There were a handful of Negroes, from small towns in the area, but I would say that it was ninety-nine percent white. The Adventist felt that we were living at the end of time, that the world was soon coming to an end.

MALCOLM X, 1965: 21

Regarding his religious life with his foster family, he remarks:

The Gohnnases were very religious people. Big Boy and I attended church with them. They were sanctified Holy Rollers now. The preachers and congregations jumped even higher and shouted even louder than the Baptists I had known. They sang at the top of their lungs and swayed back and forth and cried and moaned and beat on tambourines and chanted. It was spooky, with ghosts and spirituals and "ha'nts" seeming to be in the very atmosphere when finally we all came out of the church, going back home.

MALCOLM X, 1965: 24

These passages contain virtually everything Malcolm X has to say about his childhood religious world. His major biographers have not succeeded in supplementing the documentary record; they have not discovered significant non-autobiographical sources or obtained new insights from interviews with people who knew Malcolm as a child. As interpreters, we are equally on all fours. We are pretty much where X's autobiographical account leaves us. Putting flesh on a bare bones account requires a judicious use of inference. If we take the account that Malcolm provides in these passages at face value, then we learn several things. His father was a Baptist preacher, his mother, a Seventh-day Adventist; he never believed that Jesus was divine, found church both amazing and confusing, and encountered Pentecostalism as a foster child. To this list, I add a matter not covered in the quoted material: there was inter-religious conflict between the parents (Malcolm X, 1965: 10–12). Of all major biographers, Louis DeCaro is the most attentive to Malcolm X's religious life. He provides a sensitive inferential account of X's childhood religious life while correcting what he regards as errors in most versions. He contests the claim that Malcolm's father was a Baptist preacher and questions the authenticity of Malcolm's Christianity (DeCaro, 1996: 50, 52). In arguing that X misremembers his early childhood, DeCaro relies on the recollections of Malcolm's older brother Wilfred.[1] Since he was older, it is plausible that he was better placed to understand their father's actual status and that X confused his father's presence in various pulpits on behalf of the Universal Negro Improvement Association with the role of a Baptist preacher. This is certainly a plausible interpretation. But aside from Wilfred's emphatic claim, DeCaro does not provide evidence for choosing that over Malcolm's account. Beyond the paucity of evidence, DeCaro's fudges the matter when he remarks that "the Little family was never given to traditional Baptist beliefs." Here "traditional" does the work that a forthright claim that the Little family were not practicing Baptists would do. Baptist beliefs are not uniform (nor are beliefs definitive of religious affiliation and commitment); so what constitutes traditional beliefs is a controversial question that cannot be answered by fiat. Equally important, it is not clear to me, as a scholar, that I should baptize, pun intended, a partisan account of a particular religious tradition. I will let the Baptists sort that out among themselves. Among Baptists, practices of calling, recognizing, endorsing, and ordaining clergy can be extremely informal and idiosyncratic to a particular church. (Consider this anecdote: during the 1970's at Antioch Missionary Baptist Church in Phoenix, Arizona, my childhood church, a fellow joined one Sunday, acknowledged his call to the ministry the following Sunday, and preached a trial sermon shortly after. This phenomenon is not unusual in black Baptists churches. And this is especially true in Baptist churches where the level of educational attainment is low.) Again, Wilfred Little's recollection is plausible and may very well be true. Based on this information alone, however, there is no strong reason to accept his claim regarding Earl Little's preacherly

---

1   Jan Carew relies on the same remark and draws the same conclusion: "He was, Wilfred declared emphatically, a Garveyite activist whom sympathetic Black ministers allowed to address their congregations from time to time." Jan Carew, *Ghost in Our Blood: With Malcolm X in Africa, England, and the Caribbean* (Chicago: Lawrence Hill Books, 1994), x.

bona fides over Malcolm's claim that his father was a Baptist preacher. If we do accept Wilfred Little's claim, then it only enhances a point that I will develop extensively latter: Garveyite spirituality irradiated the conventional forms of religiosity that X inhabited. A final point: there is certainly no good reason to accept DeCaro's narrative intent which casts shade on Earl Little's Christianity and thus undermines the rhetorical power of Malcolm X's anti-Christian narrative. I make the same general claim regarding Malcolm's own Christianity. When DeCaro suggests that X was not really a Christian, he employs normative criteria, such as notions of authenticity and orthodoxy, that I find suspect.

Like most people, Malcolm did not choose his childhood religious life. He parents socialized him into that life, creating the very possibility of and, perhaps, canalizing his adult choices. As a religious subject, the choices of the child are constrained by circumstances she does not choose. Malcolm was thrown into his childhood religious world by the contingencies of birth and history. This is what we would expect in any account of a person's childhood religiosity. Malcolm's childhood religious world was complex: a black Baptist component, enveloped within a Garveyite spiritual commonwealth (I'll have more to say about this later), an Adventist component, and a Holiness Pentecostal experience. Using a travel metaphor, we might say that Malcolm, as a child, moved from one *georeligious* location to another. Without denying the fluidity among them, Malcolm inhabited different worlds, diverse pieces of imaginative geography with dissimilar relations to 'church and state.' Constitutionally, there is no established church in the United States, which is widely interpreted to mean that state and church (and its non-Christian analogues) are separate; that the state should not invest a particular religious tradition and institution with special powers or exemptions; and that 'church and state,' where possible, should avoid poaching the territory of the other. The fact of disestablishment, however, does not mean that there is not a *deep church*, that is, a set of Christian assumptions that structure interactions between state and religious actors. It prefigures the kind of answers that one can give to questions such as 'Can religion be political?' and 'Can a religion be a nation?' At my former academic institution, the University of North Carolina Greensboro, the 'spring holiday' just happens to coincide with Good Friday on the Christian calendar. Thus the university, which lies in a Protestant evangelical 'Bible belt' state, observes a Christian holy day without officially doing so. This is an example of the *deep church* at work; this structuring work eludes the reach of constitutional disestablishment and, in fact, provides its very foundation. Malcolm's entire religious life, especially his membership in the Nation of Islam, was subject to the politics of the deep church.

A Protestant consensus defined Malcolm's childhood religious world by rank-ordering various expressions of Christianity according to what its proponents regarded as fidelity to and deviation from orthodox doctrine. One sees shades of this consensus in DeCaro's skeptical account of Malcolm X's Christianity. Anthony A. Hoekema's 1963 book *The Four Major Cults: Christian Science, Jehovah's Witnesses, Mormonism, Seventh-day Adventism* expressed what was by then an unquestioned consensus. As he remarks on the very first page of this text: "One of the main purposes of this book will be to expose the pernicious anti-Christian teachings which the cults are disseminating throughout the world today" (Hoekema, 1963: 1). Hoekema writes with the confidence of a cultural consensus. While the term 'cult' is not invidious within the sociology of religion, Hoekema clearly expresses the popular association of cult with 'bad,' defective, inferior: as a perverse or faux version of religion. This consensus was in place even as Will Herberg published his influential study: *Protestant, Catholic, Jew* in 1955 and, of course, much earlier, extending back to the very founding of the nation. This title expresses a desire more than it describes sociological facts on the ground. Throughout his life, Malcolm X inhabited religious worlds that the majority culture regarded as deviant if not suspect. Within the context of these overlapping normal/deviant perspectives, black Christianity is deviant in relation to white Christianity; Pentecostals deviate from the propriety of the black Methodist and Baptist mainstream; Islam is deviant with respect to Christianity; nationalists Islam deviates from Sunni Islam; and, in the background of every geo-religious location X inhabited, the deviance of Garveyite spirituality.

Malcolm's Adult Religious World

Malcolm approaches his life like a traveler. Through the mediations of Alex Haley, he presents a travelogue of his life. I wish to play a bit with this wandering/wondering couplet. While one suspects that there has always been some ability to move among solidarities, affinity groups, and identities, the processes of space-time distantiation and disembedding that Anthony Giddens identifies as consequences of modernity renders these kinds of movement and cultural experimentation more common.[2] Modernity disorders and re-orders tradition. American religious proliferation and creativity, including the Nation of Islam, are consequences of the modernity that Giddens describes. The

---

2   Anthony Giddens.

Nation of Islam is a distinctive form of 'traveling religion.'[3] It was a religion suitable to a religious traveler such as Malcolm X. Lest I get ahead of myself. Let me note that there was no straight line from Malcolm's childhood Christianity to his adult life as a Muslim. After the death of his father, illness of his mother, and family decline, Garveyism as the organizing baseline of Malcolm's life receded. By his late teens, he appears bereft of religion except as an inverted and negative phenomenon, which is the way he imaged atheism. Thus he describes his hustling and prison life as atheist. Beyond the mere question of belief, there is little evidence of him participating in any kind of institutional religious life; no indication that he prayed, sang religious songs, or engaged in related performances; no indication of even that vague spirituality irradiated by a specific religious tradition. Performatively and pragmatically, he was not religiously engaged.

God's Angry Man, Muhammad's Sycophant

Everyone is a performer. Presumably, every normally developed adult experiences a gap between public and private personae, between the person we present to others and the person, free from observation, we take ourselves to be. This gap emerges because of a discrepancy between what we want and how the world is. We negotiate this discrepancy in various ways. Obviously, the gap is larger and the relation between personae more complicated for some than for others. The successful performance of some roles such as elected politician, especially in a heterogeneous democratic society, invariably produces and requires such a gap. One cannot simply act out the private persona without undermining one's ability to fulfill one's political obligations. One can generalize this claim to most forms of leadership. Indeed, it generally extends much further, into the everyday lives of ordinary people. Malcolm X was not ordinary. But he was a social actor just the same. He performed his piety as a member of the Nation of Islam through public acts of asceticism and sycophantic promotion of Messenger Elijah Muhammad.

To illustrate this point consider his role as publicist for the Nation of Islam. Here the focus in particular is his journalistic pieces under the byline "God's Angry Man" published in the Los Angeles Herald Dispatch in 1957 from July 18 to September 12. The recurring themes are Islam as the Dark Man's religion,

---

3   Here I signify on Edward Said's concept of "traveling theory."

Christianity as a slavemaster religion, and obsequious praise of Messenger Elijah Muhammad. In an article dated September 5, 1957, he remarks:

> Messenger Elijah Muhammad, a meek and humble little Black Man, who has been Divinely Taught and Divinely Missioned by the Supreme Being, Almighty God Allah Himself, to teach naked truth to the so-called Negroes of America and raise us from our mental sleep, is making a proclamation among us today that the world must bear witness had to come straight from the mouth of Our God. This Great Message, delivered without fear by Messenger Elijah Muhammad, is enabling the so-called Negroes to see and understand what is going on around us for the first time since we were kidnapped and brought to America 400 years ago to be made slaves to the white man.
> MALCOLM X IN LOS ANGELES HERALD, 1957

Malcolm tells the reader that Messenger Elijah Muhammad is divinely guided, and under whose leadership Islam sweeps "Black America like a 'flaming fire'"; that he is "the most revered and feared man in the Western hemisphere"; that he teaches knowledge of the so-called Negro's true nationality; and that he is Allah's "last and greatest messenger to us [black people] here in North America" (Malcolm X in Los Angeles Herald, 1957). The messenger is obviously an exceptional man and only foolish Negroes ignore or ridicule him. Maybe this reflects our knowledge of how things eventually ended between Malcolm X and Elijah Muhammad but it is hard not to think that there is more than a bit of posturing, performing, and strategic positioning at work in these articles. I am not suggesting that Malcolm's hyperbolic rhetoric is not genuine, that he did not hold the views expressed in these articles. We know that the *Autobiography* is laden with even more extravagant praise and pledges of fidelity. Beyond these views, Malcolm deeply invested in the ritual life of the Nation of Islam of which the veneration of the Messenger was one kind (here one should reference Catholic veneration of the Pope and Shi'a veneration of saints). In addition, Malcolm performed personal rites of devotion such as prayer and participated in communal rites such as the Founder's Day ceremony. He led an ascetic life that may have negatively affected the sexual and marital satisfaction of his wife; he was hyper-vigilant regarding the dietary restrictions of Nation of Islam life, and, while other members of the hierarchy enriched themselves, he practiced a sincerely motivated but reckless disregard for his family's economic security. Apparently, this is what he thought devotion to Allah and Elijah Muhammad demanded.

While the sources cannot establish this speculative claim with any confidence, it is reasonable to contend that Malcolm experienced ambivalence regarding Elijah Muhammad early; that a performative gap existed between Malcolm's public and private personae, between his role as Elijah Muhammad's chief spokesman and his private ambitions as a leader. Lest I push this argument too far consider 'Come down off the cross and get under the crescent: The Newspaper Columns of Elijah Muhammad and Malcolm X.' In this study, which considers a broader range of Malcolm X's journalism than I do, Jamie J. Wilson provides an overview of Malcolm X's ideas. He notes that Malcolm X ghost wrote some of Elijah Muhammad's columns. So these columns, even when ostensibly written by Muhammad, provide a reliable, non-*Autobiography* based source of evidence about Malcolm X's views. While the views expressed in these columns do find their way in muted form into the *Autobiography*, they do not serve the NOI-to-Sunni Islam ascension narrative that Malcolm and Haley wish to construct (Wilson, 2013: 494–495). On the contrary they underscore just how committed Malcolm X was to the ritual practices and cosmology of the NOI, including the Yacub myth: a narrative of racial treachery, genetic engineering and science run amuck; the emergence of the white (devil) race, the fall of Original (black) Man, the rise of world-wide white supremacy, and the eminent destruction of white domination and restoration of the original black world order. X was indelibly stamped by his twelve years in the Nation of Islam. "Malcolm may have questioned his faith on occasion, but even after he split with the Nation in March 1963, including the period immediately after his hajj in the spring of 1964, his public pronouncements continued to espouse, highlight, and support the Nation of Islam's worldview. These ideas were so important to him that he had difficulty setting them aside, if in fact he ever did" (Wilson, 2013: 504). To accent what I take to be the salient point of the essay, Malcolm X, for most of his adult life, even during the chaotic splint with the Nation of Islam and its immediate aftermath, was "an unapologetic prodigy of Elijah Muhammad" (Wilson, 2013: 504). To put it differently: no Elijah Muhammad, no Malcolm X.

Jesus and Master Fard

Eve was crafted from Adam's rib; Enoch ascended to heaven without tasting the bitter draught of death; Jesus was conceived by the Virgin Mary; Jesus is God incarnate, the second person of the trinity, the Son of God; Jesus is a hypostatic union – all God and all man; Isa (Jesus in the Qur'an), as an infant in the cradle, spoke with great wisdom; Muhammad Ibn 'Abdallah was the last and greatest prophet. From the perspective of members of the Nation of Islam, the claim that Wallace Fard Muhammad is Allah incarnate is no less credible or any more absurd than the preceding claims. Indeed, the claim is not absurd at all: it is true. For the purpose of his study of the Nation of Islam, Mattias Gardell sets aside skeptical theories regarding "Master Farad [Fard] being someone other than God in Person...he is irrefutably God, Allah, who came to deliver his people of choice from their exile. He was born in Mecca on February 26, 1877, and was half Original, half white, as this would allow him to travel among friends and foe alike" (Gardell, 1996: 53). Mattias' methodological decision to adopt an insider's perspective is understandable and properly motivated given a popular predisposition among some scholars and most non-scholars to accord ancient traditions, whose origins, conflicts, and sausage-making histories are less known for credibility than modern ones. Mattias will have none of that and is intent on placing inquiry into the Nation of Islam on equal footing. He inhabits the language and sensibility of NOI members so as to present their views in a manner that they would recognize. Such a fulsome and hermeneutically generous description is a necessary first move in any scholarly account.

We should note, however, that the second scholarly move is reductive analysis, an account that is adjusted (reduced) according to the evidence. While members of the NOI say that Master Fard was born in 1877 in the Holy City of Mecca, the historical record shows that he was born in 1891. It further shows that Noble Drew Ali of the Moorish Science Temple of America (MSTA) was reincarnated in the person of Master Fard on July 29, 1929 (Evanzz, 1999: 68). Or, I should say, the record shows that Master Fard claimed to be Noble Drew Ali reincarnated. Ali had recently died under mysterious circumstances. Master Fard's reincarnation claim was a bold effort to assume leadership of the MSTA. He failed, and the following year Master Fard founded the rival Muslim organization Allah's Temple of Islam. As Karl Evanzz notes, the 1920's was a time of great religious ferment in the black metropolis (Evanzz, 1999: 70). To illustrate this fact, consider the following comparative point: first century Palestine was also a time and place of religious ferment, diversity, and conflict. Palestine was crawling with bandits, healers, miracle workers, prophets, and messiahs; Jesus was merely one among many (Horsley, 1999). Figures of this type were ubiquitous. In black communities of the urban north, con men and healers, prophets and profiteers, and messiahs of all stripes were common; Master Fard, who claimed to be "a healer and miracle worker," was one among many (Evanzz, 1999: 70). With this comparative point in mind, I return to the leadership crisis in the MSTA, which was even more complicated than my spare account suggests. According to Charles Marsh, the death of Ali and deportation of Marcus Garvey left a severe leadership void among the black nationalists. Two members of MSTA, John Givens El and Master Fard Muhammad, attempted to fill the void with competing claims of being Noble Drew Ali reincarnated. "Those who believed John Givens El are present day Moorish Americans. Those who believed Master Fard Muhammad's reincarnation comprised what came to be known as the Nation of Islam" (Marsh, 1996: 35). So there is a genealogical connection between Noble Drew Ali's Moorish Science Temple, Master Fard, and the Nation of Islam.

In addition to the MSTA, the NOI is rooted in the Garvey movement and the black church. The MTSA provided black Americans with a new identity as Moors – an Asiatic black people (Clegg, 1997: 19, 20). One can certainly understand why a man of Pakistani and English descent, who appeared, phenotypically, to be white but who moved effortlessly within Blackamerican circles, might have been attracted by the Asian doctrine of the MSTA. Sans the term Moor, Master Fard recreated this doctrine of the Asiatic black man within his new organization, Allah's Temple of Islam, the future Lost-Found Nation of Islam in North America. The Asiatic doctrine and the Garveyite spirituality underlying Master Fard religious thought are evident in Louis Lomax's remark that "The sermons at Fard's meetings were always based on the same subject: the unworthiness of the white man and the need for the Negro to understand and return to his glorious history in Africa and Asia" (Lomax, 1963: 44). Another distinctive aspect of Fard's religious thought was the Ahmadiyya-derived notion of a Mahdi (savior), which eventually morphed into the notion, especially in the theology of Elijah Muhammad, that Master Fard was Allah incarnate (Clegg, 1997: 18–20).

Sunni Muslims speak, devotionally, of the ninety-nine names of Allah; Wallace Fard also has many names. The FBI identified more than forty, some owing to errors that their agents made. Regardless of the number of alias identified or misidentified by the FBI, there is one name for members of the Nation of Islam that matters the most: God (English for Allah). Just as desperate Jewish peasants in first century Palestine, subject to the awful brutalities of the Roman Empire, imagined that an equally desperate rabbi, named Jesus, recently crucified by Pontius Pilate, was more than he appeared to be, desperate black peasants and proletarians, subject to subordination and white terror in the urban north, imaged Wallace Fard Muhammad (one of the many names of Master Fard) to be more than he appeared to be. The Roman authorities saw Jesus as a criminal, an enemy of the empire, and executed him in the degrading manner reserved for such people; his followers saw him as the Son of God: God incarnate. The FBI and various local police departments saw Master Fard as a con man and petty criminal and imprisoned him on at least one occasion; his followers saw him as God incarnate.

So what did Malcolm X believe? Did he subscribe to the claim that Master Fard was Allah incarnate? The modern concept of religion is creed-focused and centers on professions of belief or non-belief in divine beings. However, people lead religious lives with a variety of subjective relations to its various components. Some are compelled by religious rules for everyday living; these rules may be as formal as laws and ethical precepts or implicit notions of good/bad, right/wrong, appropriate/inappropriate, normal/abnormal, and prudent/imprudent. Others are compelled by the rituals of communal worship or by individual expressions of devotion. Still others are compelled by stories regarding the nature and destiny of things: cosmogonies, eschatologies, and everything in between. While some religious people may equally engage all of these components, many do not. People are invested in religious traditions in different ways and degrees of intensity. Polling data shows that Americans in the ninetieth percentile profess belief in a supreme being or transcendent power. When pollsters look at participation in communal worship, the numbers drop precipitously. These questions almost always pertain to church attendance,[4] with frequency of attendance taken as a marker of intensity. Where queried more directly, respondents report levels of religious salience significantly lower than the affirmation of belief in God (Cox et al, 2014: 57–58).

Belief is a treacherous subject of inquiry. Inquirers often disagree about the object. Is belief assent to propositions – for example, there is no God but Allah and Muhammad is his Prophet – or a disposition to act in certain ways? Is belief the relationship between proposition and habitual behavior? Should we simply take a person's professions at face value? This certainly appears to be the safest and least controversial option. No matter how we think of belief, something will be left out, something that someone regards as important to an adequate understanding of the concept will fall into our blind spot. We are tempted to be too literal minded or not enough, to be too generous hermeneutically or not enough. Ultimately, no one can really know someone's subjective relationship to propositions they affirm or deny. Nor is it clear that that relationship is as important as some might think. This, among other reasons, is why some of us regard belief, as a disposition to act, as a more reliable concept. This is why some religious studies scholars focus primarily on practices and address creed within a ritual context. Whether confined to the ritual context or not, the question of what Malcolm X believed persists.

Whatever his subjective relationship (literal-minded, dogmatic, figurative, skeptical, and/or incredulous) to Nation of Islam creeds, we know with certainty that Malcolm X performed his beliefs in sermons, speeches, and the

---

4   The polling data is Christian-centered.

Autobiography. Malcolm X touches virtually every aspect of the NOI creed including the claims that Master Fard is God incarnate and Elijah Muhammad is his messenger. "Master W.D. Fard was half black and half white." This enabled black people in America to accept his leadership while he, simultaneously, moved "undiscovered among the white people, so that he could understand and judge the enemy of the blacks" (Malcolm X, 1965: 187, 193). Black people were Original Man, white people, a genetically-engineered race of devils, a science experiment go awry. Black people were a Nation of Gods among whom one person was Allah, the God of Gods. Somehow as a result of the 'tricknology' (brainwashing) of the white devil, black people had lost their way. They had forgotten their noble origins: that they descended directly from Muslims. Master Fard had come to redeem the lost Nation of Islam in North America, to "return the Negro to his true religion" (Malcolm X, 1965: 238–240). In a retrospective act of distancing from a person he once idolized and from sacred stories he now finds embarrassing, X remarks: "I was to learn latter that Elijah Muhammad's tales, like this one of 'Yacub,' infuriated the Muslims of the East" (Malcolm X, 1965: 194). Their failure to proselytize in the West had made it possible for a 'religious faker' such as Elijah Muhammad to mislead black people. But there was a time when X did not receive such tales with skepticism. When did he stop finding these tales true and compelling? It is not clear when doubt overwhelmed his faith.

Consider an earlier version of Malcolm: the young, imprisoned, recent convert to the Nation of Islam. He is troubled by the suspension of his brother Reginald from the Nation of Islam. The very person who had introduced him to the Nation had been banished for sexual misconduct. Malcolm wrote a letter to Elijah Muhammad requesting that Reginald's suspension be lifted. Tormented, he prayed and waited:

> It was the next night, as I lay on my bed, I suddenly, with a start, became aware of a man sitting beside me in my chair. He had on a dark suit. I remember. I could see him as plainly as I see anyone I look at. He wasn't black, and he wasn't white. He was light-brown-skinned, an Asiatic cast of countenance, and he had oily black hair.
> MALCOLM X, 1965: 215

Frozen in place and unable to speak, Malcolm writes that he was not afraid. The mute figure, who he did not recognize, disappeared as suddenly as he appeared. Malcolm later interpreted this encounter as a 'pre-vision' of Master Fard. To have a prevision, he writes, is to see the impossible: to see something you have never seen, exactly as it appears (Malcolm X, 1965: 215, 218). Malcolm, here, describes an uncanny encounter with Master Fard, Allah incarnate. The distancing retrospection I noted earlier is not present. There is no sense of embarrassment or suggestion that this encounter was illusory. Like Paul's post-resurrection encounter with Jesus on the road to Damascus, Malcolm X's post-disappearance encounter with Master Fard is an *authentication event* within the narrative. This silent encounter (no booming voice) authenticated his identity as a Muslim: a member of the Nation of Islam. With a 'first naiveté,'[5] he fully entered the belief world of the Nation of Islam.

Sankofa and the Nation of Islam

Chaos surrounded Malcolm's break with the Nation of Islam. Like the iconic Sankofa of the Akan people, he could not help but look backward. The Nation of Islam was too important and formative an experience for him to simply pivot and move forward. Even as he disavowed Elijah Muhammad and the Nation of Islam, he carried some things forward. Malcolm faced the task of negotiating new relations with the Nation and with Sunni Muslims both nationally and internationally. On March 19, 1964, eleven days after his split from the NOI, A.B. Spellman, a poet and jazz critic, interviewed X for the *Monthly Review* and the Revolution, regarding his organizing plans post-NOI:

> *Spellman*: Do you expect to draw from the Garveyite groups?
> *Malcolm X*: All groups – Nationalist, Christians, Muslims, Agnostics, Atheists, anything. Everybody who is interested in solving the problem is given an invitation to become actively involved with either suggestions or ideas or something.
> MALCOLM X, 2005

Regarding the approach of his new group, the Organization of Afro-American Unity, X said: "we have a problem that goes beyond religion."[6] Around the same time, he was interviewed on the Pierre Breton Show in Toronto, Canada where he offered a slightly different version: "our people have a problem in America

---

5 Here I am working inferentially from Paul Ricoeur's notion of a second naiveté that is critically mediated unlike a first naiveté.
6 http://www.onbeing.org/blog/malcolm-x-human-rights-not-civil-rights/3855. Malcolm X on Human rights, Not Civil Rights. Malcolm X on Front Page Challenge, 1965 CBC Archives. Quotation begins at 6:17. (accessed 07/24/15).

that goes beyond religion."[7] This is the post-dogmatic and ecumenical X whose expresses skepticism about the relevance of religious affiliation to political orientation and subordinates the former to the latter. Addressing a meeting of the Group on Advanced Leadership in Detroit on April 12, 1964, he remarked:

> This afternoon it's not our intention to talk about religion. We're going to forget religion. If we bring up religion, we'll be in an argument. And the best way to keep away from arguments and differences, as I said earlier, is to put your religion at home, in the closet, keep it between you and your God. Because if it hasn't done anything more for you than it has, you need to forget it anyway.[8]

By subordinating religious purity, conflict and competition to the racial struggle, he engages in a hard-learned act of political liberalism and pragmatism. With a religion first strategy, he could not do what he thought needed to be done. Malcolm X negotiated his changing Muslim identity within a contentious environment where Sunni Muslims, immigrant and native born, were stridently and persistently accusing the Nation of Islam of error. The following question from an interviewer with *Al-Muslimoon,* an Arabic language monthly published by the Islamic center in Geneva, Switzerland, captures the kind of international scrutiny that X encountered:

> QUESTION: Is it true that even after your breakaway from Elijah Muhammad you still hold the black color as a main base and dogma for your drive under the banner of liberation in the United States? How could a man of your spirit, intellect, and worldwide outlook fail to see in Islam its main characteristic, from its earliest days, as a message that confirms beyond doubt the ethnological oneness and equality of all races, thus striking at the very root of the monstrosity of racial discrimination? Endless are the texts of the Qur'an [Koran] and prophetic sayings to this effect and nothing would testify to that more than the historic fact that heterogeneous races, nations, and linguistic entities have always mingled peacefully in the homeland.
> MALCOLM X in al-Muslimoon Magazine, 1965

---

7 http://www.malcolm-x.org/docs/int_pbert.htm (accessed 07/23/15).
8 Malcolm X, *By Any Means Necessary: Speeches, Interviews and a Letter by Malcolm X* (New York: Pathfinder, 1970), 180.

The interviewer is Said Ramadan, the leader of the Geneva Islamic Center. In addition to the patronizing tone, the question betrays profound ignorance of the international dimensions of racism and the distinctiveness of its American version, the ethnic particularism (Arab-centrism) that is a constitutive element and blind spot of Islam, and the reality of anti-black racism in Arab Muslim societies. All of this is lost within the textual and historical idealism of the interviewer. As the Islam scholar Edward Curtis notes, Malcolm provided the final answers to Ramadan's questions in writing on February 20, 1965, the eve of his assassination. In response to Ramadan's provocations, he provided a different account of the relations between Islam and racial identity. He rejected a notion that he had previously affirmed as a member of the Nation of Islam: the claim that Islam was the solution to the racial problems that ailed America (Curtis, 2007: 695–696). I wish to accent a widely-cited passage that Curtis quotes from Malcolm's July 27, 1964 speech in Cairo: "My fight is twofold, my burden is double, my responsibilities multiple…material as well as spiritual, political as well as religious, racial as well as non-racial" (Malcolm X in FBI file: 47–51). Malcolm channels DuBois' notion of double consciousness and itemizes the multiples dualities that defined his life and the manner in which he lived his Islam. While not directed at Said Ramadan, Malcolm's Cairo remarks do, as Curtis' quotation of this passage underscores, render Ramadan's simplistic and Arab-centric interpretation of Islam and racial identity null and void. Summarizing Malcolm's view post Nation of Islam, Curtis remarks: "his domestic politics focused on finding black solutions to black problems, and his rearticulating of black nationalist themes included calls for racial solidarity in the face of white supremacy." While he appreciated the financial support and friendship of Arab Muslims, his conformity to their interpretation of Islam, white supremacy, and racial identity could not be bought. He embraced radicalism but not an Islamist version. He rejected a pan-Islamist response to white supremacy. "Only black people, reaching across continents and across confessional lines, could solve black problems" (Curtis, 2007: 696).

In response to a question at a February 3, 1965 speech at the Tuskegee Institute regarding Elijah Muhammad, Malcolm X remarked: "Elijah believes that God is going to come and straighten things out. I believe that too. But whereas Elijah is willing to sit and wait, I'm not willing to sit and wait on God to come." He added that God might not act soon enough. And he expressed a preference for religion that encompasses "political, economic, and social action designed to eliminate" injustice and that achieved a foretaste of paradise here on earth (Malcolm X, 1992: 22). The reader should note that this speech comes nearly a year after he broke with the NOI. And yet, he continues to look backward toward something valuable, an orientation and Garveyite-based wisdom tradition, which he could not leave behind. X's backward-looking flight from the Nation of Islam continued in a February 19, 1965 interview with famed photographer Gordon Parks. Malcolm X recalled his churlish and dismissive response to an earnest white college woman who wished to build a bridge between white people and the Nation of Islam: "I was a zombie then – like all Muslims – I was hypnotized, pointed in a certain direction and told to march. Well, I guess a man's entitled to make a fool of himself if he's ready to pay the cost. It cost me twelve years" (Malcolm X, 1992: 231). In contrast to the quotation from the February 3 speech where he appears to 'make nice,' this response feeds the anti-Nation of Islam narrative he is constructing after the break. Though his knowledge of Haitian history and culture probably did not extend beyond the stereotypical Hollywood depictions of voodoo, and while it is unfair to expect him to have been *au courant* on this topic, it is interesting that he uses a colonial trope, *zombie,* for a maligned black nation to malign the Nation of Islam.

As he pulls away from the NOI, he is pulled back. He cannot properly move forward without looking back, sorting things out and determining what he must carry forward into his life as a former member of the Nation.

Narratives, Theses, and Polemics

I have made the argument that Malcolm X was a religious peripatetic: that he traveled among religious worlds, sometimes serially, sometimes simultaneously. In his speeches, writing, and autobiography, Malcolm provides a religious travelogue. He tells us where he has been, how he lived, and what he thought about his various religious worlds. He wanders through these religious worlds with a sense of wonder. Of course, the reader must be careful when considering the narratives that he provides, since they are clearly in the service of his current interests, orientations, and rapidly evolving self-image. The most obvious narratives are those of declension and ascension. There is a bit of declension in the account of his brief travels through Seventh-day Adventism and Pentecostalism. They come off poorly in comparison with his Garveyite Baptist world. One discerns this difference in his condescending reference to the eschatology of Adventists and the 'spooky,' holy-rolling quality of Pentecostal worship. One need not question the sincerity of these characterizations to raise questions about their meaning within the narrative. There is a tension between this declension narrative where – in the golden age of early childhood – Christianity is wedded to the politics of racial uplift and African redemption and the story of X's ascent from Christianity and cocaine to Islam. There is a narrative gap between expressions of pride in his father's Baptist Garveyism and Malcolm's descent into the brainwashing world of Christianity and mind-altering drugs. Connections are missing. How should we understand Malcolm's Christianity after his father's death, during his 'wonder years,' when he wandered between Adventism and Pentecostalism? Should this be understood as the beginning of his descent? Are his comments regarding these forms of Christianity negative? As a matter of narrative, is he constructing Adventism and Pentecostalism in light of his mother's mental illness, the onset of which occurred during the Great Depression? The life of a young boy became very tough very quickly. I suspect that Malcolm X has many stories to tell and that he and Alex Haley have difficulty crafting a coherent narrative. However, in the narrative he constructs, it is hard not to see correlations among his father's death, mother's religious experimentation and insanity, the family's disintegration, his foster care experiences, drug use and criminality.

Scholars have not reflected much on the polemical context of Malcolm's adult religious life. He appears to have been constantly arguing for his tradition and against others. He employs narratives and theses (often implicit) in the polemical elaboration of his religious views. What does it mean to live one's religious life this way? The notion that religion is a battlefield is neither new nor unique. Warfare is a common trope in traditions such as Zen Buddhism, Hinduism, Judaism, Christianity, and Islam. One thinks of Arjuna and Lord Krishna in the Bhagavad Gita, conquest and genocide in the land of Canaan, Christian soldiers in the army of the lord, Crusaders and jihadis; one thinks of the 'art' of killing without attachment in Zen Buddhism. Malcolm X engages in rhetorical warfare around the topics of religious affiliation and racial identity. Religion is a matter that calls forth a militant disposition. In narrating his prison experience, X adopts a polemical attitude toward religion. Given his cultural context, he could think of nothing more powerful than the image of Satan to communicate his distance from the dominant religious tradition. Thus he signals his opposition to the normative standards of a nominally Christian culture. In his mind and the minds of fellow prisoners, Malcolm became Satan. He performed the culturally dominant stereotype of Satan as a black man. But he styled himself as an atheist as well. It does not occur to him that these two images, Satan and atheist, might be oxymoronic: that the devil is a figure within a theistic conceptual frame. But this conclusion confuses the messiness of life and the purposes of the narrative with a systematic exposition of his religious views. X was not a systematic religious (or anti-religious) thinker; consistency was not an important value. It was important, rather, to signal to the reader how wretched and anti-religious he was. Inconsistency notwithstanding, Malcolm's self-description as Satan and atheist did the necessary rhetorical work of setting the table for an ascension narrative. A narrative that begins in the degradation of Christianity, cocaine, and criminality and ends with Islam triumphant; thus Malcolm's narrative of debasement serves his narrative of exaltation. An inter-religious polemic against Christianity elevates Islam.

In his dual construction of Christianity as bad and Islam as good, Malcolm X employs a religion as hustle thesis. Religious people, he suggests, are dishonest. They are self-interested and 'on the make' – hustling wolves in sheep's wool. Presumably, Malcolm had observed the close connections between Christianity and commerce, although the contemporary church/mall culture – where church morphs into a commercial mall and the mall into a secular church – had not yet fully developed. This is the context for understanding an anecdote that he relates in the *Autobiography*. When Malcolm X first hears about Islam in the late 1940's, he initially perceives his brother's involvement as a hustle. He wants in. In the street vernacular, he wants to get paid. Of course, one gets paid by manipulating the sincere commitments of true believers. Hustlers always trade on the misplaced confidence of those they hustle. X spied an opportunity. After family members set him straight about the virtues of the Nation of Islam and their genuine commitment, he eventually develops a very different relationship with Islam. He engages it sincerely, fervently, and with great naiveté. But he does not wholly abandon the notion that religion is a hustle. Though Marxism was not his idiom, Malcolm did not abandon a Marxist-like view that Christianity is a mask, a subterfuge for white supremacy. This was a newly emergent view that he cultivated assiduously within the Nation of Islam. On this view, black Christians are brainwashed. They have lost their ability to see things as they really are. They have been hustled, pimped by white Christians, a white God, and a white Christ. They have forgotten who they really are. And, they do not know their value. As a result, they are easy targets of exploitation.

Black brainwashed Christians are often indistinguishable from that class of persons that Malcolm labels Uncle Toms, that is, race traitors. To be an Uncle Tom is to collaborate with white supremacy, to work against the rights and interests of black people. This collaboration included both outright betrayal and weak-kneed and mealy mouth opposition. Much of his criticism of civil rights clergy fell into the latter category; thus his frequent reference to the Right Reverend Bishop T. Chicken Wing. This comical appellation captures Malcolm's sense that Christian clergy such as this were pretentious and easily bought, for the mere price of chicken wings. Behind this image is the chicken-eating preacher of African American lore who eats too much at Sunday dinner leaving the poor host family hungry. Richard Wright memorializes this figure in his 1945 memoir, *Black Boy*. In this story, Wright's mother, recently deserted by her husband, invites a local preacher to dinner. The preacher settles in and begins to eat at a pace that the young Wright cannot match. Before he can even finish an appetizer of soup, the preacher has already eaten several pieces of fried chicken, a rare delicacy in an impoverished household. In exasperation, Wright blurts out: "That preacher's going to eat all the chicken!" Embarrassed by her son's lack of etiquette, Wright's mother banished him from the dinner table without the savory taste of fried chicken (Wright, 2007: 26). On X's view, this is precisely the problem with black preachers, they leave the flock hungry. Malcolm holds that black Christians are hungry, though it is their spiritual hunger, their emptiness that is the more serious issue. They are self-loathing and brainwashed; they do not know who they are.

Something curious happens as Malcolm's collaboration with Alex Haley progresses. Malcolm has a public change of heart that begins to influence in a derisive manner what had begun as a hagiography of the Honorable Elijah Muhammad. The notion that the Nation of Islam was a hustle – his instinctive initial reaction, which he abandoned in the throes of love for the NOI and the person of Elijah Muhammad – is suddenly revived. He concludes that the Honorable Elijah Muhammad is a hustler, a fake. He extends this judgment to the Chicago-based leadership of the Nation of Islam. He regrets his role in propagating what he now regards as fraudulent. His vitriol against Elijah Muhammad and the NOI nearly matches his anti-Christian invective. What explains this change? It would be naïve in the extreme to assume that this change did not have much to do with Malcolm's own interests as he then saw them. X's rhetorical battles on behalf of the NOI left him well armed in his new battle against it. In his never ending struggle to defend the NOI from its critics, he had to fight on two fronts: against Sunni Muslims who rejected the Islamic *bone fides* of the Nation of Islam and against Christian commentators who characterized nationalist Islam as pseudo-Islamic, anti-white, anti-Christian, and anti-American. Polemic was Malcolm's normal mode of inter- and intrareligious discourse. After years of public controversy, polemical engagement had become second nature. Curtis observes that Sunni Muslim critics of all kinds harshly criticized Elijah Muhammad and the Nation of Islam. "Their criticism of the NOI was a public performance of Muslim identity that expressed the growing cultural power of foreign and immigrant Muslims. By making such public pronouncements, whether they had been formally trained in the Islamic religious sciences or not, these self-appointed spokesmen for Islam attempted to define the doctrinal boundaries of Islamic religion" (Curtis, 2007: 293). As the chief publicist for the Nation of Islam, Malcolm had to defend it and the honor of Elijah Muhammad especially when he spoke on college campuses. Invariably, earnest Muslim students would take him to task for the NOI's heresies and aberrant practices. Curtis suggests that Malcolm's rhetorical skills and Qur'anic exegesis were not equal to the task, that these encounters disturbed him and probably had a role in his eventual embrace of Sunni Islam (Curtis, 2007: 692, 693). One thing is clear, after he left the NOI, X embraced many of the criticisms, including polemical and even vituperative remarks about Elijah Muhammad.

That X's polemical style provoked polemical reactions should surprise no one. This style provokes reactions among all classes of observers whether interested in his religious journey or not. The offense that he gave to Sunni Muslims for the most part was unintended. However, there were times when he and Elijah Muhammad attempted to put Muslims from the east, as the called foreign Muslims, in their place; to educate them on the distinctiveness of America and a black experience that demand a different kind of Islam on American soil. In contrast, X sought to offend black Christians and black elites: especially political and civil rights leaders, the highly educated (black PhD puppets), and the middle class. His negative tropes – black brainwashed Christian, Uncle Tom, and house Negro – are closely related. During his Nation of Islam years, one could not easily disentangle his religious and political critiques. In her analysis of Spike Lee's Bio-film, *Malcolm X*, Nell Irving Painter calls attention to the limitations of Malcolm's Black Nationalist creed. She remarks: "THE LEADING THEME IN MALCOLM'S LIFE was actually intra-racial conflict, which, in the last analysis, took his life. Like Americans who lack a conceptual category for black respectability, Malcolm X (and black nationalists generally) found it difficult to envision a Negro race made up of people of different classes and clashing convictions." This preference for uniformity, which is a standard nationalist disability, impeded Malcolm's ability to perceive intra-racial differences (gender, wealth, education) as genuine. Thus he construed intra-racial difference as a sign of race traitors "in cahoots with whites." Malcolm X identified race traitors as educated blacks and house Negroes, and he usually treated these two kinds of people as one (Painter, 1993: 438).

Subtending the tropes of black brainwashed Christian, Uncle Tom, and house Negro is a discourse of manliness. For many of his most ardent supporters, Malcolm X was 'a man's man.' Many are concerned about his legacy as contemporary analyses increasingly focus on his gender and sexual views. Commentators have noted that X expresses retrograde notions of gender in the *Autobiography*. He characterizes women as deceitful (Eve), trouble (Pandora), and dangerously seductive (Sirens). In a non-autobiographical source, he expresses gender views that are more progressive. "In every Middle East or African country I have visited, the country is as 'advanced' as its women are, or as backward as its women... An old African proverb states: educate a man and you educate an individual; educated a woman and you educate a whole family" (Malcolm X, 1992:

254). Given his patriarchal politics and allegiance to the Nation of Islam at the time Haley interviewed him, and considering the masculinist framing of the *Autobiography*, it is no wonder that a mentor such as Queen Mother Moore did not appear in Malcolm X's memoir (McDuffie and Woodard, 2013: 521). According to Erik McDuffie and Komozi Woodard, Queen Mother Moore is one of a handful of radical black women who were crucial to Malcolm's political development. They argue that the influence of these women along with Malcolm's eye-opening international travel in Africa and the Arab world pushed his gender politics in a progressive direction before his death (McDuffie and Woodard, 2013: 527). Just as his religious and political views evolved rapidly during the period immediately preceding his break with NOI and his death, it is reasonable to suspect that his gender views, which I would imagine were deeper and more tenacious, might also have begun to change.

Any suggestion that Malcolm may not have been a 'man's man,' that as a young man, a street hustler, he engaged in sexual practices that contravene this masculinist notion has provoked intense reaction, especially in the wake of Manning Marable's definitive biography, *Malcolm X: A Life of Reinvention* (2011). Khary Polk argues that those engaged in Malcolm X studies should drop the mask and stop the masculine dissemblance. This posturing gets in the way of a gimlet-eyed view of predatory capitalist social relations. She remarks: "Following Darlene Clark Hine's powerful formulation of sex-work-as rape, I submit that black fears about white consumption are at the heart of the debate over Malcolm X's sexual past – unsettling if inconclusive proof that even the best and brightest among us may not be above selling our asses to white men." Cognitive dissonance and a particular version of respectability politics make "interracial same-sexual prostitution unthinkable." It violates the hustler's code and perverts the long struggle for African American manhood rights. Polk captures that dissonance in the following question: "How could a part-time rent boy be responsible for the revolutionary transformation of black masculinity in the twentieth century?" For many scholars, this is simply unthinkable, disrespectful, and scurrilous. Those who engage in such inquiry are suspect. Polk contends that efforts to block inquiry "risks sacrificing the very kinds of subaltern knowledge that interracial sex work produces, epistemological viewpoints from below that likely played a larger role in Malcolm Little's intellectual formation – regardless of whether it was he or his friend Rudy who did the flesh-peddling – than Marable's critics acknowledge." It is likely, she argues, that X learned the same lessons about white supremacy in the Norfolk Prison library that Detroit Red had already learned on the streets: race, power, sex, consumption, and hustling are aspects of capitalism "as a performance of survival" (Polk, 2013: 579–580, 581).

I would submit that the religious subject that Malcolm X became, severe, austere, and ascetic, is inseparable from his gender views and experience in the sex trade: whether as a broker for clients seeking services and/or as a provider himself. On the latter possibility, the evidence is inconclusive.

The Garveyite Spiritual Commonwealth

In the account that I have given, Malcolm X's early childhood religious world was irradiated by Garveyite spirituality. During his teens and early adulthood, his Garveyite sensibilities became dormant; they entered a period of latency. After his conversion to Islam, this latent spirituality reemerged in mature form. In this section, I provide a genealogy (an outline) of the Garveyite spiritual commonwealth to which Malcolm X was an heir.

Wilson Jeremiah Moses notes that Marcus Garvey, Jamaica's native son, knew as little about African-based Obi worship in the Caribbean as he did about the equally African-based ecstasies of the black church in the United States. His religious sensibilities were *high church*, "more Orthodox than African" (Moses, 1993: 133). According to Rastafarianism scholar Barry Chevannes, Garvey did not think highly of the Rastafari. And yet, they are the main bearers of the oral traditions regarding Garvey's magical works and prophetic speech; they carry on his work of idealizing Africa (Chevannes, 1994: 109). Leonard Barrett remarks that "Today all Rastafarians revere Marcus Garvey as their inspirer; his picture is prominent in all homes and cult houses. His speeches are avidly read; songs and poems are written in his honor and, and in the pantheon of Rastafarians, Garvey is second only to Halie Selassie" (Barrett, 1997: 67). I should note that the Rastafari regard Selassie as God incarnate. How do we explain these facts? My notion of a 'Garveyite spiritual commonwealth' goes part of the way in providing an explanation. This commonwealth is a historical, genealogical, and analytical abstraction; a trope that I use to describe the Garvey movement's pervasive influence on Rastafarians, black Jews, black Muslims, and black Christians such as Malcolm X's parents. In standard usage, a commonwealth is a political entity, usually the political, social, economic, and cultural interrelations – the commonwealth – created by an empire, which persist long after the old order has unraveled. A preeminent example is the relationship between the Roman Empire and Europe or, in the modern period, England and her former colonies. Analogously, the Garvey movement developed a set of tropes, symbols, and ceremonies that underwrite a black spiritual commonwealth that had many black people of various religious traditions rallying to its unifying message. Garvey's Ethiopianism appears to be the most important unifying trope. A tradition of biblical interpretation among African descended people in the Americas, Ethiopianism is rooted in the seemingly prophetic words of Psalms 68:31 – "Princes shall come out of Egypt; Ethiopia shall stretch out her hands unto God." On this Blackamerican interpretation, the Bible prophesies the emancipation of black people from white domination, the rise of a 'mighty race,' and its return to former glory.

According to Randall Burkett, "The power, the religious power, of the [Garvey] movement lay precisely in its ability to relate a black nationalist ethos to a general conception of ultimate scheme of things" (Burkett, 1978a: 6). Burkett channels Protestant theologian Paul Tillich's notion of religion as ultimate concern; thus Garveyism, among other things, was a religious movement. To put a finer point on it, a recognizably Christian ethos that was nonsectarian and highly ecumenical characterized Garveyism. Using the categories of systematic theology to establish his claim, Burkett identifies doctrines of God, Christology, anthropology, soteriology, eschatology, and ecclesiology. In each case, with the exception of Garvey's Arian Christology and its effects on his doctrine of salvation, Burkett discerns theological doctrines that fall within the broad consensus of Trinitarian Christian thought. There is nothing theologically remarkable about these doctrines except for Garvey's rejection of the conventional white supremacist frame. Within this frame, God, his literal colorlessness notwithstanding, is a white man.[9] Burkett captures Garvey's opposition to this view in the following remark: "We Negroes see our God through our own spectacles. ... We Negroes believe in the God of Ethiopia, the everlasting God – God the Father, God the Son and God the Holy Ghost, the one God of all ages" (Burkett, 1978b: 47). Commenting on this passage, Leonard Barrett claims that these words are the origin point for "most Black God movements" including the "Church of the Black Madonna in Detroit, the Black Muslims of America, and the Rastafarians" (Barrett, 1997: 77). I should note that Garvey's Ethiopian God, as radical as it was for its time, has little in common with the white devil-naming theology of Elijah Muhammad (and Malcolm X) or the provocative 'if/then' of James Cone's theology: if God is not for black people and against white people, then black people should kill him; that is, "God is dead" and they should give him a proper Nietzschean send-off. As Burkett notes, Garvey's Ethiopian God (Ethiopia, a metonym for Africa) is an object of veneration and spurs black people to affirm the goodness of blackness. But Garvey's God is not a partisan in this-worldly struggles; he is not "for or against one race or another." On the rare occasions where he did make a partisan claim

---

9 Even when the views are less popular and more sophisticated, "God as beyond being, ground of being," the popular image of God as white man lurks about.

regarding God's special solicitude for black people, it was a subordinate theme (Burkett, 1978b: 52).

Complete with ceremony, Garvey re-images Jesus "as the Black Man of Sorrows." With a gesture toward Catholicism, there was also a ceremony canonizing "the Blessed Virgin Mary as a black woman." From a Garveyite lesson guide, Burkett lifts the following passage: "The Roman Catholics, therefore, have no rightful claim to the Cross nor is any other professing Christian before the Negro. *The Cross is the property of the Negro in his religion because it was he who bore it*" (Burkett, 1978b: 53; emphasis added). Lest we forget, these lesson guides were composed during the latter part of the *Nadir* (1880–1940) when lynching black people was a national sport. Though his language is reserved, those who had the ears to hear would hear: black women and men are crucified and Jesus was lynched. Garvey's assertion of the priority and propriety of the black Jesus, of the special status of black people's interpretation of Jesus and their 'ownership' of him, so to speak, is in an old tradition among African Americans. Even Malcolm X could not resist this claim of priority and propriety as his sermonette on Jesus's preferential love for black people attests. "And if Jesus was here in America today he wouldn't be going to the white man. The white man is the oppressor. He would be going to the oppressed. He would be going to the lowly. He would be going to the rejected and despised. He would be going to the so-called American Negro" (Malcolm X, PBS Video). Finally, to put a period on this point, in *The Black Messiah* (1968), the Reverend Albert Cleage, pastor of the Shrine of the Black Madonna and a devotee of Malcolm X, asserted that Jesus literally descended from black people. Fifty years earlier, Garvey remarked that "Jesus had much ... Negro blood in him" (Burkett, 1978b: 63).

Garvey's soteriology, eschatology, and ecclesiology were all of a piece. In the interest of African descendants, these doctrines promoted a Social Gospel-friendly notion of this-worldly social transformation, justice, and salvation. According to Burkett, "Garvey insisted that justice could be achieved only by a fair distribution of power" (Burkett, 1978b: 61–62). Coupled with the redemption of Africa, these goals were the very *raison d'être* of the Universal Negro Improvement Association. As most readers undoubtedly know, the importance of Africa to the Garvey movement is hard to overstate. Garveyism was part of a long tradition of back to Africa movements that ultimately extend to enslaved Africans whose desperate hope was that, through the transformative power of death, they could escape the horror of slavery and 'fly home' to Africa. Regarding the importance of Africa to Garvey's vision of the future, Burkett remarks: "This vision was embodied in the powerful image of the 'Redemption of Africa.'" St. Clair Drake demonstrated that this potent and enduring religious myth focused "meaningful activity among New World Negroes"[10] during the nineteenth century. The myth energized pre-political movements among the powerless masses of black people in the Americas and Africa as they gathered their strength for realistic political engagement. He observes that Marcus Garvey revitalized the idea of African regeneration in the early twentieth century and apparently saw it as a legitimate political objective and the definitive goal of the UNIA. "Even for Garvey, however, the 'redemption of Africa' functioned primarily in a religious sense as the eschatological goal toward which all of history was leading, and for the realization of which all one's efforts ought to be directed" (Burkett, 1978b: 63). Within Malcolm X's Nation of Islam, the territorial desires of Garvey, what Wilson Jeremiah Moses calls black imperialism and Zionism, (Moses, 1993: 132) is displaced onto a quest for separate territory in the US or elsewhere (www.noi.org/muslim-program). This is often interpreted as the demand that the government cede control of ten or so contiguous states to black people as reparations to end racial strife. To mix my religious metaphors, this Muslim Zion would become a Mecca for black people throughout the United States and contribute to the Garveyite goal of unity.

In the context of global white supremacy, with scientific racism regnant, Africa carved up by European imperial powers, Jim Crow and its "strange fruit hanging from the poplar trees," and the long dark shadow casted by the transatlantic enslavement of Africans, the old theme of Ethiopianism, revived by Garvey, was an act of psychic and material survival that promised triumph and exaltation in this world. The idea that an abject people are the special object of divine favor, despite circumstances that suggest otherwise, that powerful unseen, providential forces are working toward a dramatic reversal of fortune, is a potent elixir. Garvey is the axle on which Ethiopianism, before and after, turn. Garvey did not invent the eschatological myth of African Redemption but he shepherd, *pastored*, and institutionalized it like no one before or since.

Of the one hundred and twenty two signatories of the UNIA's Declaration of Rights (1920), Burkett identifies twenty two as clergy. He provides evidence that more than two hundred and fifty clergymen actively engaged with the UNIA and chides those Garvey scholars who underestimate the number and prominence of clergy within the movement. He traces the provenance of these clergymen to historic black Protestant denominations: Baptist, African Methodist Episcopal (AME), AME Zion, Christian Methodist Episcopal (CME), and the Protestant Episcopal Church. He also traces the participation of black Jewish clergy, which supports the claim regarding Garveyism pan-religious appeal

---

10   St. Claire Drake, *The Redemption of Africa and Black Religion* (Chicago: Third World Press, 1970), 11. Quoted by Burkett (1978b: 63).

(Burkett, 1978b: 112–113). The most important black Jew in the UNIA was Rabbi Arnold Ford. He led a small Harlem congregation named Beth B'nai Abraham. The members of the congregation regarded themselves as Ethiopian Jews. Burkett says that there is some controversy regarding which came first: Rabbi Ford's Judaism or Garveyism. He concludes that Ford became Rabbi of Beth B'nai Abraham after he joined the UNIA and remained an active Garveyite for several years. Apparently, Rabbi Ford hoped to establish Black Judaism as the UNIA's official religion. While hospitable toward religion, Garvey opposed any establishment of a specific tradition within the UNIA (Burkett, 1978a: 178–181).[11] He had previously rejected an effort by Reverend George Alexander McGuire to establish the Episcopalian-derived African Orthodox Church as the official religion of the UNIA (Burkett, 1978a: 97–99). His opposition to a black Jewish establishment notwithstanding, there were sporadic expressions of interest in Black Judaism in the Philadelphia chapter of the UNIA and in chapters elsewhere. Burkett notes that while Rabbi Ford and Prophet F.S. Cherry, leader of a black Jewish congregation in Philadelphia, are the only Jewish leaders directly affiliated with the UNIA, Garvey appropriated Jewish themes. Garveyites used Jewish history as a model for improving the status of black people, construed their back to Africa movement as black Zionism, and expressed interest in the plight of Falasha Jews. Burkett conclude that these Jewish themes and affinities created mutual interest between Garveyites and black Jews (Burkett, 1978b: 181–182). According to Moses, Ford and many members of his Black Hebrew congregation were especially taken by the UNIA's Ethiopian rhetoric. While members of Noble Drew Ali's Moorish Science Temple rejected the term 'Ethiopian' in favor of 'Moors,' they shared commonwealth ties with Garveyism as did members of the Nation of Islam (Moses, 1993: 137).

Elijah Poole, the future Elijah Muhammad, encountered the Garvey movement after fleeing to Michigan from a lynch-happy (and boll weevil-infested) Georgia (Clegg, 1997: 10–12). "Like most African Americans in the 1920's, Elijah had heard of the Black Nationalist teachings of Marcus Garvey" who advocated Pan-African solidarity, economic development, and political independence among African descended people world-wide. According to one source, "Elijah traveled to Chicago to hear Garvey speak and was greatly moved by his words" (ccnmtl.columbia.edu/projects/mmt/mxp/people/753_I.html). However, major biographers do not record any such encounter.[12] After joining the Chicago chapter of the UNIA, Poole attained the organizational rank of 'corporal.' The

---

11 Burkett, 178–181.
12 Claude A. Clegg III does not mention any encounter between Elijah Muhammad and Garvey. Karl Evanzz says explicitly that Muhammad "had never personally seen or heard

UNIA's internationalism and accent on a black global identity fascinated Poole. Garvey's deportation in 1927 left a Pan-African void that an emerging Nation of Islam filled in the 1930's. Though inflected by a peculiar 'Asiatic doctrine' that founder Wallace Fard Muhammad adopted from his earlier membership in the Moorish Science Temple (Chicago Temple 1), the Nation of Islam shared Garvey's Pan-Africanism. According to the Nation of Islam theology developed by Fard, "Original Man," aboriginal humans, was black and their descendants created African and Asian civilizations such as Egypt, Nubia, and Mecca, Islam's holiest city. Like Garvey's Universal Negro Improvement Association, the Nation of Islam advocated Pan-African (black) identification and solidarity among African descended people worldwide (ccnmtl.columbia.edu/projects/mmt/mxp/people/753_I.html).

Earl and Louise Little, the parents of Malcolm X, were contemporaries of Elijah Muhammad. Like Muhammad, Earl was a refugee from the anti-black violence of post-World War I, Jim Crow Georgia. Earl and Louise were among the earliest responders to Garvey's message. According to Manning Marable, the Georgia born Earl and Grenada born Louise met, married, and began their careers as Garveyite activists in Montreal, Canada. After living for nearly two years in Philadelphia, a city with a strong Garveyite division, the UNIA sent them to Omaha, Nebraska. There they set up shop and began to organize in mid-1921. Over the duration of the 1920's, their peripatetic lives took them to Milwaukee, Wisconsin, East Chicago, Indiana, and eventually to Lansing, Michigan. In each location, they worked on behalf of the UNIA. However, following Garvey's conviction and deportation in 1927, the movement began to disintegrate. But there were pockets in Detroit and throughout Michigan where UNIA branches remained vibrant. During the middle period of his parents UNIA activism, Malcolm X was born (Marable, 2011: 16, 20–23, 29).

Malcolm does not say much about Garvey in the *Autobiography.* But he remembers occasionally attending UNIA meetings with his father. He recalls his father preaching standard Garveyite themes such as "Africa for the Africans," the redemption of Africa, "Ethiopians, Awake!" and "Up, you mighty race, you can accomplish what you will!" He recalls the iconography surrounding the person of Garvey: the "big, shiny photographs of Marcus Garvey that were passed from hand to hand" like sacred objects. To put it succinctly, X grew up in a Garveyite household. For the better part of his adulthood, he was a member of an organization that emerged within the symbolic field and under the penumbra of the Garveyite spiritual commonwealth. A conception of African

---

Marcus Garvey deliver a speech" but did attend a lecture in 1928 by Noble Drew Ali who impressed him profoundly (65).

descended identity (blackness) as sacred defined this spirituality. Garveyism was ritually and ceremonially rich. One need only consider the liturgical character of Garveyite performances: from the ritual invocation of their motto – "One God, one aim, one destiny," to their tricolor red, black, green flag; Ethiopian hymnal-aided singing, and their catechisms regarding the virtues of blackness and destiny of Africa. Indeed, practices centered on Africa as birthplace and destiny of black people. I choose to call the commonwealth, to which Garveyism gave birth, 'spiritual' rather than 'religious' to accent its abstract, disembedded, and tradition non-specific character. Though the deep metaphors of this spirituality are Christian owing to the provenance of most participants, as a general and generalizing phenomenon this spiritually pushes against Christian capture. In this generalizing and abstract mood, participants in the Garveyite spiritual commonwealth celebrate the goodness of blackness and the blackness of the divine: of ancestors, gods, and God.

Malcolm X saw himself as carrying forward the work of Marcus Garvey. In his February 15, 1965 address at the Audubon Ballroom, "There's a Worldwide Revolution Going On," he remarks that his two newly established organizations were the first step "since Garvey died, to actually establish contact between the twenty-two million Black Americans with our brothers and sisters" in Africa. Muslim Mosque directly tied his co-religionists in America with those in Africa and Asia. He sought to alter the perception and self-perception of Blackamerican Muslims by accenting the presence of 700 Million Muslims in the world. Thus he positions his newly minted religious community as part of a powerful global communion rather than as a minority within a minority. When combined with Malcolm's new political group, the Organization of Afro-American Unity, Garvey's goal of uniting black people world-wide with "the mother continent" was only enhanced (Malcolm X, 1992: 123). Malcolm's remark about Garvey comes directly after a passage where he asserts his Muslim *bona fides*, his status, post-Hajj, as an 'authentic Muslim' in contrast to the inauthentic Muslims in the 'Black Muslim Movement' as he called the Nation of Islam. Where, earlier, he had criticized the scholar C. Eric Lincoln and media types for using the adjective 'black' when describing the Nation, he now embraces this descriptor as an important rhetorical move in the new struggle for a Muslim identity that he engages in after his break with Elijah Muhammad. He implies that authentic Muslims, Sunni Muslims rather than the nationalist Muslims of the Nation of Islam, are the true heirs of Marcus Garvey. This is quite an interpretive feat and seems more than a bit dubious. Malcolm found himself in a complex, chaotic, and rapidly changing environment. There were commitments to honor, reconfigure, or abandon. His Garveyite inheritance was chief among them. How could he truly honor those commitments while trashing the Nation of Islam, a charter member of Garveyite spiritual commonwealth? Malcolm attempted, unsuccessfully I think, to wed Garveyism and Sunni Islam. Had he not been assassinated, one wonders how long the marriage would have lasted.

Malcolm X captures quite well the cross pressures to which freedom activists within the Nation of Islam, such as himself, where subject. Their authenticity was challenged from two incompatible directions. Rejected by the so-called orthodox Muslim world that questioned its Muslim *bona fides*, the American government contemporaneously constructed them as political rather than religious. Malcolm X remarks: "We were in a religious vacuum. We were in a political vacuum. We were actually alienated, cut off from all type of activity with even the world that we were fighting against." He adds that they were forced to become "a sort of religious-political hybrid" (Malcolm X, 1992: 164). Even though he did not have the language to properly articulate the perplexity, what he adumbrates is the conflict between the Muslim notion of *din*, that is, an all-encompassing way of life that demands submission to Allah in all domains and the modern, Christian-derived notion of religion as a voluntary, nonpolitical, nonlegal, spiritual inwardness of private belief and quest for individual salvation (Malcolm X, 1992: 164). Without the requisite categories, which have only become available recently, Malcolm X did not understand the conflict between an all-encompassing Islam and (and pre-Reformation Christianity, for that matter) and the modern construction of religion as a discrete, domain specific sphere – in light of which the Nation of Islam appeared to be anomalous. Though he was not aware that he was doing so, by establishing separate Muslim and political organizations, X actually conceded to the Christian-derived notion of religion as nonpolitical. In this regard, it was a conservative step in comparison to the radicalism of the challenge to the American social order that the Nation of Islam represented. Given the power of the modernist American self-understanding where 'church and state' are independent and non-overlapping domains, a separatist understanding shared reflexively by the majority of Blackamericans, this concession was prudent. If Malcolm's Black Nationalist political project was to succeed, then it demanded the separation of religion and politics; this project could not tolerate the political establishment of a particular religious tradition. But the cost was a diminution of the radical edge of a religion such as the Nation of Islam that refuses to stay in its place. Whether that radicalism is good or bad is an open question. This concession to 'church/state' separation notwithstanding, X could not imagine a commitment to Islam that required him to abandon Garveyite spirituality.

Garveyite spirituality was the deep logic, the "changing same," running beneath, through and often ahead of Malcolm X's peripatetic religious life.

Malcolm X: A Religious Timeline

Childhood: Subject of Parental Choices

1925–1931:	Baptist (and Garveyite Spirituality)
1931–1938:	Adventism
1940:	Pentecostalism

Teens and Early Adulthood: Transitional Period

1941–1948:	Unchurched and Latent Garveyite Spirituality

Adulthood: Subject of His Own Choices

1946–1948:	Atheism
1948–1963:	Nation of Islam (Re-Emergent Garveyite Spirituality)
1964–1965:	Sunni Islam

Bibliography

Barrett, Leonard E., Sr. *The Rastafarians.* Boston: Beacon Press, 1997.

Burkett, Randall. *Black Redemption: Churchmen Speak for the Garvey Movement.* Philadelphia: Temple University Press, 1978a.

——— *Garveyism as a Religious Movement: The Institutionalization of a Black Civil Religion.* Metuchen, NJ: The Scarecrow Press, Inc. and The American Theological Library Association, 1978b.

Chevannes, Barry. *Rastafari: Roots and Ideology.* Syracuse: Syracuse University Press, 1994.

Carew, Jan. *Ghost in Our Blood: With Malcolm X in Africa, England, and the Caribbean.* Chicago: Lawrence Hill Books, 1994.

Cleage, Albert. *The Black Messiah.* Trenton: Africa World Press, 1989.

Clegg III, Caude A. *An Original Man: The Life and Times of Elijah Muhammad.* New York: St. Griffins, 1998.

Cox, Daniel Robert P. Jones, Juhem Navarro-Rivera, "I Know What You Did Last Sunday: Measuring Social Desirability Bias in Self-Reported Religious Behavior, Belief, and Identity." *Public Religion Research Institute,* 2, 57–8,11. www.publicreligion.org.

Curtis IV, Edward V. "Islamism and Its African American Muslim Critics: Black Muslims in the Era of the Arab Cold War". *American Quarterly* 59, no. 3 (Sep., 2007): 695–696.

DeCaro, Louis A., Jr. *On the Side of My People: A Religious Life of Malcolm X.* New York: New York University Press, 1996.

Drake, St. Claire, *The Redemption of Africa and Black Religion.* Chicago: Third World Press, 1970.

Evanzz, Karl. *The Messenger: The Rise and Fall of Elijah Muhammad.* New York: Pantheon Books, 1999.

Gardell, Mattias. *In the Name of Elijah Muhammad: Louis Farrakhan and the Nation of Islam.* Durham: Duke University Press, 1996.

Giddens, Anthony. *The Consequences of Modernity.* Cambridge: Polity Press, 1991.

Hoekema, Anthony A. *The Four Major Cults: Christian Science, Jehovah's Witnesses, Mormonism, Seventh-day Adventism.* New York: William B. Erdmans, 1963.

Horsley, Richard A. *Bandits, Prophets, and Messiahs: Popular Movements at the Time of Jesus.* New York: T&T Clark, 1999.

https://archive.org/stream/MalcolmX-FBI-HQ-File/100-HQ-399321-14_djvu.txt.

http://en.wikisource.org/w/index.php?title=Articles_by_Malcolm_X_from_LA_Herald-Dispatch/September_5,_1957&oldid=2327431. Last accessed: 05/01/14.

Malcolm X. *By Any Means Necessary: Speeches, Interviews and a Letter by Malcolm X.* New York: Pathfinder, 1970. http://www.malcolm-x.org/docs/int_pbert.htm.

http://monthlyreview.org/2005/02/01/interview-with-malcolm-x.

Malcolm X on Human Rights, Not Civil Rights. Malcolm X on Front Page Challenge, 1965 CBC Archives. Quotation begins at 6:17. (accessed 07/24/15).http://www.onbeing.org/blog/malcolm-x-human-rights-not-civil-rights/3855.

http://www.youtube.com/watch?v=QW-Wf9D6Wew.

http://www.noi.org/muslim-program/.

http://ccnmtl.columbia.edu/projects/mmt/mxp/people/753_I.html.

Lomax, Louis E. *When the Word is Given.* Westport, Connecticut: Greenwood Press Publishers, 1963.

Malcolm X in FBI file: https://archive.org/stream/MalcolmXFBI/malcolmx14a_djvu.txt.

Malcolm X, *February 1965: The Final Speeches.* Edited by Steve Clark. New York: Pathfinder, 1992.

Malcolm X in al-Muslimoon Magazine, 1965. http://www.malcolm-x.org/docs/int_almus.htm.

"Malcolm X: Make It Plain" Part I. Transcribed from The American Experience © 1994 WGBH, Boston, MA and Blackside. Distributed by PBS VIDEO Directed by Orlando Bagwell. Written by Steve Fayer and Orlando Bagwell.

Malcolm X and Alex Haley. *The Autobiography of Malcolm X.* New York: Ballentine Books, 1965.

Malcolm X and A.B. Spellman, *Monthly Review* 56, no. 9 (1964). http://monthlyreview.org/2005/02/01/interview-with-malcolm-x/.

Marable, Manning. *Malcolm X: A Life of Reinvention.* New York: Viking Press, 2011.

Marsh, Charles E. Marsh. *From Black Muslims to Muslims: The Resurrection, Transformation, and Change of the Lost-Found Nation of Islam in America, 1930–1995.* Landham, MD: The Scarecrow Press, Inc., 1996.

McDuffie, Erik S. and Komozi Woodard. "If You're in a Country that's Progressive, the Woman is Progressive: Black Women Radicals and The Making of the Politics and Legacy of Malcolm X." *Biography* 36, no. 3 (Summer 2013): 521. DOI: 10.1353/bio.2013.0036.

Moses, Wilson Jeremiah. *Black Messiahs and Uncle Toms: Social and Literary Manipulations of a Religious Myth.* University Park, Pennsylvania: Pennsylvania University Press, 1993.

Painter, Irvin Nell. "Malcolm X across the Genres." *The American Historical Review* 98, no. 2: (1993).

Poke, Khary. "Malcolm X, Sexual Hearsay, and Masculine Dissemblance." *Biography* 36, no. 3 (Summer 2013): 579–580,581. DOI: 10.1353/bio.2013.0029.

Wilson, Jamie J. "Come down off the cross and get under the crescent: The Newspaper Columns of Elijah Muhammad and Malcolm X." *Biography* 36, no. 3 (Summer 2013).

Wright, Richard. *Black Boy: A Record of Childhood and Youth.* New York: Harper Perennial Classic, 2007.

CHAPTER 3

On the Dialectical Evolution of Malcolm X's Anti-Capitalist Critique: Interrogating His Political Philosophy of Black Nationalism

John H. McClendon III and Stephen C. Ferguson II

Introductory Remarks

In this chapter, "On the Dialectical Evolution of Malcolm X's Anti-Capitalist Critique: Interrogating His Political Philosophy of Black Nationalism," our objective is to provide the reader with an opportunity to reflect on two major considerations regarding the complex meaning attached to his life and thought. The first part of our presentation focuses on Malcolm X's historical and political relevance for the twenty-first century. Malcolm X (El-Hajj Malik El-Shabazz) died in 1965, yet the question of his relevance for us today is not a trivial concern and indeed it is a pressing matter of highest importance. In truth for many readers, particularly the generations born since the time of his death, Malcolm X principally remains an iconic, if not a mythic, figure (Horne, 1993: 440–450; Flick, 1981: 166–181). After careful study of this section of our presentation (and especially for our younger audience) the reader will gain a substantial and critical appreciation of Malcolm's legacy for the burning political issues that we face in the United States and our world today.

The second part of our presentation is philosophical in method. This latter segment addresses the issue of interrogating Malcolm's political philosophy of Black Nationalism. Pivotal to our philosophical analysis is the critical examination of Malcolm's dialectical evolution as a Black Nationalist philosopher, which orbits around the development of his burgeoning anti-capitalist critique. The theoretical complexity of Black nationalism and Malcolm's locus as thinker, within this context, is illuminated from the perspective of dialectical and historical materialism. The critique of the false conception that Black Nationalism is strictly reducible to a race analysis serves as our presumptive context. In the last year of Malcolm's life, he expended great intellectual effort to gain new clarity about the problems ancillary with racism, national oppression, and capitalist class exploitation. We conclude that Malcolm's intellectual effort unfolds as a dialectical process of development. In his endeavor to shape the needed revolutionary weapons for African American liberation, as Malcolm X grew in his understanding, he accordingly revised his political philosophy. These revisions and corrections in Malcolm's political philosophy directly mirror how he became more profoundly engaged in his examination of the African American condition and world situation.

On Malcolm X's Relevance for the Twenty-First Century

On May 29, 1964, Malcolm X stated: "A chicken just doesn't have it within its system to produce a duck egg. It can't do it. It can only produce according to what that particular system was constructed to produce. The system of this country cannot produce freedom for an Afro-American. It is impossible for this system, this economic system, this political system, this social system, as it stands, to produce freedom right now for the black man in this country" (Malcolm X, 1966: 68–69). It appropriately follows that any consideration of Malcolm X as thinker/activist for the twenty-first century must be cognizant that some fifty years ago, he brought to our attention how the imperialist interests of the United States government and its ruling class – today often framed on the rhetoric of global capitalism/empire and the ruling one percent – in systemically hegemonic fashion remains dialectically part and parcel of the conditions of African American political impotency, social oppression, and economic exploitation. In his now well-known speech, "The Ballot or The Bullet," Malcolm explicitly states that Black people are "the victims of democracy" (Malcolm X, 1966: 26; Wolfenstein, 1993).

Malcolm keenly understands that African American oppression is not only the result of overtly individualized acts of racism; more appreciably it is structural and systemic and thus grounded in the very makeup of the U.S. political, legal, economic, and social order inclusive of an imperialist/racist international character. Malcolm opines:

> In order for you and me to know the nature of the struggle that you and I are involved in, we have to know not only the various ingredients involved at the local level and national level, but also the ingredients that are involved at the international level. And the problems of the Black man here in this country today have ceased to be a problem of just the American Negro or an American problem. It has become a problem that is so complex, and has so many implications in it, that you have to study it in its entire world, in the world context or in its international context, to really see it as it actually is.

Malcolm X continues:

> In the Black communities, the economy of the community is not in the hands of the Black man. The Black man is not his own landlord. The

buildings that he lives in are owned by someone else. The stores in the community are run by someone else. Everything in the community is out of his hands. He has no say-so in it whatsoever, other than to live there, and pay the highest rent for the lowest-type boarding place, pays the highest prices for food, for the lowest grade of food. He is a victim of this, a victim of economic exploitation, political exploitation, and every other kind.
>
> MALCOLM X, 1989: 151–152, 161

Therefore we must ask: how relevant are Malcolm's observations to our contemporary times? Does his analysis speak to developments of the past fifty years and existing circumstances as we move through the second decade of the twenty-first century? What are the present-day state of affairs surrounding African American communities with regard to housing conditions, social position, educational attainment, wage and income levels, economic conditions, and political status? Do Black working people still remain today, the victims of myriad forms of exploitation?

At present, we discover that pundits as well as scholars and activists have highlighted what becomes the mounting economic divide between those few which have wealth, power own the means of production and the increasing numbers of working people relegated to the ranks of the impoverished and powerless, who are forced to sell their labor in order to live. In January, 2014, Oxfam International reports, "The percentage of income held by the richest 1% in the U.S. has grown nearly 150% from 1980 through 2012. That small elite has received 95% of wealth created since 2009, after the financial crisis, while the bottom 90% of Americans has become poorer" (Fuentes-Nieva and Galasso, 2014).[1]

In introducing the National Urban League's analytical tool, "2014 Equality Index: Black-White," Valerie Rawlston Wilson offers the following sobering commentary: "For African Americans, these [employment] challenges

---

[1] We would like to thank Dr. Malik Simba of Fresno State University for reading several drafts of this essay and providing insightful comments and suggestions. Consult Ricardo Fuentes-Nieva and Nicholas Galasso, "Working the Few: Political Capture and Economic Inequality" *Oxfam International Report* (January 20, 2014) http://www.oxfam.org/en/policy/working--the-few-economic-inequality. Also read, Rakesh Kochlar, Richard Fry and Paul Taylor, "Twenty to One: Wealth Gaps Rise to Record Time Between Whites, Blacks, Hispanics" (Washington, DC: Pew Research Center, 2011). Derek Hamilton and William Darity, Jr., "Can Baby Bonds Eliminate the Racial Wealth Gap in Putative Post-Racial America?" *Review of Black Political Economy* 37.3–4, (2010): 207–216.

are even greater. Though Black unemployment briefly and narrowly dipped below 12 percent for the first time since 2008 at the end of last year, 42 percent of Black unemployed workers are long-term unemployed and 28 percent have been jobless for at least a year. The rate of underemployment for African Americans was 20.5 percent, compared to 11.8 percent for white workers and 18.4 percent for Hispanic workers." (Wilson, 2014: 15) Furthermore, the North Carolina based Center for Global Policy Solutions released a recent report in May, 2014: *Beyond Broke: Why Closing the Racial Wealth Gap is a Priority for National Economic Security*. The findings graphically point out, "Over a third of all African Americans (38%) and Latinos (35%) have no financial assets whatsoever, compared to only 14% of Whites. Likewise, some 33 percent of African Americans and 28 percent of Latinos have either no or negative net worth, compared to only 13 percent of Whites" (Tippett, Jones-DeWeever, Rockeymoore, Hamilton, and Darity, 2014: 3). To paraphrase Stevie Wonder, too many working people are living just enough, just enough for the city. African American working people continue to be 'victims of democracy' rather than shareholders in the American Dream. It is becoming clear that the class interest of the Black working class is incompatible with those Black individuals who have gained membership in the ruling class such as Shawn 'Jay-Z' Carter, Kenneth I. Chenault or Barack Obama.

Of particular importance is the fact that Malcolm predicts that capitalism would have such class division, with its ancillary expanding racial inequality. Malcolm X warns that without a concerted Black mass movement; class division will assume a definitively racial/national character and thereby a disproportionate number of African Americans would find themselves in the throes of shattered communities, poor achieving school systems, homelessness, incarceration, unemployment, underemployment, and poverty.[2]

---

2 Bryan Warde, "Black Male Disproportionality in the Criminal Justice Systems of the USA, Canada, and England: A Comparative Analysis of Incarceration" *Journal of African American Studies* 17.4 (December, 2013): 461–479. Robynn Cox, "Crime, Incarceration, and Employment in Light of the Great Recession." *The Review of Black Political Economy* 37.3-4, (2010) pp. 283–294. Sandra Phillips, "The Subprime Crisis and African Americans" *The Review of Black Political Economy* 37.3-4, (2010): 223–229. Gregory N. Price, "The Subprime Crisis and African Americans-Response." *The Review of Black Political Economy* 37.3-4, (2010): 231–236. Kimberly Hefling, "Disparities Remain in America's Schools" (March 21, 2014) http://news.yahoo.com/disparities-remain-americas-schools-191446916--politics.html. Rochelle L. Rowley and David W. Wright, "No 'White' Child Left Behind: The Academic Achievement Gap between Black and White Students." *The Journal of Negro Education*, V. 80, n. 2 (Spring 2011), pp. 93–107. Michele A. Gilbert, "Race, Location, and Education: The Election of Black Mayors in the 1990s." *Journal of Black Studies* 36. 3 (January, 2006): 318–333.

Malcolm's summation of capitalism is most fitting here. Malcolm argues, "Capitalism used to be like an eagle, but now it's more like a vulture. It used to be strong enough to go and suck anybody's blood whether they were strong or not. But now it has become more cowardly, like the vulture, and it can only suck the blood of those helpless" (Malcolm X, 1966: 199).[3]

Malcolm comprehends that such dire conditions facing African Americans has at root anterior economic causes as well as crucial political consequences for building the Black movement for revolutionary transformation. Malcolm concludes Black oppression issues from systemic exploitation and is not reducible to racial conflict wherein African Americans should take an essentially anti-white position. Malcolm incisively declares,

> I believe that there will ultimately be a clash between the oppressed and those that do the oppressing. I believe that there will be a clash between those who want freedom, justice, and equality for everyone and those who want to continue the systems of exploitation… It is incorrect to classify the revolt of the Negro as simply a racial conflict of Black against white, or as a purely American problem. Rather, we are today seeing a global rebellion of the oppressed against the oppressor, the exploited against the exploiter.
> MALCOLM X, 1992: 177

Malcolm repeatedly declares that it is the *United States federal government* (not just racist extremist organizations and racist local governmental agencies) that plays a pivotal role in the violent assault on the African American movement for human rights and it consequently fails to defend African-American interests. Malcolm states,

> The federal government itself is just as racist as the government in Mississippi, and is more guilty of perpetrating the racist system. At the federal level they are more shrewd, more skillful at doing it, just like the FBI is more skillful than the state police and the state police are more skillful than the local police. The same with politicians. The politician at the federal level is usually more skilled than the politician at the local level, and

---

3 See also Thomas M. Shapiro, "Policies of Exclusion Perpetuate the Racial Wealth Gap" in *One Nation Underemployed: Jobs Rebuild America*, which is the title of the National Urban League 2014 State of Black America.

> when he wants to practice racism, is more skilled in the practice of it than those who practice it at the local level.
>
> MALCOLM X, 1989: 19

Since Malcolm's assessment in 1965, how far have we advanced from the harsh reality associated with governmental (racist) actions, which he brings to our notice?

Let us consider the case of Hurricane Katrina in New Orleans. As Rodney D. Green, Marie Kouassi, and Belinda Mambo report:

> African Americans were concentrated in the most vulnerable parts of the city, located well below sea level and poorly protected by inadequate levees. The government's response to Katrina further disadvantaged black residents. The initial reaction to Katrina was *repression*; U.S. *troops* supplemented by *Blackwater mercenaries* descended on the city with an iron fist and little service. Then the city government declared a moratorium on building permits and declined to reopen schools or even restore electricity for an extended period in low-income black neighborhoods… The political leadership in local, state, and national levels and historical institutional milieu in which they functioned were not favorable to the low-income African American population; the interest of profit-oriented developers and other large businesses are better represented among these forces.
>
> GREEN ET AL, 2013: 146–147, 153. [Italics Added]

As manifested in the form of two-party politics, state power functions to preserve and enhance the dictatorship of capital and white racist ascendancy. This preservation of racism and the capitalist status quo, time and again comes at the expense (often by means of naked coercion) of the African American masses. Malcolm sharply observes,

> So today, when the black man starts reaching out for what America says are his rights, the black man feels that he is within his rights-when he becomes the victim of brutality by those who are depriving him of his rights-do whatever is necessary to protect himself. An example of this was taking place last night at this same time in Cleveland, where the police were putting water hoses on our people there and throwing tear gas at them-and they met a hail of stones, a hail of rocks, a hail of bricks.
>
> MALCOLM X, 1966: 49

As to the Black masses that on occasion erupted in militant counter-violence to state brutality, we discover Malcolm X often references this group as "the field Negroes." Malcolm's incipient class analysis of the African American community amplifies the political importance of the Black working-class masses. Drawing on the slave plantation analogy, Malcolm shrewdly notes:

> There are two kinds of Negroes. There was that old house Negro and the field Negro. And the house Negro always looked out for his master. When the field Negroes got too much out of line, he held them back in check. He put 'em back on the plantation. The house Negro could afford to do that because he lived better than the field Negro. He ate better, dress better, and he lived in a better house… If the master got sick, he'd say, 'what's the matter, boss, *we* sick?' When the master's house caught afire, he'd try to put the fire out… But then you have some field Negroes, who lived in huts, and had nothing to lose. They wore the worst kind of clothes. They ate the worst food. And they caught hell. They felt the sting of the lash. They hated their master… I'm a field Negro. If I can't live in the house as a human being, I'm praying for a wind to come along. If the master won't treat me right and he's sick, I'll tell the doctor to go in the other direction.[4]
> MALCOLM X, 1992: 27

In Malcolm X's estimation, "the field Negroes" or Black masses are the catalysts, which will push forward any program that upholds utilizing revolutionary action, with the aim of obtaining political power (Malcolm X, 1992: 26–28). Thus, Malcolm's political analysis also incisively reveals that Black dependence on liberal politicians is not a real alternative to African American political powerlessness. Malcolm X demonstrates the two-party political system fundamentally operates as an instrument for maintaining Black political dispossession. This *institutional condition* of powerlessness is chiefly responsible in facilitating the corresponding racist oppression and systemic (capitalist) exploitation of the Black working-class. Malcolm X cogently argues:

---

4 See also Robin D.G. Kelley, "House Negroes on the Loose: Malcolm X and the Black Bourgeoisie" *Callaloo* 21.2 (Spring 1998): 419–435. The idea of the "House Negro" as a tragic figure is graphically portrayed in Quentin Taratino's 2012 slavery-spaghetti Western *Django Unchained*. The character "Stephen" played by Samuel Jackson is staunchly loyal to his slave master Calvin Candie. For a critique of *Django Unchained* as part of the larger move towards "cultural politics," see Adolph Reed, "*Django Unchained*, or, *The Help*: How "Cultural Politics" Is Worse Than No Politics at All, and Why," Nonsite.org 9 (February 25, 2013) http://nonsite.org/feature/django-unchained-or-the-help-how-cultural-politics-is-worse-than-no-politics-at-all-and-why# (accessed July 10, 2014).

> You and I in America are faced not with a segregationist conspiracy, where faced with a government conspiracy. ... The same government that you go abroad to fight for and die for is the government that is in a conspiracy to deprive you of your voting rights, deprive you of your economic opportunities, deprive you of decent housing, deprive you of decent education. You don't need to go to the employer alone, it is the government itself, the government of America, that is responsible for the oppression and exploitation and degradation of black people in this country. And you should drop it in their lap. This government has failed the Negro. This so-called democracy has failed the Negro. And all these white liberals have definitely failed the Negro.[5]
>
> MALCOLM X, 1966: 30–31

Currently Malcolm's notion about the United States government, wherein Black people are in the position of 'the victims of democracy,' is under ideological attack. And this ideological perspective is especially pronounced given the election of Barack Obama, as the first Black president of the United States. For instance, in response to the 2008 election of Obama, actor Will Smith conveys: "...(a)ll of our excuses have been removed. There is no white man trying to keep you down, because if he were trying to keep you down he would have [also tried to keep] Obama down" (Hamilton and Darity, 2010: 209).

In response to Smith, first we must inquire as to why he conceives of racism as *an excuse* rather than *an explanation* for Black oppressive conditions and corresponding social status/racialized class position? Smith's notion that Obama's presidential election signals the end of white racism follows from the fact that he obviously neglects the institutional and systemic (class) character of both racism and politics in the United States. In similar fashion to Smith, Black conservative journalist Gregory P. Kane proclaims, "After 1964, after Johnson declared his 'War on Poverty,' liberals did to poor folks, especially poor black folks, the worst thing they could have done to us. They made us victims. As victims, we weren't expected, indeed not encouraged, to act responsibly."[6]

---

5 On the role of the government, by means of the legal system, in the deprivation of Black people's rights, see Malik Simba, *Black Marxism and American Constitutionalism: an Interpretive History from the Colonial Background to the Ascendancy of Barack Obama*, Second Edition, (Kendall Hunt Publishing, 2013).

6 For Gregory P. Kane's remark, consult the section on "Quote" on the website *The Black Conservative* http://blackconservative360.blogspot.com/p/quotes.html. For a scholarly treatment of 'victimized' ideology in concert with Will Smith and Gregory P. Kane's position read, Charles Johnson, "The End of the Black American Narrative: A New Century Calls for New Stories

Kane's idea of victims derives from putting the blame for Black impoverishment on the lack of *personal responsibility* among the Black poor. Kane's presumption relies on methodological individualism and what results is the view that one's socio-economic position is a matter of choice (rational choice theory) and likewise personal responsibility for such choices. At base is the perspective that the Black poor are impoverished because their values lead to bad decisions in life. This is what is known as the 'culture of poverty' thesis.[7]

In turn, with Malcolm's notion of 'victims of democracy,' we observe his idea actually highlights systemic oppression and exploitation and the onus is victimization and not how the poor Black masses fail to have the requisite values to achieve success in the capitalist/racist social order. In contrast to Gregory Kane, Malcolm's idea of 'victimization' allows for the Black masses to become conscious of the real, material conditions i.e. understand the causes of their oppression and not resort to self-blame for their social plight. For Malcolm, it is mass *social responsibility* to struggle against oppressive conditions that becomes the crucial value set for overturning the plight of the Black masses.[8]

Clearly Smith and Kane's position on Black oppression stand in stark contrast to Malcolm's systemic approach to African American exploitation as 'the victims of democracy.' For Malcolm, "The black man in North America was sickest of all politically. He lets the white man divide him into such foolishness as considering himself a black 'Democrat,' a black 'Republican,' a black 'Conservative,' or a black 'Liberal'..." (Malcolm X, 1996: 313). Accordingly, Malcolm discounts the value of the two-party political system with its liberal/conservative ideological distinctions and spectrum; we find that he aptly coins a metaphor about the fox (stipulated for liberals) and the wolf (designated for

---

Grounded in the Present, Leaving behind the Painful History of Slavery and Its Consequences" *The American Scholar* (Summer, 2008): 32–42. For a critique of Johnson read, Derek Hamilton and William Darity, Jr., "Can Baby Bonds Eliminate the Racial Wealth Gap in Putative Post-Racial America?" 209.

7   For an excellent discussion and critique of the "culture of poverty" thesis, see Alice O'Connor, *Poverty Knowledge: Social Science, Social Policy, and the Poor in Twentieth-Century U.S. History*. Princeton, N.J.: Princeton University Press, 2001; and Adolph Reed, "The 'Color Line' Then and Now: The Souls of Black Folk and the Changing Context of Black American Politics," in Adolph L. Reed and Kenneth W. Warren, eds. *Renewing Black Intellectual History: The Ideological and Material Foundations of African American Thought* (Boulder: Paradigm Publishers, 2010): 252–303.

8   Bill Cosby is another proponent of the poverty of culture thesis. For a critique, see Earl Ofari Hutchinson, "Bill Cosby's New Book Full of Racial Stereotypes" *Alternet* (October 15, 2007) http://www.alternet.org/story/65306/bill_cosby%27s_new_book_full_of_racial_stereotypes (Accessed July 10, 2014).

conservatives) as collaborating participants in the u.s. racist political arena. Malcolm states, "A fox and a wolf are both canine, both belong to the dog family. Now you take your choice. You going to choose a Northern dog or a Southern dog? Because either dog you choose, I guarantee you'll still be in the dog house" (Ellis and Smith, 2010: 15).[9]

In relatable vernacular, which reverberated with his Black grassroots constituency, Malcolm points out both fox and wolf belong to the dog family i.e. both liberal and conservatives, the Democratic and Republican parties share a robust political kinship within the prevailing framework of the two-party system. With his analysis of the two-party system and how it operates as a *racist institutional reality*, Malcolm brings into bold relief why this political system locks out the masses of African Americans from effectively engaging in the political process as means for capturing the necessary power to change their real material (life) circumstances.

The relevance of Malcolm X's political insights is perceptively affirmed in the following commentary by Black political scientist, Mack H. Jones. Jones addresses how we must analyze the nature of Black political power. He argues,

> Much of the literature on black political power will simply list the number of black voters or officeholders and suggests that they automatically demonstrate a certain level of political power. Voting, holding office, favorable population distribution, and economic wealth may be bases or sources of power – but they are only – potential sources of power... Thus voting in itself is not power; having a black majority in itself is not power; nor having black elected and appointed officials power. These phenomena become power only when they can be used to influence and effect the behavior of other actors-principally white individuals and groups. Therefore, any attempt to assess the political power of a given black community should include a discussion of the socioeconomic and political problems facing the community....[10]
>
> JONES, 1978: 93

---

9   See also Hank Flick and Larry Powell, "Animal Imagery in the Rhetoric of Malcolm X," *Journal of Black Studies* 18.4 (June 1988): 435–451.
10 Also consult, Adolph Reed, Jr., "The Black Urban Regime: Structural Origins and Constraints." In *Stirrings in the Jug: Black Politics in the Post-Segregation Era* (Minneapolis: University of Minnesota Press, 1999): 79–115. William Reed, "Profiling the Black Mayors of America." *The Hudson Valley Press* (September 11, 2013).

Citing the *Look* magazine exposé on James Meredith's integration of the University of Mississippi, Malcolm points out how the segregationist Mississippi Governor Ross Barnett and liberal U.S. Attorney General Robert Kennedy made a political deal concerning Meredith's admission and entrance into the University. As a conservative/segregationist, Barnett would openly stand at the doors of the University and obstruct Meredith's entrance. In turn, Kennedy would come with U.S. Marshals and compel Barnett to admit Meredith to the University of Mississippi. In that way, both men could sustain the political support/votes of their constituencies, i.e. liberal and conservative Democrats (Dixiecrats) respectively. In Malcolm's view Meredith's admission, as the solitary black student at the University of Mississippi, is simply a matter of tokenism and political trickery. Malcolm continues:

> So they, only come up with tokenism. In this tokenism that they give us benefits only a few. A few hand-picked Negroes gain from this; a few hand-picked Negroes have good jobs; a few hand-picked Negroes get good homes or go to a decent school... As this one or two is going to open up his mouth and talk about how the problem is being solved. In the whole world thinks that America's race problem is being solved, when actually the masses of Black people in America are still living in the ghettos and the slums; they are still the victims of inferior housing: they are still the victims of a segregated school system... They are still victims, after they get that inferior education, where they can only get the worst form of jobs.
> MALCOLM X, 1992: 59–60

Malcolm recognizes that these incorporations of a select few Black faces into political, economic and social positions of influence are only instances of tokenism, which are aimed at ameliorating mass discontent. This is because Malcolm understands that such actions did not suffice as achieving and fulfilling the critical need for Black mass-based political power. In response, to the question, about rumors that Lyndon Johnson could possibly make a Black cabinet appointment. Malcolm states:

> I just read where they planned to make a black cabinet member. Yes, they have a new gimmick every year. They're going to take one of their boys, black boys, and put him in the cabinet, so he can walk around Washington with a cigar – fire on one end and fool on the other. And because his immediate personal problem will have been solved, he will be the one to tell our people, "Look how much progress we're making: I'm in Washington, D.C. I can have tea in the White House. I'm your spokesman,

> I'm your, you know, your leader." But will it work? Can that one, whom they are going to put down there, step into the fire and put it out when the flames begin to leap up? When people take to the streets in their explosive mood, will that one, that they're going to put in the cabinet, be able to go among those people? Why, they'll burn him faster than they burn the ones who sent him.
>
> MALCOLM X, 1966: 151

No doubt, Malcolm X's cutting-edge political perspective sheds considerable light on a number of contemporary questions. As Black communist Bill Epton observes: "[Malcolm] had a clear understanding of the international situation and the class position of the African American people in the United States. He was able to take great generalities and make them quite specific and show how they applied to our situation. He could sum up complex social, political, and cultural developments in succinct phrases and explain them in clear everyday language that the masses could easily understand" (Mealy, 1993: 19). Subsequently, we can pose several key questions about Malcolm's legacy for us today.[11] How should we concretely analyze Barack Obama's presidency? Does Obama's presidency indicate political and social progress for the African American working-class? Have we really reached the status of post-racial society?

Regarding Obama's election and the idea of racism's declining significance and hence the achievement of a post-racial society, economists Derek Hamilton and William Darity Jr. argue:

> The post-racial ideology represents a shift from some acknowledgement of a social responsibility for the condition of black America to a position where blacks need to "get over it" and "take personal responsibility"... Moreover, blacks are enjoined to stop making particularistic claims on America and solely pursue programs of social change designed to reach all Americans. All of these sentiments were expressed plainly by Barack Obama in his "More Perfect Union" speech in Philadelphia during the campaign... Both implicitly and explicitly, Obama is arguing that there is nothing unique about the discriminatory barriers faced by black Americans today, and further, whatever discriminatory barriers that they may face, are at their lowest point ever. However, Obama does seem to

---

11 See, for example, Malcolm's analysis of the Mississippi Freedom Democratic Party read, Malcolm X, "With Mrs. Fannie Lou Hamer," in George Breitman, ed., *Malcolm X Speaks* (New York: Grove Press, 1966): 108–114.

uniquely target his personal responsibility rhetoric to blacks. What is lacking from his discrimination narrative is the empirical evidence which indicates that since the mid to late 1970s black-white wage inequality, along with the measured component of that inequality attributable to discrimination, has remained roughly flat.[12]

HAMILTON AND DARITY, 2010: 208

Additionally we must raise the question, why do we have not only growing income differentials between whites and African Americans, but also an increasing income/wealth gap between the Black 'middle-class' and African American masses?[13] Despite an unprecedented sum of Black officeholders, along with the emergence of Black mayors from Cleveland and Gary to Atlanta and Los Angeles, why are the Black masses without political power? Why are Black elected and appointed officials virtually powerless in halting the erosion of African American communities – such as we find in Detroit – a city where Malcolm X once resided?[14]

In 2006, Michele Gilbert informs us, "To many in our country, the structural significance of race in society is eroding. However, when examining race in the election of Black mayors, I find that it is still a primary factor in the determination of political success for Black candidates… Essentially, my research has confirmed that the legacy of racism in our country is still a primary factor in

---

12   Also see, Robert Staples, "The Post Racial Presidency: The Myths of a Nation and its People" *Journal of African American Studies* 14.1 (March 2010): 128–144. For the classic study on the declining significance of race consult, William Julius Wilson, *The Declining Significance of Race: Blacks and Changing American Institutions*, 3rd edition, (Chicago: University of Chicago Press, 2012). For leftist critiques of Wilson, see Thomas D. Boston, *Race, Class, and Conservatism*. Boston, Massachusetts: Unwin Hyman, 1988; and Steven Rosenthal, "How Liberal Ideology Assists the Growth of Fascism: A Critique of the Sociology of William Julius Wilson," *Journal of Poverty* 3.2 (1999): 67–87.

13   See Bart Landry and Kris Marsh. "The Evolution of the New Black Middle Class." *Annual Review of Sociology* 37 (2011): 373–378, C1-C3, 379–394. See also Eugene Robinson, *Disintegration: The Splintering of Black America*. New York: Doubleday, 2010.

14   Devitt, Caitlin. "Detroit Mayor Cuts Wages, Benefits." *Bond Buyer* 381.33750 (July 19, 2012): 1–8. See also Lisa Saunders, "Employment and Earnings: A Case Study of Urban Detroit," *The Review of Black Political Economy* V. 39.1 (March, 2012): 107–119. Michael Bonds, "Black Political Power Reassessed: Race, Politics, and Federal Funds," *Journal of African American Studies* 11.3-4 (December 2007): 189–203. Neil Kraus and Todd Swanstrom, "Minority Mayors and the Hollow-Prize Problem," *Political Science and Politics* 34.1 (March 2001): 99–105. Johnnie Dee Swain, Jr., "Black Mayors: Urban Decline and the Underclass," *Journal of Black Studies* 24.1 (September 1993): 16–28.

the political arena" (Gilbert, 2006: 331). With respect to his political analysis, Malcolm's sharp arguments – about the two-party political system and the exercise of state power – perceptively capture our existing circumstances and we must recognize this system as a formidable obstacle to our advancing a political agenda for Black liberation.

Also regarding Malcolm's continued relevance for the twenty-first century; we have the recent and sustained debates surrounding Manning Marable's biography, *Malcolm X: A Life of Reinvention* (2011). The critical response to this less than credible biography unmistakably illustrates that a significant host of activists and scholars are aware Malcolm's political and intellectual heritage is an existing issue of monumental proportions. Arguably, these debates are the most noteworthy polemics to emerge, in several years, among the ranks of the Black liberation movement and in African American Studies.[15]

In the twenty-first century, another way Malcolm's legacy remains as relevant is by way of the continual surfacing of Black Nationalist formations.[16]

---

15   Manning Marable, *Malcolm X: A Life of Reinvention* (New York: Penguin Group, 2011). One of the authors of this chapter offers critical remarks, on Marable's biography, in an interview for an article by Bill Castanier, "Debate Still Rages over Malcolm X: A New Biography Reignites Old Controversies Surrounding the African American Leader," *City Pulse* (Wednesday, April 27, 2011). Also read, V.P. Franklin, "Introduction: Reflections on the Legacy of Malcolm X," *The Journal of African American History*, 98.4 (Fall 2013): 562–564. Phillip M. Richards, "Marable's Malcolm and the Myth of the Folk," (Review of *Malcolm X: A Life of Reinvention* by Manning Marable) *The Journal of African American History* 98.4, (Fall 2013): 573–578. Abdul Alkalimat, "Rethinking Malcolm Means First Learning How to Think: What Was Marable Thinking? And How?" *The Black Scholar*, 41.2 (Summer 2011): 2–10. William W. Sales Jr., "Manning Marable's Reinvention of Malcolm X: The Biography that Hype Couldn't Save," *The Black Scholar*, 41.2 (Summer 2011): 26–33. Jared A. Ball and Todd Steven Burroughs, eds., *A Lie of Reinvention: Correcting Manning Marable's Malcolm X* (Baltimore: Black Classic Press, 2012). Herb Boyd, Ron Daniels, Maulana Karenga and Haki R. Madhubuti, eds., *By Any Means Necessary: Malcolm X – Real, Not Reinvented: Critical Conversations on Manning Marable's Biography of Malcolm X*. Chicago: Third World Press, 2012.

16   Eddie Glaude, *Is it Nation Time? Contemporary Essays on Black Power and Black Nationalism* (Chicago: University of Chicago Press, 2002). Melanye T. Price, *Dreaming Blackness: Black Nationalism and African American Public Opinion*. (New York: New York University Press, 2009). Kevin Rashid Johnson, "Black Liberation in the 21st Century: A Revolutionary Reassessment of Black Nationalism" *Kasama Project* (February 20, 2012) http://kasamaproject.org/race-liberation/3911-43black-liberation-in-the-21st-century-a-revolutionary-reassessment-of-black-nationalism. Daryl Augusta Hugley, *The State of Black Nationalism in 21st Century Urban America* (MS Thesis: Southern Connecticut State University, 2012).

However, given the influence of the hegemonic ideological myth of the nation-state, the dominant schools of political philosophy have virtually ignored the impact and importance of Black Nationalism in African American intellectual thought. From the inception of the 'Revolution' of '76 and the subsequent formation of the bourgeois state under the U.S. Constitution, the myth that the United States is a (singular) nation-state has had an overriding ideological influence.[17]

The prima facie neglect of the reality of the multinational state is not an oversight of imprecision; rather it follows the nation-state's putative ideological objective of individual assimilation which functions as the guiding principle of social and political integration. As Rudolph O. de la Garza, Z. Anthony Kruszewski, and Tomás Arciniega state, "For centuries, Anglo Americans have felt it necessary to rationalize the relationship between America's native peoples and the Anglo majority. The way to resolve the Mexican and Indian 'problem' was to make them 'Americans'" (Garza et al, 1973: 7).

With African American national oppression in mind, we can see why Malcolm X repeatedly argues that Black people in the United States are 'victims of Americanism' and thus his adoption of the political philosophy of Black Nationalism. Accordingly, Malcolm's political and intellectual legacy vibrantly persists in the twenty-first century and it demands our upmost intellectual efforts and critical attention; that is to say if we are, in this century, to begin paving our road for liberation.

Interrogating Malcolm's Political Philosophy of Black Nationalism
In this section of our essay, the primary objective is to explore how Malcolm X addresses the complex philosophical ramifications embodied in the very nomenclature and substance of the concept, "Black nationalism."[18] After his break from the Nation of Islam, Malcolm X argued that Black Nationalism served as his political philosophy. Beyond personal differences with Elijah Muhammad, prima facie this declaration about Black Nationalism tells us very little as to

---

17 For an extended discussion on the myth of the nation-state as political ideology, see John H. McClendon III, "Jazz, African American Nationality, and the Myth of the Nation-State," *Socialism and Democracy* 18.2 (December 2004): 21–36.

18 For discussions of Black nationalism, see James Lance Taylor, *Black Nationalism in the United States: From Malcolm X to Barack Obama* (Boulder: Lynne Rienner Publishers, 2011); E.U. Eissen-Udom, *Black Nationalism: The Search for an Identity in America* (Chicago: University of Chicago Press, 1962); St. Clair Drake, *The Redemption of Africa and Black Religion* (Chicago: Third World Press, 1970); and Robert Allen, "Racism and the Black Nation Thesis," *Socialist Revolution*, 6.1 (January/March 1976).

why the break. The consensus scholarship explicitly illustrates the Nation of Islam is preeminently nationalist in its makeup, albeit cast in religious/theological form.[19] Consequently, Malcolm's break from the Nation of Islam is not ostensibly an ideological departure from Black Nationalism, instead it is a split directed at Elijah Muhammad's particular version of it.[20]

Our general analysis of Black Nationalism begins with the background assumption there are specific and multifaceted forms of it. Given this starting point, our overriding question becomes: how are we to philosophically assess and ideologically characterized Malcolm's conception of Black Nationalism vis-à-vis Muhammad's views. Are their differences about nationalism, more personal (that is, subjective) or philosophical in character? In the same way, how do such considerations factor into Malcolm's departure from the Nation of Islam? In play here is the need to specify the concrete forms of nationalism, which are in contention and why did this ultimately lead to the fractured bond and ultimately an ideological, political and epistemological break between Malcolm X and Elijah Muhammad?[21]

We contend that within Malcolm's thought process, there is a dialectical tension between the *nomenclature* 'Black nationalism' and its *substantive content*. As nomenclature, on the one hand, 'Black Nationalism' functions as an *apparent form*, which nominally remains *constantly* and *consistently* his ideological point of departure. While, on the other, we discern 'Black Nationalism' in its *substantive content* functions *dynamically* and this element represents his continuous political and ideological process of growth qua philosophical formation.[22]

---

19 See, for instance, Lewis Edward Wright, *The Political Thought of Elijah Muhammad: Innovation and Continuity in Western Tradition* (Doctoral Dissertation: Howard University, 1987).

20 Ernest Allen, Jr., "Religious Heterodoxy and Nationalist Tradition: The Continuing Evolution of the Nation of Islam" *The Black Scholar* 26.3-4, (Fall-Winter 1996): 2–34. E.U. Eissen-Udom, *Black Nationalism: The Search for an Identity in America* (Chicago: University of Chicago Press, 1962). William L. Van Deburg, ed., *Modern Black Nationalism: from Marcus Garvey to Louis Farrakhan* (New York: New York University Press, 1997).

21 Karl Evanzz, *The Judas Factor: The Plot to Kill Malcolm X*. New York: Thunder's Mouth Press, 1992. Robert L. Jenkins and Mfanya Donald Tryman, ed., *The Malcolm X Encyclopedia* (Westport: Greenwood press, 2002).

22 See also W. Marvin Dulaney, "Documenting the Life and Legacy of Malcolm X" (Review of Manning Marable and Garrett Felber, eds., *The Portable Malcolm X Reader*) *The Journal of African American History,* 98.4 (Fall 2013): 602–608. Kevin Ovenden, *Malcolm X: Socialism and Black Nationalism* (London: Bookmarks, 1992). Hank Flick, "Malcolm X: The Destroyer and Maker of Myths" *Journal of Black Studies* 12. 2 (December, 1981): 166–181

When undertaking philosophical inquiry into the substantive aspect of his thought, we find that the nomenclature 'Black nationalism' remains an inadequate depiction of Malcolm's political philosophy. Indeed precisely due to his evolving (substantive) political thought, Malcolm X reaches, in due course, the conclusion that the very nomenclature 'Black nationalism' is really problematic. Malcolm believes that continued use of the 'Black nationalist,' moniker actually hinders his internationalist aspiration to forge revolutionary struggle on a global scale. This is why as a matter of our method of inquiry, we must critically interrogate the various meanings affixed to Malcolm's notions about Black nationalism. (Collins, 1992: 59–85).[23]

When dialectically investigated, we disclose that Black Nationalism is not monolithic; rather it is multifaceted, variegated and historically specific. From the 19th century until our current-day, there have been *historically specific* and *varying forms* of Black Nationalism. These different cultural, economic, religious, and political forms of nationalism repeatedly emerge on the horizon of African American thought. In material terms, these multifaceted forms of nationalism reflect the political and social reality of African American national oppression in the United States.[24]

In most circumstances, these multiple forms are configured such that they are not always mutually exclusive but tend to be amalgamated and oftentimes are manifested by accenting one form over the others. Consequently, religiously anchored Black Nationalism can also assume cultural, economic, and political expression. (Smith, 1998: 533–547).[25] When religiously oriented nationalist groups, organizations or individuals put forth economic and politically directed programs, such expressions do not undermine or negate what are basic religious obligations. In our appraisal of the Nation of Islam, we do not

---

23   See also George Breitman, *The Last Year of Malcolm X* (New York: Merit Publishers, 1967), 64–65. Robert Terrill, ed., *The Cambridge Companion to Malcolm X* (Cambridge: Cambridge University Press, 2010). Anthony Marcus, *Malcolm X and the Third American Revolution: The Writings of George Breitman* (Amherst: Humanity Books, 2005).

24   See also I.K. Sundiata, *Brothers and Strangers: Black Zion, Black Slavery, 1914–1940* (Durham: Duke University Press, 2003); Wilson Jeremiah Moses, *Classical Black Nationalism: From the American Revolution to Marcus Garvey* (New York: New York University Press, 1996); Wilson Jeremiah Moses, *The Golden Age of Black Nationalism, 1820 – 1925* (New York; Oxford: Oxford University Press, 1988); Tunde Adeleke, *UnAfrican Americans: 19th Century Black Nationalists and the Civilizing Mission* (Lexington: University Press of Kentucky, 1998); and John H. Bracey, Jr., August Meier, and Elliot Rudwick, ed., *Black Nationalism in America* (Indianapolis: Bobbs-Merrill, 1970).

25   See also Joseph R. Washington, Jr., *The Politics of God* (Boston: Beacon Press, 1969).

presume that its claims to religious status are effectively undercut, due to the propagation of nationalist social-political analysis and economic programs.[26]

Further, although we maintain that varied forms of Black Nationalism are without fail on the horizon of African American thought, we are not suggesting some type of form/content dialectic; wherein these forms are manifestations of some underlying (prototypical) content. In *Black Nationalism in American Politics and Thought*, Dean E. Robinson brings this important point home: "There is no 'essential' black nationalist tradition, despite similarities; the positions of nationalists of different eras have diverged because their nationalisms have been products of partly similar but largely unique eras of politics, thought, and culture. Missing this point can result in an ahistorical, teleological interpretation of black nationalism as a historical phenomenon" (Robinson, 2010: 6).

The concrete historical response and presence of multiple forms of Black Nationalism is crucial to apprehending the dialectical nature of Malcolm's progression vis-à-vis his own adherence to Black Nationalism as political philosophy.[27] Malcolm's dynamic and evolutionary comprehension of Black Nationalism is at root an instance of succession that conflicts and contradicts with several key factors relating to the Nation of Islam and Elijah Muhammad's nationalist ideology.[28]

For instance, we think because Elijah Muhammad's religiously derived Black Nationalism is based on his inimitable slant on Islamic theology; it follows that adjoining political, economic, historical, and racial analyses are theoretically dependent on the various components of that uniquely fashioned theological framework. In large measure, Elijah Muhammad's Black religious

---

26   See C. Eric Lincoln, *The Black Muslims in America* (Boston: Beacon Press, 1961); and Nathaniel Deutsch, "The Approximate Other: The Nation of Islam and Judaism" in Yvonne Patricia Chireau and Nathaniel Deutsch, eds. *Black Zion: African American Religious Encounters with Judaism* (New York: Oxford University Press, 2000): 91–117.

27   See James Lance Taylor, *Black Nationalism in the United States: From Malcolm X to Barack Obama* (Boulder: Lynne Rienner Publishers, 2011). Roderick D Bush, *We Are Not What We Seem: Black Nationalism and Class Struggle in the American Century* (New York: New York University Press, 1999). Alphonso Pinkney, *Red, Black, and Green: Black Nationalism in the United States* (New York: Cambridge University Press, 1976). John H. Bracey, Jr., August Meier, and Elliot Rudwick, ed., *Black Nationalism in America* (Indianapolis: Bobbs-Merrill, 1970).

28   After Malcolm's break from the Nation of Islam, he actually makes a conceptual distinction between Black nationalists and the Nation of Islam, wherein he amplifies the conservative apolitical nature of NOI vis-à-vis Black nationalists. See Malcolm X, "The Black Muslim Movement: An Assessment" in *February 1965: The Final Speeches* (New York: Pathfinder, 1992): 211.

theology frames his nationalist political outlook. Subsequently, Muhammad's religiously-based Black nationalism constitutes what can be best described as political theology (Smith, 1998: 533–547).

Malcolm's efforts at developing an independent viewpoint on Black nationalism – away from Elijah Muhammad's position – necessitated an ideological rupture, and in the instances of both theology and politics. Malcolm successively moves away from NOI political theology. But, also more notably, he rejects political theology in principle. In Malcolm's demarcation of his own type of Black Nationalism from the Nation of Islam's, he observes, "[T]he Black Muslim movement teaches that every white individuals that comes into the world is the devil by nature... And the black nationalists don't do that. The black nationalists judge people by their behavior, by their deeds, not by the color... The Black Muslim movement is a hybrid, a hybrid, political religious hybrid..." (Malcolm X, 1992: 211). Instead of starting with political theology – as the theoretical underpinning for Black Nationalism – Malcolm envisions that his type of nationalism is more prominently in concert with secular political philosophy (Malcolm X, 1992: 251–252).

In line with his new grounding, wherein he distinguishes theological commitments from his political philosophy, Malcolm founded the Muslim Mosque Inc. (for the purpose of his Islamic ministry) and the Organization of Afro-American Unity as the political arm for his social activist/revolutionary work. These qualitatively different organizational bodies, for Malcolm X, are both vital. Their different organizational missions reflect practical concerns and philosophical considerations, which we must examine carefully.[29]

Malcolm's evolving view of Black Nationalism is best understood as successive motion toward 'left-wing' nationalism. In essence, left-wing nationalism is anti-imperialist and anti-capitalist in content and this is why the dialectical unfolding of Malcolm's views on capitalism and imperialism comprise the pivotal substance of his evolving nationalism. We submit that Malcolm's political philosophy of Black Nationalism includes his internationalist call for human rights and his vision of the Pan-Africanist scope of African American liberation. Thus, we do not counter-position Malcolm's Black Nationalism to

---

29 See, for example, Benjamin Karim, with Peter Skutches and David Gallen, *Remembering Malcolm: The Story of Malcolm X from inside the Muslim Mosque by his Assistant Minister Benjamin Karim* (New York: Carroll and Graf Publishers, Inc., 1992); "Basic Unity Program, Organization of Afro-America Unity" in Steve Clark, ed., *The Final Speeches, February 1965*, (New York: Pathfinder, 1992): 257–269; and William W. Sales, Jr., *From Civil Rights to Black Liberation: Malcolm X and the Organization of Afro-America Unity* (Boston: South End Press, 1999).

his Pan-Africanist and internationalist position.[30] We contend that if we start from the vantage point of the dialectical evolution of Malcolm's Black Nationalism; what we can discern is a salient and compelling progress in the direction of Pan-Africanism and internationalism. Thus, Malcolm broadens his view on Black Nationalism to include Pan-Africanism and more generally internationalism of the 'oppressed.'[31]

A chief issue in Malcolm's evolution is the challenge of moving away from Elijah Muhammad's blanket condemnation of the entire white race. The blanket condemnation of the entire race is a cardinal principle of Muhammad's political theology and his adjoining "Message to the Black man" (Muhammad, 1965). In his role as the chief spokesperson of the Nation of Islam, Malcolm came to be identified as the most prominent Black leader to espouse the idea that all white people were devils and enemies of the Black race.

The ideological break from the Nation of Islam and Muhammad's political theology mandates that Malcolm – in a philosophically substantive manner – could no longer conflate the critique of racism with an anti-white posture. Malcolm's formidable philosophical challenge to transform his critique of racism and his very notion of race is an essential aspect of his substantive thought. Moreover, since Malcolm in principle does not draw on political theology, as the source for his explication of racism, the need to find new ground for his political perspective is decisive. The political framework that Malcolm develops is *leftist* in character and this directly corresponds with his anti-capitalist and anti-imperialist formulations about Black Nationalism. We can only grasp the *substantive meaning* of Malcolm's rejection of the blanket condemnation of white people, from the standpoint of this leftward turn. George Breitman correctly states,

> Malcolm came to the conclusion that the Black Muslims had gone as far as they go, and he wanted to go further. He wanted to get into the active struggle, influence it ideologically, and revolutionize it. He wanted to build a new movement, on new foundations, and therefore he reviewed

---

30 In counter-positioning of Malcolm's concept of Black nationalism to Pan-Africanism, Wolfenstein argues, "In less than a year Malcolm X had shifted from black nationalism to Afro-American internationalism. The first of these positions was racial-religious in nature; and the more political-culture." See Eugene Wolfenstein, *The Victims of Democracy: Malcolm X and the Black Revolution* (New York: the Guilford Press, 1993): 313.

31 See, for instance, Roderick D. Bush, The *End of White World Supremacy: Black Internationalism and the Problem of the Color Line* (Philadelphia: Temple University Press, 2009); George Breitman, *Malcolm X: the Man and His Ideas* (New York: Pathfinder, 1965).

all of his ideas – keeping some, modifying others, casting aside still others. He began to move to *the left*... The main allies of Afro-Americans, he decided, are the black, brown, yellow, and red people of the world; but then he also began to see the possibility of alliances with what he called 'militant white' Americans... None of this made him an 'integrationist.' But it did make him go beyond the simple formula, the white man is the enemy... It did make him think about and study the causes of racism and see the possibilities of its elimination some day. It led him to study the nature of American capitalist society, and the world capitalism-always from the point of view of how the interests of black people could be promoted and protected

BREITMAN ET AL, 1991: 122–124.[32] [Italics Added]

The reader should keep in mind that we are not arguing that Malcolm adopted a form of scientific socialism or communism. All available information clearly points out that Malcolm did not have the opportunity to systematically study Marxist political economy. And, Malcolm had not progressed to the point of recognizing that the Black working class and the Black bourgeoisie had mutually exclusive class interests. For instance, Malcolm's construction of the difference between the 'house Negro' and the 'field Negro' was not reflective of a Marxist class analysis.[33] Rather, we should note that Malcolm had shed any previous anti-communism of his previous NOI period and openly espoused an anti-imperialist critique.

Although he is in concert with rejecting blanket condemnation, Malcolm's 'left-wing' Black nationalism discards the liberal inference that follows with that concurrence; namely the liberal view that better race relations is a sufficient

---

32 For Breitman's entire discussion of this matter, read "Myths about Malcolm X" in George Breitman, Herman Potter, and Baxter Smith, *The Assassination of Malcolm X* (New York: Pathfinder Press, 1991) cited quotations from pages 122–124.

33 For an analysis of the house Negro/field Negro concept in Malcolm's political philosophy, see Adolph Reed, "The Allure of Malcolm X and the Changing Character of Black Politics," in *Stirrings in the Jug: Black Politics in the Post-Segregation Era* (Minneapolis, MN: University of Minneapolis Press, 1999), 220–221 and Patricia Hill Collins, "Learning to Think for Ourselves: Malcolm X's Black Nationalism Reconsidered" in Joe Wood, ed., *Malcolm X: In Our Own Image* (New York: St. Martin's Press, 1992): 59–85. For an Afrocentric reading of Malcolm X, see Molefi Asante, *Malcolm X As Cultural Hero: And Other Afrocentric Essays* (Trenton, N.J.: Africa World Press, 1993); Molefi Asante, *Afrocentricity: A Theory of Social Change (Revised and Expanded)* (Chicago, Illinois: African American Images, 2003), 26–27; and Oba T'Shaka, *The Political Legacy of Malcolm X*. Richmond, California: Pan Afrikan Publications, 1983.

condition for the termination of racism. In its place, Malcolm seeks to advance Black Nationalism as a weapon against racism, national oppression, capitalism, and imperialism (Baraka, 1992: 29). Nevertheless, when Malcolm adopts 'left-wing' Black Nationalism, he also realizes there are fetters appended to the signifier 'Black' in 'Black Nationalism.' In his international travels and communication with revolutionaries around the globe that were not Black, Malcolm had to consider the question, what does 'Black' as a descriptor signify for his nationalism?

Malcolm struggles with the possible implications of advocating a principle of racial exclusiveness. Malcolm realizes that if a principle of racial exclusion is affixed to Black Nationalism, then his efforts at broadening his nationalism to the stature of an international movement are effectively thwarted. Why he struggles with such implications is precisely because as anti-imperialist revolutionary, Malcolm intends to join in the vanguard, fighting for "A Global Rebellion of the Oppressed against the Oppressor" (Malcolm X, 1992).

For the purposes of our discussion, we will highlight the following areas for review: Malcolm's Black Nationalism and his conception of race and racism contra Elijah Muhammad and the Nation of Islam and their corresponding racialist theological groundwork; Malcolm's views on capitalism and imperialism and their affiliation to Black or African American identity. While not exhaustive, we do think these subject areas collectively and organically provide a coherent analytical framework for our query into Malcolm's efforts at constructing a leftist form of Black Nationalism as a viable political philosophy of liberation.

With this composite analytical tool, we can hopefully capture why Malcolm X's political philosophy projects toward 'left-wing' rather than 'right-wing' Black Nationalism. By left-wing Black Nationalism, I mean definitive types of nationalism that are essentially anti-imperialist and anti-capitalist in character. The recognition that national oppression/racism is intimately connected to capitalism/imperialism is one of the cardinal aspect of left-wing nationalism.[34]

By 'right-wing' Nationalism, I intend specific kinds of nationalism that tend to be accommodative with capitalist/imperialist structural conditions. I presume that racialist ideologies – even those under the guise of Black Nationalism – instead of undermining the capitalist/imperialist status quo

---

34 See Malcolm X, "There Is a Worldwide Revolution Going On" in Malcolm X and Bruce Perry, *Malcolm X: The Last Speeches* (New York: Pathfinder Press, 1989); and Kevin Ovenden, *Malcolm X: Socialism and Black Nationalism* (London: Bookmarks, 1992).

actually affirm it, either in a benign or explicit manner.[35] It is Malcolm's adoption of left-wing Black Nationalism that propels him from Elijah Muhammad's racialist political theology to actively joining the ranks of the anti-imperialist revolutionary movement.

Malcolm X on Race and Racism

From Racialist Theology to Anti-Imperialist Revolutionary Thought
In *The Autobiography*, Malcolm states that his split from the Nation of Islam was due to several objective reasons. We do not believe that Malcolm's break from the NOI was merely subjective in nature based on his personal shock about revelations concerning Muhammad's infidelity. First, outsiders often viewed Malcolm as the principal leader of the group and the upper echelon within the NOI grew jealous of his growing celebrity status. Second, as Elijah Muhammad's national spokesperson, the same elements were threatened by Malcolm's increased stature within organizational ranks, and feared he would inherit Elijah Muhammad's mantle. Third, we have Malcolm's own disenchantment with Elijah Muhammad's moral corruption and departure from NOI ethical standards. Lastly, and we argue the most decisive reason is that Malcolm remains disgruntled that despite the use of militant rhetoric, the Nation of Islam in actuality was a politically conservative organization governed by political quietism. In particular, Elijah Muhammad failed to respond to police brutality and the murder of NOI members. All of the above, undoubtedly, substantially forced Malcolm to make an objective break from the Nation of Islam and Elijah Muhammad's leadership.[36]

---

35   For discussions of right-wing nationalism in African-American intellectual thought, see Hayward Farrar, "Radical Rhetoric Conservative Reality: The Nation of Islam As an American Conservative Formation" in Peter Eisenstadt, ed., *Black Conservatism: Essays and Intellectual and Political History* (New York: Garland Publishers, 1999) pp. 109–130: Judith Stein, *The World of Marcus Garvey: Race and Class in Modern Society* (Baton Rouge: Louisiana State University Press, 1986); Stephen W. Angell, "Henry McNeal Turner – Conservative? Radical? Or Independent?" in Peter Eisenstadt, ed., *Black Conservatism: Essays and Intellectual and Political History* (New York: Garland Publishers, 1999): 25–50; and Nell Irvin Painter, "Martin R Delany: Elitism and Nationalism" in Leon Litwack and August Meier, eds., *Black Leaders of the Nineteenth Century* (Urbana: University of Illinois press, 1988): 149–172.

36   Malcolm's commentary on the Kennedy assassination is the speech that led to his suspension from the NOI. It is a critique of the U.S. political system and its auxiliary violence, see Malcolm X, "God's Judgment of White America (The Chickens Come Home

While *The Autobiography* is a necessary source, for grasping the contradiction, it is not sufficient reference for comprehending the impediments surrounding the incompatible philosophical viewpoints, brought by Malcolm's burgeoning nationalism. Before his departure, we contend that Malcolm's conception of Black Nationalism gradually evolved and was even restrained by the organizational limitations of the Nation of Islam. As Malcolm's older brother, Abdul Aziz Omar (Philbert X) states,

> The Honorable Elijah Muhammad was teaching us that our place was not to fight the Caucasian-leave them alone. Just give 'em back everything they gave you, like whiskey, wine, beer, and learn how to take care of your own homes, your own family. And he said, 'You don't have to test them, Allah will destroy them. Allah will destroy the devil.' In fact, he had to admonish Malcolm many times, because Malcolm, when he really got going, you'd have thought he had an army in the back room to come and get you.
> STRICKLAND, 1984: 66

Omar's reflections shed light on the internal tension generated by Malcolm's efforts to go beyond the limits of Muhammad's political theology of quietism. The right-wing nature of NOI nationalism is marked by how the locus of Allah/God's primacy, within Muhammad's political theology, is inversely proportional to actual political activism. The continuation of this point is most evident in the Ronald Stokes case. In 1962, the Los Angeles police attacked the LA mosque and murdered Ronald Stokes, a member of the NOI.[37] In the wake of Stokes' murder, Malcolm expected Elijah Muhammad's command to affect a concerted and mass response to the attack. Instead Muhammad stated:

> In the case of the so-called American Negro, we have nothing to fight back with. If you come to the door shooting, we have no guns here to shoot back so, therefore, the right is with God, as it is written in the book.

---

to Roost)," *The Black Commentator* (December 4, 1963) http://www.blackcommentator.com/91/91_malcolm_pf.html. Malcolm X, *By Any Means Necessary; Speeches, Interviews, and a Letter*, George Breitman, ed., (New York, Pathfinder Press, 1970).

37 For a substantial treatment of the Stokes case, see Frederick Knight, "Justifiable Homicide, Police Brutality, or Government Repression? The 1962 Los Angeles Police Shooting of Seven Members of the Nation of Islam" *The Journal of Negro History* 79.2 (Spring, 1994): 182–196.

> He will defend us if we believe in Him, and we're going to start fighting with anyone to have Him to defend us. But if we are attacked, we depend on him to defend us....[38]
>
> KNIGHT, 1994

Elijah Muhammad's failure to call for any action about the murder of Ronald Stokes and the assault on NOI Los Angeles members, graphically illustrated his conservative political theology (Farrar, 1999: 109–130). As national spokesperson and in line with NOI organizational discipline – before a mass rally in Harlem – Malcolm gave the humiliating proclamation "We are going out into the streets to begin war with the devil. Not the kind of war he expects... No, we are going to let the world know he is the devil: we are going to sell newspapers."[39] Although, at that time, Malcolm made no public declaration of disagreement with Elijah, he was quite disgruntled about Muhammad's directive.

Benjamin Karim later shares Malcolm's private remarks, at that point, about the Stokes case, "We spout our militant revolutionary rhetoric and preach Armageddon... [B]ut when our brothers are brutalized or killed, we do nothing... We just sit on our hands" (Karim et al, 1992: 138). Later in 1965, Malcolm publicly expressed his earlier dissension. "Black Muslim movement has never any time been involved in any kind of strike against the Ku Klux Klan or the Citizens Council. Even in the South or the North. But they give the order to fight each other. When the brother [Stokes] was killed in Los Angeles, no order was given. In fact, the brothers who wanted to go into action were restrained-many of them right here in New York..." (Malcolm X, 1992: 212).

Previously we argued that in its substantive content, Malcolm's Black nationalism precedes to change from its initial pedigree within Elijah Muhammad's political theology to the theoretical boundaries of secular political philosophy. After the first 'pedigree' stage of Malcolm's ministry, some members noticed his gradual evolution away from Muhammad's political theology. Malcolm's elder brother Abdul Aziz Omar notes,

---

38 The quotation from Elijah Muhammad is cited in Frederick Knight, "Justifiable Homicide, Police Brutality, or Government Repression? The 1962 Los Angeles Police Shooting of Seven Members of the Nation of Islam" *The Journal of Negro History* 79.2 (Spring, 1994): 191.

39 Frederick Knight points out that "Under pressure from Mayor Yorty, Elijah Muhammad admonished Malcolm to tone down his rhetoric." Frederick Knight, "Justifiable Homicide, Police Brutality, or Government Repression? The 1962 Los Angeles Police Shooting of Seven Members of the Nation of Islam" *The Journal of Negro History* 79.2 (Spring, 1994): 191. The quotation from Malcolm is on page 190 of the Knight article.

> Malcolm began to talk less and less about how God was going to get rid of the Caucasians, and began to talk about how we were gon' to be able to go into court and bring them to justice, that they are guilty according to the law of the land-which was not our argument at all. Our argument was that we were divine people and that we would be protected and finally delivered put in the seat of authority by Allah. That was our teaching at the time.
> STRICKLAND AND GREENE, 1994: 132

In speaking less about Allah/God's intervention – as the primary and ultimate source of Black liberation – signals Malcolm's leftward direction and movement beyond the boundaries of the political theology of the NOI. This direction of less 'God talk' in Malcolm's thinking, brings to the fore the theological question; in practical terms, what characterizes the manner of Black people's ontological dependence on God/Allah? Are we to wait on Allah's actions; must Allah's divine intervention have priority over Black people fighting their own battles?

Elijah Muhammad argues, "Allah (God) is completely self-independent – having infinite knowledge and power over all – yet he is the most loving, the most merciful. But we are not self- independent; we are dependent on Allah. Only the foolish disbelievers think and feel they are self-independent and not dependent upon Allah" (Muhammad, 1957: 9). This answer to the aforementioned question is the primary basis for Malcolm's discontent with Elijah Muhammad's political theology of pacifism and quietism.

Although the previous discussion accents the gradual progression of Malcolm's secular (materialist) political philosophy contra Elijah's political theology; Malcolm's early years, in the NOI ministry, quintessentially represented Muhammad's racialist theology of nationalism. In 1962, Malcolm states:

> I might stop right here to point out that some of you may say, 'I came up here to listen to some religion about Islam, but now all I hear you talk about is black.; We don't separate our color from our religion. The white man doesn't. The white man never has separated Christianity from white, nor has he separated the white man from Christianity. When you hear the white man bragging, 'I'm a Christian,' he's bragging about being a white man. Then you have the Negro. When he is bragging about being a Christian, he's bragging that he's a white man, or he wants to be white... So the religion that we have, the religion of Islam, the religion that makes us Muslims, the religion that The Honorable Elijah

Muhammad is teaching us here in America today, is designed to undo in our minds what the white man has done to us.

MALCOLM X, 1971: 37–38

To better appreciate the complexity of Malcolm's dialectical development, we should provide a summary examination of Muhammad's political theology with its ancillary theological anthropology and theodicy. Elijah Muhammad's political theology – and NOI politics – is anchored in his particularistic Black interpretation of Islamic theology. Muhammad's idiosyncratic interpretation of Islamic theology pivots on a presumed dialectic of Black/white racial antagonism of cosmic proportion. The analysis of this cosmic antagonism is set within a mythic religious account, which seeks to explain the basic (racist) character of the entire white race, in terms of theological anthropology.[40]

In explaining what he thinks is the true nature of white people; Muhammad's theological anthropology first embarks on how white people came to inhabit the world. It not only outlines Muhammad's arguments about the essential nature of white people and why they are inherently racist but also he seeks to describe the 'true' nature of Black people in cosmic as well as historical terms. In volume one of *The Supreme Wisdom*, Muhammad states,

> If you understand it right, you will agree with me that the whole Caucasian race is a race of devils. They proved to be devils in the garden paradise and 4000 years later they were condemned by Jesus. Likewise they are condemned today by the great Mahdi Muhammad as the nothing but devils in the plainest language... After the righteous black nation has labored under the wicked rule of the devils for 6000 years, the return to a righteous ruler, under the God of righteousness, the people must be reorganized to live under such government.
>
> MUHAMMAD, 1957: 26–27, 38

This composite account on the cosmic origin and historical plight of Black people, functions as the eschatological vision that Muhammad deems as the 'true knowledge' of the Black man's history and future. It functions as Muhammad's prophetic "Message to the Black man."[41]

---

40   For detailed and critical discussion of the Nation of Islam theology, see Zafar Ishaq Ansari, "Aspects of Black Muslim Theology" *Studia Islamica* 53 (1981): 137–176.

41   Edward E. Curtis IV, "Islamizing the Black Body: Ritual and Power in Elijah Muhammad's Nation of Islam" *Religion and American Culture: The Journal of Interpretation* 12.2 (2002): 167–196; Richard Brent Turner, *Islam in the African-American Experience* (Bloomington:

Now we ask, how does Muhammad's nationalism inform his political theology? Subsequently in what way does Elijah's political theology shape his notion of Black Nationalism? The notion that Elijah Muhammad's nationalism assumes *religious form* presumes that nationalism provides the *basic content* for his political theology. Black Nationalist principles, as understood by Muhammad, serve as NOI religious tenets. In turn, political theology fashions Muhammad's politics in a manner that secular/political concerns are ultimately reducible into his Black conception of Islamic articles of faith.[42]

This interrelated character of Elijah's version of Black Nationalism and political theology has immediate practical utility for his followers. Elijah Muhammad's theology is not merely a composite of abstract formulations; more essentially it provides guiding principles for his followers in the pursuit of their daily lives. Such guiding principles have an explanatory function and assist followers in relating their day-to-day existence to a broadly conceived view of life, reality, history, self-identity and even "how to eat to live" (Muhammad, 1957; Muhammad, 1965; Muhammad, 1967).

Thus, we have the following questions: If Black nationalism is a response to national/racist oppression then how do we come to grips with the very basis for national/racist oppression? What causes racism and national oppression? Why have – and do – Black people suffer at the hands of white people? When such questions are posed within the framework of theology, it follows we have ancillary concerns about the attributes of God, along with God's place in human history and specifically Black history. As a minister and spokesperson for Elijah Muhammad and the Nation of Islam, Malcolm X sought to answer these questions and provide explanations consistent with the Nation of Islam's Black Nationalist theology.

This theological focus on why suffering and evil in the universe and concretely in the Black world, brings us to a core subject area of theology, namely theodicy. The late Black philosopher and theologian, Dr. William R. Jones astutely states:

> Theodicy, from the Greek theos, God, and dike, justice, is the common term for the field of inquiry that deals with the issue of evil and human suffering. Most often it signifies the attempt to account for human

---

Indiana University Press, 1997); Claude A. Clegg III, *An Original Man: the Life and Times of Elijah Muhammad* (New York: St. Martin's Press, 1997).

42 One of the first scholarly works on Elijah Muhammad's introduction to Nation of Islam theology, see Erdmann Doane Beynon, "The Voodoo Cult among Negro Migrants in Detroit" *American Journal of Sociology* 43. 6 (May-1938): 894–907.

> suffering and evil in the framework of one's affirmations about the nature and activity of God. I shall use the term, however, in a different sense. The centrality of theodicy concludes that the unique character black suffering forces the question of divine racism, and to pose this question is to initiate the theodicy debate. The black theologian is obliged to reconcile the inordinate amount of black suffering, which is implied in his claim that the black situation is oppressive, with his affirmations about the nature of God and God's sovereignty over human history.[43]
>
> JONES, 1998: XXXVI

Since the Black experience is replete with multiple kinds (Jones's 'inordinate amount') of suffering as oppressive: slavery, segregation, lynching, police brutality, meager or no health services and facilities, racial discrimination, shattered communities, poor achieving school systems, poverty, powerlessness and so on; poses the question, how must we comprehend God's presence in the midst of this reality? What is God's relationship to Black people and their oppression and suffering? What is God's connection to whites and the evils of racism?[44]

Let's analyze how Elijah Muhammad and the Nation of Islam interpret the problem of what Jones identifies as divine racism and the problems attached to theodicy. Subsequently we must examine the manner in which Elijah Muhammad determines God's relationship to Black people and how he answers the question, why the historical and persistent circumstances of Black oppression and racism?

In view of these oppressive circumstances, does Muhammad assume that God is omnipotent (all-powerful), omnibenevolent (all-good), omnipresent (always present) and omniscient (all-knowing)? For the Nation of Islam, are Black people ontologically (in the most fundamental sense of reality) dependent on God's will for their liberation? In what way is God connected to Black lives and oppression as well as the path to liberation?

---

43   For interpretive analysis of Jones' work and legacy, see Stephen Ferguson, "On the Occasion of William R. Jones's Death: Remembering the Feuerbachian Tradition in African-American Social Thought," APA Newsletter on Philosophy and the Black Experience 12.2 (Spring 2013): 14–19; John H. McClendon and Brittany L. "William R. Jones and Philosophical Theology: Transgressing and Transforming Conventional Boundaries of Black Liberation Theory," APA Newsletter on Philosophy and the Black Experience 13.1 (Fall 2013): 19–34.

44   For an attempt to analyze these questions in the context of Hurricane Katrina, see Ferguson, Stephen. "Teaching Hurricane Katrina: Understanding Divine Racism and Theodicy," APA Newsletter on Philosophy and the Black Experience 7.1. (Fall 2007): 1–5.

When Malcolm was fully in concert with Elijah Muhammad's theodicy, we observe that, in a discussion about Christianity, Malcolm deals with the above questions. He argues,

> If Christianity hasn't *always* been the name of God's religion it isn't *now* the name of God's religion. God doesn't change His religion; God doesn't change His mind; God's mind is made up from the beginning. He doesn't have to change His mind because He knows all there is to know all the way down the wheel of time. He never has to change His mind, His mind is made up, His knowledge is complete, all encompassing. Do you understand? So once you can see, and I think you can, then it's almost impossible for God to call *Christianity* His religion.
>
> MALCOLM X, 1971: 44

Elijah Muhammad's theology argues that Allah/God's relationship to Black people is both cosmic and concretely historical. On the cosmic level, Allah created the universe and has the power to destroy the world. Muhammad declares, "Allah has warned us of how he would (one day) destroy the world with bombs, poison gas, and would destroy everything of the present world. Not anything of it (the present world of white mankind) would be left" (Muhammad, 1957: 14).

In referring to the white man, Muhammad states, "He [the white man] is the devil in person, who was made of sin, not anything that was good in the essence that he was from" (Muhammad, 1957: 17–18). Theologically the cosmic battle against sin and evil is fulfilled by the destruction of the white man for that reason this destruction of white civilization is Muhammad's eschatological event. Muhammad's eschatology is race specific, this is because evil and sin are characteristics that emanate from the white race and the end event for whites is the rebirth of the Black nation. In NOI theology racism and whiteness are inseparable categories and in fact synonymous.

From the standpoint of NOI theodicy, the expression 'white racism' is actually a redundant locution. Hence, Muhammad's theodicy explains that the oppression/suffering of Black people is the product of the very nature and makeup of white people. White dominance over Black people follows from the evil power, which the white man possesses over Black people. The very existence of racism is both cosmic and natural and both F. D Muhammad (Allah) and Elijah Muhammad (his Messenger) have prophetically announced its termination. Malcolm voices Elijah Muhammad's position:

> And six thousand years ago, a scientist named Yacub created another tribe on this Earth... It was made different from all of the twelve tribes

> that were here when it arrived. A new tribe, a weak tribe, a wicked tribe, a devilish tribe, a diabolical tribe, a tribe that is devilish by nature. So that before they got on the scene, The Honorable Elijah Muhammad says that when we came with the Earth, the oldest city on the Earth is the Holy City... Mecca is the city that is forbidden. No one can go there but the black man.
>
> MALCOLM X, 1971: 70–71

This theological summation means that in terms of the cosmic nature of evil, God/Allah is not directly responsible for Black oppression. The devil (the white man) is the immediate catalyst for Black suffering. Therefore, in answer to Jones's question, "Is God a white racist?" Elijah Muhammad would respond by saying that God is not a white racist; however, the devil holds that responsibility. That is to say, Black misery/oppression follows from the actions of the white man and precisely because he is white, he is consequently racist. Ultimately, Allah/God will destroy white people and in turn eliminate racism.

This raises the question, what evidence do we have that God is on the side of oppressed Black people? Moreover, who is God/Allah? The concrete historical dimension of Muhammad's theodicy comes with his conception of Allah and how God intervenes in human history. First, Allah/God is a human person rather than a spiritual/transcendent being. Muhammad rejects the notion that God is a non-material/spiritual entity that is transcendent yet immanent in the world. In volume 2 of *The Supreme Wisdom*, Muhammad claims this idea of God as spiritual being is no more than rendering Him as a 'spook' (Muhammad, 1957: 9).[45]

Second, Allah/God is not beyond human comprehension and concrete grasp because he actually came to the United States (in 1930) to prepare Black people for their liberation. In the first volume of *The Supreme Wisdom* Elijah Muhammad explains, "Mr. Fard Muhammad (God in Person) chose to suffer one-half years [sic] to show his love for his people who have suffered over 300 years at the hands of the people who by nature are evil, wicked, and have no good in them" (Muhammad, 1957: 15). Muhammad continues to clarify:

---

45   On the issue of an immaterial God, Zafar Ishaq Ansari states, "As for the God of the spirit, how can such a formless God, asks Elijah Muhammad, be interested in human affairs? And what glory will such an immaterial God get out of the material world. As distinguished from this spooky God, the God of the Nation of Islam is so human that he would even die." Zafar Ishaq Ansari, "Aspects of Black Muslim Theology" *Studia Islamica* 53 (1981): 143.

> [The One Hundred and Forty-four Thousand] This number 144,000 is a prophecy about the future in symbolic terms refers to the vision by Yakub, father of the white race, which he had seen on the island of Patmos or Pelah 6,000 years ago. He was warning his people of that which would come at the end of this time. The number 144,000 in mathematics means a SQUARE which is a perfect answer for the spiritual work of Allah with that number of people. They are the first (Negro) convert them among the wicked to Allah (God) and His messenger, referred to as the first ripe fruit... After the righteous black nation has labored under the wicked rule of the devils for 6000 years, the return to a righteous ruler, under the God of righteousness, the people must be re-organized to live under such government. The All-Wise God, to Whom praises is due, who came in the person of Master W.F. Muhammad, seeking us, the lost and last numbers of a chosen nation, is building a new world of Islam out of the old. Therefore, He lays the base of his Kingdom with a squared number of mathematics which represents TRUTH.
>
> MUHAMMAD, 1957: 23–24

In regard to Elijah Muhammad's theodicy, he claims that Yakub created the white race. Yakub is a Black man and a lesser deity or Black scientist of immense genius. It was out of the desire to create a different race of people, from the original Black people of the planet that Yakub decided to genetically engineer the white race.

Thus, the existence of evil in the world, which is synonymous with racism, is actually the creation by a Black man, whom operated as a lesser deity. Ironically, in terms of Muhammad's theodicy, the Black man is ultimately responsible (and the white man penultimately) for the very racism that Black people face today. In the context of Muhammad's theology, we can see that the problem of theodicy does not undermine the omnipotence of God. However, this claim does make the issue of God's omnibenevolent character logically problematic.

The theology of the Nation of Islam initially provides Malcolm X with a worldview that sufficiently explained for him, why the dire conditions of his life; by specifically outlining the root causes for Black impoverishment and powerlessness. Elijah Muhammad's conception of Black theodicy is the framework for Malcolm X to bring together not only an integrated and comprehensive conception of his own personal life but also the ability to recognize the core issue surrounding the general plight of African Americans.

In 1952, Malcolm attended a Sunday rally on Labor Day where Elijah Muhammad spoke to his followers. Malcolm informs us about his first personal encounter with Elijah Muhammad. Malcolm reports,

> Elijah Muhammad spoke of how in this wilderness of North America, for centuries the "blue eyed devil white man" had brainwashed the "so-called Negro." As one result, the black man in America was "mentally, morally and spiritually dead." Elijah Muhammad spoke of how the black man was the original man, who had been kidnapped from his homeland and stripped of his language, his culture, his family structure, his family name, until the black man in America did not realize who he was. He told us, and showed us, how his teachings of the true knowledge of ourselves would lift up the black man from the bottom of the white man's society and place the black man where he had begun, at the top of civilization.
> MALCOLM X, 1966B: 197

One of the cardinal features of the Nation of Islam's theology is that it explicitly provides an explanation for racism as an intrinsic characteristic that is endemic to the white race as an entire group. Generally speaking this kind of argument stands in stark contrast to most African American Christian denominations and theologies. However, we must add the utilization of theological anthropology to account for the very notion of the origins of races is not foreign to Black Christian thinkers. Written within the genre of race vindicationist historical literature, Martin R. Delany's 1879 tract, *Principia of Ethnology: The Origin of Races and Color*, fosters the idea of the unity and equality of the races and attempts to provide a critique of white racial superiority (Delany, 1879).

The significance in referencing Delany is that he is generally thought of as the 'father' of Black Nationalist thought and therefore a predecessor to Muhammad within this tradition.[46] Hence, we have the opportunity to compare – within the philosophical framework of Black nationalism – Delaney and Muhammad's treatment of the origins of the races within the philosophical framework of Black nationalism. Grounding his claims on biblical Scripture, Delany develops an argument for the origins of the races. An early proponent of the back-to-Africa movement, Delany sets out to refute the racist (Christian) myth concerning the curse of Ham, which was widely used to justify the enslavement of African Americans.[47] By way of theological anthropology, social science and Egyptian hieroglyphics, Delany argues,

---

46   See Robert S. Levine, ed., *Martin R. Delany: A Documentary Reader* (Chapel Hill: University of North Carolina Press, 2003).

47   For a treatment of Black biblical scholarship and the curse of Ham myth, read Michael Joseph Brown, *Blackening of the Bible* (New York: Trinity Press International, 2004): 26–30, 62–63.

> Adam, and his complexion to have been clay color or yellow, more resembling that of the lightest of the pure-blooded North American Indians. And there is no doubt in our mind that the peoples from Adam to Noah, including his wife and his sons' wives, were all one and the same color... The sons of Noah were three in number: Shem, Ham and Japheth. That these three sons were the active heads of the people as directors and patriarchal leaders, there is no doubt. There is to us another fact of as little doubt; that is, that these three sons of Noah all differed in complexion, and proportionate numbers of the people – their dependants... And these different complexions in the people, at that early period, when races were unknown, would have no more been noticed as a mark of distinction, than the variation in the color of the hair of those that are white, mark them among themselves as distinct peoples.[48]
>
> DELANY, 1879: 12, 20, 21

While Delaney argues that the original man was of dark complexion (not white), he does not presume that people of color are superior and argues that differences in skin color actually precede the very notion of race.[49] It is transparent that Delaney and Elijah Muhammad are both Black nationalists and each are clearly responding to the matter of white racist claims about Black inferiority, via discourse on the origin of the races. Despite this commonality, we can see that they are in fundamental disagreement respecting the idea of racial supremacy.

What is the significance of our foray into how these two Black nationalists respond to white racism? For our analysis of Malcolm X's political philosophy, there are two primary considerations. First, we see that not all Black nationalists presume they must anchor their philosophy in Black racial superiority. Hence, Delany offers a historical precedent for Malcolm's post-NOI conception of nationalism sans racism. Second, while both Delany and Muhammad treat the problem of racism and Black existence in theological terms, Malcolm departs from this line of thinking. Although Malcolm states that his initial move away from racialist theology results from encounters with

---

48   For critical look at the class nature of Delany's Black nationalism read, Nell Irvin Painter, "Martin R Delany: Elitism and Nationalism" in Leon Litwack and August Meier, eds., *Black Leaders of the Nineteenth Century* (Urbana: University of Illinois press, 1988): 149–172.

49   For a treatment on Delany's defense of Black people and his use of Egyptology read, Mario A. Beatty, "Martin Delaney and Egyptology" *Ankh Revue d'égyptologie et des civilisations* n. 14/15 (2005–2006) www.ankhonline.com/ankh_num_14_15/ankh_14_15_m_beatty (Accessed July 10, 2014).

traditional Islam in Mecca, his post-NOI political philosophy of nationalism and the adjoining treatment of racism, assumes a secular character. I believe it is this second consideration, which has greater significance for our deliberation.

While Elijah Muhammad's racialism is reducible to and anchored in theology, Malcolm demarcates his religious commitments from political philosophy. Correspondingly, while Malcolm becomes a Sunni Muslim, his notions about Black Nationalism are not based on theological presumptions or reducible to his religious commitment. This is because Malcolm ultimately jettisons political theology as the substantive content for his conception of Black Nationalism.[50]

Malcolm's secular/sacred demarcation has an adjoining organizational obligation; namely he must establish two groups in alignment with this separation. Therefore, the establishment of both Muslim Mosque Inc. and the Organization of Afro-American Unity derives not only from practical concerns but also philosophical imperatives. As to the practical issues, the former devotees of the NOI that joined Malcolm were not of necessity parting on strictly theological grounds. Most were disillusioned about the corruption within the NOI and Elijah Muhammad's moral indiscretions. This reality is also coupled with the fact that the Muslim Mosque Inc. was a religious organization; this consequently means that non-Muslims open to Malcolm's leadership, were not permitted to join.

The theoretical imperatives are at root philosophical in nature. As previously mentioned, Malcolm could not simply replicate the religious nationalism of Elijah Muhammad. The ideological rupture encompassed more than the immediate matter of personal differences with Elijah Muhammad and the Nation of Islam hierarchy. Malcolm had to rethink Black Nationalism in terms of fashioning a secular (materialist) political philosophy. Where Elijah Muhammad's religious Black Nationalism reduced the political dimension into his theological foundation, Malcolm's political philosophy of Black Nationalism had to be strictly separated from any theological admixture. The theology affixed to the Muslim Mosque Incorporated could not serve as the secular philosophy guiding the Organization of Afro-American Unity.

In view of the fact that Elijah Muhammad's form of Black Nationalism was anchored in racialism; we think it is of no coincidence that after Malcolm X left

---

50   On Malcolm's Sunni Muslim experience and how the Sudanese Sheik Ahmed Hassoun guided his theological transition within the Muslim Mosque Inc., read Malik Simba, "Sheik Ahmed Hassoun" in Robert L. Jenkins and Mfanya Donald Tryman, ed., *The Malcolm X Encyclopedia* (Westport: Greenwood press, 2002): 266–267.

the NOI, he increasingly became critical of the thesis that white people were blue-eyed devils. When Malcolm visited Mecca and thereafter adopted Sunni Islam, he publicly criticized NOI and Elijah Muhammad's racialism. Speaking about Elijah Muhammad's racialist conception of Islam, Malcolm noted: "No Arab or Asian Muslims were ever permitted in his [Elijah Muhammad's] temples or places of worship. In fact, his doctrine is as anti-Arab and anti-Asian as it is anti-white" (Malcolm X, 1992: 249).

Malcolm eventually ceased to make blanket condemnations of white people. In Malcolm's metamorphosis we witness the transition in philosophical anthropology from the Nation of Islam's incommensurability and mutual exclusion among races to the principle of universality and mutual inclusion. Malcolm's principle of mutual inclusion is anchored in his growing realization that the international struggle against imperialism must be established on materialist (philosophical) grounds.

Shortly before his assassination, Malcolm stated "The worst form of human being, I believe, is one who judges another human being by the color of his skin" (Malcolm X, 1992: 160–161). Armed with a new (non-racialist) perspective on Black Nationalism, Malcolm X embarks on rethinking the political-economic dimension of the Black liberation struggle. Rather than solely depend on theological principles, Malcolm's process of rethinking Black nationalism; consequently surfaces as philosophically driven by an increased reliance on the materialist analysis of the political economic nature of Black oppression and exploitation. Without religious mythos to account for racism and national oppression, Malcolm turns to secular (materialist) political philosophy for his concept of Black Nationalism. Now, he must grapple with identifying the structural features and systemic character of capitalism and imperialism and especially the problem of their intricate (material) connection to racism and national oppression.

The Dialectical Evolution of Malcolm's Anti-Capitalist Critique

Black Nationalism, Pan-Africanism and Anti-Imperialist Struggle

In a television interview (January 19, 1965), a month prior to his tragic murder, Malcolm offers a bluntly honest assessment on Muhammad's overwhelming influence:

> Well, he [Elijah Muhammad] represented himself to us as a prophet who had been visited by God, who had been taught by God, who had been given an analysis of the problems concerning black people in America by

God, and also a solution by the same God, as long as I believe in him as a man, I actually thought that he had been taught and commissioned by God to solve the problems of our people in America.[51]

GALLEN, 1992: 179–180

In the opening stage of his transformation, from NOI racialism, Malcolm's conception of the principle of universality is expressed through embracing traditional Islam as the basis of equality among various racial groups, throughout the world. In turn, Malcolm's secular (materialist) political philosophy of Black Nationalism expands his views on the universality of humanity and the equality of the races beyond the framework of Islam to embracing anti-imperialist internationalism.

Along with his rejection of mutual exclusion (racialist) principles, Malcolm also progressively gives voice to human rights as the cardinal aspect of the African American liberation struggle. In fact, Malcolm's human rights campaign prominently emerges as the centerpiece of his political philosophy.[52] While in Egypt, Malcolm announces: "The common goal of 22 million Afro-Americans is respect as human beings, the God-given right to be a human being. Our common goal is to obtain the human rights that America has been denying us. We can never get civil rights in America until our human rights are first restored. We will never be recognized as citizens there until we are first recognized as humans" (Clarke et al, 1969: 304).

Standing on new philosophical ground, regarding racialist dogma, Malcolm now must grapple with identifying the structural features and systemic character of capitalism and imperialism; that is, if he especially aims to determine what the intricate (material) connection may be to racism and national oppression. If we grant that NOI Black nationalism is right-wing in content and racialist in form; it follows that Malcolm's left-wing nationalism – in its anti-imperialist and anti-capitalist bearing – must shift toward a different political-economic course as well as non-theological direction.[53]

---

51 See also Wilson Jeremiah Moses, *Black Messiahs and Uncle Toms: Social and Literary Manipulations of a Religious Myth*. (University Park: Pennsylvania State University Press, 1982).

52 This is reflected in the following historical accounts and personal memoirs: George Breitman, *The Last Year of Malcolm X*, 64–65; William Strickland, *Malcolm X Make It Plain* (New York: Viking, 1994): 154–155, 176–177; and Gerald Horne, *Race Woman: The Lives of Shirley Graham Du Bois* (New York: New York University Press, 2000): 187–188.

53 See Malcolm X, "There Is a Worldwide Revolution Going On" in Bruce Perry, ed., *Malcolm X: The Last Speeches* (New York: Pathfinder Press, 1989): E.U. Eissen-Udom, *Black Nationalism: The Search for an Identity in America* (Chicago: University of Chicago Press, 1962): 164–167;

It ought to be equally noted that Malcolm's critical investigation of this complex relation also has profound sway on the meaning affixed to African American identity, particularly in light of the context of African cultural roots and the politics of the Pan-African movement. This political importance is above all due to the anti-imperialist temper of the African liberation struggle and Pan-African movement.[54] On May 13, 1964, during a talk at the University of Ghana, Malcolm comments on imperialism in Africa and also reflects on the significance of African political and cultural achievement for African Americans and unity with Africa. Malcolm declares:

> [A]s long as the Americans or other imperialists or twentieth-century colonialists could continue to make the Africans measure wealth in terms of gold and silver, they never would have an opportunity to really measure the value of the wealth that is in the soil, and would continue to think that it is they who need the Western powers instead of thinking that it is the Western powers who need the people and the continent that is known as Africa.

Malcolm added,

> President Nkrumah is doing something there that the government in America does not like to see done, and that is he's restoring the African image. He is making the African proud of the African image; and whenever the African becomes proud of the African image and this positive image is projected abroad, then the Black man in America, who up to now has had nothing but a negative image of Africa – automatically the image that the Black man in America has of his African brothers changes from negative to positive, and the image that the Black man in America has of himself will also change from negative to positive.[55]
>
> MALCOLM, University of Ghana, 1964

---

and Earl Ofari Hutchinson, "The Continuing Myth of Black Capitalism" *The Black Scholar* 23.1 (Winter-Spring 1993): 16–21.

54   Malcolm X, "Our People Identify with Africa" in Bruce Perry, ed., *Malcolm X: The Last Speeches* (New York: Pathfinder Press, 1989): 91–107; and Malcolm X, "Educate Our People in the Science of Politics" in Steve Clark, ed., *February 1965, The Final Speeches: Malcolm X* (New York: Pathfinder, 1992): 93–95. For a scholarly secondary source of Malcolm's dialectical progression on Black identity, read Liz Mazucci, "Malcolm X, Going Back to Our Own: Interpreting Malcolm X's Transition from 'Black Asiatic' to Afro-American" *Souls* 7.1 (2005): 66–83.

55   Malcolm X at University of Ghana (May 13, 1964) http://malcolmxfiles.blogspot .com/2013/07/university-of-ghana-may-13-1964_1.html (Accessed July 10, 2014).

In Malcolm's view, Nkrumah's efforts constituted a blow against the racism adjoined to cultural imperialism. "Having complete control over Africa, the colonial powers of Europe projected the image of Africa negatively. They always project Africa in a negative light: jungle savages, cannibals, nothing civilized" (Malcolm X, 1970: 73). Malcolm's revelation about the cultural worth of the African image is another area of philosophical exodus from Muhammad. Malcolm's exit centers on rejection of Muhammad's mythic (idealist) account of why and how Black people, in the United States, are descendants of Africans. Claude Clegg, a leading scholar on Muhammad, explains that according to Muhammad's myth, the Shabazz tribe was the first to inhabit Africa – south of Egypt/Ethiopia. This migration in turn results from how a Black scientist of the name:

Shabazz proposed that the tribe of Shabazz explore the rest of Africa, which heretofore had been uninhabited for humans. He theorized that if the tribe lived in the jungles of the continent long enough, it will become tougher and better able to deal with the rigors of life in any setting... Over thousands of years, the immigrants changed phenotypically, only vaguely resembling their ancestors. Their hair, which had been straight, coiled and became kinky; their thin lips swelled, and their noses became broader. The original people who settled in the jungles of Africa did, indeed become more rugged physically, but at a cost: they lost the cultural legacy of their forefathers, which resulted in a precipitous decline in their civilization. In the end, the scientist Shabazz made a monumental mistake in leading his people into the woodlands of Africa (Clegg, 1997: 47).[56]

Although Elijah Muhammad advocates Black pride, his cultural perspective on Africa and Africans is stereotypically racist. In the views of the nineteenth century Black nationalists such as Alexander Crummell and Henry McNeal Turner, along with Marcus Garvey in the twentieth century, we will find important precursors to Muhammad's views on African culture.[57]

---

56 In 1968, Elijah Muhammad responded to the growing sense of African identity and cultural nationalism, within the African American community, by instructing NOI members not to wear African garb and Afros. He deemed such displays of African culture to be an example of the "'savage' and 'uncivilized' cultures invading black America." See Edward E. Curtis, ed., *Encyclopedia of Muslim-American History* (New York: Infobase Publishing, 2010): 157.

57 For a fuller discussion of this point, see Tunde Adeleke, *UnAfrican Americans: 19th Century Black Nationalists and the Civilizing Mission* (Lexington: University Press of Kentucky, 1998): Wilson Jeremiah Moses, *Classical Black Nationalism: from the American Revolution to Marcus Garvey* (New York: New York University Press, 1996); and Judith Stein, *The World of Marcus Garvey: Race and Class in Modern Society* (Baton Rouge: Louisiana State University Press, 1986).

Malcolm's ideological and ultimately epistemological break from Muhammad's reactionary views on Africa and Africans are a vital piece of his critique of Elijah's political theology.[58] Malcolm conveys, "Elijah Muhammad has never made one statement that is pro-African. And he is never, in any of his speeches, or written or oral, said anything to his followers about Africa... He was as anti-African as he was antiwhite" (Malcolm X, 1992: 205). Consequently, Malcolm's exodus from Muhammad's political theology begins with the reappraisal of Elijah's idiosyncratic racialist notions about Africa and Islam, along with the ancillary theodicy of dependency on God's intervention. The editor of Elijah Muhammad's *The Theology of Time*, pejoratively notes this last ideological difference. Nasir Makr Hakim states, "In a nutshell, Malcolm believed in the ballot or the bullet, both controlled by the enemy, and Elijah Muhammad believed in the power of Allah, Master Fard Muhammad, on which Malcolm vacillated." (Muhammad, 1997: xv) Moreover, Muhammad argues, "By now it should be ever so clear that politics will no more solve our problem then it did the difficulties facing Israel during her bondage to Egypt."[59] This apolitical stance, wrapped in theological garb, has definitively economic grounding and specifically immediate ramifications. After the break, this capitalist economic dimension becomes the critical ideological hurdle that Malcolm has to confront.[60]

In no manner does Muhammad's right-wing nationalism attempt to link racism to capitalism. Instead Muhammad presumes that the issue with capitalism is simply the requirement to establish and support Black businesses. (Muhammad, 1965) NOI political theology, its programmatic policies and practical actions do not address the systemic character of capitalism and its institutional impact on the African American community and Black working-class masses (Clegg, 1996: 49–59).

---

58 As late as December, 1962, Malcolm argued, "The Honorable Elijah Muhammad says that the only hair that the black man has today that looks now like it looked prior to fifty thousand years ago is your and my eyebrows. Right here, you notice, all Negroes has straight – I don't care how nappy their hair is – they have straight eyebrows. When you see a nappy-hair-eyebrowed Negro you got somebody. But all of this took place back in history, and everything The Honorable Elijah Muhammad teaches is based on history." See Malcolm X and Karim, 72.

59 Elijah Muhammad, *The Fall of America* (Chicago: Muhammad's Temple of Islam No. 2, 1973): 2. For Malcolm's contrasting view on politics, Malcolm X, "Educate Our People in the Science of Politics " in Steve Clark, ed., *February 1965, The Final Speeches: Malcolm X* (New York: Pathfinder, 1992).

60 Claude Andrew Clegg, "Rebuilding the Nation: The Life and Work of Elijah Muhammad" *The Black Scholar* 26. 3–4, (Fall-Winter 1996): 49–59. (See note 8 in Clegg about payment to workers in NOI businesses.)

With Malcolm's leftward turn, the critique of the NOI bourgeois (capitalist) feature yet lingers on; it is the more complex philosophical challenge. Rooted in the viewpoint of Black capitalism, Muhammad's right-wing nationalism is located in the classical tradition of Black nationalists such as Martin R. Delany, Alexander Crummell, Henry M. Turner and Marcus Garvey.[61] Despite the concerted emphasis on Black racial pride, Muhammad voiced an essentially conservative (rightist) form of Black Nationalism. (Farrar, 1999: 109–130) Wilson J. Moses states, "His [Muhammad's] programs were essentially conservative, although his rhetoric was militant. The Nation of Islam attempted to withdrawal from American society on a symbolic level, while accommodating bourgeois values on a practical level. It was never stringent in its attempt to modify the environment or make it more hospitable to black Americans" (Moses 1982, 208).[62]

Muhammad's declaration for racial separation involves building the Black nation through Black businesses. Such economic autonomy, he believes would leave the white man to his own devices and Black people freed from economic exploitation. The underlying presumption is that the economic makeup of the African American community is essentially separate yet dependent on white capital i.e. the Black political economic order is essentially a form of domestic or internal colonialism.[63]

In consequence, Muhammad's political theology has both its religious and political-economic aspects. The possibility for the realization of Black economic independence comes in adopting NOI political theology and hence pooling individual resources for the collective cause of escaping from white (capitalist) control. In real political-economic terms, given the reality of monopoly

---

61 Nell Irvin Painter, "Martin R Delany: Elitism and Nationalism" in Leon Litwack and August Meier, eds., *Black Leaders of the Nineteenth Century* (Urbana: University of Illinois press, 1988): 149–172; Wilson J. Moses, *Alexander Crummell: A Study of Civilization and Discontent* (New York: Oxford University Press, 1989); Stephen W. Angell, "Henry McNeal Turner – Conservative? Radical? Or Independent?," 25–50; Judith Stein, *The World of Marcus Garvey: Race and Class in Modern Society* (Baton Rouge: Louisiana State University Press, 1986); Earl Ofari Hutchinson, *The Myth of Black Capitalism* (New York: Monthly Review Press, 1970).

62 For a similar point, see Lawrence L. Tyler, "The Protestant Ethic among the Black Muslims" *Phylon* 27.1 (1st quarter, 1966): 5–14.

63 Charles Pinderhughes, "Toward a New Theory of Internal Colonialism" *Socialism and Democracy* 25.1 (March, 2011): 235–256; Donald J. Harris, "The Black Ghetto As Internal Colony: a Theoretical Critique and Alternative Formulation," *The Review of Black Political Economy* 2.4 (September 1972): 3–33; and J.H. O'Dell, "Colonialism and the Negro American Experience," 6.4, *Freedomways* (Fall, 1966): 296–308.

capitalism, Muhammad's economic policy amounts to no more than an escapist illusion.[64] The political-economic aspect is no more than Black capitalism in nationalist façade.[65] Hayward Farrar insightfully comments, "The Nation of Islam's programs of economic self-sufficiency based on petty entrepreneurial capitalism plus its insistence on petty bourgeois values and behavior and its repudiation of racial integration are rooted in not only classical black nationalist thought but more also in the agenda of Booker T. Washington" (Farrar, 1999: 125).

Before his exit from the NOI, Malcolm is in accord with Muhammad's economic analysis. He states,

> He [Muhammad] shows us how to pool, and to work together toward a common objective. Among other things, we have small businesses in most cities in this country, and we want to create many more. We are taught by Mr. Muhammad that it is important to improve the black man's economy, and his thrift... We must learn to become our own producers, manufacturers and traders: we must have industry of our own, to employ our own. The white man resists this because he wants to keep the black man under his thumb and jurisdiction in white society. He wants to keep the black man always dependent and begging-for jobs, food, clothes, shelter, education.
>
> GALLEN, 1992: 111

On March 8, 1964, Malcolm formally announces his break from the Nation of Islam. Within that month, Malcolm gives his first extended discussions of his independently emerging philosophy of Black Nationalism. On April 3, 1964, Malcolm further elaborates on his economic philosophy with the speech, "The Ballot or The Bullet." Now let us examine this lecture in terms of Malcolm's evolving economic views. What is foremost in our examination is to compare Malcolm's post-NOI nationalist perspective on the Black economic condition vis-à-vis our previous summation of Muhammad's Black capitalist view of nationalism, which Malcolm was in agreement. Now Malcolm argues,

---

64 Wilson Jeremiah Moses, *Black Messiahs and Uncle Toms: Social and Literary Manipulations of a Religious Myth* (University Park: Pennsylvania State University Press, 1982): 208; and Frank M. Wright, "The National Question: A Marxist Critique," *The Black Scholar* 5.5 (1974): 45–53.

65 Lawrence L. Tyler, "The Protestant Ethic among the Black Muslims" *Phylon* 27.1 (1st quarter 1966): 5–14; Robert L Allen, *Black Awakening in Capitalist America* (Garden City, New York: Doubleday, 1969); and August Meier, *Negro Thought in America, 1880–1915: Racial Ideologies in the Age of Booker T. Washington* (Ann Arbor: University of Michigan Press, 1966).

> The economic philosophy of black nationalism is pure and simple. It only means that we should control the economy of our community. Why should white people be running all the stores in our community? Why should white people be running the banks of our community? Why should the economy of our community be in the hands of the white man? Why? If a black man can't move his store into a white community, you tell me why a white man should move his store into a black community… Our people have to be made to see that any time you take your dollar out of your community and spend it in a community where you don't live, the community where you live will get poorer and poorer, and the community where you spend your money will get richer and richer.
> MALCOLM X, 1966A: 38–39

This argument is directly in alignment with Muhammad's stance on domestic colonialism. White ownership over businesses in the Black community is identified as the main problem at the foundation of African American economic woes.[66] Malcolm's economic analysis does not, at this point, present a critique of capitalism in its basic composition. In Malcolm's estimation, the overriding issue remains white control over businesses in the Black community and not the systemic nature of capitalism. Malcolm continues:

> So the economic philosophy of black nationalism means in every church, in every civic organization, in every fraternal order, it's time now for our people to become conscious of the importance of controlling the economy of our community. If we own the stores, if we operate the businesses, if we try and establish some industry in our own community, then we're developing to the position where we are creating employment for our own kind. Once you gain control of the economy of your own community, then you don't have to picket and boycott and beg some cracker downtown for a job in his business.
> MALCOLM X, 1966A: 39

It is transparent – at this point in Malcolm's political evolution – he had not in substance departed from Elijah Muhammad's nationalist conception of Black

---

66 Donald Harris, "The Black Ghetto as Internal Colony: A Theoretical Critique and Alternative Formulation," *The Review of Black Political Economy* 2.4 (Summer 1972): 3–33; James Boggs, "The Myth and Irrationality of Black Capitalism" *The Review of Black Political Economy* 1.1 (Spring-Summer 1970): 27–35.

capitalism. After his immediate exit, Malcolm was incapable of rethinking the core premises that buttress Muhammad's thinking about the economics of Black Nationalism. The dialectical formation of Malcolm's philosophy of nationalism was uneven and his economic viewpoint lagged behind advances made pertaining to the refutation of Muhammad's views on Africa, political theology, theological anthropology, and racialism.

It is our main thesis that the configuration of anti-capitalist and anti-imperialist thought comprises the *substantive content* of Malcolm's *left form* of nationalism. In view of Malcolm's disregard for the critique of capitalism, prima facie, we are unable to firmly establish – that at this stage of his thought – what we claim, for Malcolm, is *left-wing* nationalism. Therefore we ask, why and how is it that Malcolm ultimately achieves his advocacy of left-wing nationalism? In view of our dialectical materialist method, we cannot presuppose in some teleological sense that Malcolm – despite the absence of an anti-capitalist critique – must arrive at this left form of Black Nationalism.[67]

There are several factors which function as means for Malcolm's leftward projection. Since along with anti-capitalism, anti-imperialism is one of the two prime components respecting the substance of Malcolm's political philosophy; anti-imperialism is the starting point of our analysis. Although, the conceptual disconnect between anti-imperialism and anti-capitalism is quite evident; nevertheless, we think it can be demonstrated that Malcolm's *very growth and development* as anti-imperialist thinker, actually propels his leftward movement to anti-capitalism.[68]

---

67   For an example of post-Malcolm right-wing Black Nationalism, which is based on Black capitalism, see "Roy Innis: From Left-wing Radical to Right-wing Extremist" *The Journal of Blacks in Higher Education* 30 (April 30, 2003): 69. Roy Innis, "Separatist Economics: A New Social Contract" in William F. Haddad and G. Douglas Pugh, ed., *Black Economic Development* (Englewood Cliffs: Prentice-Hall, 1969): 50–59. Also read, Joshua D. Farrington, "'Build Baby Build': Conservative Nationalist, Free Enterprise, and the Nixon Administration" in Laura Jane Gifford and Daniel K. Williams ed., *The Right Side of the Sixties: Examining Conservatism's Decade of Transformation* (New York: Palgrave Macmillan, 2012): 61–80.

68   Here we are in agreement with George Breitman's assessment, "And from his [Malcolm's] thought and study – especially from the thinking initiated through his discussions with African revolutionaries (whose impact on him far exceeded the influence of the religious Muslims in Mecca) – he came to the conclusion that capitalism is the cause of racism, that you can't have capitalism without racism, and therefore socialism should seriously be considered as an objective by black Americans as well as by Africans and Asians and Latin Americans." George Breitman, Herman Porter, and Baxter Smith, *The Assassination of Malcolm X* (New York: Pathfinder Press, 1991): 124.

Why does anti-imperialism function in this manner? Because of the impact of racialism on his anti-imperialist views – during his NOI membership – Malcolm gradually subordinates Muhammad's political theology to more secular (materialist) yet racially focused anti-imperialist thinking. It brings forth a qualitatively different result than it had on his strictly theological viewpoint. The racist character of imperialism forces Malcolm to adjust NOI racialism to the material and ideological aspects of imperialism.

By highlighting the racial dimension of the anti-imperialist struggles, Malcolm tacitly accommodates to – yet ultimately comes into tension with – NOI racialist political theology. In this adjustment, Malcolm achieves a certain degree of flexibility in his political analysis; yet simultaneously, he strains NOI racialist constrictions. Malcolm not only spoke out against U.S. and western imperialism but he also met with prominent anti-imperialist fighters. For example, we find that Malcolm publicly made pronouncements on the importance of the Bandung Conference; critiqued U.S. intervention in the Korean War; met with Fidel Castro in 1960 and voiced support for the Cuban revolution. Additionally, in 1960, Malcolm met with African leaders Kenneth Kaunda, Gamal Nassar, Sékou Touré and Alex Quaison Sackey. He also organized a Harlem Rally for Kwame Nkrumah.

In public lectures, Malcolm also brought attention to the Mau Mau in Kenya, and weighed against the assassination of Patrice Lumumba and the nefarious role of U.S. and western imperialism. Further, Malcolm linked these two events as parallel with the varied confrontations of the Black liberation movement. Given Muhammad's reactionary 'jungle' depiction of Africa, Malcolm's consistent involvement with African leaders and issues considerably pushed the limits of NOI political theology.

Before his Mecca revelations – about the non-racist manner of whites – which he encountered under the banner of traditional Islam, Malcolm was quite favorable toward Castro and the Cuban revolution. Despite his concurrent espousal of Muhammad's theodicy and white demonology, Malcolm does not identify Castro as a white man and hence a devil. After his Hotel Theresa meeting with Fidel (September, 1960), Malcolm states, "Any man who represents such a small country but who would stand up and challenge the country as large as the United States on behalf of his people must be sincere" (Evanzz, 1992: 85). Yet, Malcolm follows with a statement, which clearly maintains NOI theological posture, "The Nation of Islam is not an alliance with Mr. Castro or with any foreign powers on earth. The Nation of Islam is allied with Allah. Hence, we cannot be affiliated with Communism since it's atheistic" (Evanzz, 1992: 85).

Malcolm stretches the limits of NOI racialism. By ignoring the fact that Castro is a white man, it is apparent that considerably before Malcolm's trip to

Mecca, he abandons, in this instance, Muhammad's racialism and affirms anti-imperialism. In concert with the African liberation movement, Malcolm locates Castro and the Cuban revolution on the side of the anti-imperialist forces (Reitan, 1999). As Black communist Bill Epton observes on the significance of Malcolm's meeting with Castro:

> For those of us who subsequently met, had conversations with, and came to know Malcolm, it becomes obvious in hindsight that his days in the Nation of Islam were limited. He had a clear understanding of the international situation and the class position of the African American people in the United States...He was politically and intellectually far beyond the myopic outlook of the Nation of Islam.
> MEALY, 1993: 19

Malcolm's conferring with Castro and his attempted strategy of tacit accommodation, nevertheless, created a tension with Muhammad's conservative apolitical position. Karl Evanzz notes, "From the wiretap on Elijah Muhammad's telephone the FBI discovered that the Messenger was furious about Malcolm meeting with Castro on September 20. Muhammad, it seemed, was afraid the American government would try to link the Nation of Islam with Communism and use this as an excuse to decimate the sect as it had done in 1942" (Evanzz, 1992: 85).

In its campaign of misinformation, the FBI, in fact, leaked a story to the New York *Journal American* falsely accusing Malcolm of joining in an international conspiracy. Evanzz outlines the story: "'Malcolm X and his Chicago headquarters' had been linked by the intelligence community in 'international intrigue' with Nassar, Castro, and Nikita Khrushchev of the Soviet Union in a plot to win the minds of America's 20 million Negroes to use them in winning the allegiance of the newly independent dark-skinned nations in Africa'" (Evanzz, 1992: 87).

The conduit for Malcolm's meeting with Castro was the Welcoming Committee of the 28th Precinct Community Council and as a result of the news article; Malcolm resigned from the group (Evanzz, 1992: 87). With Malcolm's prior affirmation of Castro and his subsequent resignation, from the group that facilitated the meeting, we have the dialectical contradiction; where Malcolm both stretches the limits of NOI racialist political theology and his accommodation to organizational discipline. In spite of Muhammad's concerns, we observe Malcolm embraces Castro as an anti-imperialist fighter and his whiteness is not a deterrent.

By May 29, 1964, Malcolm's knowledge of the mechanics and complexity of imperialism rapidly advanced to connecting imperialism to capitalism and racism:

> [A]ll of the countries that are emerging today from under the shackles of colonialism turning towards socialism. I don't think it's an accident. Most of the countries that were colonial powers were capitalist countries, and the last bulwark of capitalism today is America. It's impossible for a white person to believe in capitalism and not believe in racism. You can't have capitalism without racism.
> MALCOLM X, 1966A: 69

It is evident that Malcolm's anti-imperialism is pivotal to his motion toward grasping anti-capitalism. George Breitman correctly states,

> Malcolm came to the conclusion that the Black Muslims had gone as far as they can go, and he wanted to go further. He wanted to get into the active struggle, influence it ideologically, and revolutionize it. You wanted to build a new movement, on new foundations, and therefore he reviewed all his ideas – keeping some, modified others, casting aside still others. He began to *move to the left*... The main allies of Afro-Americans, he decided, are the black, brown, yellow, and red people of the world; but then he also began to see the possibility of alliances with what he called 'militant white' Americans... None of this made him into an 'integrationist.' But it did make him go beyond the simple formula, the white man is the enemy... It did make him think about and study the causes of racism and to see the possibility of its elimination some day. It led him to study the nature of American capitalist society, and world capitalism – always from the viewpoint of how the interests of black people could be promoted and protected
> BREITMAN ET AL, 1991: 122–124.[69] [Italics Added]

This progression further accelerated with Malcolm's two trips to Africa. In his journeys, Malcolm had numerous encounters with anti-imperialist socialists

---

[69] For the entire summation of Brightman's analysis, read the chapter "Myths about Malcolm X" in George Breitman, Herman Porter, and Baxter Smith, *The Assassination of Malcolm X* (New York: Pathfinder Press, 1991): 109–130. The cited quotation is from pages 122–124.

in Africa. Many of these revolutionary thinkers/activists were staunch anti-capitalists. Malcolm's understanding begins to extend beyond imperialism in Africa:

> Among the Asian countries, whether they are communist, socialist-you don't find any capitalist countries over there too much nowadays. Almost every one of the countries that have gotten independence and devise some kind of socialist system, and this is no accident... None of them are adopting the capitalistic system because they realize they can't. You can't operate a capitalistic system unless you are vulturistic....
> MALCOLM X, 1966A: 120–121

These encounters aided Malcolm's understanding of the organic ties not only to racism but also of imperialism to capitalism. One of the most important relationships that Malcolm cemented was with Abdul Rahman Muhammad Babu of Tanzania. A comrade of Babu remembers:

> Babu and Malcolm X met in Cairo in July 1964 at the second Summit of the newly-formed Organisation of African Unity (OAU) which was followed by a Summit of the Non-aligned Movement. As the two revolutionaries were meeting, Malcolm X's community, Harlem, New York, was burning... Babu helped Malcolm X realise the two objectives: meeting and discussing with anti-imperialist leaders (including President Julius Nyerere) of the Third World and heading home to lead his people in battle.[70]
> MALCOLM X AND ABDUL RAHMAN BABU

On December 13, 1964, subsequently, Malcolm invited Babu to give a lecture before his Organization of Afro-American Unity (OAAU). Babu, the Tanzanian Minister of Economic Development, was a revolutionary anti-imperialist and socialist. Furthermore, Babu's anti-capitalist position was thoroughly grounded in the Marxist critique of capitalism.[71] Babu led the revolution in Zanzibar and united the island with Tanganyika, to become Tanzania. Babu also played a

---

70 "Malcolm X and Abdul Rahman Babu" in *Assata Shakur Forums* (August 12, 2006) http://www.assatashakur.org/forum/shoulders-our-freedom-fighters/20686-malcolm-x-abdul-rahman-babu.html.

71 For a sample of Babu's socialist views, see Abdul Rahman Mohamed Babu, Salma Babu, and Amrit Wilson. *The Future That Works: Selected Writings of A.M. Babu*. Trenton, NJ: Africa World Press, 2002; Abdul Rahman Mohamed Babu, *African Socialism or Socialist Africa?* London: Zed Press, 1981.

role in gaining African (heads of state) support of Malcolm's resolution before the OAU; which condemned Black oppression in the U.S. Malcolm's resolution before the OAU was a crucial part of his efforts to expand the civil right movement to the internationalist platform of human rights.

At the same December 13, 1964 meeting, Chè Guevara was also scheduled to speak before the OAAU. He could not attend but Chè sent a message of solidarity. Given Malcolm's earlier period of accommodation to the NOI, on the Cuban revolution, Malcolm's response is most instructive. In reference to Chè as an ally, Malcolm declares:

> You and I should practice the habit of weighing people and weighing situations and weighing groups and weighing governments for ourselves. And don't let somebody else tell us who our enemies should be and who our friends should be. I love a revolutionary. And one of the most revolutionary men in this country right now was going to come here along with our friend, Sheik Babu, but he thought better of it.
>
> MALCOLM X, 1966A: 102

Malcolm continues to reassess the nomenclature 'Black Nationalism' especially given the anti-capitalist impulse as substantive content. Ultimately, Malcolm questions the viability of the nomenclature 'Black Nationalism' as a revolutionary appellation that would sufficiently convey his political philosophy. Malcolm reflects:

> I used to define black nationalism as the idea that the black man should control the economy of his community, the politics of his community, and so forth. But when I was in Africa in May, in Ghana, I was speaking with the Algerian ambassador who is extremely militant and a revolutionary in the true sense of the word.... When I told him that my political, social and economic philosophy was black nationalism, he asked me very frankly, well, where did that leave him? Because he was white. He was an African, but he was an Algerian, and to all appearances he was a white man. And he said if I define my objective as the victory of black nationalism, where does that leave him? Where does that leave revolutionaries in Morocco, Egypt, Iraq, Mauritania? So he showed me where I was alienating many people who were true revolutionaries, dedicated to overthrowing the systems of exploitation that exist on this earth by any means necessary. So, I had to do a lot of thinking and reappraising of my definition of black nationalism.
>
> BREITMAN, 1967: 64–65

We must conclude that any critical study of Malcolm's political philosophy must of necessity acknowledged that Malcolm's dialectical process of revolutionary formation remained an ongoing project. With respect to Malcolm's assassination, one of the great tragedies is that it robbed him of the possibility of further developing the substance and form of his political philosophy. In light of his tragic demise, the nomenclature left-wing Black Nationalism is, in many ways, inadequate; an abrupt and frozen moment, in his dialectical movement toward revolutionary thought.

Bibliography

Adeleke, Tunde. *UnAfrican Americans: 19th Century Black Nationalists and the Civilizing Mission*. Lexington: University Press of Kentucky, 1998.

Allen, Jr., Ernest. "Religious Heterodoxy and Nationalist Tradition: The Continuing Evolution of the Nation of Islam." *The Black Scholar* 26, no. 3–4 (Fall/Winter, 1996): 2–34.

Angell, Stephen W. "Henry McNeal Turner – Conservative? Radical? Or Independent?" in Peter Eisenstadt, ed., *Black Conservatism: Essays and Intellectual and Political History* (New York: Garland Publishers, 1999): 25–50.

Baraka, Amiri. "Malcolm as Ideology" in Joe Wood, ed., *Malcolm X: in Our Own Image*. New York: St. Martin's Press, 1992.

Bracey, Jr., John H. August Meier, and Elliot Rudwick, eds., *Black Nationalism in America*. Indianapolis: Bobbs-Merrill, 1970.

Breitman, George. *The Last Year of Malcolm X*. New York: Merit Publishers, 1967.

George Breitman, Herman Potter, and Baxter Smith, *The Assassination of Malcolm X*. New York: Pathfinder Press, 1991.

Bonds, Michael. "Black Political Power Reassessed: Race, Politics, and Federal Funds." *Journal of African American Studies* 11, no. 3–4 (December, 2007): 189–203.

Bush, Roderick D. *The End of White World Supremacy: Black Internationalism and the Problem of the Color Line*. Philadelphia: Temple University Press, 2009.

Clarke, John Henrik, A. Peter Bailey, and Earl Grant. *Malcolm X: The Man and His Times*. New York: Macmillan, 1969.

Clegg III, Claude A. "Rebuilding the Nation: The Life and Work of Elijah Muhammad" *The Black Scholar* 26, no. 3–4 (Fall/Winter, 1996): 49–59.

Clegg III, Claude A. *An Original Man: the Life and Times of Elijah Muhammad*. New York: St. Martin's Press, 1997.

Curtis IV, Edward E. "Islamizing the Black Body: Ritual and Power in Elijah Muhammad's Nation of Islam." *Religion and American Culture: The Journal of Interpretation* 12, no. 2 (2002): 167–196.

Collins, Patricia Hill. "Learning to Think for Ourselves: Malcolm X's Black Nationalism Reconsidered" in Joe Wood, ed., *Malcolm X: In Our Own Image* (New York: St. Martin's Press, 1992): 59–85.

Delany, Martin R. *Principia of Ethnology: The Origin of Races and Color With an Archaeological Compendium of Ethiopian and Egyptian Civilization, From Years of Careful Examination and Enquiry.* Philadelphia: Harper & Brother, Publishers, 1879.

Dulaney, W. Marvin. "Documenting the Life and Legacy of Malcolm X" (Review of Manning Marable and Garrett Felber, eds., *The Portable Malcolm X Reader*) *The Journal of African American History* 98, no. 4 (Fall, 2013): 602–608.

Eissen-Udom, E.U. *Black Nationalism: The Search for an Identity in America.* Chicago: University of Chicago Press, 1962.

Ellis, Catherine, and Stephen Smith. *Say It Loud: Great Speeches on Civil Rights and African American Identity.* New York: New Press, 2010.

Evanzz, Karl. *The Judas Factor: The Plot to Kill Malcolm X.* New York: Thunder's Mouth Press, 1992.

Farrar, Hayward. "Radical Rhetoric Conservative Reality: The Nation of Islam As an American Conservative Formation" in Peter Eisenstadt, ed., *Black Conservatism: Essays and Intellectual and Political History* (New York: Garland Publishers, 1999): 109–130.

Flick, Hank. "Malcolm X: The Destroyer and Maker of Myths." *Journal of Black Studies* 12, no. 2 (December, 1981): 166–181.

Flick, Hank and Larry Powell. "Animal Imagery in the Rhetoric of Malcolm X." *Journal of Black Studies* 18, no. 4 (June, 1988): 435–451.

Fuentes-Nieva, Ricardo and Nicholas Galasso. "Working the Few: Political Capture and Economic Inequality." *Oxfam International Report* (January 20, 2014) http://www.oxfam.org/en/policy/working--the-few-economic-inequality.

Gallen, David. *Malcolm X: As They Knew Him.* New York: Carroll & Graf, 1992.

de la Garza, Rudolph O., Z. Anthony Kruszewski, and Tomás Arciniega, eds., *Chicanos and Native Americans: The Territorial Minorities.* Englewood Cliffs: Prentice Hall, 1973.

Gilbert, Michele A. "Race, Location, and Education: The Election of Black Mayors in the 1990s." *Journal of Black Studies* 36, no. 3 (January, 2006).

Green, Rodney D., Maie Kouassi and Belinda Mambo. "Housing, Race, and Recovery from Hurricane Katrina." *The Review of Black Political Economy* 40, no. 2 (June, 2013): 145–163.

Hamilton, Derek and William Darity, Jr. "Can Baby Bonds Eliminate the Racial Wealth Gap in Putative Post-Racial America?" *Review of Black Political Economy* 37, no. 3–4 (2010): 207–216.

Horne, Gerald. "'Myth' in the Making of 'Malcolm X,'" *The American Historical Review* 98, no. 2 (April, 1993): 440–450.

Pedro de la Hoz, *Africa in the Cuban revolution: Our Search for Full Justice*. Habana: Instituto Cubano Del Libro, 2005.

Jenkins, Robert L. and Mfanya Donald Tryman, ed., *The Malcolm X Encyclopedia*. Westport: Greenwood press, 2002.

Jones, Mack H. "Empowerment in Atlanta: Myth and Reality Black Political Empowerment in Atlanta: Myth and Reality." *Annals of the Academy of Political and Social Science* 439 (September, 1978).

Jones, William R. *Is God a White Racist? A Preamble to Black Theology*. Boston: Beacon Press, 1998.

Karim, Benjamin, Peter Skutches, and David Gallen. *Remembering Malcolm: The Story of Malcolm X from inside the Muslim Mosque by his Assistant Minister Benjamin Karim*. New York: Carroll and Graf Publishers, Inc., 1992.

Knight, Frederick. "Justifiable Homicide, Police Brutality, or Government Repression? The 1962 Los Angeles Police Shooting of Seven Members of the Nation of Islam" *The Journal of Negro History* 79, no. 2 (Spring, 1994): 191.

Kochlar, Rakesh, Richard Fry, and Paul Taylor. "Twenty to One: Wealth Gaps Rise to Record Time Between Whites, Blacks, Hispanics." (Washington, DC: Pew Research Center, 2011).

Kraus, Neil and Todd Swanstrom. "Minority Mayors and the Hollow-Prize Problem." *Political Science and Politics* 34, no. 1 (March, 2001): 99–105.

Malcolm X. "God's Judgment of White America (The Chickens Come Home to Roost)," *The Black Commentator* (December 4, 1963) http://www.blackcommentator.com/91/91_malcolm_pf.html (Accessed July 10, 2014).

——— Malcolm X Speech at University of Ghana (May 13, 1964) http://malcolmxfiles.blogspot.com/2013/07/university-of-ghana-may-13-1964_1.html (Accessed July 10, 2014).

——— *By Any Means Necessary; Speeches, Interviews, and a Letter*. New York: Pathfinder Press, 1970a.

——— *Malcolm X on Afro-American History*. New York: Pathfinder Press, 1970b.

——— *Malcolm X Talks to Young People*. New York: Pathfinder Press, 1989a.

——— *February 1965: The Final Speeches*. New York: Pathfinder, 1992.

——— *Malcolm X Speaks: Selected Speeches and Statements*. George Breitman (Ed.) New York: Rove Press, 1966a.

——— (as told to Alex Haley). *The Autobiography of Malcolm X*. New York: Random House, 1966b.

——— *The End of White World Supremacy*. New York: Merlin House, 1971.

——— *Malcolm X: The Last Speeches*. Bruce Perry (Ed.) New York: Pathfinder, 1989b.

Marable, Manning. *Malcolm X: A Life of Reinvention*. New York: Penguin Group, 2011.

Marcus, Anthony. *Malcolm X and the Third American Revolution: The Writings of George Breitman*. Amherst: Humanity Books, 2005.

Mealy, Rosemari. *Fidel & Malcolm X: Memories of a Meeting*. New York: Ocean Press, 1993.

Moses, Wilson Jeremiah. *Black Messiahs and Uncle Toms: Social and Literary Manipulations of a Religious Myth*. University Park: Pennsylvania State University Press, 1982.

Moses, Wilson Jeremiah. *The Golden Age of Black Nationalism, 1820–1925*. New York; Oxford: Oxford University Press, 1988.

Moses, Wilson Jeremiah. *Classical Black Nationalism: from the American Revolution to Marcus Garvey*. New York: New York University Press, 1996.

Muhammad, Elijah. *The Supreme Wisdom, Vol. 1: Solution to the So-Called "Negroes" Problem*. Chicago: University of Islam, 1957a.

Muhammad, Elijah. *The Supreme Wisdom, Vol. 2: What Every American So-Called Negro Should Know About*. Chesapeake, Virginia: ECA Associates, 1957b.

Muhammad, Elijah. *Message to the Black Man in America*. Chicago: Muhammad Mosque of Islam, No. 2, 1965.

Muhammad, Elijah. *How to Eat to Live, Book 1*. Phoenix, Arizona: Secretarius MEMP Ministries, 1967.

Muhammad, Elijah. *The Theology of Time: (The Secret of the Time)*. Atlanta: Secretarius M.E.M.P.S, 1997.

Ovenden, Kevin. *Malcolm X: Socialism and Black Nationalism*. London: Bookmarks, 1992.

Painter, Nell Irvin. "Martin R Delany: Elitism and Nationalism" in Leon Litwack and August Meier, eds., *Black Leaders of the Nineteenth Century* (Urbana: University of Illinois press, 1988), 149–172.

Reitan, Ruth. *The Rise and Decline of an Alliance: Cuba and African American leaders in the 1960s*. East Lansing: Michigan State University Press, 1999.

Robinson, Eugene. *Disintegration: The Splintering of Black America*. New York: Doubleday, 2010.

Robinson, Dean E. *Black Nationalism in American Politics and Thought*. New York: Cambridge University Press, 2001.

Stein, Judith. *The World of Marcus Garvey: Race and Class in Modern Society*. Baton Rouge: Louisiana State University Press, 1986.

Sales, Jr., William W. *From Civil Rights to Black Liberation: Malcolm X and the Organization of Afro-America Unity*. Boston: South End Press, 1999.

Saunders, Lisa. "Employment and Earnings: A Case Study of Urban Detroit." *The Review of Black Political Economy* 39, no. 1 (March, 2012): 107–119.

Smith, R. Drew. "Black Religious Nationalism and the Politics of Transcendence." *Journal of the American Academy of Religion* 66, no. 3 (Autumn, 1998): 533–547.

Strickland, William, and Cheryl Y. Greene. *Malcolm X, Make It Plain*. New York: Viking, 1994.

Sundiata, I.K. *Brothers and Strangers: Black Zion, Black Slavery, 1914–1940.* Durham, North Carolina: Duke University Press, 2003.

Swain, Jr., Johnnie Dee "Black Mayors: Urban Decline and the Underclass." *Journal of Black Studies* 24, no. 1 (September, 1993): 16–28.

Taylor, James Lance *Black Nationalism in the United States: From Malcolm X to Barack Obama.* Boulder, Colorado: Lynne Rienner Publishers, 2011.

Terrill, Robert ed., *The Cambridge Companion to Malcolm X.* Cambridge, MA: Cambridge University Press, 2010.

Tippett, Jones-DeWeever, Rockeymoore, Hamilton and Darity. *Beyond Broke: Why Closing the Racial Wealth Gap is a Priority for National Economic Security.* Washington D.C.; Center for Global Policy Solutions, 2014.

Turner, Richard Brent. *Islam in the African-American Experience.* Bloomington: Indiana University Press, 1997.

Van Deburg, William L. ed., *Modern Black Nationalism: from Marcus Garvey to Louis Farrakhan.* New York: New York University Press, 1997.

Washington, Jr., Joseph R. *The Politics of God.* Boston: Beacon Press, 1969.

Valerie Rawlston Wilson, "Introduction to the 2014 Equality Index." in Hardy, Chanelle P., ed. *2014 State of Black America: One Nation Underemployed: Jobs Rebuild America.* New York: National Urban League, 2014.

Wolfenstein, Eugene. *The Victims of Democracy: Malcolm X and the Black Revolution.* New York: The Guilford Press, 1993.

Wright, Lewis Edward. *The Political Thought of Elijah Muhammad: Innovation and Continuity in Western Tradition.* Diss. Howard University, 1987.

CHAPTER 4

Malcolm X and Revolutionary Religion: Christianity, Islam and their Emancipatory Potentials

Dustin J. Byrd

Many recent books on Malcolm X focus on the biographical transformations of his thought and religious praxis. Malcolm, they demonstrate, like a good scientist or dialectical philosopher was not afraid to change his mind as he was introduced to new evidence, better arguments, and a deeper understanding of the subject confronting him. Yet, I do not want to focus on the determinate negations prevalent within his biography. Rather, in this essay, I will focus on what remained consistent from his days in the Nation of Islam to his embrace of Sunni Islam. One of these themes was his critique of Christianity and other forms of what can be defined as 'positive' religion, or forms of religion that have abandoned the prophetic concern for social dynamics for the priestly investment in social statics. Like other faiths, Christianity abdicated its early oppositional nature towards the state, power, and social idolatry, Malcolm X understood Islam to be the *inner-critique* of the Abrahamic traditions (Horkheimer, 1974: 34–37). As such, Islam was the conceptual 'other' that embodied, augmented, and implemented that which the previous religions either failed to realize and/or had abandoned, i.e. radical equality or, as Malcolm described it, the *true spirit of brotherhood*. Just as the Qur'an regards itself as *al-furqan* (the criteria) by which to judge all other revealed scriptures, Islam, especially in its most conceptually pure form, served as the measure by which the other Abrahamic religions were judged, regardless of the imperfect ways in which it was and is actualized throughout the Muslim world both then and now. Malcolm X saw that Islam was a religion pregnant with the potential to do that which the others failed to do, change the social dynamics of a given civilization, especially in terms of its racial antagonisms. For him, the persuasive power to erase away the "cancer of racism" that is often found within antagonistic civil society made Islam attractive beyond contemporary Christian thought and praxis (Malcolm X, 2013: 40).[1] Christianity, at least in its dominant Western

---

1 It also has built within it certain mechanisms to mitigate the disastrous effects of class divisions. However, these have not always had the desired effect. The extreme poverty that can be found within the Muslims world within the shadows of extreme wealth is no different than

manifestations, despite its radical communitarian origins, failed to bring about a society of equality, solidarity, and brotherhood, but rather gave birth to a society of systemic violence, brutal imperialism, slavery, genocide and systematic racism, or at minimum justified such a society.[2] For Malcolm X, African-Americans were just one among many victims of the so-called 'Christian' society, but were nevertheless the subject of his immediate concern.

With the help of the Critical Theory of Religion, as developed by the Frankfurt School for Social Research, especially via the religious thought Max Horkheimer, Theodor Adorno and Walter Benjamin, I will reexamine Malcolm X's critical analysis of Christianity, its social and moral failures, and its functionalization as ideology within the American bourgeois 'white society.' Malcolm X was not a critical theorist in the academic sense, but his keen observations, his penetrating analysis, and his uncompromising praxis embodies the spirit of the radical critique of non-conformist intellectuals; a spirit that recalcitrantly says 'no' to stale ideologies that justify exploitation, oppression, systematic hatred and unwarranted violence against the innocent victim, and the struggle for a more reconciled, equal and peaceful future society. Because of this confluence, the Critical Theory of Religion can help us illuminate the already defiant stance of Malcolm X towards the 'world-as-it-is' and aid in the struggle, not only for recognition of the victims of history, i.e. racial minorities, the poor, the marginalized and all others who have been left in the ditch of 'civilization,' but it can contribute to bringing about a new society rooted within the Prophetic and Socratic ideals for which he and many other revolutionaries were martyred.

Three Periods of Christianity in Malcolm's Biography

Malcolm X's relationship with Christianity can be broken down into three distinct periods in his biography. First, his growing up in the home of his parents and their combination of the Black Nationalism of Marcus Garvey and the Baptist denomination (Malcolm X, 1992a: 7). Additionally, this period extends

---

in the non-Muslim world; a phenomenon that many more leftist Muslims see as a failure of the Muslims to implement true Islamic values. In many ways, Muslim society has been influenced by the brutality of aggressive capitalism more so than capitalism has been influenced by Islam.

2 If we cannot say that it was totally responsible for this phenomenon, and I don't believe it was, then we can at least say that it failed to arrest them.

into his wayward days as a minor hustler, pimp, drug dealer, etc., when he became hostile to questions of religion, until he was introduced to the teachings of Elijah Muhammad while in Norfolk Prison Colony in 1948.[3] His most vivid experience with Christianity in this first period began with his father's religious preaching, which left him unimpressed. In his autobiography, Malcolm recalls his church experiences,

> My brother Philbert...loved church, but it confused and amazed me. I would sit goggle-eyed at my father jumping and shouting as he preached, with the congregation jumping and shouting behind him, their souls and bodies devoted to singing and praying. Even at that young age, I just couldn't believe in the Christian concept of Jesus as someone divine. And no religious person, until I was a man in my twenties – and then in prison – could tell me anything. I had very little respect for most people who represented religion.
> MALCOLM X, 1992A: 7

It is doubtful that Malcolm developed any real critique of the core concept of Jesus' divinity at such a young age, but we have no reason to doubt his youthful skepticism of this particular form of Christian worship, especially the charismatic aspect. It may have been the case, as others have claimed, that he was projecting his adult critique of Christianity into his childhood experiences, or, he may simply be recalling a time period in his life that was confusing, offputting and for some unarticulated reason uncomfortable for the youngster in church.[4] However, Malcolm did express his approval of his father's ethnopolitical views on Marcus Garvey, which were delivered in a more "intelligent" and "down to earth" manner, saying "the image of him that made me proudest was his crusading and militant campaigning" which scared "these white folks to death" (Malcolm X, 1992a: 9). As we can see, the period between 1925, the

---

3 In 1950 Malcolm was transferred back to Charlestown State Prison, where he was originally incarcerated, for refusing to be inoculated for typhoid. Since he objected on religious grounds, he was returned to Charlestown. However, by April of 1950, he and other NOI converts were demanding *halal* (permissible by Islamic dietary laws) meals and jail cells facing east towards Mecca (Marable and Felber, 2013: xxx).

4 William David Hart has suggested that this may be a case of Malcolm's "auto-biographical memory," wherein his present opinions are projected back into his biography (William David Hart, 2008: 26–27). If this is the case, it simply further emphasizes Malcolm's later rejected the divinity of Jesus of Nazareth in conformity with the Islamic tradition's insistence on Jesus' mere humanity.

year of Malcolm's birth, to sometime in 1948, when he was introduced to the Nation of Islam by family members, was filled with many experiences with Christianity. If we take Malcolm's writings verbatim, most of these experiences left him unimpressed or with a negative impression.

Second, Malcolm X experienced Christianity through the lenses of the Nation of Islam as being a totally 'racialized' religion. Having just accepted the teaching of Elijah Muhammad in prison, Malcolm relates an insight in his autobiography. He states,

> And where the religion of every other people on earth taught its believers of a God with whom they could identify, a God who at least looked like one of their own kind, the slavemaster injected his Christian religion into this "Negro." This "Negro" was taught to worship an alien God having the same blond hair, pale skin, and blue eyes as the slavemaster.
>
> MALCOLM X, 1992A: 188

During this time period, certain aspects of Christian history were cleverly integrated into the NOI's mythological anthropology, its 'Yacub's history' (Malcolm X, 1992a: 190–194). While certain 'historical' facts about Christianity and its origins were maintained, others are simply devoid of any truth, thus producing a sacred myth with a few scattered historical references within. Although the NOI often focused on the entwinement of Christianity, slavery, and white supremacy, Elijah Muhammad's peculiar Christology was half historical fact and half fiction. Without a shred of credible scholarship behind his claims, he made Jesus of Nazareth into the "illegitimate son of Joseph and Mary," and a "black prophet" who preached "the essence of the original Islam to the whites" (Clegg, 1997: 54). For having told the Jews about their "evil origins," Jesus was "skewered" with a knife, "pinned...to a wooden wall," his body being contorted into the shape of a cross, until "Joseph claimed his corpse" (Clegg, 1997: 55). According to Claude Andrew Clegg, "The prophet [Jesus] was prepared for burial by Egyptians and interred in Jerusalem. His sepulcher, guarded by Fruit of Islam, could be freely visited and viewed by Muslims; however, others would have to pay six thousand dollars and secure a certificate from the pope of Rome to gain entrance to the site" (Clegg, 1997: 55). The "tricknology" of evil whites, as Elijah Muhammad called it, resulted in the "unholy conspiracy" called Christianity, which was the evil religion of whites who were attempting to obscure the real religion of Islam, the religion of the original Asiatic Black man (Clegg, 1997: 55; Evanzz, 1999: 75). As such, Master Fard Muhammad, whom the Nation of Islam believed was God incarnated and the teacher of Elijah Muhammad, was sent to save the Black race from the evils of the whites, including their religion.[5] While the NOI's mythical telling of Christianity's origins is rather peculiar and mostly absent of verifiable history, it was designed primarily based on the *needs* of its audience and not *truth*. First, it was an attempt to divorce African-Americans from Christianity and bring them into the fold of the Nation of Islam. Second, such a *sacred story* provided as sense of worth, historical pride, and racial dignity that traditional Christianity failed to do – or intentionally took away – as it had become so indistinguishable from a society dominated by the ideology of white supremacy, the very society that victimized Black folk both physically and psychologically. In this sense, the truth of the myth was not important; what it *did* for Black folk, as it answered a *need*, was the prevailing factor. The 'brainwashing,' which had been done for hundreds of years by white 'Christians' to Black folk, had to be undone, and that was the intent of Yacub's anthropological mythology (Malcolm X, 1992a: 188).

Lastly, as Malcolm emancipated himself from the constrictions of the Nation of Islam's ideology, he divorced his understanding of Christianity from Elijah Muhammad's Dr. Yacub; he began to recognize the emancipatory potentials in Christianity, especially in light of the prophetic courage of the Black Church, led by Dr. Martin Luther King Jr., but nevertheless continued to maintain the idea that Christianity was inadequate in the struggle for human rights in the United States and abroad.[6] As such, Malcolm could appreciate the faith of millions of Black folk who looked to the religious opposition of Jesus of Nazareth to the empire of Rome and his subsequent martyrdom as *prophetic religion* – that it was a religion that could resist the *world-as-it-is*, as it was done by his most courageous mother and father. Nevertheless, he could not come to the conclusion that such a religion, so infused and disfigured by the untrue white-bourgeois-society, could bring about a society of peaceful coexistence, racial equality and true justice, similar to the one he witnessed while on pilgrimage to Mecca. Neither could a religion committed to the principle of non-violence engage in the necessary revolutionary praxis that was needed in the United States, as "revolutions are never fought by turning the other cheek [and] revolutions are never based upon love-your-enemy

---

5   For a much more comprehensive accounting of the NOI's mythological anthropology and its teachings on Christianity, see Clegg's extremely well written and research book, *An Original Man: The Life and Times of Elijah Muhammad*, pg. 1–73.
6   In a moment of contrition, Malcolm writes in his autobiography that "I was to learn later that Elijah Muhammad's tales, like this one of 'Yacub,' infuriated the Muslims of the East. While at Mecca, I reminded them that it was their fault, since they themselves hadn't done enough to make real Islam known in the West. Their silence left a vacuum into which any religious faker could step and mislead our people" (Malcolm X, 1992a: 194).

and pray-for-those-who-spitefully-use-you" (Malcolm X, 1965: 50). Christianity, even if stripped from the tyranny of white supremacy, was ill equipped for revolution, for within its foundation was the principle of non-violence. Islam, he believed, was the only religion that contained the moral, ethical, and political-economic vision to bring about a future reconciled, peaceful and just society, precisely because of its dual commitment to 'principled violence' (when necessary and as a last resort) and to its vision of a just and equitable society.

Positive and Negative Religion

From the perspective of the Frankfurt School's Critical Theory, the history of religion is dialectical in nature. There is always a dialectical tension between the religion that resists the world (*adversus mundi*) and the religion that conforms and compromises (*pro mundi*) with the world (Boer, 2012: 11–14). All three Abrahamic faiths, beginning with their founders (or initiators) Moses, Jesus and Muhammad, are by nature and design resistant towards conforming or compromising with the 'fallen' world and all its wickedness. Moses fights against the brutality of the slave holding society of Egypt; Jesus resists the unjust and oppressive empire of Rome and the collaborating Jewish authorities; and Muhammad fights against the pagan barbarity of *Jahaliyya* (Arabian age of ignorance). In their purest of essences, they are in a perpetual state of what Max Horkheimer calls the 'longing for the totally other,' (*die sehnsucht nacht dem ganz anderen*) opposed to the already established history of torture, terror, suffering and misery that this world breeds. In this sense, the given world is always in contradiction to the world-as-it-should-be, and the prophetic voices are those that make this distinction painfully clear to the masses, thus disturbing their sense of security, their invested-ness in the status quo, and/or their complacency in the face of suffering, poverty, misery and social despair. They are also the uncompromising voices that confront the brutal powers behind the status quo; those ruling classes, ideologies, governments and groups that depend on the status quo for their position, wealth, and authority. Nevertheless, as history has demonstrated too often, these faiths can be co-opted by the worldliness of power, status, and wealth, and abandon the very vision of the 'other' society that once made them so attractive to the victims of history. When these Abrahamic faiths abandon this 'otherness,' when it compromises with earthly power, the state, or the status quo, it loses its revolutionary and emancipatory potentials; it deflates into mere ideology – no longer concerned with *social dynamics* but rather with the preservation and reproduction of *social statics*. *Positive religion*, therefore, is any form of religion, whether it be an institution, belief and/or belief attitude, that embraces, justifies and sanctifies the given, especially the political, economic and social status quo, which includes the social antagonisms that lead to the reproduction of unnecessary suffering, despair, and oppression (Adorno, 2005: 135–142). It is a religion that has abandoned its revolutionary and prophetic core, and is left exhausted and facile, or worse, it becomes a "whitened sepulcher" – holy and pure on the outside but hollow and dead in the inside: a reduction to mere formalism (Matthew 23:27). From the perspective of the critical historian, this form of religion is often embraced by those who are the 'winners' of history, i.e. the feudal lords, the aristocracy, the bourgeoisie, and the dominant 1% in today's society, who are rarely ever concerned with the *content* of religion, but rather the *appearance*. This form of religion has a dual function. First, it fails to threaten the social status and wellbeing of the ruling class, i.e. it is defanged and made into *harmless* religion. Secondly, as Vladimir Lenin pointed out, it serves as a outlet for their guilt-consciousness (if it is present), by offering the ruling class opportunities for social absolution through meaningless compromises with altruism (the social appearance of which is more important than the altruistic act itself) (Lenin in Schapiro and Reddaway, 1967: 108–109). Despite its origins in radical Prophetic equality, most notably with Jesus of Nazareth and continuing through the early Christian tradition, this form of religion reifies the unjust conditions which are already established, making any thought of radical transformation within the given impossible as it is often perceived to be perverse and/or unnatural to attempt to change that which has a fixed nature. In an attempt to naturalize – and therefore legitimate – the socially constructed, Jesus of Nazareth is often quoted saying "the poor will always be with you" while failing to ask *why* such poor are always with us and whether or not Jesus meant they *should* always be a permanent fixture in the society of man (Mark: 14:7). If even the 'son of God' believes the poor will always be with us, they coyly say, then who are we to disagree, or God forbid, proving him wrong!

In this slumber-induced religiosity, associated with the 'Uncle Tom,' the victims of history are routinely asked to *suffer peacefully* while they are victimized – what Malcolm X referred to as "Novocaine" religion (Malcolm X, 1965: 12). In his *Message to the Grass Roots,* delivered in Detroit on November 10, 1963, Malcolm spoke of the religion of passivity, stating that,

> It's like when you go to the dentist, and the man's going to take your tooth. You're going to fight him when he starts pulling. So he squirts some stuff in your jaw called novocaine, to make you think they're not doing anything to you. So you sit there and because you've got all of that novocaine in your jaw, you suffer – peacefully. Blood running all down your jaw, and

> you don't know what's happening. Because someone has taught you to suffer – peacefully.
>
> MALCOLM X, 1965: 12

In other words, the social imperative instilled in the victim is to *suffer well*, forget this life, and be content to be rewarded after death (Malcolm X, 1992a: 188). In this passive ideology, revolutionary and emancipatory potentials quickly evaporate as the victims are made immobile, apathetic, and unwilling to engage in their own struggle for liberation; they are in affect *paralyzed in their lamentations*. By only gazing inward, and seeing salvation exclusively in the realm of the eschatological, the status quo remains unmolested, unmodified, and entrenched, and most perversely, serviced and maintained by the victims themselves. Although they remain extremely conscious of their deplorable conditions, their second-class citizenship, and their absence of substantive freedom, the victims nevertheless hopelessly rely on a remedy outside of history for their miserable condition. Revolution, as Malcolm X advocated, was barred from serious consideration by those hooked on novocaine religion.

However, the Abrahamic religions, especially Christianity, were not always world-confirming, but had a negative or world-defying aspect from its very inception. Although it has been forgotten, submerged within the ethical and moral bog of bourgeois society, Christianity inherited its inherent negativity from Messianic Judaism (Scholem, 1971: 1–36). For example, remembering the social implication of the belief in a divine being, the Critical Theorist Max Horkheimer writes,

> The concept of God was for a long time the place where the idea was kept alive that there are other norms besides those to which nature and society give expression in their operation. Dissatisfaction with earthly destiny is the strongest motive for acceptance of a transcendental being. If justice resides with God, then it is not to be found in the same measure in the world. *Religion is the record of the wishes, desires, and accusation of countless generations.*[7]
>
> HORKHEIMER 2002: 129

For the philosopher Horkheimer, the concept of God was the repository of all hope – 'hope' being the entrenched and undiminished longing or desire to negate what is the case, i.e. the unnecessary suffering and misery of created

---

7 My emphasis added.

by the perpetual catastrophe of nature and history, what liberal-capitalist and fascist society calls *progress*. (Benjamin, 1969: 257). If perfect justice did not reside within this world, whether its absence is in any given society's justice system or in the day-to-day lifeworld, then it could only be found in the negation of this world, through the perfect justice of the divine. Where this world fails to bring about this perfect justice, the perfect creator of justice remained the only possibility for global reconciliation, and all hope is placed within that potential. The space between this world, with all its deficiencies, ugliness, and unwarranted violence, and the concept of God, allowed the believer to continue to hope for the coming of God and his kingdom, which would create *on earth as it is in heaven*. The idea of an eschatological rupture of history by the divine, either through the Messiah or Mahdi, expressed the longing for the negation of this fallen and cruel world and the misery it imposes on its finite inhabitants. In other words, the broken and abused wish to end the tragic suffering embedded not only in the general human condition, but especially within the communities who feel the wrath of unjust oppression, as well as systemic and direct violence, i.e. the very condition that African-Americans endured (and still endure) in the United States for centuries, with the perverse brutality of slavery, Jim Crow and the 'New Jim Crow' of the American Industrial Prison Complex. As long as this world was not thought to be identical to the *other* world; as long as the 'other' expressed its dissatisfaction and disappointment with the worldliness of the earth-bound, than the oppressed and battered could hope to be on the side of the 'totally other,' who represented absolute and perfect justice and therefore the hopeful end of their unspeakable suffering. As such, *negativity* towards the destructiveness and brutality in the world, with its unbalanced and unjust social relations, animated the thought of those believers who hoped for an *apocatastasis* (ἀποκατάστασις), or a restitution of the primordial condition of mankind and his creator – a state of *being-with* the divine outside of the ugliness of 'history as Golgotha.' Therefore the world-as-it-is could not be embraced, but rather the suffering, the brokenness, and the martyrs that this cruel world created, symbolized and witnessed for – through their misery – the opposite of such misery: the *world-as-it-should-be*. That *otherness* was the world that the Abrahamic faiths embraced and held up as the standard of judgment for this world. If world history was world judgement, as Hegel believed it was, then the Abrahamic religions were supposed to be the *grand inquisitors*, as they expressed the ideals of absolute justice, unconditional love, and limitless compassion in the name of history's victims. Christianity, especially in its earliest articulations, expressed this longing to transcend the world and all its ugly brokenness; it attempted to actualize that utopic nature of the 'other' in its religiously inspired – and radically communistic – communities, which could not embrace, to Nietzsche's disappointment, the heroic (and brutal) *ethos* of the pagan Roman empire.

In looking at why the post-Nation of Islam Malcolm X rejected Christianity as an agent for radical social change, despite the fact that Jesus of Nazareth was certainly an advocate of such change in his own time, we must examine the history of Christianity. We must ascertain what drove the prophetic, Socratic and revolutionary nature in Jesus of Nazareth and the first martyrized Christian community to embrace the worldly, the mundane, and the barbaric status quo in nature and history. What brought the religion of freedom, as Hegel described it, to legitimate a society of slavery? What brought the iconoclastic religion of anti-idolatry to idolize power, wealth, greed and unjust violence?

Looking in to early Christian history, we witness the negativity of the early Christian Church towards the world-as-it-is swiftly giving way to the *world-ing* of the church via the imperial embrace of Emperor Constantine in 313 CE. The heavenly words he heard at the Milvian bridge, *In Hoc Signo Vinces* (In this sign conquer) speaks of *conquering* this world, it did not speak of *overcoming* or *transcending* (*aufhebung*) it. To conquer was to embrace, and to embrace was to deflate Christianity of its eschatological other-worldiness, as it delivered Christianity to the machinations of the state – a very world-affirming institution.[8] Lamenting this sudden and devastating evaporation of Christianity's negativity, Horkheimer writes,

> But the more Christianity brought God's rule into harmony with events in the world, the more the meaning of religion became perverted. In Catholicism God was already regarded as in certain respects the creator of the earthly order, while Protestantism attributed the world's course directly to the will of the Almighty. Not only was the state of affairs on earth at any given moment transfigured with the radiance of divine justice, but the latter was itself brought down to the level of the corrupt relations which mark earthly life. *Christianity lost its function of expressing the ideal, to the extent that it became the bedfellow of the state.*[9]
> HORKHEIMER, 2002: 129

---

8   Although we can be critical of how Christianity embraced the empire of Rome, we do have to remember that Emperor Constantine represented to many Christians the end of oppression and systematic violence against their communities within the Roman empire. Making Christianity legal, which happened through the Edict of Milan (*Edictum Mediolanense*) in 313 CE, meant safety and security for the first time within the empire – a prospect that seemed extremely desirable after nearly three hundred years of persecution.

9   My emphasis added.

It is in the final passage of this last quote from Horkheimer that we can see a similar observation of Malcolm X and even the Nation of Islam, who often expressed the idea that Christianity had become the ruling and legitimating ideology of the white racist society. Making the state and the religion identical inherently deflated Christianity of its liberational potentials; it had become the dominant ideology of a dominating state edifice, which was created by slaveholders. The very Constitution reflected their interests, not the interests of their victims. In modern times, despite the official separation of church and state, that American state has failed its Black citizens.[10]

Once the Constantinian state appropriated Christianity, it was no longer 'the other' world that was emphasized, nor was it the utopian vision of a world without suffering that it advocated, but rather it became entangled in its own reproduction, maintenance and advancement. Because of the *parousia delay* (tardiness of the messianic presence of God), it was not the Messiah that comforted the people, but rather the institution of the church. The worldly church, with all its hierarchy and bureaucracy, became the center of religious life, not the longing for the negation of this earthly and suffering-bound life. In this transformation something radically altered the constitutional and liberational potentials of Christianity. This constitutional change within Christianity had a lasting effect up to the modern period and Malcolm X, both while in the Nation of Islam and after his defection, was keenly aware of this distortion, and this knowledge contributed to his overall critique of Christianity.

It is easy to see that Horkheimer's critique of religion is partially rooted in Karl Marx's famous passage from his *Contribution to the Critique of Hegel's Philosophy of Right,* where he states that,

---

10   Malcolm X didn't allow individual politicians to take the blame for the plight and predicament of its Black citizens; it was not a particular party, a particular election or candidate that was responsible, the whole of the government was responsible. He said in *The Ballot or the Bullet* speech, "it is...the government of America...that is responsible for the oppression and exploitation and degradation of black people in this country. And you should drop it in their lap. This government has failed the Negro. This so-called democracy has failed the Negro. And all these white liberals have definitely failed the Negro" (Malcolm X, 1965: 31). One can't help but to wonder had the state actually embodied the values of Jesus of Nazareth, would it not have been on the side of those who were enslaved from the beginning. Malcolm X was keenly aware of this cleavage between "Christian" values and the dominant ethos of America, thus his critique of America never blames Jesus of Nazareth, who he believed to be a prophet in accordance with Islamic beliefs, for the sin of the "Christian" nation.

religious suffering is at the same time an expression of real suffering and a protest against real suffering. Religion in the sign of the oppressed creature, the sentiment of a heartless world, and the soul of a soulless condition. It is the opium of the people.

MARX, 1978: 54

Many religious critics and followers of Marx have taken this as proof of his anti-religious stance, but this was no mere reactionary critique of religion. Marx fully understood that the origins of religions lie within the existential *needs* and *experiences* of mankind, especially in the face of suffering and despair, thus religion is both the "expression of real suffering" and the "protest against real suffering" (Marx, 1978: 54). Religion was consolation in the face of real disappointment, comfort in the face of brokenness, and solace in the face of misery, and thus Marx took religion as a human phenomenon seriously. He understood that at least in its origins, religion was partially the product of oppressive and exploitative conditions. Just as he attempted to answer the question of injustice in this world under the conditions of capitalism with his historical materialist philosophy, he understood religion to be an inadequate attempt of others to address those very same or similar conditions, albeit via eschatology. With this in mind, *negative religion* can be understood as a form of religion that both realizes the suffering of the finite individual and longs for its negation. As such, recognition of the unjust conditions and the longing to negate them are the preconditions for revolutionary praxis, whether the theory and method is secular or religious. What Marx failed to conceive adequately was the possibility that religion could play a positive role in the negation of the cruel conditions mankind finds itself trapped within. It seemed impossible to Marx that religion, a symptom of a disease (capitalism, exploitation, oppression, alienation and class domination), could be an active ingredient in the overcoming of the disease. In short, Marx's analysis of religion was insufficiently dialectical.

Following Ludwig Feuerbach, Marx conceived of religion as a product of man's alienation which serves the purpose of justifying and legitimating his condition, but unlike Feuerbach, he did not believe the critique of religion was the end point. Religion was the first object of critique for Marx, as the task of liberating man's mind from his religious illusions was the necessary condition for his political, economic and existential liberation on earth, but it was not the end of critique (Marx, 1978: 143–145). In other words, in order to bring "criticism of earth" to bear, one must first engage in a "criticism of heaven" (Marx, 1978: 54). Outside of Friedrich Engel's work on Thomas Müntzer, who argued for *omnia sunt communia* (all things in common), Marx remained unaware of the liberational qualities and potentials of religion, or rather saw those potentials as passé and/or utopian. His analysis was rooted in science, reason, and *dialectical materialist* (*diamat*) thought, which did not sympathize with theology or even with Hegelian metaphysics, as they remained too abstract and abeyant from the concrete conditions of humanity. The tools of the Enlightenment, albeit often used against the Enlightenment itself, were the tools of Marx's philosophy, and he refused to *retreat* into obscurantist metaphysics, religious or otherwise.

Regardless of Marx's dogmatic materialism, a hint of his critique of religion can also be found pulsing through Malcolm X's critical analysis of religion, especially Christianity. Malcolm X rarely tired of pointing out the opiate-qualities of the form of Christianity embraced by the overwhelming number of Black folk, while knowing there was also a more prophetic side of the Black Church, in part due to the memory of his Garveyite father Earl Little (DeCaro, 1996:38–47). Nevertheless, the question for Malcolm X was whether or not Black Christianity would aid just as vigorously in the liberation of Black bodies as it did for Black souls, or would it continue to preach the opiate religion of 'pie in the sky when you die'; would it engage in more radical praxis, or was it hopelessly ineffective because of its commitment to the Gospel tradition of non-violence? If Black Christians continued to take seriously the constitutional ban on the *lex talionis* (law of retaliation), even in the face of White America's complete abandonment of Jesus' *contra lex Talionis* (against the law of retaliation), then for Malcolm X Christianity could not successfully aid in the liberation of Black folk from White oppression, White supremacy, and the racist American social order. It appeared to him to hopelessly handicap itself with its ethical commitment to non-violence amidst a struggle for life and death, and thus Malcolm X was not prepared to join the self-sacrificing nature of Black Christianity. He said in his *Message to the Grassroots* that,

> the white man does the same thing to you in the street, when he wants to put knots on your head and take advantage of you and not have to be afraid of your fighting back. To keep you from fight back, he gets these old religious Uncle Toms to teach you and me, just like novocaine, to suffer peacefully. Don't stop suffering – just suffering peacefully... There's nothing in our book, the Koran [Qur'an], that teaches us to suffer peacefully... if someone puts his hand on you, send him to the cemetery. That's a good religion.
>
> MALCOLM X, 1965: 12

For Malcolm, the religion that cannot match the language of the violent other is an ineffective religion, and a religion that could communicate better with the violent nature of white society was necessary for the liberation of African-Americans. For non-violence to work against the brut there must be a sense of shame within the nation that brutalizes. This sense of shame is what Gandhi was able to bring out in the British people, when they saw the peaceful non-violent resistance of the Indians, Hindu, Muslim and Sikh, when they were slaughtered, abused, and beaten by the colonial police. *Shame* was the essential ingredient in changing the minds of the average British citizen on the question of Indian home rule. Nevertheless, there seemed to be no overwhelming sense of shame among the American oppressors, the lynch mob, rapists and murderers, nor the general public outside of the American liberal, whom Malcolm frequently accused of being a hypocrite. This liberal would condemn racism in words but failed to live his views in deeds (Malcolm X, 1992a: 33). Therefore, the condition of *shamelessness,* rooted in American pride, racial pride and the sense of being chosen by the divine – the new Augustinian "City of God" – blinded many in the United States to the plight and predicament of Black people and the suffering they endured. Yet, even Mahatma Gandhi, believed the shamelessness of White supremacy should not be succumbed to, but rather should be resisted at all costs. Sounding much like Malcolm, he said to a group of West African soldiers that

> The moment the slave resolves that he will no longer be a slave, his fetters fall. He frees himself and shows the way to others. Freedom and slavery are mental states. Therefore, the first thing is to say to yourself: "I shall no longer accept the role of a slave. I shall not obey orders as such but shall disobey them when they are in conflict with my conscience." The so-called master may lash you and try to force you to serve him. You will say: "No, I will not serve you for your money or under a threat." This may mean suffering. Your readiness to suffer will light the torch of freedom which can never be put out.
> GANDHI, 2002: 282–283

What Malcolm understood through his own experiences, regardless of Elijah Muhammad's peculiar mythical anthropology, was that the thoroughly 'whitened' African mind was incapable of saying 'no' to the slave master. The 'white' in 'White Christianity' so thoroughly deflated the prophetic negativity of Christianity, which he had seen in his parents' political-theology, that Christianity became synonymous with White society, i.e. the rules, regulations, social norms, and values of the present American Bourgeois order. To be a *real*

Christian was to accept, not reject, this unjust order, believe it to be divinely ordained, and to forego any substantive critique of such an order. This social imperative within this social order not only infected the minds of Black Christians, but also saturated the minds of what Malcolm called 'bourgeois Blacks,' who were happy to be 'tokens' and accept token measures in the struggle for equal rights (Malcolm X, 1992b: 45–46). Speaking to a mostly white audience on the campus of Michigan State University, on January 23, 1963, he spoke of this kind of "negro" and his acceptance of white Christianity. He said,

> This type has blind faith in your religion. He's not interested in any religion of his own. He believes in a white Jesus, white Mary, white angels, and he finally gets to a white heaven. When you listen to him in his church singing, he sings a song – I think they call it – "Washing him white as snow." He wants to be clean white so he can go to heaven with the white man. It's not his fault...for this is the state of his mind. This is the result of four hundred years of brain-washing here in America. You have taken a man who is black on the outside and made him white on the inside. His brain is white as snow. His heart is white as snow.[11]
> MALCOLM X, 1963

For Malcolm, 'white' Christianity was the most effective vehicle through which the Black man was integrated into the bourgeois order. Through this, he was domesticated, politically castrated, and made docile, and therefore was unable to resist the demands of the 'slave master' as Gandhi and others insisted. Content to accept the crumbs of the American bourgeois society, just as the 'house negro' was content to accept the crumbs of his slave master, Malcolm advocated a religion that would liberate this house negro from the American "brain-washing," and bring him to the side of the 'field negro,' who was prepared, like Nat Turner, to burn down the master's house. However, if such a 'house negro' failed to see the light, and insisted on maintaining his chains, Malcolm was fully prepared to burn the house down with the house negro still inside.

While Malcolm was prepared to take radical action against White supremacy in the United States, as well as lend his support to Third World liberation movements, both the Black Church and the Nation of Islam were reticent to follow him. From their own ethical commitments, they could not accede to

---

11   This is my transcription of a youtube video. A parody of this type of 'negro' can be seen in an episode of Aaron McGruder's *Boondocks*, where 'Uncle Ruckus' plays the part of the white-infatuated 'house negro' who visits 'white heaven' and meets its real 'St. Peter at the Pearly Gates,' Ronald Reagan.

Malcolm's radical call for the overthrowing of White supremacy *by any means necessary*. While the NOI cowered from the thought of real revolutionary action, waiting rather for an eschatological rapture-like event to rescue them (or simply to secure the riches they had acquired), and the Black Church remained dedicated to the Gospels rejection of violence, Malcolm X forged ahead with his political-theology, which brought together the Islamic sense of justice and the political struggle of Black Americans in the United States (Evanzz, 1999: 310–335).

However, despite Malcolm's damning critique of Christianity, many forms of the Prophetic Black Church preserved within itself the *negativity* of the early Christians and its martyrs, much more so than many of the predominantly 'White' denominations, whose affirmative religiosity embraced the world-as-it-is precisely because it was effectively *their world*.[12] Naturally, the Old Testament stories of enslaved Hebrews rang more true to those in bondage rather than to those who bound the slaves, and the desire to liberate the *eternal soul* from the torment of the *finite flesh* was a message that was painfully felt with every wound brought by the slave master's whip, every laceration created by vicious police dogs, and with every 'strange fruit' harvested by the lynch mob. The longing to negate this world of torment, the longing for the end of suffering, and the longing for perfect and absolute justice – that the innocent victim shall someday triumph over their abuser and/or murderer – remained engrained within those who suffered from the viciousness of slavery, Jim Crow, and the systematic ghetto-bound racism of the urban north. Witnessed through the hymns, the 'down-trodden' hermeneutics of sacred scripture, and the transcendent nature of Black worship, the negativity that Christianity once revealed through its persecuted martyrs and saints of the first centuries, was rediscovered and relived with the victims of America's racist society. Christianity was once again returned to the victims of history, just as it was in its beginning with its initiator (*stifter*) Jesus of Nazareth. With the victims it was a prophetic religion once again; with the victors it was a stale ideology that legitimated their barbaric rule. As such, those who were lynched embodied in their torment the suffering of the crucified just as forcefully as those who did the lynching embodied the sadism and cruelty of the Roman executioners.

---

12   Clearly not all forms of Christianity fall into the denomination of "white" and "black" as there were many White Christians who identified more with the slave and the victims of Jim Crow than they did with the White dominated social order. John Brown, a dedicated Calvinist and radical abolitionist, would be the best example of this. See Louis A. DeCaro, Jr. *Fire from the Midst of You: A Religious Life of John Brown*. New York: New York University Press, 2002. Also see W. E. B. DuBois, *John Brown*. New York: International Publishers, 1996.

Yet, if we accept the argument that the negativity of Christianity could still be found within the ever-suffering Prophetic Black Church, that it held within itself a deep desire to negate the given-ness of the world, especially racist America, then what drove Malcolm X to reject Black Christianity as an inadequate or unviable source for liberation? If he too wished to transcend or overcome the iron cage of American capitalism, and its original sin of racism, genocide and slavery, then what made Islam a more viable option in the struggle against those things? Given the intricate similarities between Christianity, especially in its negative form, and Islam – both having roots in the prophetic faith of Abraham – what dynamics did Islam provide which proved to Malcolm X that it was more capable of bringing about a society of justice and equality? In essence, we must ask: why Islam and not the Prophetic Black Church?

Context

Malcolm X's critique of racism, imperialism, and dollarism (capitalism) matured during a period of radical social and political transformation throughout much of the world. The old edifices of Western imperialism were beginning to crumble from within, especially after the devastation of the Second World War, and more importantly from the growing pressure from the subjugated peoples themselves. As Malcolm X stated on February 18, 1965, "we are today seeing a global rebellion of the oppressed against the oppressor, the exploited against the exploiter" (Malcolm X, 1992b: 177). Struggles to liberate the minds and bodies of Africans, Arabs, and Asians from the repressive grip of imperial powers, whether it be through various forms of nationalism, socialism, communism and/or religio-political thought, grew to the point where dozens of nations were able to emancipate themselves from their former imperial masters. Even the Frankfurt School's Herbert Marcuse, who was deeply rooted in Marx's class analysis, believed the agent of social revolution had shifted from the working class, most associated with white workers, to communities on the margins of liberal capitalist society, i.e. ethnic minorities, women, students, etc. (Marcuse, 2005). In this sense, Malcolm X understood the struggle for the basic Human Rights of the Afro-American in the United States as being intimately connected with the liberation struggles in Africa, the Middle East, and in other parts of the world, especially those in which the primary subject of oppression was people of color. Forging a solid connection between these two struggles was one of the primary reasons for his extensive travel in 1964 and 1965 (Malcolm X, 1992a: 366–418; Malcolm X, 2013).

By bringing the struggle of African-Americans to the attention of revolutionaries in other parts of the world, Malcolm X joined the liberation struggles being fought by various revolutionaries, including the Argentinian/Cuban Commandante Ernesto 'Che' Guevara, who in early 1965 went to the Congo to help the Simba Movement and their struggle against the counter-revolutionary forces that overthrew the leftist freedom fighter and later President Patrice Lumumba (Anderson, 1997: 621–670; Reitan, 1999). Remembering the 1954 CIA led coup d'état of the revolutionary President Jacobo Árbenz in Guatemala, Guevara understood that the murder of Lumumba was an counter-revolutionary act that all leftists should learn from; the imperial powers, and their friends in Washington D.C., would not allow leftist liberation movements to simply destroy the structure of domination that the West had for centuries built and maintained. All attempts to overthrow the imperial powers were met with substantial and brutal resistance, either overtly or covertly. Che, having already fought and defended the Cuban Revolution from American aggression, joined forced with the Congolese communists in their attempts to liberate the Congo from Western domination and their African 'House Negroes' who were the black façades of white control. He would eventually be executed at the hands of the Bolivian government and the CIA while attempting to start a continent-wide revolution in South America, a prospect the capitalist Euro-north could not tolerate (Ratner and Smith, 2011).

Malcolm X also joined the ranks of the Algerian revolutionary leader Ahmed Ben Bella, who led a successful revolution against the French colonial power in Algeria in the late 1950's and early 1960's. Through his *Front de Liberation Nationale* (FLN), Ben Bella was able to defeat the French forces who had occupied this North African nation since the mid-19th century, and who regarded Algeria simply as another 'province' of greater France. Regarding himself as a moderate 'Islamist,' Ben Bella engaged in a war against oppression that many in the West viewed as being 'terroristic' in nature. However, Ben Bella never tired of pointing out the true terroristic nature of imperialism, racism, and capitalism, and believed that armed struggle against such oppression was the only way to liberate the nation from the clutches of imperial France. Malcolm X was later invited by Ben Bella to his February 1965 international conference of world revolutionaries, at which he and Che Guevara would have been the keynote speakers (Jenkins, 2002: 96). According to Mfanya Donald Tryman, Malcolm X and Che Guevara were to cooperate and coordinate the African-American involvement in the global struggle for emancipation for all oppressed people of color; a conflation that would have alarmed the American political establishment (Jenkins, 2002: 97). The 'internationalization' of the struggle for human rights in the United States by finding common cause with those groups who had already successfully liberated their countries from the allies of the United States, was a major concern for Washington D.C., as some of these nations had liberated themselves with the help of the Soviet Union and other communist factions. However, Malcolm's death and the overthrow of Ben Bella's presidency cancelled the promise of their cooperation.

Malcolm X was also impressed by the revolutionary efforts of Gamal Abdel Nasser, the young military officer who overthrew King Farouk of Egypt and established a socialist but non-Aligned secular government in 1952–1953 in the North African country. Nasser, refusing to ally himself with the intrusive policies of the Soviet Union, while at the same time refusing the manipulative support of the U.S. and its monetary 'aid,' steered his country on a path towards modernization, while at the same time attempted to alleviate the entrenched inequality that had plagued Egypt under colonialism and monarchy. As he embraced Malcolm X as a fellow freedom fighter, he offered Malcolm twenty scholarships to Al-Azhar University in Cairo for African-Americans to study Sunni Islam, as a way of bringing orthodox Islam to the United States and strengthening the fledging Muslim community in the United States to traditional 'Azhari' style Islam. This would also strengthen the bonds between those who were fighting for a new socialist reality in their countries and the struggle for substantive emancipation and the realization of human rights in the United States. Additionally, it would interject the revolutionary potential of Islam into the struggle of the African-American more adequately, as Malcolm X would begin to have a more Islamically educated cadre serving as the basis for his movement.[13] This was especially important as it would have been the counterpoint to the NOI's version of Islam and would have surely eclipsed the luster of Elijah Muhammad within the Black community, especially among militants.

Needless to say, Malcolm X's involvement with groups and individuals that were fundamentally against U.S. policies in their regions and countries only heightened the American government's fear that Malcolm X was quickly becoming a threat to the status quo. In his debate with Louis Lomax on May 23,

---

13   Malcolm X's embarrassment stemming from his lack of knowledge of orthodox Sunni Islam and the Arabic language is evident in his autobiography and his travel journal. This was something that he was determined to remedy and his hajj was partially an attempt to do just that (Malcolm X, 1992: 366–393). He states "not being able to speak the language is like being in a fish bowl: everyone looking at me, talking about me and to me, and me not able to understand (hear) or answer back. Never have I felt so deaf and dumb, and I'm thankful I am among friends and brothers whose very religion compels them to be patient with my ignorance, my 'crippled condition' and take me by the hand at every step" (Malcolm X, 2013: 15).

1964, as a reminder of the revolutionary change that was sweeping across the globe, Malcolm emphasized to his American audience that his methods were not the same as Dr. Martin Luther King's methods, and that the growing impatience of the twenty-two million Black people in the United States could lead them to "adopt the guerrilla tactics of other deprived revolutionaries" (Marable and Felber, 2013: 332). Not only that, his attempts to bring charges against the United States in the United Nations was not only an embarrassment for the government, but would also have undermined the dominant narrative that was publicly peddled by Washington's propagandists: that the United States was the epicenter of the 'free world' in distinction to the 'tyranny' of communism. Malcolm X demonstrated to all who would listen the 'hypocrisy of American democracy' – while the United States condemned other countries for their violation of human rights, twenty two million African-Americans languished in poverty, second-class citizenship, and systematic racism; while they fought for so-called 'freedom and democracy' abroad, in far off places such as Germany, France, Japan, Korea, and Vietnam, they enforced barbaric and unfree conditions at home, thus fighting against the 'rule of the people' (especially people of color) within their own borders. While liberals extolled the virtues of the free markets, they simultaneously attempted to mute the victims of those free markets. 'Free' in this sense was relative to whom one was speaking of. For Malcolm, the 'free world' was the world free of racism, exploitation and oppression – that was the world he found in Mecca, not within the ugliness of the entrenched race and class antagonisms of the United States of America.

For the U.S. government of the time, Malcolm X was Che Guevara, Ahmed Ben Bella, and Gamal Abdel Nasser with an American passport. He was not a Dr. Martin Luther King Jr., whose religious faith only allowed him to slightly modify the system through non-violent resistance, but was rather a man of religion whose faith radically embraced revolutionary theory, revolutionary praxis, and a revolutionary-humanistic vision that was intricately saturated with third-world liberation thought. The internationalizing of the struggle for Human Rights for the African-American population brought the anti-colonial and anti-imperial fight of Cairo, Algiers, Brazzaville, Conakry, Dakar, Havana, to the streets of Detroit, Chicago, New York, Los Angeles and Washington D.C. In this sense, Malcolm X was the door way for the global struggle against white supremacy via European and American imperialism to enter into the ghettos of the United States, which were already on the verge of exploding in the mid-1960's as he had predicted. Malcolm testified in his 1964 diary that "freedom comes only from the efforts made [by] those who themselves tire of oppression and themselves take action against it" (Malcolm X, 2013: 171). With their common weariness born of exploitation, denigration, and oppression, Malcolm X, more than anyone else, blurred the multiple visions of emancipatory praxis into one push towards liberation. Just as the Bandung conference of 1955 had done, he *deemphasized* the differences of the oppressed of various nations in order to highlight the similarities of those same *wretched*; all were brutalized and disfigured by the international status quo and thus all had a common enemy to fight against (Malcolm X, 1992b: 158–159).

By looking into the world context, and seeing that the world was lit by the fire of revolution during Malcolm X's public life, we can get a better understanding of his thoughts on both religion and political praxis. We can begin to answer the question as to why a revolutionary faith was needed for Malcolm X and why Christianity wasn't adequate for the task of liberating the twenty-two million African-Americans in his understanding.

Inadequacy of Christianity as Revolutionary Praxis

In the chapter entitled "1965" in Malcolm's autobiography, he remarks that he knew that most 'Afro-Americans' would be reticent to support taking the United States to the international courts of the United Nations to demand justice for themselves. In other words, they were not prepared to see their struggle as being anything beyond the realm of civil rights, which was only a matter of *reform* and not *revolution*. He also opined the improbability of African-Americans following him into Islam, remarking that "American Negroes – especially older Negroes – are too indelibly soaked in Christianity's double standard of oppression" (Malcolm X 1992: 419). For Malcolm, the whites man's religion, i.e. Constantinian-turned-Bourgeois-Christianity, not only sapped the revolutionary and emancipatory potentials from the victims of history by teaching them to be passive and to love their enemies, but it also indelibly bound them to the ideology that justified the cruel and barbaric treatment which they experienced every day in both the urban north and the rural south of America (Malcolm X, 1992a: 46). They were emotionally, spiritually, and eschatologically invested in Jesus Christ, who, most cruelly, only seemed to offer consolation in the face of suffering and not earthly liberation from that suffering. However, Malcolm knew that if he were to push his own Islamic faith, which "had given [him] the insight and perspective...that black men and white men truly could be brothers," it would surely be met with hostility from other African-Americans who were distrustful of other religious faiths, seeing them as dangerous cults whose insistence on empowering Black people could threaten their own stable but marginal place in white society (Malcolm X, 1992a: 419). It was also a simple matter of faith; they wholeheartedly believed in the *content* of their religious tradition, which, in an era of *neutralized religion,* already makes them "non-conformists" (Adorno et al, 1950: 731). However, religious hypocrisy *is* constitutional within White "Christian" society, as Horkheimer wrote, "it is not part of life in this civilization to take religion seriously. Only the powerful have to be respected; the poor and powerless are worshipped in religion, i.e., in spirit, but mistreated in reality" (Horkheimer, 1978: 91). The 'double standard' of Bourgeois Christianity, that preached brotherhood on Sunday but failed to practice it on any day, would remain the dominant reality among his Christian listeners, despite their attraction to his political program. Therefore, as Malcolm wrote, he "did not immediately attempt to press the Islamic religion, but instead [began] to embrace all who sat before [him]," as discussions of religion would only create new fissures between himself and others (Malcolm X, 1992a: 419). As he became increasingly more interested in engaging in a forceful praxis against white supremacy and white bigotry by joining other African-American leaders, he refused to allow his Islamic beliefs, which still struck 1960's America as being exotic and outside of the mainstream, to become a point of contention that would drive away otherwise willing participants to his burgeoning movement. Common cause against the brutality of racism would unite the various factions, not religion. Yet, after experiencing an enormous frustration with the political castration of the Nation of Islam, which, by Elijah Muhammad's orders, didn't allow him to join with reform minded movements, his new independence in 1964/1965 would not allow the age-old trick of *divide et impera* (divide and conquer) to separate him from other leaders (Malcolm X, 1992a: 417). Despite the pragmatics of continuing his socio-political work without *dawa* (Islamic evangelizing), he nevertheless remained deeply critical of the American and/or Western articulation of Christianity and its social and moral failures. For Malcolm, just as the Black man's traditional leaders failed to inspire a revolutionary spirit in the community, so too did "the religion of Christianity...fail him. The black man was scarred, he was cautious, he was apprehensive," and that had to be remedied (Malcolm X, 1992a: 420). But in the immediate struggle, it would not be remedied through the mass conversion of Black folk to Islam. What Malcolm had to do was appeal not only to their innate sense of moral justice, but to the deep seated longing to see that justice actualized. This longing was found both in Christianity and Islam, as well as in the secularized political theories which animated the various entities which comprised *The New Left.*

Behind the historical confluence of religion and the state, religious legitimation of criminal activities, and clerical support of unspeakable violations of human sovereignty, dignity, and autonomy, such as one witnessed in the genocide of the Native American, slavery and Jim Crow, there is a foundational dynamic that helps explain why religion, and Constantinian-turned-Bourgeois-Christianity in particular, has so often taken the side of those with the biggest battalions (Voltaire).[14] Again, the Critical Theorist Max Horkheimer points out that

> when the authoritarian state seems to engage in a historic conflict with religion, the essential issue is whether the two shall compete, be coordinated, or go their separate ways. A bureaucracy au courant with the contemporary situation takes over and reorganizes the old ideological apparatus in which the church had its share. Even if it involves hardship the church must ultimately see that *its own social position depends on the continued existence of the basic traits of the present system.* If these were to change, the church would lose all and gain nothing. *Its position rests on the belief that absolute justice is not simply a projection of men's minds but a real eternal power; a future society, however, would cease to perpetuate this belief.*[15]
>
> HORKHEIMER, 2002: 130

Horkheimer gives us a keen insight into the nature of the church as an institution; although there may be individual clerics, movements, and or orders that wish to arrest, abate, and/or transcend the present social order, the institution itself is dependent on the status quo for its own continual existence. Here we can see the function of the church: it is not only to pacify the victims of the history, who, according to Marx, possess the greatest potential for revolutionary change, but also to guarantee its own survival by binding itself to the already established society. In this sense, the church as an institution is inherently conservative, reactionary, and counter-revolutionary, as it must preserve the situation that allows it to remain relevant. However, it is not the case that the church has been merely the dependent entity in society, as the state often looks to the church for its blessing to engage in various activities. In other words, "God is on the side of those with the biggest battalions" as long as the battalions worship at God's *carroccio* (portable war altar). As such, there is a symbiotic relationship between the state and church; the state provides the space and stability for the church to reproduce itself while the church provides legitimation and justification for the activities and policies it engages in.

---

14 "On dit que Dieu est toujours pour les gros bataillons." (It is said that God is always on the side of the biggest battalions).

15 My emphasis added.

This dynamic even transcends the secular constitution of the United States, in which the government, which is supposed to be neutral in matters of religion, is barred from engaging in religious activities, but nevertheless benefits from the opiate work of the church, especially in Black and other disenfranchised communities. However, the function of the church, especially in Bourgeois society, remains the same; it is there to forestall any revolutionary movement from the population as revolution could mean the end of the religious institution, as happened in during the Bolshevik revolution in Russia (Froese, 2008). The Bolsheviks, having inherited the vision of a fully reconciled future society, as expressed by Marx, one in which mankind no longer lives in alienation from himself, his labor, nature, and others, which itself was a semblance of the Jewish, Christian and Islamic vision of a peaceful and reconciled society, attempted to bring such an existence into being without the help of religion. Indeed, had their attempts been fully realized, it was claimed, the heavenly vision of such a society would no longer be relevant; what the Messiah was once tasked to do mankind had now done – all the Messiah had to do is put his stamp of approval on it. In this sense, following the long path of the Bourgeois Enlightenment to the Marxist Enlightenment, eschatology was humanized.

Horkheimer highlights this dynamic in the last passage of the above quote; a future reconciled society, one that has embraced and actualized the principles and ideals of equality, fraternity, and justice, would leave no real place for the imagined *paradisio* of the post-apocalypse. If such a society could be brought about by the hands of man without the guidance or labor of the Holy Spirit, the Messiah, etc., than the need for such a religious institution would cease to be. In this sense, Malcolm X understood that the religion was, (1) a possible force for the bringing about a future reconciled society – like he saw in Mecca, but that it could also be done through more secular 'revolutionary' means, and (2) that some forms of religion are heavily invested in making sure the status quo remains unmolested, because only within the social chaos of racism, sexism, class domination, etc., is the power of the utopian 'pie in the sky' motif effective. Malcolm pointed out this dynamic when he ruminated over the status of the "most fervent Christians" in America, the Black man. He wrote,

> The Black man needs to reflect that he has been Americas most fervent Christian – and where has that gotten him? In fact, in the white man's hands, in the white man's interpretation...where has Christianity brought this world?
>
> MALCOLM X, 1992A: 424

In a FBI summary report dated April 30th, 1958, the devoted NOI spokesman, Malcolm X, is recorded to have said to his Detroit audience,

> the so-called Negro had really been taken for a ride by accepting a religion which teaches that there is life after death. He said the very phrase "life after death" is self-revealing if put in its proper prospective. He told those in attendance that they should immediately dispense with this false religion which is a throwback of the days of slavery and accept Islam which "is the religion of the black man."
> MANNING AND FELBER, 2013: 114

If Malcolm believed that African-Americans are the most committed group of people to Christianity, and Christianity served as the legitimating ideology of white supremacy and white domination, then where did that leave the believing African-American Christian? In one phrase, they were the most enslaved community in America, partially by their own doing. Without explicitly conceptualizing it, he fully understood the nature of *positive religion* within the American context, that the greater the misery of the African-American, the greater their attachment to the consoling effects of Christianity; the greater their attachment to Christianity, the greater they were bound to the status quo. The prophetic Black Church (as an institution), as Malcolm frequently pointed out, perpetually failed to follow Toussaint L'Ouverture, Nat Turner or John Brown into revolutionary praxis, but too often passively dreamed of better tomorrows within America, despite their deep seated longing to transcend the barbarity and butchery of American society.

Because of Malcolm's travels in the Muslim world, in which he saw the revolutionary potential of *negative* and therefore revolutionary religion, he could not go the way of the secular Marxist, who discarded religion all together as being a force for reactionary status quo reproduction. He saw in Islam a religion that embraced the revolutionary spirit, acted upon it, and wasn't afraid to struggle for it, even if it was through violent means. Christianity, despite Jesus of Nazareth's and the early Christian community' radical negativity, remained inadequate for the liberation of the African-Americans. By nature and by history, it's most dominant orientations had been functionalized and transformed into a force for enslavement. In Malcolm's view, it could not liberate itself from the clutches of white supremacy, European culture, and its cruel legacy of violence against the poor, the broken, and the downtrodden, and therefore it could not contribute adequately to the real emancipation of Black folk and the Third World from the clutches of white supremacy, capitalism, and Western imperialism.

The True Terror in American Society

In a dialogue with Louis Lomax in 1964, Malcolm X elaborated on the aims of African-Americans in their struggle with the society and government of the United States. He said,

> The 22 million Afro-Americans...seek recognition and respect as human beings and when you think in terms of segregationist or rather separationists or integrationists, it actually clouds the issue. Integration is only a method that is used by some Negroes to get what they really want – recognition and respect as human beings.
> MARABLE AND FELBER, 2013: 336

He continues,

> I differ...greatly [on] this stress on civil rights and in acceptance in the American society as citizens before the society itself has even permitted itself to recognize us as human beings, and I very much doubt that you can make a citizen out of anyone that you don't regard as a human being.
> MARABLE AND FELBER, 2013: 337

Here, I think Malcolm articulated his ideas in an inadequate liberal idiom, despite the fact that the reality of his own life taught him otherwise. Malcolm expressed the idea that the *dehumanization* (lack of recognition and respect) of African-Americans by white people is what allows them to engage in discriminatory and oppressive behavior. In other words, because African-Americans were not considered sufficiently human by white society, they were not afforded recognition and/or respect. The assumption in this line of thinking is that if whites could fully realize the humanity of Black people they would no longer engage in such hateful activities. However, from my own experience dealing with white racists and bigots, I think Malcolm underestimated the nature of their hatred: the *true terror* is not that the racist denies the humanity of the other, thinking them to be something other than humans, even if they tell themselves that, but rather that they fully realize the humanity of the other, but continues to engage them *as if* they were less then human, *as if* they were life unworthy of life. This wasn't a mistake of *consciousness*, but a *conscious* choice to hate, brutalize and murder other humans, whom they fully recognized as humans. Recognition, as Malcolm declared as being a precondition for civil rights, was not the problem, as such recognition did not necessarily lead to better relationships between the races. Racism is more insidious than just a problem of recognition and citizenship – it is a blunt conscious decision to hate the other who is *fully human* despite the recognition that they are full human. Racists hate a portion of humanity precisely because they are a portion of humanity which the racist feels should not be a part of humanity. The closeness of the other to the humanity of the racist himself motivates his attempt to exile the other from the species. In other words, dehumanization, although as a method of making it psychologically easier to brutalize a group of people, does not necessarily make the aggressor more aggressive, as one can be dehumanized to something non-threatening, such as benign object. However, it is because the hated other is a part of one's same species – and thus biologically and psychologically too close to the one who's hating – that the hatred is so deep and encompassing. We should not be fooled by the linguistic absurdity of dehumanizing language; the white racist psychologically comforted himself when describing Black people as being sub-human, but those very accusations betrayed the uncomfortable truth that what they really feared (and knew), that Black people were just as human as whites. As such, hatred for other species rarely invokes such a response as hatred for a certain group *within* one species, a dynamic the Nazis demonstrated in their idea that Jews were "of our species but not of our race." Most perversely, the hatred for Black people by the white supremacist was the very way in which they recognized the humanity of Black people. A negative recognition for sure, but a recognition of their full humanity – and therefore perceived threat – nonetheless. Therefore, the violence done to Black people was conversely the translation of such negative recognition into praxis. As such, the precondition for a more peaceful and reconciled society was not simply recognition of the humanity of Black people, but the recognition that Black humanity equally affords Black people *the same rights and respect due to all members of the human race*. The 'otherness' of the 'other' must be decoupled with hatred, and for Malcolm, there was only one force that could adequately do that: the egalitarian nature of Islam.

Islam as Revolutionary Force

On his way to Mecca to perform the hajj, Malcolm was stopped in Jedda and his passport inspected. Reflecting on the irony of this small gesture, he said "I'm handing them the American passport which signifies the exact opposite of what Islam stands for" (Malcolm X, 1992: 373). For Malcolm X, America was the "other" to Islam, the *hubris* and the *nemesis*, the enslaver and the liberator, and it seems he felt a certain level of embarrassment for carrying the passport of the most aggressive imperial power, especially in light of the unbridled cruelty

America perpetrated upon African-Americans and other people of color, as well as poor people around the world, which was always done most hypocritically in the name of 'freedom, justice and democracy.' In light of this micrological moment – which was clearly saturated with comedic tragedy for Malcolm – we have to investigate what it is about Islam that made it the "exact opposite" of America. Through this investigation we can obtain a better understanding of why Malcolm X believed Islam was the answer to many of the deeply entrenched problems plaguing the West and America in particular, as well as why he was convinced of its corrective potential.

According to the Critical Theorist Max Horkheimer, the urge to engage in radical praxis towards the realization of a fully reconciled future society remains ever present in the contemporary moment. However, as much of the world increasingly moves through the secularization process, the religious veneer that once shrouded this longing for a society devoid of hatred, violence, alienation, and antagonisms, has been shed and the task has been left primarily to secular revolutionaries. Horkheimer writes,

> A purely spiritual resistance becomes just a wheel in the machine of the totalitarian state. True discipleship, to which many Christians may once again be called, does not lead men back to religion. Yet that image of perfect justice, the spreading of which brings neither power nor respect in the world or the beyond and which is accompanied by a growing awareness of its own vanity, may be more attractive to disillusioned believers than the empty self-satisfaction which religion in the last century either did not see within itself or else tolerate as well intentioned.

He continues,

> Mankind loses religion as it moves through history, but the loss leaves its mark behind. Part of the drives and desires which religious belief preserved and kept alive are detached from the inhibiting religious form and become productive forces in social practice. In the process even the immoderation characteristic of shattered illusions acquires a positive form and is truly transformed. In a really free mind the concept of infinity is preserved in an awareness of the finality of human life and of the inalterable aloneness of men, and it keeps society from indulging in a thoughtless optimism, an inflation of its own knowledge into a new religion.
> HORKHEIMER, 2002: 130–131

What I find most enlightening about Horkheimer's critique here is his keen awareness of the effect the process of secularization has upon religion and religious believers. Although they may be forced to abandon their faith in religion and metaphysics, as Nietzsche so clearly pointed out as being impossible to maintain after the *death of God*, i.e. the impossibility of faith post-Enlightenment, they nevertheless cannot abandon their longing for absolute justice. For Horkheimer, the "inhibiting religious form" has been cast off from the disillusioned former believer while simultaneously the longing and commitment to a world in which the ills of the given are transcended remains branded upon their consciousness. Religion, for Horkheimer, is no longer adequate for revolutionary praxis in the modern period – it simply cannot persevere having lost all its rearguard-struggles against secular modernity. In this sense, the former believer has *determinately negated (bestimmte negation)* religion; having both preserved its negativity within secular revolutionary praxis while at the same time allowing religion's criminality, obscurantism, divisive sectarianism, and most of all its self-defeating positivity, to recede into the forgotten pages of history. Yet, does this pessimistic diagnosis of religion and religion's future apply to all religions, or does it apply only to western Christianity (which Horkheimer was writing about)? More specifically, has Islam fallen victim to the same secularization process as has Christianity in the West, wherein the only way to rescue the liberational and emancipatory potentials of the religion is to translate them into secular ideals, principles, and goals (Benjamin, 1969: 253)? The answer to this question weighs heavily on why Malcolm X was attracted to Islam.

Through a detailed study of Malcolm X's autobiography and his travel journal, as well as other major works that have contributed to our understanding of the religious aspects within his biography, we can see that Malcolm X was interested in Islam especially for two important reasons. The first, Malcolm was attracted to the theological dogma of *tawhid,* the oneness of God that is at the theological core of the Qur'an, and second, the socio-political and moral imperatives that Muslims derive from the *Qur'an*, the *Sunnah* (way) of Prophet Muhammad, and the example of the *Sahaba* (Muhammad's companions). These two aspects of Islam are interlinked and cannot be artificially divorced from each other for the devote Muslim. The ethical norms of Islam are rooted in the idea of God's oneness; as God is one so too is humanity, his religion, and his vision for what *ought* to be the case in the world are also one. It is certainly a fact that Muslims, just like every other religious community, have too often failed to embody those norms, values, and principles, and that *fitnah* (division) within the global Muslim *ummah* (community) has been a source of major historical conflicts, but regardless of the shortcomings, the sense of *'asabiyya* (solidarity) within the ummah remains much stronger than it does in the now secularized Western world, which, since the beginnings of Protestantism, places emphasis on individual autonomy rather than social solidarity.[16] However, such individual autonomy has failed to block the mass madness of extremist political movements in the 20th century, such as fascism, the consumer society (where one appears to be an individualist while consuming the same mass produced and mass marketed products as everyone else), and various forms of nationalism.

In his journal, Malcolm writes of the connection between the theology of Islam and its social implications which he juxtaposed to the reality of racial brutality in the United States. He says,

> I have not bitten my tongue once, nor passed a single opportunity in my travels to tell the truth about the real plight of our people in America. It shocks these people. They knew it was 'bad' but never dreamt it was as inhuman (psychologically castrating) as my uncompromising projection of it pictures it to them. These people have a tender heart for the unfortunates, and very sensitive feelings for truth and justice. The very essence of the Islam religion in teaching the Oneness of God gives the believer genuine voluntary obligations toward his fellow men (all of whom are one family, brothers, sisters to each other)...and because the True Believer recognizes the Oneness of all humanity the suffering of others is as if he himself were suffering, and deprivation of the human rights of others is as if his own human rights (right to be a human being) were being deprived.
>
> MALCOLM X, 2013: 26–27

In this brief passage, Malcolm highlighted one of the most important aspects of the Qur'an's teaching about the divine intelligence embedded within creation. The Qur'an states,

> O mankind! We [Allah] created you from a single male and female and fashioned you into nations and tribes, that you should know each other (and not hate each other). Indeed, the most honored of you in the sight

---

16 For a classical Islamic conception of 'asabiyya, see Ibn Khaldun's *The Muqaddimah: An Introduction to History.* Trans. Franz Rosenthal, Ed. N. J. Dawood. Princeton, NJ: Princeton University Press, 1989. For a discussion of Protestantism's influence on the idea of individualism, see Alister McGrath's *Christianity's Dangerous Idea: The Protestant Revolution – A History from the Sixteenth Century to the Twenty First.* New York: HarperOne, 2007.

of Allah is the most righteous among you. And Allah is omniscient and is well acquainted (with all matters).[17]
QUR'AN: 49: 13

In this passage, the Qur'an establishes two important things. First, that Allah is the author of the racial, linguistic, and regional differences within mankind, and thus those differences represent the way Allah wants the world's population to be. Additionally, these differences are not reasons for discord, but rather are invitations to discourse, dialogue, and mutual friendliness; to use them as points of contention is a violation of Allah's design for mankind. Second, righteousness has something to do with understanding the divine design and living in accordance with it. According to the Qur'an, Allah reminds his followers that he is fully aware of all things they do, especially those that contradict the meaning and goals of human diversity. In light of this one Qur'anic passage, artificial antagonisms based solely on race, ethnicity, gender, and nationhood are to be struggled against, as Muhammad taught in his "final sermon." In other words, these social ills are a part of the personal and collective *jihad* (struggle) within the lifeworld (*lebenswelt*) – the world in which the individual experiences himself/herself and struggles against themselves within their worldly context. *Nationalism*, or the sense of superiority, whether it be by race or region, has no part in a transcendent and internationalist understanding of Islam, which sees the whole of humanity as a family created by the divine.[18] The measurement of man, as Malcolm learned in Mecca, was in his deeds, his righteousness, and how he lives his faith, and not in his race, which he could not control. Therefore, '*asabiyya* (solidarity), or in the Christian lexicon *agape*, plays a major role in the way the *Muslim* is to live their life; they are to live in *sympathy* (to suffer with) with those who have been left in the ditch of history;

---

17 My translation.
18 This was a rather difficult lesson for Malcolm X to learn. Despite his first idea to bring both Black Nationalism and Islam to the African-Americans, the limits of Black Nationalism was brought to his attention by an Algerian Ambassador in Ghana, who Malcolm X regarded as racially 'white' but was both a Muslim and a successful Algerian revolutionary (Malcolm X, 2013: 19; Barnes, 2010: 47–48). The Ambassador expressed his disagreement with Malcolm X over the appropriateness of Black Nationalism, which would leave no part for men like him because of his pale complexion. By limiting his political, economic, and social philosophy within the confines of *race*, Malcolm stated in an interview to the *Young Socialist* magazine that he "was alienating people who were true revolutionaries dedicated to overturning the system of exploitation that exists on this earth..." and that he "had to do a lot of thinking and reappraising of [the] definition of Black Nationalism" (Barnes, 2010: 47–48).

those who have been marginalized and/or excluded; those who suffer from poverty, sickness, and oppression, as Muhammad did during his prophetic life. While Christians are to engage in a radical *imitatio Christi* (imitation of Christ's earthly life), Muslims too are to live in accordance with the *sunnah* (way) of Prophet Muhammad, who harbored a inextinguishable "being-with" ethic even before his prophetic call in 610 CE. Indeed, Malcolm X, like Muhammad, was for all intents and purposes an orphan after his father, Earl Little, was assassinated by the Black Legion and his mother, Louise Little, was so cruelly detained by the State of Michigan and committed to the Kalamazoo State Hospital for twenty four years (Marable and Felber, 2013: 15–16, 24, 26–32). Without his parents, Malcolm was forced to live in a foster home in Mason, a small rural town just outside of Lansing, Michigan, where he was the "token" Black boy: the perpetual 'outsider.' This experience of being without the family anchor, being without unconditional love, and being vulnerable to the corrupting brutality of civil society due to the loss of familial protection, shaped both Muhammad and Malcolm's life's trajectories. 20th century America and the Arabian *Jahaliyya* (age of ignorance) had much in common, including the dominance of greed, violence, racial antagonism, misogyny, and *necrophilia* (love of dead material things) as determining aspects of the society. These contexts made them both keenly sensitive to the plight and predicament of those who were vulnerable, but it also bore in them the willingness to dedicate their lives to the furthering of justice – a struggle that serves the goal of a fully reconciled future society, in which families are not torn apart by the inhumanity of the state and civil society, but are once again cherished, nurtured and protected as the basis of a healthy society.

Rooted in this 'being-with' ethic is the Qur'anic vision of the *world-as-it-ought-to-be*. For Islam, this vision remains the main interrogator of the *world-as-it-is*; it is the source of Islam's negativity. 'Revolution,' within the context of Islamic thought, does not simply mean the overthrow of one government for the purposes of installing another, it means the implementation of a vision of the way the world-ought-to-be based on the Qur'anic – and humanistic – precepts of absolute justice, equality, mutual recognition, mercy, compassion, solidarity, friendly-living-together, the absence of alienation and the balance between individual autonomy and collective solidarity. Freedom cannot be achieved within the ancient cages of heteronomy, alienation, injustice, and disrespect, and neither can it be found through the necrophilic *having-mode of existence* (consumerism), but rather through a modern transcendence of such constrictions does one find subjective and substantive freedom. Malcolm X explicitly understood this when he spoke of so-called 'civil rights' laws, as well as the Emancipation Proclamation, the Constitution of the United States, and the Declaration of Independence, as not being true sources of freedom; they were empty documents loaded with false promises that failed to change the material and spiritual conditions for African-Americans. It was not the passing of more superfluous laws that would change the ugly reality for the victims of America, but a change in the fundamental constitution of the American people – they had to go through a revolution of consciousness which, according to Malcolm X, was possible only through the conversion to Islam, which was a religion that would *sharpen their consciences* towards the suffering of others, and not *dulls the conscience* so that they can sleep blissfully next to the slums of their cities (Kant, 1998: 93). He wrote in his letter home from Mecca that,

> I could see from this, that perhaps if white Americans could accept the Oneness of God, then perhaps, too, they could accept *in reality* the Oneness of Man – and cease to measure, and hinder, and harm others in terms of their 'differences' in color.
>
> MALCOLM X, 1992: 392

For Malcolm, the 'white' in 'white Americans' impeded their ability to see the diversity of God's human creations. Islam was that religion that could still wipe this 'white' away.[19] Additionally, he wrote

> With racism plaguing America like an incurable cancer, the so-called "Christian" white American heart should be more receptive to a proven solution to such a destructive problem. Perhaps it could be in time to save America from imminent disaster....
>
> MALCOLM X, 1992: 392

In this optimistic moment, Malcolm seems to be scaling back his wholesale condemnation of America, but rather looking for a cure for the ills that have infected it from the beginning – the cure being the acceptance of Islam and its radical sense of brotherhood beyond the boundaries of race. In this sense, Islam is the only viable option for America if it wants to eradicate the plague of racism. We have no reason to believe that Malcolm X was optimistic about the prospects of America embracing the Islamic path and therefore rescuing itself from itself, but he would remain a "prisoner of hope" nevertheless (Zachariah 9:12). Thus, while he struggled for human rights in the United States, he simultaneously made modest contributions to the correcting of the Nation of Islam's distortion of Islam, both in his own organization *Muslim Mosque*

---

19   Malcolm is clearly talking about a 'white' that has nothing to do with pigmentation of the skin, but rather a socio-political concept of white in which it means to be 'superior,' or 'boss' as he often pointed out.

Incorporated (MMI), but also in his public speeches and interviews, through which he emphasized Islam's racial inclusivity.

Along with its vision of a world without racism, Islam, throughout its history, has advanced a more pragmatic understanding of violence as a means for social progress. Unlike Jesus of Nazareth's complete negation of violence as a way of solving conflicts, the Prophet Muhammad never made such a prohibition as long as the violence is confined by moral considerations and Qur'anic principles. However, against the Islamophobic claims of the critics of Islam, Muhammad's preference for peaceful means of conflict resolution can be demonstrated through any cursory study of his *seerah* (biography). Nevertheless, violence as a means of restoring justice, freedom, addressing grievances, and championing the poor, the marginalized, the broken, and the brutalized has always been reserved as a possible avenue of praxis within Islamic thought. Muhammad himself engaged in violent actions when compelled to do so by the antagonistic forces surrounding him. In this sense, if the negativity of Islam – its insistence on saying 'no' to the unjust conditions of the world-as-it-is – is at the core of the Islamic way-of-being-in-the-world – and it is willing to fight against those unjust and unfree conditions peacefully, or with violence if necessary, than Islam, unlike Christianity, offers the revolutionary Muslim more options through which he can struggle against the brutality of tyrants and unjust systems of control. Islam offers a very similar recalcitrant and resistant negativity as Christianity – at least Jesus of Nazareth – but it also encourages its members to engage in a *jihad* (struggle) against the hypocrisy and mendacity of tyrants, oppressors and despots. If "oppression is worse than death," as the Qur'an tells us in Surat al-Baqarah 2:191, than it is incumbent on Muslims to change the social, political and economic situations that maintain and/or produce such oppression, even if it is through violent means. In this sense, the *negative vision*, i.e. the utopic *sum of all oughts*, remains the blueprint for the longing for absolute justice, equality and freedom from alienation and oppression, and this vision is brought into existence through *revolutionary praxis* when it cannot be done through any other means (Malcolm X, 1965: 45–57).

Malcolm X understood clearly that the Christian language of the *contra lex talionis*, the ethic of 'turning the other cheek' and 'loving thine enemies' was not the political-theology of the so-called 'Christian' America, who had long since abandoned this ethic but, being a bourgeois nation, did not discard the ideological functionalization of it. Through secularization and the accumulation of wealth, American elites had become *securi adversus Deum*, not troubled about the status of their souls in the eyes of religion.[20] Although they

---

20   "Indifferent towards God."

never believed in it, the ruling bourgeoisie in Europe and in America never failed to functionalize the statements of Jesus of Nazareth when it suited their interests, especially when it pacified their would-be hangmen: the poor, the workers, abused, oppressed, marginalized, colonized and the excluded. Similar to Marx, Malcolm understood this functionalization as an powerful tool for turning the potential for a revolution into a mild reform; without violence and the overthrow of the American political system, there was no chance for a true emancipation of African-Americans, as that system itself was entrenched within systematic and structural forms of racism, as well as the class antagonism, which was often camouflaged by the race problem. The only way to eliminate the tyranny of the system was, like Samson, to bring down the whole edifice. With this in mind, Malcolm was geared towards a religion of action, a religion of radical praxis, and religious believers who were not willing to compromise on the freedom of African-Americans. In this sense, he was looking for a 'John Brown' form of religion to ally himself with; one which did not see the American government, nor the Constitution, as being somehow sacred, but rather as a very human document constructed by a certain class for the benefit of a certain class. As he said on July 5, 1964, in his second OAAU rally,

> We've got to seek some new methods, a reappraisal of the situation, some new methods for attacking it or solving it, and a new direction, and new allies. We need allies who are going to help us achieve a victory, not allies who are going to tell us to be nonviolent. If a white man wants to be your ally, what does he think of John Brown? You know what John Brown did? He went to war. He was a white man who went to war against white people to help free slaves. He wasn't nonviolent. White people call John Brown a nut. Go read the history, go read what all of them say about John Brown. They're trying to make it look like he was a nut, a fanatic. They made a movie on it, I saw a movie on the screen one night. Why, I would be afraid to get near John Brown if I go by what other white folks say about him.[21]
> MALCOLM X, 1964

---

21 http://malcolmxfiles.blogspot.com/2013/07/the-second-oaau-rally-july-5-1964.html The fact that Malcolm knew that some Christians, like John Brown and his family, could overcome the imperative to "turn the other cheek" against the brutality of white supremacy and consequently take up arms against it, must only have solidified his belief that most Christians were not committed to the non-violence principle, but were simply not prepared to sacrifice their own life and treasure for the African-American as John Brown had done. In this sense, their insistence on non-violence was a cover for their cowardice, duplicity, or lack of true commitment. Where actions were needed, too many stopped at words, using the Bible as their legitimation.

Through Dr. King's non-violent approach to the struggle for African-American emancipation, the Black community would become experts at 'revolts' and 'rebellions,' but never revolutions; the constitutional strictures of Constantinian-turned-Bourgeois-Christianity would never allow for such questionable activity, as violence, even in self-defense was suspect on the basis of the Gospels. Yet for Malcolm, White folks had already liberated themselves from the Christian ethics of charity, compassion, and solidarity with the suffering and oppressed, while African-Americans continued to chain themselves to the ideology of non-violence at their own peril. While it certainly meant that the Black Church was more exemplary of Christian ideals, it did not emancipate African-Americans from the burden of White supremacy. Therefore, non-violence with those who are violent against you was the wrong language, it was incomprehensible to the violent other, and would only lead to further brutality. It taught the brute how he could treat the brutalized; it normalized his injustice and it perpetuated his rule. Only Islam, in Malcolm's mind, provided for both the spiritual life of the African-American as well as the tools for his physical emancipation, which indelibly included the use of principled violence to achieve a just solution to an unjust society (Malcolm X, 1992: 390–393).

Redemption of the Dead: Memory and Mimesis

Malcolm's political-theology resided in the present; it was a future-oriented struggle for the benefit of oppressed peoples, especially those who were the victims of white supremacy. Nevertheless, an important component of his political-theology remained underdeveloped, even if it was simply appropriated from the Islamic tradition, i.e. the redemption of the previous generations of victims. In other words, Malcolm X's attempts to bring about a society that transcends racism, oppression, and alienation was directed towards the contemporary and those yet-to-come, but world history is saturated with the innocent who were abused, tormented and murdered simply because of their race, class, gender, and religious affiliation and they also cry out for redemption from the brutality of our depraved history. Yet, as a philosophical and theological question, we must ask: in light of Malcolm's prophetic way-of-being-in-the-world, what can the living do today to redeem the multitudes of innocent victims from history, and how can the innocent victim ultimately triumph over their abuser and murderer? Additionally, how can we today, in the shadow of Malcolm X, redeem his suffering at the hands of an unjust and vicious system of exploitation and murder, as he too became a victim of that hateful system?

Returning to the critical theorist Max Horkheimer, he writes most pessimistically that,

> It is impossible that such justice should ever become a reality within history. For, even if a better society develops and eliminates the present disorder, there will be no compensation for the wretchedness of past ages and no end to the distress in nature... Yet the urge to such a conceptional transcending of the possible, to this impotent revolt against reality, is part of man as he has been moulded by history. What distinguishes the progressive type of man from the retrogressive is not the refusal of the idea but the understanding of the limits set to its fulfillment.
> HORKHEIMER, 2002: 130

From the perspective of Horkheimer's Critical Theory of Religion, man's praxis is inherently incapable of bringing about a full redemption of the dead, for they are lost to history and their lives full of suffering remain the ugly disfigurement they have taken to their grave. Nevertheless, Horkheimer gives the revolutionary a certain semblance of *hope* (the undeterred longing to negate what is the case in history and nature) that can guide him in his attempts to "transcend the possible," to "revolt against the reality of unnecessary suffering," and to embrace and embody the negative principle of both Prophet Muhammad, which Malcolm X courageously followed until his murder on February 21st, 1965, as well as a guide towards the recovery and resurrection of the latent negativity of the prophetic Jesus of Nazareth. Even if the fatigue associated with the *parousia delay* (delay of the Messiah/Mahdi) weighs heavily on the members of the Abrahamic faiths, through this radical praxis, combined with the sensitivity for the suffering of the finite individual – which resides most fervently within the consciousness of the historical materialists – revolutionaries may bring about what the critical theorist Walter Benjamin described as earthly *jetztzeit*, or "now-time" or *nunc stans* (eternal now) – a messianic-like breaking of the present conditions through an aggressive actualization of the utopian other (Benjamin, 1969: 261). While Horkheimer believes in the concrete limits to the redemption of the dead through the radical praxis of the living, Benjamin optimistically believes that each generation is endowed with a "weak messianic power, a power to which the past has a claim," the likes of which "cannot be settled cheaply" (Benjamin, 1969: 254). In other words, if Golgotha history weighs heavily on the revolutionary today, so too does their responsibility to transcend the history of brutality and oppression. This imperative/endowment gives each passing generation the ability to redeem the dead through the construction of a future society based on the realm of freedom beyond the realm of necessity, the realm of autonomy beyond the realm of heteronomy, and the realm of love and solidarity beyond the realm of hate and division, starting with a recovery of memory of past sacrifices and prophetic *mimesis* (μίμησις – imitation). What Benjamin thought, while facing the rising tide of fascism that would eventually take his life in Portbou, Spain, in 1940, was that the living can modify the past through a future-oriented remembrance of past suffering coupled with a radical commitment to bring about the society that redeems the blood, misery, and despair of the victims of the past. It is true that in the Abrahamic faiths of Judaism, Christianity and Islam that "only the messiah himself consummates all history, in the sense that he alone redeems" and therefore "nothing historical can relate itself on its own account to anything Messianic," but what Malcolm X has taught the revolutionary is that the messianic notion of the totally other society – other than what is already the case – must remain as the yardstick which stands as the grand inquisitors of the world and all it contains (Benjamin, 1978: 312). If the revolutionary cannot see the Kingdom of God as the *telos* of history, because it is by definition the breaking of the continuity of history, then he must see Malcolm X and other revolutionaries for what they are: the voices that expresses the longing for absolute justice and the example of those who strive to bring it about in hopes that the Messiah will someday complete and/or endorse the job.

Malcolm Today

As the world becomes increasingly enveloped by the disfiguring forces of racism, capitalism, neo-imperialism, and other systems of exploitation and brutality, it becomes ever more important that we both *remember* Malcolm X and engage in a radical *mimesis* of his radical and prophetic praxis. Not only are the living and the soon-to-be-living dependent upon us for sculpting the conditions for a future reconciled society, and leading humanity away from the totally administered society, but so too do the dead look to us for their redemption, even if it is incomplete. Only on the foundations of the great prophetic and revolutionary voices like Malcolm X are we to ever achieve such transcendent goals. And so as Ossie Davis' eloquent eulogy for Malcolm X should not be the final word on him, so too should the grief-filled eulogies of history not be the final word on the innocent victims; the horror and terror of slavery, Jim Crow and new Jim Crow, the pain and agony of First Nation Americans, the destitution of the poor white worker, and the misery of all the oppressed should be given bold expression if only to rescue them from the shackles of history itself. The legacy of Malcolm X impels us not to forget the wretched, but to remember them within our daily praxis. His *dies irae* (day of wrath) has yet to come, but now we – in the shadow of this great revolutionary – are tasked to be its instrument.[22]

Bibliography

Adorno, Theodor. *Critical Models: Interventions and Catchwords.* New York: Columbia University Press, 2005.
Adorno, T.W., Frankel-Brunswik, Else, Daniel J. Levinson. *The Authoritarian Personality.* New York: Harper&Row, 1950.
Anderson, Jon Lee. *Che.* New York: Grove Press, 1997.
Benjamin, Walter. *Illuminations: Essays and Reflections.* New York: Schocken Books, 1969.
——— *Reflections: Essays, Aphorisms, Autobiographical Writings.* New York: Harcourt Brace Jovanovich, 1978.
Boer, Roland. *Criticism of Theology: On Marxism and Theology III.* Chicago: Haymarket Press, 2012.
Clegg III, Claude Andrew. *An Original Man: The Life and Times of Elijah Muhammad.* New York: St. Martin's Press, 1997.
DeCaro, Louis A. *On the Side of my People: A Religious Life of Malcolm X.* New York: New York University Press, 1996.
Evanzz, Karl. *The Messenger: The Rise and Fall of Elijah Muhammad.* New York: Vintage Books, 1999.
Froese, Paul. *The Plot to Kill God: Findings from the Soviet Experiment in Secularization.* Berkeley: University of California Press, 2008.
Horkheimer, Max *Critique of Instrumental Reason.* New York: The Seabury Press, 1974.
———. *Critical Theory: Selected Essays.* New York: Continuum, 2002.
Ibn Khaldun. *The Muqaddimah: An Introduction to History.* Franz Rosenthal (Trans.), N.J. Dawood. (Ed.) Princeton, NJ: Princeton University Press, 1989.
Jenkins, Robert L, ed. *The Malcolm X Encyclopedia.* Westport, CT: Greenwood Press, 2002.
Kant, Immanuel. *Religion within the Boundaries of Mere Religion.* New York: Cambridge University Press, 1998.
Malcolm X. *Malcolm X – at Michigan State University,* January 23, 1963. youtube.com video.
——— *Malcolm X: Second OAAU Address: July 5,* 1964. http://malcolmxfiles.blogspot .com/2013/07/the-second-oaau-rally-july-5-1964.html.

---

22 "Day of wrath."

―― *Malcolm X Speaks: Selected Speeches and Statements.* George Breitman (Ed.) New York: Grove Weidenfeld, 1965.
―― *The Autobiography of Malcolm X.* New York: Ballantine Books, 1992a.
―― *February 1965: The Final Speeches.* Steve Clark, ed., New York: Pathfinder, 1992b.
―― *The Diary of Malcolm X (El-Hajj Malik El-Shabazz): 1964.* Herb Boyd and Ilyasah Al-Shabazz, eds., Chicago: Third World Press, 2013.
Marable, Manning & Felber, Garrett. *The Portable Malcolm X Reader.* New York: Penguin Classics, 2013.
Marcuse, Herbert. *Herbert Marcuse: The New Left and the 1960s.* Douglas Kellner, ed., New York: Routledge, 2005.
Marx, Karl and Engels, Friedrich. *The Marx-Engels Reader.* Robert C. Tucker, ed., New York: W. W. Norton & Co., 1978.
McGrath, Alister. *Christianity's Dangerous Idea: The Protestant Revolution – A History from the Sixteenth Century to the Twenty First.* New York: HarperOne, 2007.
Ratner, Michael and Smith, Michael Steven. *Who Killed Che? How the CIA Got Away with Murder.* New York: OR Books, 2011.
Reitan, Ruth. *The Rise and Decline of an Alliance: Cuba and African American Leaders in the 1960s.* East Lansing: Michigan State University Press, 1999.
Schapiro, Leonard and Reddaway, Peter. *Lenin: The Man, the Theorist, the Leader: A Reappraisal.* New York: Frederick A. Praeger, 1967.
Scholem, Gershom. *The Messianic Idea in Judaism: And Other Essays on Jewish Spirituality.* New York: Schocken Books, 1971.

CHAPTER 5

Malcolm X and the Meccan Epistle

Seyed Javad Miri

Introduction

Malcolm X is not very well known in Iran. I searched in vain for relevant literature on him at the Iranian libraries but the result was negative. I could not find anything related to him. As a matter of fact, in Iran, when you ask about Malcolm X people turn the question by answering that they have seen the movie *Malcolm X* starred by *Denzel Washington*. In other words, despite the official anti-Americanism of the Iranian governing body the majority of Iranians rely on Hollywood's narratives on Islam and key Muslim thinkers in America or elsewhere in the globe. This is to argue that there is little done by the Iranian scholars on Islam and Muslims in America. To be honest, many people – even the educated elites – are surprised when you mention to them that Malcolm X converted to Islam and his adopted name was el-Hajj Malik el-Shabazz. To put it differently, this is not only a nominal problem but demonstrates how orientalistic the Iranian narrative on Malcolm X is. By 'orientalism' here I refer to the dominant outlook within the humanities and social sciences which condition our preferences as far as the subjects and problems of research and study are concerned. For instance, one of the most challenging questions before Muslim communities around the globe is the challenge of Islamism, which in every state is internally expressed in terms of merging nationalism with Islamic principles and externally expressed as Islamic Internationalism. In this chapter, I am not much concerned with the internal dimensions of Islamism; what is of interest for me is the internationalism of Islamism which can be discerned in Malcolm X's political biography. In addition, it should be stated that Malcolm X's Islamic Internationalism is not understood in a dogmatic fashion or an orthodox manner by me. Here I am not intending to reconstruct Malcolm X's legacy in an ideological fashion or sectarian mode. On the contrary, I think his legacy is best understood in terms of what he himself conceptualized – but less developed and hence under-theorized – as *the intelligible search for truth*. By this concept, Malcolm X has not only entered the stage as a political activist (with Internationalist-Islamic inclinations) but also put forward a sociological concept which could assist us in reconceptualizing social issues within the parameters of an alternative social science *à la* Ali Shariati, Fanon, Jalal

Ale Ahmad, Murtada Muttahari, Mohammad Beheshti, Syed Hussein Alatas, Syed M. Naguib Al-Attas, Allama Tabatabai, Ayatollah Taleghani, Syed Farid Alatas, Said Nursi, Seyyed M.B. Sadr, Imam Musa Sadr, Allama Jafari and Malek Bennabi. I would like to assert at the outset that Malcolm X's legacy is deeply under-theorized globally, in general, and in the Muslim World, in particular. As a matter of fact, in Iranian sociological discourses, he is totally absent due to the fact that Iranian social scientists do not follow research programs which are not considered as 'mainstream' by Euro-Atlantic social scientists. In other words, post-colonial frameworks, subaltern discourses, post-racial theories, post-ethnic paradigms and post-positivistic research programs are not often welcome in Iran due to the fact that Iranian social scientists take the Eurocentric body of theories as inviolable sacred canons which should be followed literally and internalized religiously. This outlook has hindered many sociologists in Iran from developing their own research programs which could be sociologically significant but peripheral in terms of Eurocentrism. In other words, if, for instance, the legacy of Malcolm X is not theoretically appropriated in Iran – the reasons being multifarious – but one which must be mentioned in this context is that many Iranian sociologists seem to be choosing between being relevant in a Eurocentric frame of reference and/or they wish to be intellectually relevant within global multipolar frames of references (which are surely larger than the Eurocentric vision of the world). This is to argue that they have chosen so far to be relevant in the former at the expense of the latter.

The irony is that in Iran social scientists and theorists argue that they are in search of alternative modes of theorizing but I do not quite understand how we could achieve this without building upon thinkers such as Malcolm X and those who left an arsenal of conceptual material behind? This is a question which needs to be addressed properly and surely it falls outside the major concern of the debate here. However it is important to realize that if we do not take the imaginative configurations envisaged by thinkers such as Malcolm X seriously, then the political modalities of Islamic Internationalism could easily turn into alienation, violence, sectarianism and hate-mongering, as it has been the case in the past decade, wherein the spirit of Islamic Internationalism has distanced itself from enlightened discourses of Islamism and instead left the stage for obscurantist interpretations of the revealed tradition. In other words, the state of the Muslim world today is not an accident, but rather it is clearly evident that we should take the relation between theory and praxis as well as visionary thinkers of the Islamic traditions seriously.

Islamic Internationalism

Islamic Internationalism is one of the most progressive movements which is indebted to the nineteenth century Iranian visionary intellectual Seyyed Jamal al-Deen Asadabadi. By raising the collective consciousness among diverse Muslim nations, Islamic internationalist activist-intellectuals attempted to overcome oppressive international colonial and imperial regimes, on the one hand, and internal despotism/inertia/regressive mode of social organization, on the other hand. However, in countries outside the traditional Islamic world, there were other oppressive issues which made the nature and scope of the fight against injustice more dramatic. In America, people like Malcolm X came to realize that they had to fight a different battle than their brethren in Africa, Asia and/or the ex-Soviet Union. The central question before Malcolm X, unlike intellectuals like Ali Shariati or Allama Iqbal, was the racial question and the oppressive segregative system which brutally and violently discriminated against Black People. As a matter of fact, in an interview on Chicago TV with Jim Hurlbut, Malcolm X described his early childhood and explained that his house was burned down by the Ku Klux Klan and that they murdered his father. The brutality of a racially oppressive system was not only an *intellectual question* for Malcolm X, it was a *vital question* which enveloped all his existential being until he was assassinated in the Audubon Ballroom in Harlem. In order to understand the type of Islamic Internationalism which occupied the mind and heart of Malcolm X, we need to reread certain dimensions of his life through a *personal narrative approach*. Although he does not use this term in his work, one can see how eloquently he has applied this approach in his discourses on the racial problems of the United States and the world at large. The concept is mine but one could see this approach, for instance, in his Meccan Epistle as early as 1964.

A Shariatian Approach for Deciphering the Biography of X

How could we decipher the political biography of Malcolm X? Dr. Ali Shariati has a very interesting interpretation of the Islamic Calendar. He argues that the beginning of Islamic era does not referred to the birth of Muhammad; the ordainment of Prophet Muhammad; the *tanzil* (descent) of Qur'an in the Cave of Hira or any other Arabic symbols which people around the globe, for many cultural reasons, may not be able to associate with. On the contrary, the beginning of the Islamic Calendar is coincided with the *hijra* or 'migration.' Consequently,

Islam started to become a world religion when Muslims migrated outside the boundaries of their inhabited lands and culturally acquired habits which had previously shackled them. In other words, one of the significant characteristics of human life is the question of exodus, but this should not be considered in an almanac-ian fashion, as though this was an event which happened centuries ago. On the contrary, Shariati argues that this is an event which could occur every day and in any place for any human who is ready for transformation (Shariati, 1980). In other words, *hijra* is not a simple physical evacuation but a spiritual mode of transformation which could have far-reaching consequences for the individuation process. If we take this definition of *hijra*, which has been eloquently elaborated by Shariati, then we can approach the departure of Malcolm X from the United States to Africa and finally to Mecca in a different fashion. To say it otherwise, the almanac-ian date when Malcolm X moved out from the United States in April 1964 has a symbolical importance as this was not just a physical move from America to Saudi Arabia. On the contrary, this was a *hijra* in its truest sense of the term, i.e. a *spiritual transformation* which changed Malcolm forever. However what we need to understand is the fact that Malcolm X was a social thinker who believed that the realms of theory and praxis are inseparable and in this fashion he approached the realities of life based on a method which he conceptualized as *the intelligible search for truth*. Of course, it is incumbent upon critical thinkers to ask what the fundamentals of this approach are or how Malcolm X applied this method on social issues which occupied him as a social theorist.

I think it would be a mistake to fathom this approach as a method within the parameters of a positivistic/legislative frame of reference. On the contrary, it seems Malcolm X was years ahead of his contemporaries who were attempting to reduce the complexity of human life both individually and collectively into quantitative realms as these domains were understood in terms set by the natural sciences. He seems to have envisioned the 'cultural turn' in humanities as depicted marvellously by Zygmund Baumann, who argued that social sciences were long accustomed to view human societies through the prism of legislative paradigms, but now we all have grown up to realize that the epoch of legislation in humanities is long gone and an era of interpretative social sciences has set in (Baumann, 1990). In other words, Malcolm X's theory of intelligible search for truth (or his theory of the *House Negro* and the *Field Negro*) is one of those theories which need to be worked out thoroughly but outside the parameters of legislatively-designed naturalistic social sciences. In this method, the experiential dimensions of the scholar are not underrated; rather it constitutes a significant aspect of engaging with the human condition in all its complexity. To put it otherwise, the relation between the subject and the question under investigation is not conceptualized in a positivistic fashion which is current in disciplinary approaches to human questions and quests. This mode of engagement is expressed in various phases of Malcolm X's life and works but here I would only focus on one instance: his *Meccan Epistle*.

By purpose I term this letter as *epistle* due to the fact that this was not a simple note but a writing directed and sent by Malcolm to a person (in this context his wife Betty Shabazz) and a group of people (i.e. the wider community in the USA and/or even the global audience), in an elegant and formal didactic fashion. In addition, it was not didactic in the formal sense of being *instructive* and educational as we understand these terms in academia today. On the contrary, it was *edifying*, i.e. it was a mode of deconstructing patterns of normalcy in regards to racial questions in United States as well as constructing future strategies for a post-racial society. This epistle is one of the most inspiring pieces of imaginative theories which have gone unnoticed by social thinkers, sociologists and social theorists who are accustomed to find sociologically relevant works in disciplinary journals and articles published by prestigious publishing houses in the U.S., the U.K. and the E.U. Fortunately, this epistle was not published initially by Eurocentrically endorsed houses which work within the frames of 'normal science.' The *Meccan Epistle* of Malcolm X transformed the intellectual as well as the political landscapes in America and the world beyond for time to come.

I am writing this chapter while I am sitting at the skirts of Alborz Mountains in Tehran. I looked at the literature which was available on Malcolm X but found nothing which I could relate to existentially and in a meaningful intellectual fashion. I did not want to produce an article for the sake of publication as I relate to Malcolm X as an inspiring intellectual who has re-fathomed the parameters of the sociological imagination in an authentic fashion. I do not think that a new volume on Malcolm X should reproduce existing patterns of researches or popular Eurocentric research programmes which are not existentially relevant anymore due to the fact that they have lost touch with the real and vital miseries of humanity today. It seems issues that matter existentially are not relevant scientifically and problems which matter academically are not relevant existentially. This is a paradox of relevancy which has conditioned the human soul existentially and I do not see any exit based on the existing paradigms in academia – which grows more and more alienated from the wider realities. Malcolm X's intelligent search for truth as expressed in his Meccan Epistle may be a way out of these dilemmas, paradoxes and problems. I have tried to look at Malcolm X in a different fashion than we have been taught in academia which belittles personal biographical narratives at the expense of naturalistic/scientific language which is quantified and precise but empty and hopeless. The human life is possible when it imbues hope in the hearts of people and this is what one can see in the Meccan Epistle but nobody, as far as I know, have worked on this in the way I think it would be constructive and hope-generating.

The Meccan Epistle

Every thinker has a central problem or key questions which occupy a primary importance in their theoretical framework. Malcolm X is not an exception in this regard as he grew up in a society where racial questions were the dominant problem. Here I would like to focus on a letter he wrote in April 1964 from Mecca to his wife in the United States which should not be treated as a simple letter, but rather I think it is Malcolm X's manifesto where his theory, praxis and methodology is expressed in the most succinct manner. The letter begins with a reference to race and color as key points which have obstructed the emergence of the sane society. Malcolm X argues that I have never witnessed

> such sincere hospitality and overwhelming spirit of true brotherhood as is practiced by people of all colors and races here in this Ancient Holy Land, the home of Abraham, Muhammad and all the other Prophets of the Holy Scriptures. For the past week, I have been utterly speechless and spellbound by the graciousness I see displayed all around me by people of all colors.
> MALCOLM X, 1992: 390

Race is the central issue through which Malcolm X has approached social problems. For instance, the sociological point of departure of Karl Marx is not race but *class*; Max Weber's sociology is premised upon *rationality*; Durkheim's sociological point of view is not rationality but *anomie*; Jalal Ale Ahmad's sociological viewpoint is not anomie but *westoxification* and so on and so forth. But Malcolm X needs to be reconceptualized as a social thinker who has taken the question of race as a key social problem which has overshadowed dominant trends in modern Western countries such as England, the United States, Germany, Sweden and Canada.

Although Malcolm X takes the American society as his case study, the questions of disunity of humanity and conflict in the *world society* are issues that have preoccupied him in a serious fashion. On his pilgrimage to Mecca he states that there

> were tens of thousands of pilgrims, from all over the world. They were of all colors, from blue-eyed blonds to black-skinned Africans. But we were all participating in the same ritual, displaying a spirit of unity and brotherhood that my experiences in America had led me to believe never could exist between the white and non-white.
>
> MALCOLM X, 1992: 390–391

The modern world came to being through three lofty ideals: *fraternity, liberty* and *equality*. These three notions build the discursive backbone of the Enlightenment which was supposed to transform the world and make it a more humane place for humanity at large. But the place Malcolm X came to experience as a kid and later as an adult did not demonstrate any of these ideals which were supposed to be the pillars of democracy. In 1956, Frantz Fanon, before the First Congress of Negro Writers and Artists in Paris, argued that racism "is not the whole but the most visible, the most day-to-day and, not to mince matters, the crudest element of a given structure" (Fanon, 1956). Malcolm X shared the same view; that in reality, the American social structure was not built upon the Enlightenment ideals of fraternity, equality and liberty. On the contrary, it was a racist, unequal and oppressive system which was far from a democratic political system. In other words, when Malcolm was writing to his wife from Mecca about the 'spirit of unity and brotherhood' (1964) he had the 'American Nightmare' in mind. This led him to believe for quite a long time that the white and non-white populations could never coexist in peace. Slavery had given birth to an oppressive structure which was not only of an external nature but also had an internal dimension, that in the Fanonian perspective, Malcolm X considered as 'cultural' (Fanon, 1956). Fanon in his memorable speech in Paris in 1956 argued that

> to study the relations of racism and culture is to raise the question of their reciprocal action. If culture is the combination of motor and mental behavior patterns arising from the encounter of man with nature and with his fellow-man, it can be said that racism is indeed a cultural element. There are thus cultures with racism and cultures without racism.
>
> FANON, 1956

Malcolm realized the cultural dimension of racism when he encountered societies where the 'race problem' was not their central dilemma and this too made him move away from the biological reductionism of the Nation of Islam which considered 'whiteness' as a biological derivative which should be treated as a plague. Malcolm, by employing a *personal narrative approach,* attempts to demonstrate that even the race-obsessed society of the United States could be redeemed if we could read human biography from a different point of departure, which, in his case, is Islam. For example, he uses a personal narrative approach in telling a different story about human fellowship, where he relates that

> throughout my travels in the Muslim world, I have met, talked to, and even eaten with people who in America would have been considered 'white' – but the 'white' attitude was removed from their minds by the religion of Islam. I have never before seen sincere and true brotherhood practiced by all colors together, irrespective of their color.
> MALCOLM X, 1992: 391

What Fanon considered as a 'cultural element,' Malcolm X conceptualized as a 'white attitude,' which could be removed if we were to accept the natural facts of life and not submit to the fabricated fictions of power, which portrayed the 'other' as an object which should be tamed, trained and civilized by superior masters. But how could we change our attitudes which are so deeply ingrained in the fabric of our societies and minds? Malcolm is not a simple man but a very complex intellectual and the way he approaches riddles of society is also complex. He knows that the racial question is one of the most intractable questions which lie before the American and even capitalist system and it would not be easy to overcome this for a nation which has grown accustomed to the separation of whites and blacks. He argued that "my experiences in America had led me to believe never [a spirit of unity and brotherhood] could exist between the white and non-white" (Malcolm X, 1992: 391). But the problem which he was talking about was not solely the problem of white people. On the contrary, this is a problem which concerns humanity as such due to the fact that every single person could act unintelligently in the face of facts. Malcolm X depicts this question in a very beautiful manner which I have termed the *personal narrative approach*. He states you

> may be shocked by these words coming from me. But on this pilgrimage, what I have seen, and experienced, has forced me to re-arrange much of my thought-patterns previously held, and to toss aside some of my previous conclusions. This was not too difficult for me. Despite my firm convictions, I have always been a man who tries to face facts, and to accept the reality of life as new experience and new knowledge unfolds it. I have always kept an open mind, which is necessary to the flexibility that must go hand in hand with every form of intelligent search for truth.
> MALCOLM X, 1992: 391

Here Malcolm X demonstrates clearly that we need to have certain universal criteria which would enable us to live by truth and act in accordance with intelligence. This method is what he terms the 'intelligent search for truth' (Malcolm X, 1992: 391). The first principle is that one should have firm convictions but one's convictions should not be based on blind faith. On the contrary, one should face facts and realize that facts are not fabricated mental illusions. In other words, when one see facts as realities of life then one can see new dimensions which would touch the experiential aspects of one's being as a human person. Additionally, these realities could increase one's cognitive capacities as an individual. However, one needs to keep broad-mindedness and flexibility which, in an integral fashion, would create an inclination in the human self which Malcolm X conceptualizes as 'intelligent search for truth' (Malcolm X, 1992: 391). In other words, the intelligent search for truth is what characterizes the true spirit of Islamic Internationalism. Although other internationalists of the Islamic Movement did not express this formula so clearly, Malcolm X expressed this as a criteria which could bring Muslims (and even non-Muslims) together in a spirit of fraternity. To put it differently, the spirit of Islamic Internationalism has turned today into sectarian violence and hatred, but the question is why has the Muslim Community fallen into such a horrible ditch? I think here we can be inspired by Malcolm X's practical theory of intelligent search for truth. The Muslim Community has been inclined toward violence, hatred and extremism due to the lack of principles which Malcolm had already elaborated six decades ago. These ideals include (1) considering facts as realities of life; (2) realities as instruments of cognitive-expansion; (3) broad-mindedness; (4) flexibility; and (5) the intelligent search for truth. In other words, convictions are respectable when they express realities of life, but when they are not demonstrating such realities, we then must

> rearrange much of [our]...thought-patterns [which we]...held [dear]... and [we should]...toss aside [our previous]...conclusions [as we have to be ready to]...face facts, and accept the reality of life as new experience and new knowledge unfolds it. [In other words,] we should keep... an open mind, which is necessary to the flexibility that must go hand in hand with every form of intelligent search for truth.
> MALCOLM X, 1992: 391

In summary, the Islamic Internationalism of the 21st century is in dire need of an intelligent approach to reality, religion, humanity, politics, differences, others, diversity, and culture in the fashion that Malcolm X demonstrated in his Meccan Epistle. In other words, every change starts from within and without that type of transformation it is an illusion to think that we can bring about a *sane society* in the style articulated by Erich Fromm (Fromm, 1955), or an *intelligible society* in the Jafarian style (Jafari, 2012). Malcolm X's theory of intelligent search for truth was aimed at overcoming the race problem in the United States but this does not mean that this theory is confined to that issue alone. On the contrary, we can approach differences and diversities in an intelligent fashion which may finally yield into constructive results and make our society a better place to live. This is how I think we can build upon Malcolm's intelligent theory of truth.

Bibliography

Baumann, Z. *Thinking Sociologically. An introduction for Everyone.* Cambridge, MA: Basil Blackwell, 1990.

Fanon, F. *Racism and Culture.* "A speech delivered before the First Congress of Negro Writers and Artists in Paris in September 1956." http://tamilnation.co/ideology/racism.htm.

Fromm, E. *The Sane Society.* New York: An Owl Book, 1955.

Jafari, M. T. *Intelligible Life.* Bloomington, IN: Xlibris, 2012.

Malcolm, X. *Letter from Mecca.* 1964. http://www.malcolm-x.org/docs/let_mecca.htm.

Shariati, Ali. *Religion versus Religion.* Collected Works (22). London: Mona Publishing House, 1980.

CHAPTER 6

Malcolm X – A Martyr of Freedom

Rudolf J. Siebert

In the perspective of the comparative, dialectical religiology, the charismatic leader Malcolm Little, or Malcolm X, or finally El-Hajj Malik El- Shabazz, from Lansing, Michigan, was like many other martyrs of freedom of the 19th, 20th, and 21st centuries, an American citizen, and thus his life and his work, including his tragic death can be understood and comprehended only in the wider context of the overwhelmingly European-American civil society and state, to which he, the passionate African-American, belonged, and which shaped him, and which he reflected, and which he influenced. As such, he must be seen *contextually*. Malcolm X's home was not only the planet earth, or Western Civilization, but most specifically his African-American family – including his parents, his marriage with his beloved wife, *Sister Betty*, familial property (or the lack of), and the education of his six children, in the overwhelmingly European-American civil society, which includes the need system, administration of justice, the professional organizations and most of all the police. This society includes the liberal constitutional state, internal state law, i.e. the constitution, external state law, and national and international history, as well as culture, including art, religion, philosophy, and science. No matter how much and how radically he may sometimes have criticized them – and justifiably so – these aspects of modern society remain necessary.

Search for a New World

Particularly since the Vietnam War, and then even more so since the beginning of the Second Gulf War, socially conditioned discomfort and discontent in the Western Civilization during its present historical transition-period from modernity to post-Modernity, happened to express itself in an animosity against the United States of America, even inside itself, which seems to have produced many of the present martyrs of freedom: including Malcolm X, and his revolutionary vision. But the War in Vietnam, or the Second Gulf War, or the Afghan War, rational or irrational, justified or unjustified as they may have been, may have been less than a motivation but rather a rationalization of hostility against the United States in Europe, the Near East, Africa, Central and Latin America, and elsewhere. What, however, moved people in the 1960's not only in Europe but in all civilized countries of the earth, was the horror and terror which they shared with America about the murder of Malcolm X, only shortly after the assassination of President John F. Kennedy, and only shortly before the murder of Dr. Martin Luther King and Robert Kennedy, the brother of the murdered President, and the democratic candidate for the Presidency in Washington D.C. (King, 1963a-b; 1967; 1986; Dyson, 2000; 2008; Waldschmidt-Nelson, 2012; Cone, 1992). Robert Kennedy wrote in his book *In Search for a New World*, that moral goals must point the way to, and must be the guideline of human praxis (Kennedy, 1968: 248). Robert Kennedy confessed and witnessed that the faith, the passion, and the conviction of man were ultimately more powerful than all calculations of national economists and generals. Robert Kennedy declared that pure instrumental or functional reason, or mere suitability, could lead into post-modern alternative Future I – the totally administered society, characterized by work and death camps like Auschwitz and Treblinka, or into post-modern alternative Future II – an entirely militarized society, dominated by what former General and then outgoing President Eisenhower had called the 'military-industrial-congressional-complex,' producing one non-constitutional and unjust war after the other.[1] In other words, Robert Kennedy declared his support for the policies and politics of his brother, the martyrized President John F. Kennedy. While Malcolm X was a Muslim, and came from the lowest level of the rather rigid American class society, the proletariat or precariat, and while Robert Kennedy was a Christian, a Catholic, and came from the upper middle class, or bourgeoisie, they both shared the longing for the post-modern alternative Future III: a new society, characterized by mimetic and communicative rationality, faith, passion, morality, conviction, personal autonomy and universal, i.e. anamnestic, present, and proleptic solidarity. Both were murdered for their common revolutionary vision of the freedom of all. When Robert Kennedy came to Kalamazoo, Michigan, on his Presidential campaign trip, where this chapter is written, and where I at the time served as the connection between Western Michigan University and the *Students for a Democratic Society* (SDS) in Detroit and the student movement, as well as the campaign manager of the Third Congressional District for Presidential candidate George McGovern, who advocated the Roosevelt-Liberal political vision and message of Dr. Martin Luther King, and the Kennedy's, and where I received my police file, he was received by a large crowd not only of European-Americans, but also of African-Americans so enthusiastically, that on the joyful ride from the airport to Bronson Park, he lost his shoes, which are still preserved in the city today by faithful Democrats (Bonfiglio, 2005; Siebert, 2010b).

---

1 See U.S. President Dwight D. Eisenhower's "Farewell Address" on Jan. 17, 1961.

Liberal Men and Women

Whoever is concerned with the history of assassinations, and in general of the political murders, will find out that most of all relatively innocent, humane and liberal men and women have belonged to the victims. These liberal men and women have been the objects of threats, of marginalization, of hindrances in professional life, of force and violence in general. The critical theorist of religion remembers liberal men and women in Europe, such as Rosa Luxemburg, Karl Liebknecht, Jean Jaures, Walther Rathenau, and of the Near East or the Far East, such as Mahatma Gandhi, and Ali Shari'ati. In contemporary American civil society, truly liberal men and women can be found less among conservative or neo-liberal Republicans, who attempt to retreat back into the 18th and 19th centuries, and more among Democrats, who remember President Roosevelt's New Deal, in which he modified the socially atomistic liberalism in conformity to the principle of subsidiarity, which he took from the Papal Encyclical *Quadragesimo Anno* of 1931. Liberal leaders have been infinitely more threatened and less protected than the dictators such as Stalin, Hitler, Mussolini, Franco, Salazar, or Pavelić. In America, Abraham Lincoln, the President who led the war for the rescue of the Union, and the liberation of the African slaves, became the victim of murder in 1865. President James Garfield was assassinated in 1881. President William McKinley was murdered in 1901. President John F. Kennedy was assassinated in 1963. There were also assassination attempts on President Theodore Roosevelt, who followed the slain President McKinley into office, and President Franklin D. Roosevelt, and President Harry S. Truman. They all were devoted servants of their liberal state. Long before – as well as after – Malcolm X or Martin Luther King leveled their prophetic accusations against the United States, white men were highly critical of the antagonistic American civil society, constitutional state and history. Without pausing, they continue to do so today. There were not only immoral and criminal slave-traders and holders, but also brave liberal men, the abolitionists in England and America, and President Lincoln, and most importantly John Brown, who helped to emancipate the black slaves to some extent, but unfortunately very slowly. Today, liberal men like Chris Hedges and Charles Mercieca ask African-Americans and European-Americans to teach their children that there is no glory in war, that there are no heroes in war, but that the glory comes from the actions that prevent war, and the heroes are the ones who implement those actions (Mercieca, 2014a; Hedges, 2003; 2006; Hedges/ Al-Arian, 2008). Both liberal men describe the apparent present *status* of the United States, criticizing the departure of the American nation from itself in the following way:

> We now live in a nation
> where doctors destroy health,
> lawyers destroy justice,
> universities destroy knowledge,
> governments destroy freedom,
> the press destroys information,
> religion destroys morals, and
> our banks destroy the economy.
>
> MERCIECA, 2014A; HEDGES, 2003; 2006; HEDGES/AL-ARIAN, 2008

While this may sound like an exaggeration, the Critical Theorist Theodor W. Adorno was correct when he stated that the truth lays precisely in the exaggeration. Today liberal men like Hedges and Mercieca also present a solution for various problems, including the Israel-Palestine Conflict – in which the United States has been so deeply involved up to the present – the moral and humanitarian catastrophe of Gaza, the hellish conflagration in Syria and Iraq – where a new Islamic State or Caliphate has come into existence through the 'Islamic State in Iraq and Syria' (ISIS) – and in Afghanistan, Libya, and the Ukraine (Mercieca, 2014a; Hedges, 2003; 2006; Hedges/Al-Arian, 2008). Ironically, they recommend relocating Israel into the United States:

> Highlights:
> Israelis are most loved by Americans.
> Americans will welcome Israelis with open arms into their homes.
> America has plenty of land to accommodate Israel as its 51st state.
> Israel can have a real safe Jewish state surrounded by friendly states.
> America will no longer have to spend $3 billion taxpayer money per year for Israel's defense.
> The transportation cost will be less than three years of defense spending.
> Palestinians will get their land and life back.
> Middle East will again be peaceful without foreign interference.
> Oil prices will go down, inflation will go down, the whole world will be happy.
>
> MERCIECA, 2014A; HEDGES, 2003; 2006; HEDGES/AL-ARIAN, 2008; CHAICHIAN 2014

Beyond the irony of this proposal for the solution of the Israel-Palestine Conflict lays the truth, that Israel has the right to defend itself and Palestine has the right to rebel against the military occupation, because no nation has the right to occupy the other. Likewise, Malcolm X and his followers, while still in the Nation of Islam, also dreamed sometimes of a separate state for African Americans in the United States.

Symbols

While some religious leaders like the Maccabees, Thomas Müntzer, the Brothers Cardinal and Malcolm X, were willing to engage in violent revolt and revolution if there was no other way to solve the contemporary unjust race, national, or class problems, others like Mahatma Gandhi, the Berrigan Brothers and Martin Luther King opted for a non-violent method in order to overcome the outrageous social injustices. In the 1960's, two religious leaders became victims and the definitive symbols of political murder: the African-Americans Malcolm X and Martin Luther King; both became members of the community of martyrs of freedom. Malcolm X, the son of Earl Little, a Baptist minister and follower of Marcus Garvey – who was assassinated because he wanted to take the Afro-Americans back to their homelands in Africa, and whose wife spent 25 years in the insane asylum here in Kalamazoo, Michigan – converted in prison to Islam, the *Religion of Law*, and became an agitator for the Black Muslims, the union of African Americans who converted from Christianity, the Religion of Freedom, to Islam (Hegel, 1986q; Haley, 1992; Marable, 2011). In opposition to Martin Luther King, Malcolm X preached for twelve years unyielding, inexorable, revolutionary power, force and self-defense in the service of the Nation of Islam and its founder and leader Elijah Muhammad, the 'Messenger of Allah' (Haley, 1992; Marable, 2011). As long as Malcolm X served the Black Muslims well, as agitator and demagogue, he was welcome. However, in 1964, one year before his death, Malcolm X converted from the *Lex* or *Jus Talionis* to the *Golden Rule*, which all world religions share. He also became more hopeful about the prospects for peace between the races (Haley, 1992: 367; Marable, 2011). On the basis of personal experiences in America, in the Middle East, particularly in Jeddah and Mecca, and in Africa, particularly in Ghana, Malcolm X gained the insight into the evilness of barbarism. He had already left the irreconcilable Nation of Islam for the true and global Islam of Muhammad ibn Abdallah in the full consciousness of the danger of being killed by his former brothers, the Black Muslims, to which he exposed himself. Malcolm X confessed that now, in 1964/1965, was the *time of martyrs* (Malcolm X, 1966: 385; Breitman, 1990; Haley, 1966; 1992: Chaps. 16–19; 441–523, 524–527; Marable, 2011). In case he himself had to become a martyr, then this should happen for the sake of the *cause of brotherhood*, always including *equality* and *freedom*.

For Malcolm, nothing else could rescue America. Malcolm X had to learn that arduously enough, but he had learned it.

Brotherly Love

In contrast to Malcolm X, Dr. Martin Luther King, also the son of a Protestant minister, was recognized and respected in the world; he became a recipient of the Noble Peace Price in 1964. Martin Luther King studied for the Christian ministry and then earned his doctorate at Boston College. Here a professor introduced him to Hegel's *Philosophy of History*: the goal of history was the alternative Future III – the realm of the freedom of all, and the means to it were only too often violent revolutions (Hegel, 1986 g; l; King, 1963a-b; 1967; 1986; Dyson, 2000, 2008; Waldschmidt-Nelson, 2012; Cone, 1992). The alternative Future III was not the ultimate kingdom of God, a final theocracy, a Messianic apocalyptic-eschatology, which was rather the goal of the history of religions. Already for Hegel, a century before Ernst Bloch and Walter Benjamin, the theocracy could only be religious and spiritual and not political; the world spirit was not the absolute Spirit (Hegel 1986a; c; g; l; p; q). The modern dichotomy between the sacred and the profane had become too deep, in order to allow for a political theocracy any longer. The goal of history was finite human happiness, not the kingdom of Heaven (Benjamin, 1968; Siebert, 2010b; 2013b; 2014c). But the secular and the religious, politics and theology, moving in a different direction, could still support each other – toward the silent approach and arrival of the kingdom of God in which the human realm of universal freedom would be concretely superseded (Hegel, 1986a; g; l; p; q; Benjamin, 1968). Theocracy had been the form of the patriarchal relationship and theocracy had been the constitution of the old Oriental World. The old Jewish theocracy meant the identity of state and religion. That precisely is the problem of contemporary Iran and Iraq and the new Islamic state, the Caliphate, that their theocracies are not only religious but also still political, economic, and military, as ISIS shows only too clearly. For King and Malcolm X, political theocracy had come to its end. Theocracy was merely a religious issue. Their striving for the freedom of all was political, and could not be bound within the confines of religion. But the politics of the universal liberation and the tendency toward spiritual theocracy, could still promote each other. While Malcolm and King, the Muslim and the Christian, had in common their political goal, they differed in their methodology toward achieving it. Mahatma Gandhi enlightened Martin Luther King, but not Malcolm X, about what neither the Jewish, Christian, or Islamic tradition, nor Hegel, could teach them: the possibility of non-violent means to reach the goal of universal freedom (Hegel, 1986a; g; l; p; q; King, 1963a, 1963b; 1967; 1986; Dyson, 2000; 2008; Waldschmidt-Nelson, 2012; Cone, 1992; Küng, 1970; 1991a-b; 1994a-b; 2004). Jews, Christians, and Muslims had 'just war' theories but no theories of non-violent 'just revolutions.' Mahatma Gandhi, who belonged to the Hindu faith, the *Religion of Imagination* according to Hegel, had accepted the fourth commandment of Rabbi Jesus of Nazareth's so called *Sermon on the Mount*:

> You have learnt how it was said: Eye for eye and tooth for tooth. But I say this to you: offer the wicked man no resistance. On the contrary, if anyone hits you on the right cheek, offer him the other as well; if a man takes you to law and would have your tunic, let him have your cloak as well. And if anyone orders you to go one mile, go two miles with him. Give to anyone who asks, and if anyone wants to borrow, do not turn away.
> MATTHEW 5:38–42

According to Mahatma Gandhi, to follow the *Jus* or *Lex Talionis* – eye for eye – would make the entire world blind. While Malcolm X and Martin Luther King shared the same goal – the emancipation of the African-Americans in the United States and finally of all people – they differed sharply concerning the means by which they would reach this goal. Malcolm X did not think that the dogs of the white police could be encountered effectively by holding up the other cheek. It was simply not practical. Malcolm X did not only convert to Islam because the American slaveholders had been Christians, and most white men he knew were Christians, but most of all because of the Christian prohibition against the *Lex Talionis*, which Islam, like Judaism, the *Religion of Sublimity* according to Hegel, subscribed to, and he remained a Muslim to the end of his life, even after he separated from the Nation of Islam. Later he would develop his own democratic strategy, informed by the newly discovered principle of universal brotherhood, through the epiphany of Mecca (Hegel, 1986a; q; Breitman, 1990: Chaps. I–III; Haley, 1992: Chaps. 17–18; Marable, 2011: Chaps 11–16). Even after his conversion, Malcolm X could still not follow entirely the forth commandment of the *Sermon on the Mount*. He now, nevertheless, was ready paradoxically enough, to embrace the fifth commandment, preached by the *Prophet* or *Messenger Jesus of Nazareth* in his *Sermon on the Mount* concerning neighborly and brotherly love:

> You have learnt how it was said: you must love your neighbor and hate your enemy. But I say this to you: love your enemies and pray for those who persecute you; in this way you will be sons of your Father in heaven,

for he causes his sun to rise on bad men as well as good, and his rain to fall on honest and dishonest men alike. For if you love those who love you, what right have you to claim any credit? Even the tax collectors do as much, do they not? And if you save your greetings for your brothers, are you doing anything exceptional? Even the pagans do as much, do they not? You must therefore be perfect just as your heavenly Father is perfect.
MATTHEW 5: 43–48

The second part of Jesus' commandment of neighborly and brotherly love – *hate of the enemy* – cannot be found in the Mosaic Law, but it was a popular Aramaic way of saying: *you do not have to love your enemy*. The principle of brotherhood brought Malcolm X closer to Martin Luther King whom he had secretly admired from the start, in spite of tensions and controversies (Waldschmidt-Nelson, 2012; Cone, 1992). In the 18th century, the Western bourgeoisie – the third estate – had promised *fraternite, egalite, and liberte*, principles rooted originally in the Abrahamic religions, but it failed to apply them in practice to the fourth estate, the proletariat, or precariat, white and black alike, not to speak of the slaves. Malcolm X and Martin Luther King tried to help correct this deficiency, and precisely in this attempt were connected with genuine liberals and humanistic socialists, despite the fact that their main issue was first of all the race struggle. Slowly they turned their attention toward the class struggle in direction of post-modern, alternative Future III – universal emancipation and liberation, which is not possible without brotherhood and equality.

Model

Dr. Martin Luther King reached the climax of his worldly recognition when he received the Noble Peace Price in Oslo, Norway, in December of 1964. He stood up for the demand, the fight, battle, contest, struggle, and war for the improvement and correction of the situation of the African-Americans that should certainly be carried out with all the energy possible, but, nevertheless, should only be done so through peaceful means. The radical Euro-Americans, or Whites, hated King's imperturbability. The radical African-Americans hated his lack of brutality. For 12 years, Malcolm X was one of these hating radicals, which only abated after his conversion to true orthodox Islam (Breitman, 1990; Haley, 1992; Marable, 2011). Those liberal leaders like Martin Luther King and the converted Malcolm X, who wanted what was good, were persecuted. As such, Jesus of Nazareth served as a model for their revolutionary and humanitarian theory and praxis; not only for the Christian Dr. Martin Luther King, but even for the Hindu Mahatma Gandhi, who also became a martyr of freedom. Even the martyrized Muslim Malcolm X, or now *El-Hajj Malik El-Shabazz*, saw the martyr Jesus of Nazareth as a model of social justice, even if he could not accept the counter-revolutionary use of Jesus' memory. Not an assassination, but the judgment of the ruling class, and the state, in Jerusalem and Rome took the Nazarene's young life, after he had challenged and provoked them in the name of the Truth, which they did not understand, and which they continually violated (Matthew, 5–7; 26–28; Mark, 14–16; Luke, 6; 22–24; John, 18–21; Horkheimer, 1974a: 96–97; Küng, 1970; 1994a-b; 2012; Pope Francis I, 2013). The love which Rabbi Jesus preached was always more dangerous for those who practiced it than for those who merely confessed to it; the latter professed *agape* without drawing the consequences from this confession in real practical witness. Love realized itself in these ideas, secular and theological, which today in late capitalist society are in a process of decline and dissolving (Horkheimer, 1974). The Catholic Robert Kennedy belonged, in spite of all his weaknesses, to those liberal leaders who were still connected not only with words, but seriously with the threatened Western culture. As candidate for the highest office in the USA, Robert Kennedy had the right thing in mind, particularly to end the war in Vietnam. His death was a new proof that the good everywhere had brought more sacrifices in this world than the bad. The same is true for the Muslim Malcolm X and the Baptist-Christian Martin Luther King. Malcolm X had his own Islamic *Christology* from below (Malcolm X, 1965; 1966; Breitman, 1990; Haley, 1992: 345–346; Marable, 2011).

After his turning away from the *Cross* to the *Crescent*, Malcolm X never returned to untrue *white* Christianity. He nevertheless, followed before, and particularly after his physical and psychological divorce from the Black Muslims, and his conversion to genuine *true Islam*, the theory and praxis model of the Prophet Muhammad, and the Messenger Jesus of Nazareth, in his most heroic struggle for the poor in a rich, white, so called Christian country. Malcolm X fought rightly against the *white man's* untrue *Christianity*. Long before Malcolm X, white men had already struggled against bad religion, opium religion, and ideological religion. Kant, Hegel, Marx, and Freud had understood that 'opium religion' made people feel good, while at the same time it dulled their conscience so that they could live quietly side by side by the most exploitative and degrading slavery, serfdom, and wage labor. They understood bourgeois religion as ideology in the critical sense: as false consciousness, as the cover-up and masking of particular racial, national, or class interests, or as wishful, illusionary, or delusionary phantasies: shortly as *untruth*. Malcolm X grew up in a rich, white, so-called Christian country, in which a President, who confessed to be a Christian, and to hold on to the Mosaic Law and to the Sermon on the Mount, but nevertheless allowed two atomic bombs, blessed by a Catholic priest, to be dropped on two cities that were full of innocent civilians, women and children. This killed 140,000 people but was considered to be *the lesser evil* in terms of Catholic morality. According to that claim, the bombing of Hiroshima and Nagasaki prevented the third, fourth, and fifth bomb, etc., to be thrown on other cities, as well as a possible American invasion of the Japanese home islands. In light of this, how could Malcolm X possibly know of a *true* Christianity? Astonishingly enough, Malcolm X differentiated no less between true and untrue Christianity, as he did between true and untrue Islam, in terms of an *inner criticism*, which compares a religion with its own original notion, confession, witness, cognitions, values and norms, and expressive symbols; he always remembered his own martyrized father, a Christian minister, even after he had become the Islamic minister Malcolm X, and even after he had turned to true orthodox Islam (Haley, 1992; Marable, 2011; Breitman, 1990; Waldschmidt-Nelson, 2012; Cone, 1992).

Non-violence

In 1963, when Malcolm X began to separate himself slowly from the Nation of Islam and began to move toward the true orthodox Islam, President James Miller of Western Michigan University, Kalamazoo, Michigan, invited Reverend Dr. Martin, Luther King, a Baptist minister, motivated by Hegel's *Philosophy of History* and by Mahatma Gandhi's teaching on non-violence as means for liberation, to speak to the academic community (The Western Michigan University Magazine, 2013: 10–13). At the time, the University's Psychology Department was making substantial contributions to the training of soldiers for the Vietnam War: peaceful accountants were conditioned, through B.F. Skinner, and transformed into aggressive marines in the shortest possible amount of time. President Miller invited Dr. King on suggestion of the Governor of Michigan in order to balance a very hawkish speaker who had previously addressed the academic community. Dr. Martin Luther King visited the University and announced his *Dream* in a peaceful speech and in a subsequent discourse with faculty, students, and newspaper/radio reporters. He told the students and faculty what Malcolm X would comprehend fully only a year later in Jeddah and Mecca, namely, that all people must learn to live together as brothers, or they would all perish together as fools. More than ever before, men and women were challenged to develop a world perspective. Through their scientific genius, people had made a neighborhood of this world. Now, through their ethical and moral commitments, people had to make of it a universal brotherhood.

For Dr. Martin Luther King this was the great challenge; what the Christian theologian, philosopher, and psychologist, Paul Tillich, called for on the same Western Michigan University Campus and in the same year 1963, with the New Testament, the present, historical *Kairos*, or *hour*. For Dr. Martin Luther King, this *Kairos* was valid and true for individuals as well as for whole nations. Of course, this existential, or historical *Kairos* presupposed Providence, goal, plan, and means in all three Abrahamic religions: the Universal appeared in the singular (Tillich, 1963a-b; 1966; 1972; 1977; Siebert, 2010).

According to Dr. King, professors and students were challenged, after having worked in the realm of ideas, to move out into the arena of social action, and to work passionately and unrelentingly to make social justice a reality. Dr. Martin Luther King confessed that it was always a rich and rewarding experience for him when he could take a brief break from the day-to-day demands of his struggle in the South, the old and new Confederacy, to discuss the issues involved in this struggle with college and university students and professors. Thus, he was very pleased to be at Western Michigan University. According to Dr. Martin Luther King, all people were challenged to get rid of the notion, once and for all, that there were superior and inferior races. Unfortunately, this notion still lingered around in various quarters of American civil society and constitutional state, despite the fact that certain intellectual disciplines, like the anthropological sciences, have said that there was not any truth to this doctrine of racial inequality. For Dr. King, there could be no gainsaying of the fact that the American system of segregation was on its deathbed in 1963. The only thing uncertain about it was how costly the segregationists would make the funeral. If an opponent, so Dr. Martin Luther King argued with the Gospels to students and faculty, set out to beat the Civil Rights movement, they would develop the quiet courage to accept blows without retaliating (Matthew 5–7; Luke 6; The Western Michigan University Magazine, 2013: 10–13; King, 1963a-b; 1967; 1986). If the opponent put them in jail, they would go in that jail, and they would transform it from a dungeon of shame to a haven of freedom and human dignity. Non-violent resistance, rooted in Christian and Gandhian praxis, would disarm the opponent which would leave him confused and morally deflated. Dr. Martin Luther King had seen this so many times in his own struggle in the South. He often thought that when the African-Americans came to see the true meaning of nonviolence, and to see that this is a strong method for liberation, and not a do-nothing method, then they would follow his peaceful 'turn-the-other-cheek' philosophy. It did not mean that people sat down and just passively accepted evil. In reality they courageously stood up against evil, but they would come to see that they had a more powerful weapon when they stood up against evil through non-violent methods. People stood up against evil, without using methods of violence – by boycotts if necessary; by picketing if necessary; by sit-ins if necessary; by mass pilgrimages if necessary. All of these things were methods of non-violent direct action, in which individuals and groups were able to do something; yet, they were doing it non-violently. Martin Luther King believed firmly that the *Negro* had come to see the power of this approach even though he had a legitimate summer of discontent in 1963. According to Dr. King, this was the final thing that he wanted to say at Western Michigan University.

Sometimes a man does more in his death than he could have ever done in life. Sometimes people have to take an evil situation and wring the good out of it. Dr. Martin Luther King considered it to be possible that the assassinated President Kennedy would be able to do more for civil rights in death than he could have ever done in life; the same was true for the later assassinations of Robert Kennedy, Dr. Martin Luther King himself, and Malcolm X. Reverend King's concluding remarks may have been among the most poignant and prophetic words he uttered, even about his own life and death five years later in 1968. Dr. Martin Luther King's *polemics* did not only include his non-violent struggle for social justice between the races and the classes, but also the violent conflicts in Vietnam, and potentially the later wars and civil wars in Nicaragua, El Salvador, Guatemala, Yugoslavia, Afghanistan, Iraq, Syria, Palestine, Pakistan, Iran, Libya, Ukraine, and all over Africa.

At Western Michigan University, Reverend Dr. King spoke for 48 minutes on the philosophy of non-violence, race related legal decisions, and the imperative of passing civil rights legislation without delay. He decried tactics which delayed civil rights legislation that, as it turned out, would pass in the following year in 1964. He spent time explaining how non-violence was an effective and *moral* tool for the civil rights movement. On *Martin Luther King Day* in 2014, Martin Luther King's son, MLK III, remembered and confessed on MSNBC that his father was murdered during a non-violent garbage collector strike in Memphis, Tennessee, because he stood up for the *redistribution of wealth* in the most unequal modern civil society; he defended not only the African American workers, but also the European American workers, and even for Asian, Vietnamese workers, and this while the Vietnam war was still raging (King, 1963a-b, 1967, 1986; Dyson, 2000; Waldschmidt-Nelson, 2012; Cone, 1992). Dr. Martin Luther King did not only stand up for the redistribution of wealth, but also for the recognition of the humanity and the dignity of all workers in the antagonistic civil societies around the globe: against alienation, reification, commodification, disrespect, disregard, narcissism, necrophilia, and against the pathology of normalcy, reason, and freedom. He connected the American race struggle with the national and international class struggle. There was at least one African-American who learned to see the power of his non-violent method of emancipation and brotherly reconciliation during 1963's summer of discontent, Malcolm X, who converted to true Islam in 1964, and witnessed his new confession to universal brotherhood, including equality and freedom, through his martyr death in February of 1965.

Today, fifty years after Malcolm X's and Martin Luther King's martyr/death for freedom, and civil rights legislation, the shooting of unarmed young black men by white policemen, and the consequent protests and riots still continue. Thus again, on August 11, 2014, in Ferguson, near St Louis, Missouri, the white policeman Darren Wilson, 28 years old, divorced, and father of a child, shot multiple times and killed the black 18 years old Michael Brown, a high school graduate. There followed two weeks of non-violent and violent protests, with agitators coming from the outside of town, even from the West and East coast, from Miami and Chicago, including so-called *anarchists* and *communists*. The Nation of Islam, now led by Louis Farrakhan, and the New Black Panther Party were present as well. Black groups protested in the name of the victim and his family while many other white groups took the side of the policeman. The latter collected $400,000 for Wilson's legal defense, had he been indicted by the grand jury. The black groups wanted the policeman to be suspended without pay and to be charged with murder. They were driven to protest by the longing that the murderer should not triumph over his innocent victim (Horkheimer 1970a-c; 1985g). A militarized police force tried to control the crowd with tear gas, but the shooting, the throwing of Molotov cocktails, the looting, and the vandalizing continued. Finally, the National Guard had to be called in by the Governor of Missouri, Jay Nixon. The journalists and the press felt like they were operating in a war-zone similar to Afghanistan or Iraq. They asked the African-American President Barack Obama, the Commander in Chief of the American armed forces, and the likewise African-American Attorney General, Eric Holder, to come to Ferguson and bring justice and make peace. The Attorney General came but the President did not. The tragedies, pain, and suffering, in American civil society and state, and on the slaughterbench and Golgatha of history – at the Mexican border, in the Eastern Ukraine, in Palestine (particularly Gaza), in Syria, in Iraq, in the new Caliphate, in the whole Arab world and all over Africa, etc. – were too great to bear for many. A few days after Michael Brown's killing, a European-American member of the Ferguson Police Department declared in public that *he was a believer in Jesus Christ, but that he was also a killer, and that he had killed a lot, and that he would continue to do so*. It is this kind of pathological untrue Christianity which failed to prevent the annihilation of the Native Americans and the enslavement of the African-Americans in the past 400 years. It also made the once-Christian

Malcolm Little into the Muslim Malcolm X and later into El-Hajj Malik El-Shabazz. The police officer, Darren Wilson, was relieved of his duties with pay and his actions were later found to be *legally* justified.

From the very origins of civil society in the ancient city states, civil society, situated in between the family and the state, had a tragic character, which not even the most optimistic anthropology or theology could completely overcome, and only too often its most beautiful dreams turned into nightmares. The Abrahamic religions have always recognized this tragic character and condition of civil society in spite of their firm trust in God and their rather positive, at least practical theodicies, which often embody severe contradictions, e.g., from Psalm 22:

> My God, my God, why have you deserted me?
> How far from saving me, the words I groan!
> I call all day, my God, but you never answer,
> all night long I call and cannot rest.
> Yet, Holy One, you
> who make your home in the praises of Israel,
> in you our fathers put their trust,
> they trusted and you rescued them;
> they called to you for help and they were saved,
> they never trusted you in vain.
>
> PSALM 22: 1–2; MATTHEW 26–28; MARK 14–16

March on Washington

In 1963, the American Federal Government was trying, without making fundamental changes in antagonistic civil society, to control an explosive racial and class situation. The Federal Government tried to channel the anger into the traditional formal democratic cooling mechanisms of the ballot box, the polite petition, the officially endorsed quiet gathering, the peaceful town hall meetings, the transformation of class problems into racial problems, etc. When the black civil rights leaders planned a huge *March on Washington* in the summer of 1963, to protest the failure of the nation to solve the race problem, which was really a class problem, it was quickly embraced by President John F. Kennedy and his brother Robert Kennedy, the Attorney General, and other national leaders, who turned it into a friendly assemblage. Dr. Martin Luther King's speech during the *March on Washington* thrilled 200,000 African-American and European-Americans: *I have a dream....* It was admittedly magnificent oratory. However, it was devoid of the anger which many African-Americans felt, including Malcolm X and the Nation of Islam. When John Louis, a young Alabama born *Student Non-Violent Coordinating Committee* (SNCC) leader, who had been often arrested and beaten, tried to introduce a stronger note of outrage at the meeting, he was censored by the leaders of the March on Washington, who insisted he omit certain sentences critical of the national Government. He would not be allowed to urge militant action for fear of alienating the support of white liberals. Eighteen days after the March on Washington, almost as if in deliberate contempt for its moderation, a bomb exploded in the basement of a black Baptist church in Birmingham, Alabama, and four girls attending a Sunday school class were murdered. President Kennedy had praised the deep fervor and quiet dignity of the March on Washington. According to Malcolm X, when a high-powered-rifle slug tore through the back of the NAACP Field Secretary Reverend Medgar Evers in Mississippi, he wanted to say the blunt truths that needed to be said (Breitman, 1990; Marable, 2011; Haley, 1992: 338–339). When the bomb exploded in a Negro Christian church in Birmingham, Alabama, ending the lives of those four beautiful little black girls, Malcolm X made comments that the American white man was generating and nourishing race hatred (Haley, 1992: 346–349). The more hate was permitted to lash out, when there were still ways it could have been checked, the more bold the hate became. At last it struck the white man's own kind, including his own leaders. In Dallas, Texas, the Vice President and Mrs. Johnson were vulgarly insulted. The U.S. Ambassador to the United Nations, Adlai Stevenson, was spat upon and hit on the head by a white woman picketer. Finally, that very hate killed President Kennedy. It was in this context that Malcolm X used the fateful phrase that *The Chickens*, i.e. the necrophilic white hate, were *Coming Home to Roost*. Mr. Muhammad and the Nation of Islam used this misunderstood phrase as a pretense to eliminate Malcolm X from their community, and which became an important step in his conversion to the genuine, true form of orthodox Islam, and to the confession and witness to universal brotherhood, including freedom and equality, as once understood by the three Abrahamic religions, as well as by the deist and enlightener, Thomas Paine, who was one of the initiators of the American independence from the British colonial power, which had brought *race* slavery to the American colonies and into the cotton fields of the old Confederacy.

Black Revolution

But the black militant Malcolm X, the black people's *tribune*, was nevertheless closer to the real mood of the African-American community in American civil society in 1963 and 1964 than the Nation of Islam, or even Dr. Martin Luther King. Speaking in Detroit two months after the March on Washington, which he had critically observed from a distance, and the Birmingham bombing, and one year before his conversion to true orthodox Islam, Malcolm X stated in his powerful and icy-clear rhythmic style, that the *Negros* were out on the streets and were talking about how they were going to march on Washington D.C., and on the Senate, and on the White House, and in the Congress, and how they wanted to tie it up and bring it to a halt, effectively shutting down the capital. The center of the 'free world' would not be free until their demands were met. They even said they would go to the airport and lay down on the run ways, and not let any planes land. For Malcolm X, that meant they were preparing for a *black revolution*, not just reform. It was the grass roots of the African-American people out there in the street, and it scared to death the white man and his white power structure in Washington D.C. According to Malcolm X, when the white man and the white power structure found out that that Black people were going to protest in the streets of the capital, it called in Uncle Tom to help placate and manage the Black rage that was sure to materialize. In Malcolm X's interpretation, President Kennedy's and other white liberal's involvement in the March on Washington watered down its militancy, and it ceased to be angry and uncompromising. It even ceased to be a revolutionary movement and became just another flaccid stroll down the street with a few lukewarm speeches. It became a picnic and a circus with clowns. For Malcolm X, the March on Washington was a sell-out and a shrewd take-over by moderates and liberals. The white establishment controlled the march on Washington so tightly that they told those national *Negro* leaders what time to hit town, where to stop, what signs to carry, what song to sing, what speech they could make, and what speech they could not make, and then told them to get out of town by sundown (Malcolm X, 1965:17).

Shortly, in Malcolm X view, the black revolution was co-opted and integrated and killed by the white man, the white ruling class, and its political representatives. For Malcolm X, revolution meant, *a la* Thomas Paine, Cornel West, or Chris Hedges, the qualitative change of *systems* not only in nature, the systems of which went through innumerable revolutions since the Big Bang 14 billion years ago, but also and particularly so in human history, in which primitive social systems were concretely superseded by slave holder systems, slaveholder systems by feudal systems, feudal systems by capitalist systems, and more recently capitalist systems by socialist systems (Siebert, 2010b). The structure of systems embraced according to Hegel's new, idealistic, revolutionary *Science of Logic* –

A. Universal: culture, including, art, religion, philosophy, and science.
B. Particular: civil society, state, and history,
C. Singular: individual and family.

Or according to Marx's inverse, materialistic, revolutionary, dialectical logic –

A. Singular: individual and family.
B. Particular: civil society, state, and history.
C. Universal: culture, including art, religion, philosophy and science.

Counter-revolution meant the attempt to return to a social paradigm which had already been concretely negated by a revolution, i.e. the liberal, and fascist, and neo-liberal, conservative, or counter-revolutions of the 1920's, 1930's, 1940's, and 1980's, and once more at the second decade of the third millennium, i.e. in the Ukraine. For Malcolm X, the *long hot summer of 1964* in which he converted to universal brotherhood, had given him the idea of a general post-liberal, black revolution in globalizing white civil society. Yet this remained only an idea. This idea of a general black revolution was only an idea, because all of those riots which took place in 1964 were kept contained within the particular ghettoes in which African Americans lived. If, so Malcolm X argued, "any of these bitter, seething black ghettoes all over America [would] receive the right igniting incident, and become really inflamed, [they would] explode, and burst out of their particular boundaries into where whites live," and that could lead to a general black revolution (Haley, 1992: 360). If in New York City enraged blacks would pour out of Harlem across Central Park, and fan down the tunnels of Madison, and Fifth and Lexington, and Park Avenues, they could lead to a general black revolution (Hedges, 2003, 2006; Hedges/Al-Arian, 2008; Breitman, 1990; Haley, 1992: 360–361; Marable, 2011; Siebert, 2010b). Malcolm X remembered that Detroit had already seen a "peaceful massing of more than a hundred thousand blacks" (Haley, 1992: 360). "Black social dynamite" was already festering in many other cities in the nation (Haley, 1992: 360).

Democratic Coalition

The accuracy of Malcolm X's caustic and ironical description of the March on Washington was corroborated in the description from the other side of the race and class warfare in the antagonistic American civil society of 1963: the white Establishment. The White House advisor Arthur Schlesinger wrote in his book *A Thousand Days*, how President Kennedy met with the civil rights leaders, and said that the March on Washington would create an *atmosphere of intimidation*, just when Congress was considering civil rights bills (Schlesinger, 1965). The civil rights leader, A. Philipp Randolph, replied to the President Kennedy that the *Negros* were already on the streets and that it was likely impossible to get them off the streets. According to Schlesinger, the conference with President Kennedy did persuade the civil rights leaders that they should not lay siege to Capitol Hill. Schlesinger described the March on Washington admiringly, and then concluded that in 1963 President Kennedy moved to incorporate the *Negro* revolution into his democratic coalition. But things did not work out completely. The African-Americans could not be easily brought into the *democratic coalition* when bombs kept exploding in churches and when new *civil rights* laws did not change the root condition – the low class condition – of the African-American people, with the exception of a small black bourgeoisie. In the spring of 1963, the rate of unemployment for whites was 4.8 percent and for non-whites it was 12.1 percent. According to government estimates, one fifth of the white population was below the poverty line, and thus belonged to the lowest level of the proletariat, or precariat, while one half of the black population was below that line. The civil rights bills emphasized *formal, not material democracy*: i.e. voting rights. But voting was not a fundamental solution to racism, or poverty, i.e. low class status. In Harlem, African-Americans, who had voted for years still lived in rat-infested slums, in tenement houses, and high-rise apartment buildings, also known as 'vertical ghettos.' As such, the *democratic coalition* could not provide an adequate post-liberal critique of the American power structure. It could not accomplish an adequate distribution of wealth. It could not heal the socially torn-apart civil society, its pathology of individual freedom, and its rationality. It could not generate a dynamic communitarianism and a new moral foundation for individual, family, society, state, history, and culture. It could not give a moral grammar for conflict resolution in the general struggle for recognition. It could not overcome disrespect. It could not stop the social dynamics of disregard, uneasiness, discontent, social deformity, disapproval, abuse, assault in urban and rural slums and beyond. It could not resolve the enormous paradoxes of late capitalism, with its massive reification and commodification of human life, and its high level of necrophilia. No matter how rich modern civil society had become on both sides of the Atlantic in the past 400 years, it had never been able to solve its enormous poverty problem (Siebert, Ott, Byrd, 2013). In precisely those years, when civil rights legislation coming out of the American Congress reached its peak, in 1964–1965, there were black outbreaks in every part of the country. In Florida they were set off by the killing of an African-American woman and a bomb threat against an African-American high school; in Cleveland they were set off by the killing of a white minister who sat in the path of a bulldozer to protest discrimination against African-Americans in construction work; in New York they were set off by the fatal shooting of a fifteen year old African-American boy during a fight with an off-duty policeman. There were riots also in Rochester, Jersey City, Chicago, and Philadelphia. These were also the years in which Malcolm X converted – paradoxically enough – to universal brotherhood, equality, and freedom, the principles of the modern bourgeois revolutions, up to the American civil war. However, genuine reconciliation could come about in the extremely antagonistic American commodity-exchange-society only through the emancipation of all people.

Black Power

During the years of 1963–1965, *Black Power* became the new revolutionary slogan. It was an expression of distrust of any *progress* given or conceded by the European-Americans. It was a powerful rejection of white paternalism. Few African or European Americans knew then the statement of the British writer Aldous Huxley: liberties are not given, they are taken. But the idea of autonomous freedom was there among African-Americans in the Black Power movement. There was also a pride in race – *black is beautiful* – and insistence on black independence, and often, on black separation, which was seen as the vehicle for achieving this independence as well as personal and collective autonomy. Malcolm X was the most eloquent spokesman for this African-American independence before and after his conversion to universal brotherhood. After Malcolm was assassinated, as he spoke on a public platform in New York in February 1965, according to a plan, the origins of which are still obscure today, he became the martyr of this Black Power-independence movement (Breitman, 1990; Haley, 1992; Marable, 2011; Waldschmidt-Nelson, 2012; Cone, 1992). Hundreds of thousands of people, black and white, read Malcolm X's *Autobiography*, which had been edited by an undercover FBI agent, Alex Haley, in whom he trusted and to whom he dictated his life story over several years up to his death (Marable, 2011). Malcolm X was like President Kennedy, his brother Robert Kennedy, and Dr. Martin Luther King, even more influential in death than during his life time despite of all attempts to suppress him.

Radical Attitude

In 1964–1965, Dr. Martin Luther King, although still respected in America and worldwide, was slowly being replaced by new and more militant heroes such as Huey Newton of the *Black Panthers*. Unlike Dr. King, the Black Panthers had guns and thought blacks should defend themselves if needs be. In late 1964, Malcolm X had spoken to African-American students from Mississippi, visiting Harlem, about the struggle for freedom. Malcolm X told the black students that they shall get freedom by letting their enemy know that they would do anything necessary to get their freedom. This willingness to fight for freedom was the only way to guarantee it. However, Malcolm X knew that students with such an attitude would be discredited by being labeled extremists, subversives, crazy or even terrorists. But when the students would remain resolute in their convictions, and would meet critical mass, they would gain their freedom. Since Malcolm X had been converted to universal brotherhood in 1964, he was still, like Dr. Martin Luther King, most seriously and radically committed to the goal of freedom, but he did not speak any longer of violent means in order to reach this goal in the United States (Haley, 1992; Marable, 2011). *Radical* came from Latin *radix, the root*. The *root* of the African-American struggle was man's *natural freedom* and *potential*, which is realized in his/her individual biography, family, civil society, constitutional state, world-history and culture, including art, religion, philosophy, and science.

Judgment

Many times since President Kennedy's assassination in Dallas, Texas, on November 22, 1963, Malcolm X looked at the speech notes he had used that day, which had been prepared at least a week before the murder. The title of Malcolm's speech had been *God's Judgment of White America*. It was on the Hebrew Bible and New Testament theme which was very familiar to Malcolm X: *as you sow, so shall you reap*, or in other Biblical words:

> I speak of what I know: those who plow iniquity
> and sow the seeds of grief reap a harvest of the same kind
> (Proverbs, 22:8).

> Wind they sow, and storm they shall reap (Hosea, 8:7).

MALCOLM X – A MARTYR OF FREEDOM 161

> Don't delude yourself into thinking God can be cheated: where a man sows, there he reaps: if he sows in the field of self-indulgence he will get a harvest of corruption out of it; if he sows in the field of the Spirit he will get from it a harvest of eternal life. We must never get tired of doing good because if we don't give up the struggle we shall get our harvest at the proper time. While we have the chance, we must do good to all, and especially to our brothers in faith.
> GALATIANS, 6:7–10

Malcolm X applied the agricultural, Biblical image of plowing, sowing, and reaping to the hypocritical American white man: he was reaping precisely what he had sowed. Then, when Malcolm X was asked by the press – *What do you think about President Kennedy's assassination?* – "without a second thought," he said what he "honestly felt," namely that it was "a case of *the chickens coming home to roost*" (Haley, 1992: 347). Malcolm said that "the hate in white men had not stopped with the killing of defenseless black people, but their hate, allowed to spread unchecked, finally had struck down this country's Chief of State" (Haley, 1992: 347). Malcolm said that "it was the same thing as had happened with Reverend Medgar Evers, with Patrice Lumumba," with Fidel Castro, "with Madame Nhu's husband," and all other emancipatory movements that had been attacked by America (Haley, 1992: 347).

Later, when Malcolm X visited Mr. Muhammad, the latter told him that he had made a profound mistake. The country admired President Kennedy despite his faults and weaknesses. The whole country was in mourning. Despite the fact that the Nation of Islam often spoke negatively about President Kennedy, Malcolm's statement seemed ill-timed and in defiance of Elijah's direct orders to remain silent on the issue. Elijah took that opportunity to silence Malcolm X for the ninety days, supposedly so that the Black Muslims could dissociate themselves from his public faux-pas. Malcolm went numb, but he obeyed with great difficulties and trepidations (Haley, 1992: 348). Three days later, the first word came to Malcolm X that a Mosque Seven official, who had been one of his most immediate assistants, was telling certain Mosque Seven brothers, "if you knew what the Minister, Malcolm X, did, you would go out and kill him yourself" (Haley, 1992: 349). Then Malcolm X knew, "as any official in the Nation of Islam would instantly have known," that any discussion of Malcolm's death could only be approved of by one individual: Elijah Muhammad (Haley, 1992: 349). Malcolm X's ultimate break with the Nation of Islam was unavoidable. Naturally, Malcolm suspected that the *chicken coming home to roost statement* had been only an excuse to put into action the plan for getting him out of the Nation of Islam. However, Malcolm had already outgrown the confines of Elijah's organization.

Religious Pathology

After his conversion to the *orthodox Islam* in 1964, Malcolm X thought of the possibility of a peaceful, nonviolent general black revolution through a new political organization, which was to heal the African-Americans' pathologies. Converted Malcolm X did not only know of the many mental illnesses, neuroses, and psychoses of individuals in American, atomistic, liberal society, which suffers from insufficient solidarity, but also of America's collective religious, economic, and political pathologies. In his response to them, Malcolm X felt the challenge to plan and build an organization in competition with the Nation of Islam that could help to cure the black man in North America of the sicknesses which had kept him under the white man's heel since the beginning of slavery. According to Malcolm X, the black man and woman in North America was religiously and/or spiritually sick; for centuries they had accepted the white man's Christianity, or better Christendom, an untrue slave holder, feudal, or bourgeois religion. The slaveholder and bourgeois Christendom asked the black so-called Christians to expect no true *Brotherhood of Man*, including *Freedom* and *Equality*, but rather to "endure the cruelties of the white so-called Christians" (Haley, 1992: 361). Untrue slave holder and bourgeois Christendom had made black men confused in their thinking. "It had taught the black man to think if he had no shoes, and was hungry, 'we gonna get shoes, and milk, and honey, and fish in Heaven'" (Haley, 1992: 361). That precisely was bad, slaveholder and bourgeois, ideological, *opium* religion, which has not only been fed to the African-American but also to the European-American proletariat, or precariat, in modern civil society. Malcolm X shared this inner criticism against bad religion with the Prophets and Messengers Abraham, Moses, Jesus of Nazareth, and Muhammad, and with their serious Jewish, Christian, and Islamic followers, as well as with the modern enlighteners. There was not only a modern dialectic between the sacred and the profane, but also a dialectic in the religion, and in the secular enlightenment (Horkheimer, 1970a-d; Adorno, 1951). Not only enlightenment but also religion could turn against itself and betray itself. The religion of truth could turn into the ideology, i.e. false consciousness – the masking of racial, and national, and class interests, untruth, of slaveholders, feudal lords, and capitalists. The religion of love could turn into Crusades, Anti-Semitism, Holy Inquisition, heresy trials, witch hunts, water boarding, and other forms of torture. The secular enlightenment instead of freeing people from their fears and making them masters of their fate, or instead of moving *Ego* to where *Id* was, or consciousness to where the unconscious was, could terrorize them, and make them more dependent and more unconscious (Horkeimer/Adorno, 1951). In this sense, there was not only a true and untrue Islam, but also a true and untrue Christianity, or a true and untrue Judaism. Malcolm X moved from an untrue Christianity through an untrue Islam to a true Islam. Therefore Malcolm X was less interested in the idealistic (moving from the Universal to the particular) shell of the mussel of religion –

> Set your hearts on his (the heavenly Father's) kingdom first, and on his righteousness, and all these other things (life, eating, drinking, body, clothing, life span) will be given you as well. So do not worry about tomorrow: tomorrow will take care of itself. Each day has enough trouble of its own –

than in its materialistic (moving from the particular to the Universal) shell "Set your hearts first on food and clothing, then the kingdom of God will fall to you by itself" (Acts, 17:11). While Malcolm X became finally a strong believer in the true, orthodox Islam, and had a deep faith in Allah, he was as critical of bad and untrue religion, and religious pathologies, as any traditional or modern atheist: e.g. Richard Dawkins, Sam Harris, Christopher Hitchins, etc. While Malcolm X stood firmly on the religious side and believed strongly in the Providence of Allah in the individual biography, as well as in the history of nations, he was enlightened enough to allow for a relative autonomy, not only of nature, but also of the individual person, the family, civil society, constitutional state, history, and culture, and to give room for a relative secularization. The believers did not have to ask the rabbi, minister, or priest every minute what to do in the world; the world had its own laws which man could discover through his reason and conscience. The reconciliation of the antagonism between the religious and the secular, expressed in the continuous culture wars, could contribute much to the curing and healing of the religious pathology of the African-Americans.

Economic Pathology

According to Malcolm X, the black man and woman in North America were mentally ill not only through their cooperative sheep-like acceptance of the white man's culture, his religion, i.e. white bourgeois Christianity, but they were also economically sick. The black man's economic illness "was evident in one simple fact: as a consumer he got less than his share and as producer he gave *least*" (Haley, 1992: 361). The African-American in 1964 showed Malcolm X the perfect parasite image: "the black tick under the delusion that he is progressing because he rides on the udder of the fat three-stomached cow that was white America" (Haley, 1992: 361). It was because black men did not own and control their own communities' retail establishments for automobiles, or Scotch whisky, not to speak of businesses employing over ten people, that they could not control their own communities (Haley, 1992: 361). The problem was the absence of a larger African-American bourgeoisie, including patricians like the Roosevelt's, the Kennedy's or Bush family on the European-American side. Black folks were not the owners of the means of production. The black proletariat shared this problem with the much larger white proletariat. The solution of this problem needed more than mass anger; it needed thought as well – critical biology, anthropology, psychoanalysis, economics, sociology, philosophy, religiology, and even theology. The angry fanaticism of freedom given into the hand of the masses of the black or white people could easily become awful, as indeed it did during the great bourgeois revolution in France in 1789, or during the bourgeois-revolutionary American civil war of 1865, which cost almost one million casualties from at the time a 40 million population; the Union could no longer endure two ruling classes, thus the Northern bourgeoisie, better equipped, annihilated the Southern slaveholder class and thus *liberated* the slaves into wage laborers. Only through the liberation of the black and white precariat, also the black and white bourgeoisie could become really free: the freedom of All instead of the always endangered freedom of the One, or of the Few, the so called *masters of mankind* (Marx/Engels, 1953a-c; Lenin, 2014). The black revolution would have to extend into a multi-ethnic revolution, since the pathology of reason and freedom is widely spread among the classes in civil society. Despite the fact that there was indeed a small African-American bourgeoisie, the problem remained the absence of the black ownership of the means of production. As stated above, this problem was commonly shared with the white precariat, and the solution of this problem needed a common – but hopefully – non-violent revolution. Malcolm X, despite the fact that he was not a Marxist, was nevertheless fully aware that he could not speak about the economic pathology of the African-Americans without speaking about capitalism as the private appropriation of collective labor Malcolm examined the dark side of democracy and showed how the demands of globalizing capitalism had subjugated billions of black, brown, and white people on all continents to the highest and most intense forms of racism and exploitation (Breitman, 1990; Haley, 1992; Marable, 2011; Waldschmidt-Nelson, 2012; Cone, 1992). A new balance between democracy and capitalism was necessary. As such, Malcolm X looked behind the scene of the information – and communication – economy. He wanted to move from the industrial or late capitalist society, towards a lasting and persistent economy (Breitman, 1990; Haley, 1992; Marable, 2011; Waldschmidt-Nelson, 2012; Cone, 1992). He looked for a democratic way toward something like an African-American, humanistic communitarianism. Therefore he envisioned the African-American emancipation from the commodity-exchange society toward a sane society. He participated, consciously or unconsciously, in the long ideology-critical discourse on the *market totalitarianism* of high-tech capitalism, which reached from Hegel, and Marx, to Adorno and Horkheimer, from Lenin to Gramsci, and from Foucault to Butler, and which explained the ideological reasons for the relative stability of the highly alienated, and subjecting, late industrial society, in spite of all its most painful crises, from which the African-American proletariat suffered even more than the European-American precariat. Since the rich classes in civil society want rather *to be rich than right*, as a Fortune 500 member was reported by CNN on Labor Day 2014, to have confessed, therefore things are so wrong for labor, black and white alike; since the 2008 depression, increase in income for the CEOs, owners and stockholders rose 850%, and increase in salaries and wages for labor rose 5.4%. The CEO earned over 200 times more than his workers, black and white alike.

Political Pathology

In Malcolm X's view, the black man and woman in North America were sickest of all politically. The black man allowed the "white man to divide him into such foolishness as considering himself a black 'Democrat,' or a black 'Republican,' or a black 'Conservative,' or a black 'Liberal'" – *divide et impera* – "when a ten million black vote bloc could be the deciding balance of power in American politics, because the white man's vote was almost always evenly divided" (Haley, 1992: 361). Strangely enough, Malcolm X did not notice the unusual lack of a viable labor party in the USA, which made it necessary that the 250 million African-American and European-American workers were represented in Congress by two bourgeois parties: one liberal – Roosevelt-liberalism – and the other conservative and/or neo-conservative. For Malcolm X, the polls were one place where every black man could fight for the black man's cause with dignity, and with the power and the tools that the white man understood, respected, feared, and cooperated with (Haley, 1992: 361). If a black bloc committee would tell Washington's worst racists that they represent ten million votes, he would leap up and welcome them (Haley, 1992: 362). Otherwise he would not survive in office. If that was not so, racist politicians would not fight so hard to keep black men and women from the poles and continue to do so in many states of the Union up to the present. According to Malcolm X, "whenever any group could vote in a bloc, and therefore decide the outcome of elections, and fails to do this, then that group is politically sick" (Haley, 1992: 362). In Malcolm X's view, America's black man, voting as a bloc, could wield an even more powerful force than the Irish Catholics, and so they did when he helped to vote in the first African-American President Obama in 2008. Malcolm X could not witness this great event but he had – like Martin Luther King – contributed to it through his life, work, and martyr death for freedom, equality, and brotherhood.

Malcolm X was keenly aware that U.S. politics was ruled by special interest blocs and lobbies. No interest group needed not only a bloc, but also a lobby more urgently, than the black man. Malcolm X was keenly aware, that U.S. politics was ruled by special interest blocs and lobbies. Malcolm X remembered the labor lobby. It owned one of Washington's largest buildings close to the White House (Haley, 1992: 362). Malcolm X mentioned the Big Oil lobby, which continually got its depletion allowances from Congress. Malcolm knew of the very successful farmer lobby. In Malcolm X's view, the medical doctor lobby was powerful enough to postpone the Medicare program for decades, despite the fact that it was wanted and needed by millions of other people. Malcolm X knew of the Beet Growers' Lobby, the Wheat Lobby, the Cattle Lobby, and the China Lobby (Haley, 1992: 362). There were all the small countries' special interest lobbies. The Government had departments to deal with many of these special interest lobbies. There was a Department of the Interior, in which the Indians, or Native Americans, were included. For Malcolm X, the black man was a much greater problem than farmers, medical doctors, or Indians, and therefore needed their own lobby and their own Pentagon-sized Washington department which would deal with every segment of their problems. According to Malcolm X, in 1964, twenty two million black men had given America four hundred years of free labor and toil (Haley, 1992: 362). They had bled and died in every battle, since the American War of Independence. They were in America before the pilgrims, and long before the mass immigrations of European Americans. But in 1964, they were still at the very bottom of everything, i.e. of the American class system. In Malcolm X's view, the cornerstone of America's operation was economic and political strength. The black man did not have the economic strength yet; it would take time for him to build it. But right now – in 1964 – the American black man had the political strength and power to change his destiny overnight: e.g. through building a skyscraper lobbying building in Washington DC (Waldschmidt-Nelson, 2012; Cone, 1992; Marable, 2011).

Political Organization

For the converted Malcolm X of 1964, the black man and woman needed a political organization in order to form a voting block and a lobby to gain political and economic power. Malcolm X was very much aware that this organization, which he was creating in his mind, had the potential for important change. It was to help "challenge the American black man and woman to fight for their human rights" and to aid in the alleviation of their "mental, spiritual, economic, and political" pathologies (Haley, 1992: 363). Malcolm X started the political organization not only with an idea but also with a concrete plan. The organization, which Malcolm X hoped to build, would differ substantially from the Nation of Islam – which he had left already physically and psychologically – in that it would embrace all religious faiths of black men, and it would carry into practice what the Black Muslims had only preached: it would be ecumenical, and it would solve the very difficult theory-praxis problem (Haley, 1992: 363). The first thing Malcolm X was going to do was to "attract far more willing heads and hands" than his own (Haley, 1992: 363). In 1964, each day more militant-oriented brothers, who had been with him in Mosque Seven in New York, announced their break from the Nation of Islam in order to join his cause. Malcolm X's political organization would not only include the proletarian or precariat class of African Americans, but also the lower and middle – middle class. While the political organization would not adequately engage in the redistribution of wealth among African-Americans, it would, nevertheless, work for equal recognition and respect among all of them. Astonishing numbers of European-Americans called and wrote to Malcolm X and offered contributions to his organization. The European-Americans also asked if they could join the organization. Malcolm answered with a categorical *no*; the organization was to be purely African-American for philosophical reasons. But if the consciences of the European-Americans dictated it, they could financially help the organization and its constructive approach to America's race problem. For his prophetic and uncompromising speech and deeds, Malcolm was invited to many speaking engagements, which he rarely rejected as they were opportunities for him to reach larger audiences. It was startling for Malcolm that an "unusual number of the requests came from groups of white Christian ministers" (Haley, 1992: 364). To be sure, for Malcolm there was not only an untrue, but also a true Christianity in America, and he was willing to ally with it, while he was fighting the untrue Christianity, as well as the untrue Islam. Malcolm announced that he was organizing and heading a new mosque in New York City, known as the *Muslim Mosque Inc* (Haley, 1992: 365). It would give to Malcolm X a religious basis for his political organization and it would provide it with the spiritual motivation necessary to alleviate the vices that destroy the moral adhesives of African-American communities (Haley, 1992: 365).

Malcolm went few places without constant awareness that any number of his former brothers in the Nation of Islam would make heroes of themselves among the Black Muslims if they would kill him (Haley, 1992: 365). Malcolm X also knew how Elijah Muhammad's followers thought. He was their master-teacher before he left the organization. Therefore, he knew that "no person would kill you quicker than a Black Muslim" if he felt that was the will of Allah (Haley, 1992: 365). While Malcolm X wrote his *Autobiography*, he continually had the premonition that he would be murdered before the book appeared. Unfortunately this came to pass. The political organization which Malcolm X wanted to continue to build after his pilgrimage to Mecca was sociologically situated at the fringe of the lifeworld in the American overwhelmingly white action system. From there the political organization was to fight the *colonization* of the life world, which was still characterized by mimetic or communicative rationality and practice, rooted in the human potential of language and memory, and in the evolutionary universal of recognition and respect, which was still mediated through ethical and moral norms: an internal *colonization*, carried out by the economic subsystem, characterized by instrumental rationality and action, rooted in the human potential of work and tool, and mediated through the medium of money, and by the political subsystem, also characterized by functional rationality, but mediated through the medium of power. As Malcolm X's political organization would fight the economic and political *colonization* of the lifeworld in the American action system, it would do that not only in the interest of the African-Americans, but also of the European Americans as well. Malcolm X did not opt for the market economy, or for state socialism, and he did not engage in the infantile disorder of 'vulgar' communism, but rather chose to struggle with his political organization through the democratic channels that already existed in the American federal state. This was as an essential step toward a black revolution. As Hegel, Marx, Bourdieu and Garcia Linera have suggested in their reflections on personality, civil society, class, indigenous identity, state, and history, and their relevance to social struggles, in the united American World, the religious, economic and political pathologies could be healed only through plebeian power, collective action, the indigenous working class, and popular identities.

Pilgrimage

There was one further major preparation for the formation of his political organization that Malcolm X knew he needed to make: the pilgrimage to

Mecca – the origin of true orthodox Islam. Malcolm X was aware, that the pilgrimage to Mecca, known as Hajj, was a religious obligation, one of the Five Pillars, and that every orthodox Muslim fulfilled at least once in their life. Wanting to always know more about his religion, Malcolm had had this pilgrimage to Mecca in his mind for a long time. But it would require money that Malcolm did not have. Now in 1964, Malcolm received the money for the pilgrimage to Mecca from his half-sister Ella in Boston: a strong, big, black, Georgia woman who greatly resembled Malcolm's father Earl (Haley, 1992: 367). She also had left the Nation of Islam. She had studied under orthodox Muslims and founded a school where Arabic was taught (Haley, 1992: 367). She had originally been brought into Islam by her brother Malcolm. Now she financed Malcolm's pilgrimage to Mecca, instead of herself. Malcolm X believed that this was providential; Allah always gave signs to believers when they were with Him, to remind them of his presence (Cone, 1992; Haley, 1992, Marable, 2011). Likewise, for Malcolm X, as for the orthodox Muslims, such as Dr. Mahmoud Youssef Shawarbi, *no man was a Muslim until he wished for his brother what he wished for himself*. Faith in Allah became perfect only through the practice of the *Golden Rule*, which all great world religions have in common (Küng, 1970; Siebert, 2011).

Hospitality

On his way to Cairo, Jeddah, and Mecca, Malcolm X landed with Lufthansa Airlines on the airport of Frankfurt a.M., Germany. He and a brother Muslim had a few hours layover before they would take another plane to Cairo. They decided to go sightseeing in Frankfurt (Haley, 1992: 368). I grew up in Frankfurt and I had experienced in the city the worst kind of racism before, during, and after the *Kristall Nacht* of 1938, when I saw its famous synagogue being burned down and all the Jewish stores on the *Zeil*, the main street, being looted; and when over 30,000 Jews were imprisoned just less than three decades earlier. However, now in the almost rebuilt Frankfurt of 1964, which had been destroyed up to 80% by the American and British air forces, Malcolm X and his Muslim brother were amazed by the friendly hospitality of the Frankfurters (Haley, 1992: 369). People who had never seen Malcolm X and his Muslim brother before, and knew they were strangers, and members of another race, would nevertheless greet them most cordially. In America, so Malcolm remembered, he would walk into a store and spend a hundred dollars and would still be a stranger; this being a part of the condition of economic alienation (Haley, 1992: 369). According to Malcolm X, the Europeans acted more humane. In one little shop in Frankfurt the shopkeeper "leaned over his counter" towards Malcolm X and his Muslim brother and "waved his hand, indicating to the German people passing by outside the store: *This way one day, that way another day*" (Haley, 1992: 369)! Malcolm and his Muslim brother understood what the shopkeeper was indicating: German would rise again (Haley, 1992: 369). The German economic miracle, initiated and supported by the Marshall Plan, had just started to come into its own. The Germans began to forget their racist past and its horrible crimes, or to repress it, and they became more and more unable to mourn, and concentrated more and more their energies on economics and business, and became very successful in doing so (Mitcherlich, 1993; 1994; Kogon, 1965). Malcolm X and his Muslim brother did not have time enough to visit the Institute for Social Research at the Johann Wolfgang Goethe Universität, the so called Frankfurt School, from where came Max Horkheimer and Theodor W. Adorno, Erich Fromm and Herbert Marcuse, who would become the intellectual leaders of the worldwide student movement, and where Angela Davis, the African-American Marxist and activist, would study.

Prayer Ritual

In the Jeddah airport, Malcolm X heard large groups of Muslims chanting a prayer in unison which summed up what true Islam was all about, particularly in differentiation from the untrue nature of Bourgeois Christianity. According to Malcolm X's reading, the core of the prayer was the absolute Oneness of God – *Tawhid* – the belief all three Abrahamic religions, and even the bourgeois deistic enlightenment, have in common. In spite of his great faith in Allah, Malcolm was nervous at Jeddah airport, waiting for having his passport inspected (Haley, 1992: 373–378). He was apprehensive concerning his American passport. He was aware, that he was right at *The Fountain* of the Muslim world. He was handing the Jeddah airport officials his American passport, which "signified the exact opposite of what Islam stands for": the deep antagonism between the American and the Near Eastern World, between West and East, and between nationalism and the internationalism of Islam (Haley, 1992: 373). However, the pilgrimage to Mecca would teach Malcolm that the American value system, rooted in its antagonisms between races and classes, had its limits; it failed to penetrate into the social solidarity that was integral to Islam and the Muslims.

Idealism

In Jeddah, Malcolm X encountered for the first time in his life what is popularly and ironically and sometimes cynically, called *idealism*: namely genuine, practical, religious idealism, closely connected not only with Islam, but also with Judaism and Christianity, as well as with modern, classical, theoretical and practical, transcendental, subjective, objective and absolute idealism, and proletarian idealism. "Nothing in either of [his] two careers as a black man in America had served to give [Malcolm X] any *idealistic* tendencies. [Malcolm X's] instincts automatically examined the reasons, the motives, of any person who did anything they didn't have to do for him. Always in [his] life, if it was any white person, [Malcolm] could see a selfish motive": bourgeois materialism, selfishness, self-interest, egoism, alienation, narcissism, instrumentalization, functionalization, reification, and commodification (Haley, 1992: 383).

Grand Mufti of Jerusalem

One day Malcolm X had the opportunity to meet Hussein Amini, the Grand Mufti of Jerusalem. For Malcolm, the Grand Mufti of Jerusalem was a 'cordial man of great dignity,' who was interested in the divisions between himself and the Nation of Islam (Haley, 1992: 385). Malcolm did not remember that the Grand Mufti's likewise blue-eyed and blond-haired predecessor had been a friend of the blue-eyed Adolf Hitler and that he visited him in Berlin and hoped to find in him an ally against England. The blue-eyed *Führer*, who had refused to shake hands with victorious African athletes during the Olympics in Berlin in 1936, filmed by Leni Riefenstahl, and made into a famous movie named *The Will to Power*, had, nevertheless, a great preference for Islam, because it did not invert the order of the rich and poor classes, and because it did not demand to hold up the other cheek, but affirmed the *lex talionis – eye for eye, tooth for tooth* – and because it still had a concrete, sensuous image of Paradise, or Heaven, in which Huris would be present, and streams of wine would flow. Hitler preferred the Islamic Paradise and rejected the Christian Heaven particularly the even more abstract Protestant Heaven, in which he supposedly was to sing eternally Alleluia, after throughout his life he had listened and played the beautiful music of Richard Wagner.

To be sure, Hitler was like, according to the Roman historian Tacitus, the Germanic tribes men who were *securi adversus deos*, and like, according to Hegel's *Philosophy of History*, the whole modern enlightenment *securus adversus Deum*: without any fear of God, which would have been the beginning of all wisdom according to the Jewish Religion of Sublimity, the Christian Religion of Freedom, and the Islamic Religion of Law (Hegel, 1986; Hitler, 1943). Hitler would not have minded if Europe had become Islamic rather than Christian (Hitler, 1943). With his great philosopher Arthur Schopenhauer,

Hitler considered Judaism to be a lie. The baptized Catholic, friend of priests, partner to the Empire Concordat, employer of army chaplains, and of nuns as nurses in his field hospitals, Hitler, nevertheless, considered a Christianity to be the source of the Roman and the Russian *atheistic bolshevism*, which he now fought at the Eastern Front with 3 million soldiers from all over Europe, most of them baptized Christians, who would kill 27 million so called Slavs and communists, and 6 million Jews. For Hitler, the Grand Mufti of Jerusalem was a principle actor in the Near East. In the realm of politics, he was seen as a realist rather than a dreamer. With his blond hair and blue eyes, the Grand Mufti gave Hitler the impression that he was, despite of his sharp and mouselike countenance, a man with more than one Aryan among his ancestors, and one who may well have descended from the best Roman stock. In conversation with Hitler, the Grand Mufti showed himself to be a pre-eminently sly old fox. When the Grand Mufti spoke, he weighed each word very carefully. According to Hitler, the Grand Mufti's quite exceptional wisdom put him almost on equal terms with the Japanese, who were supposedly almost on equal terms with the Germans, and the Aryans. In Malcolm X's view, informed and inspired by the new Grand Mufti of Jerusalem, with the kind of "racism plaguing America like an incurable cancer, the so-called 'Christian' white American heart should be more receptive to the proven Islamic solution," and accept the Oneness of God and the reality of the Oneness of Man, 'to such a destructive problem' as racism (Haley, 1992: 392). Perhaps Islam could rescue America from imminent disaster brought on by the same racism which eventually destroyed the Germans themselves (Haley, 1992: 392).

Hitler wanted to produce the final solution of the religious problem in his retirement, after the end of the War. But – against his philosopher Schopenhauer's advice – Hitler committed suicide before the war ended, in the hope for the Hindu migration of the soul: *nemesis* met *hubris*.

Civil Rights Act

Three years after Malcolm X's assassination, the American Congress responded to the riots of 1967 by passing the Civil Rights Act of 1968. By doing so, the Federal State interfered into the racial and class antagonisms of civil society. The Civil Rights Act was supposed to make stronger the laws prohibiting violence against African-Americans. One section actually increased the penalties against those European-Americans who would deprive African-Americans of their human and civil rights. However, the Civil Rights Act also said that the provisions of this same section would not apply to acts, or omissions, on the part of law enforcement officers, members of the National Guard, or members of the Armed forces of the United States, who were engaged in suppressing a riot or civil disturbance. Furthermore, the Civil Rights Act of 1968 added another section. It was agreed to by liberal members of Congress, in order to get the whole bill passed. The new section provided up to five years in prison for anyone travelling interstate or using interstate facilities, including mail and telephone, in order to organize, promote, encourage, participate in, or carry on a riot. The new section defined a riot as an action by three or more people which involve threats of violence. The first person prosecuted under the Civil Rights act of 1968 was a young black leader of SNCC, H. Rap Brown, who had made a militant angry speech in Maryland, just before a racial disturbance there. At the time, I was teaching about the events at Loyola College, in Baltimore, Maryland. Later on, the Civil Rights Act was used against Anti-Vietnam War demonstrators in Chicago – the *Chicago Eight* – one of whom, Tom Hayden, is still active today in matters of social justice. Around the same time I accumulated a large police file under the Civil Rights Act (Bonfiglio, 2005). To be sure, despite of all the heroic martyrs of freedom, like Malcolm X and Martin Luther King, John and Robert Kennedy, etc., their confessions and witnesses, no violent or non-violent, black or white, revolution (or better still *pro-volution*), took place in American civil society or in liberal state in the 1960's. President Nixon's and President Reagan's neo-liberal counter-revolution became victorious over Adorno's, Marcuse's, Fromm's and Habermas' humanist-socialist revolution or *pro-volution* at home and abroad. Post-modern alternative Future III – the reconciliation of the races and the classes through emancipation remained a distant goal in the American, European, and now also Slavic icy cold commodity exchange societies. Without doubt, the Civil Rights Act improved the situation of the African-American population to some extent, and thus re-stabilized American civil society. However, this re-stabilization and improvement also helped to prevent rather than promote the black or white revolution, or *pro-volution*, for the time being, and the eradication of the root causes of the present chronic race and class-conflicts at home and abroad.

Poor Peoples' Encampment

Like Malcolm X years earlier, so in spring of 1968 Martin Luther King became more concerned with problems untouched by civil rights laws: problems coming out of poverty shared by African-Americans as well as by many European-Americans, i.e. class problems rather than race problems (King, 1963a-b; 1967; 1986; Cone, 1992). Martin Luther King also began to speak out – against the advice of some African-American leaders who feared losing friends in the Washington political establishment – against the War in Vietnam: against a finally victorious communist movement and revolution; against French and American colonialism; against a Catholic fascist dictator, Diem, who had studied in Lansing, Michigan; and against mass poverty in the country (King, 1963a-b; 1967; 1986; Waldschmidt-Nelson, 2012; Cone, 1992). Dr. King most prophetically connected war and poverty. According to Martin Luther King, it was inevitable that he and the black leadership had to bring out the question of the tragic mix-up in priorities in the American federal state. In the present Vietnam War, the American government was spending all this money for death and destruction and not nearly enough for life and constructive development. When the guns of war became a national obsession, social needs inevitably suffered. Of course, Dr. King could not speak about war and poverty without speaking directly or indirectly about capitalism. As Malcolm X before, Martin Luther King now became a chief target of the FBI and the national security state, which tapped his private phone conversations long before that became customary for average citizens after the catastrophe of September 11, 2001. They sent him fake letters; threatened him; blackmailed him; and even once suggested in an anonymous letter, that he, the Christian minister, commit suicide (King, 1963a-b; 1967; 1986; Waldschmidt-Nelson, 2012; Cone, 1992). FBI internal memos discussed finding a black leader to replace Dr. King. A U.S. Senate report on the FBI said in 1976 that it tried to destroy Dr. Martin Luther King. The FBI had tried to do that to Malcolm X as well. As a result of their opposition to the humane vision forwarded by these two most courageous leaders, some force within the security state succeeded in destroying both martyrs of freedom. Without doubt, Dr. King was, like Malcolm X before, turning his attention to troublesome social questions and problems: from the race struggle to class struggle. However, Martin Luther King still insisted up to his violent death on non-violence as the most adequate method to resolve social problems. As such, Dr. King thought that riots were self-defeating. However, they did, nevertheless, express a deep feeling of discontent among the African-American poor which could not be ignored. Thus, according to Martin Luther King, non-violence had to be militant, massive, but still non-violence. Thus, Dr. King planned a *Poor Peoples' Encampment* in Washington D.C. (King, 1963a-b; 1967; 1986; Waldschmidt-Nelson, 2012; Cone, 1992). This time it was to happen without the paternal and manipulative approval of the President. Obviously, Dr. King had heard Malcolm X's critique in Harlem of the march on Washington. Malcolm X would probably have agreed with the new project against poverty, at least to some extent. Thus, Martin Luther King went to Memphis, Tennessee, in order to support a strike of black and white sanitation workers in that city. There, standing on the balcony outside his hotel room, Dr. King was shot to death by an unseen marksman (King, 1963a-b; 1967; 1986; Waldschmidt-Nelson, 2012; Cone, 1992). The *Poor Peoples' Encampment* went on, nevertheless. But it was broken up by police action, like the World War I Veterans' Bonus Army of 1932 was dispersed and driven out of Washington by the Generals Marshall and Eisenhower, who, nevertheless, after World War II initiated the GI Bill: they had learned from history. The murder of King, like that of Malcolm X before, brought new urban outbreaks of riots and violence all over the country. Thirty-nine people were killed; thirty-five of the victims were African-Americans. At the same time, evidence was piling up that even with all of the civil rights laws which were promulgated and were now on the books, the courts would not sufficiently protect African-Americans against violence and injustice. This situation continues to prevail today – in 2014 – in American civil society and elsewhere. It will probably take more than human and civil rights legislation, symbolical poor peoples' marches and encampments, and even more than the great martyrs of freedom, like Malcolm X, and Martin Luther King, and the Kennedy family, in order to change the race and class system of the affluent capitalist society, so that poverty in all its terrible, murderous forms may be conquered, as far as humanly possible toward post-modern alternative Future III: the realm of the brotherhood, equality, and freedom of All on the basis of the realm of natural and economic necessity. Alternative Future III remains valid for all martyrs of freedom; for the Muslim Malcolm X and the Christian Martin Luther King, and for all martyrs of freedom. The very Jewish *Revelation states,*

> When he (Messiah) broke the fifth seal, I (John) saw underneath the altar the souls of all the people who had been killed on account of the word of God, for witnessing to it. They shouted aloud, "Holy, faithful Master, how much longer will you wait before you pass sentence and take vengeance for our death on the inhabitants of the earth?" Each of them was given a white robe, and they were told to be patient a little longer, until the roll was completed and their fellow servants and brothers had been killed just as they had been.
>
> In my vision, when he (the Jesus – Messiah) broke the sixth seal there was a violent earthquake... Then all the earthly rulers, the governors and the commanders, the rich people and the men of influence, the whole population, slaves and citizens, took to the mountains to hide in caves and among the rocks. They said to the mountains and the rocks,' Fall on us and hide us away from the One who sits on the throne and from the anger of the Lamb (Messiah). For the Great Day of his anger has come, and who can survive it?

......and the One (God) who sits on the throne will spread his tent over them. They will never hunger or thirst again; neither the sun nor scorching wind will ever plague them, because the Lamb (Messiah) who is at the throne will be their shepherd and will lead them to springs of living water; and God will wipe away all tears from their eyes.

REVELATION 6: 9–17; 7: 15–17; 18–22

Dies Irae! Dies Illa! Believers and enlighteners are united in their longing and hope for the imageless and nameless utterly Other than the horror and terror of nature and history, the Negation of all negativities, including the racial and class antagonisms, Perfect Justice and Unconditional Love, and in their firm expectation, that history remain open, and that the murderer shall not triumph over his innocent victim, at least not ultimately.

Bibliography

Adorno, Theodor W. *Minima Moralia*. Frankfurt a.M.: Suhrkamp Verlag, 1951.

Benjamin, Walter. *Illuminations*. New York: Schocken Books, 1968.

Bonfiglio, Olga. *Heroes of a Different Stripe: How One Town Responded to the War in Iraq*. Kalamazoo, MI: Fidlar Doubleday Inc., 2005.

Breitman, George. *The Last Year of Malcolm X. The Evolution of a Revolutionary*. New York: Pathfinder, 1990.

Chaichian, Muhammad A. *Empires and Walls: Globalization, Migration and Colonial Domination*. Chicago: Haymarket Books, 2014.

Cone, James H. *Martin and Malcolm and America: A Dream or a Nightmare*. Maryknoll, New York: Orbis Books, 1992.

Dyson, Michael Eric. *I May Not Get There with You: The True Martin Luther King Jr*. New York: A Touchstone Book, 2000.

——— *April 4, 1968: Martin Luther King, Junior's Death and How it Changed America*. New York: Perseus Book Group, 2008.

Haley, Alex. *The Autobiography of Malcolm X*. New York: Grove Press, 1992.

Hedges, Chris. *War is a force that gives us meaning*. New York: Anchor Books, 2003.

——— *American Fascists: The Christian Right and the War on America*. New York: Free Press, 2006.

Hedges, Chris and Laila Al-Arian. *Collateral Damage: America's War against Iraqi Civilians*. New York: Nation Books, 2008.

Hegel, Georg W.F. *Frühe Schriften*. Frankfurt a. M.: Suhrkamp Verlag, 1986a.

——— *Phänomenologie des Geistes*. Frankfurt a. M.: Suhrkamp Verlag, 1986b.

——— *Grundlinien der Philosophie des Rechts oder Naturrecht und Staatswissenschaft im Grundriss*. Frankfurt a. M.: Suhrkamp Verlag, 1986c.

―――― *Vorlesungen über die Philosophie der Geschichte*. Frankfurt a. M.: Suhrkamp Verlag, 1986d l.

―――― *Vorlesungen über die Philosophie der Religion I & II*. Frankfurt a. M.: Suhrkamp Verlag, 1986e.

Hitler, Adolf. *Mein Kampf*. Boston: Houghton Mifflin Company, 1943.

―――― *Hitler's Secret Book*. Translated by Salvator Attanasio. New York: Grove Press, 1986.

Horkheimer, Max. "Bemerkungen über Wissenschaft und Krise." In *Zeitschrift für Sozialforschung*, München: Kösel-Verlag, 1970a.

―――― "Geschichte und Psychologie." In *Mitteilungen des Instituts für Sozialforschung*. München: Kösel-Verlag, 1970b.

―――― *Kritische Theorie: Eine Dokumentation*. Frankfurt a. M.: Fischer Bücherei, 1970c.

―――― *Die Sehnsucht nach dem ganz Anderen. Ein Interview mit Kommentar von Helmut Gumnior*. Hamburg: Furche Verlag, 1970d.

―――― *Critique of Instrumental Reason*. New York: The Seabury Press, 1974a.

―――― *Eclipse of Reason*. New York: The Seabury Press, 1974b.

―――― *Notizen 1950 bis 1969 und Dämmerung: Notizen in Deutschland*. Frankfurt a. M.: Fischer Verlag, 1974c.

―――― *Vorträge und Aufzeichnungen: 1949–1973*. Frankfurt a. M.: Fischer Taschenbuch Verlag, 1985g.

Horkheimer, Max and Theodor W. Adorno. "Vorurteil und Charakter." *Frankfurter Hefte: Zeitschrift für Kultur und Politik* 7, no. 4 (1951):284–291.

Kennedy, Robert. *Auf der Suche nach einer neuen Welt*. Gütersloh, 1968.

King, Martin Luther. *Why We Can't Wait*. New York: New American Library, 1963a.

―――― *Strength to Love*. Minneapolis, MN: Fortress Press, 1963b.

―――― *Where do we go from here? Chaos or Community*. Boston: Beacon Press, 1967.

―――― *A Testament of Hope. The Essential Ways and Speeches of Martin Luther King*. Edited by James M. Washington. New York: Harper Collins, 1986.

Kershaw, Ian. *Hitler. 1889–1936 Hubris*. New York: W. W. Norton and Company, 1999.

―――― *Hitler 1936–1945 Nemesis*. New York: W.W. Norton and Company, 2000.

Kogon, Eugen. *Der SS – Staat. Das System der Deutschen Konzentrationslager*. Frankfurt a. M.: Europäische Verlag, 1965.

Küng, Hans. *Menschwerdung Gottes: Eine Einführung in Hegel's Theologisches Denken als Prolegomena zu einer künftigen Christologie*. Freiburg: Herder Verlag, 1970.

―――― *World Religions: Universal Peace: Global Ethic*. Tübingen: Foundation Global Ethic, 1991a. www.weltethos.org/pdf_dat/ausstellung_eng. pdf.

―――― *Das Judentum*. München: Piper Verlag, 1991b.

―――― *Das Christentum: Wesen und Geschichte*. München: Piper Verlag, 1994a.

―――― *Grosse Christliche Denker*. München: Piper Verlag, 1994b.

―――― *The Catholic Church: A Short History*. New York: The Modern Library, 2003.

―――― *Der Islam. Geschichte, Gegenwart, Zukunft*. München: Piper Verlag, 2004.

―― *Jesus*. München: Piper Verlag, 2012.
Lenin, Vladimir I. *Left-Wing Communism: An Infantile Disorder*. Chicago: Haymarket Books, 2014.
Malcolm X. *Malcolm X speaks*. New York: Meret, 1965.
Marable, Manning. *Malcolm X: A Life of Reinvention*. New York: Viking, 2011.
Marx, Karl and Friedrich Engels. *Ausgewählte Schriften,* (Band I). Berlin: Dietz Verlag, 1953a.
―― *Ausgewählte Schriften, Band II*. Berlin: Dietz Verlag, 1953b.
―― *Die Heilige Familie und andere Philosophische Frühschriften*. Berlin: Dietz Verlag, 1953c.
Mercieca Charles. "Great Food for Thought." Personal email from mercieca@knology.net August 11, 2014.
―― "Practical Solution to the Middle East Conflict." Personal email from mercieca@knology.net August 10, 2014b.
Mitscherlich, Margarete. *Erinnerungsarbeit. Zur Psychoanalyse der Unfähigkeit zu trauern*. Frankfurt a. M.: Fischer Verlag, 1993.
―― *Über die Mühsal der Emanzipation. Die Frau in der Gesellschaft*. Frankfurt a. M.: Fischer Verlag, 1994.
Schlesinger, Arthur. *The Age of Jackson*. New York: Little and Brown, 1945.
―― *A Thousand Days*. New York: Houghton Mifflin, 1965.
Siebert, Rudolf, J. *Manifesto of the Critical Theory of Society and Religion: The Wholly Other, Liberation, Happiness and the Rescue of the Hopeless*. Leiden: Brill Publisher (Vol. 1–3), 2010.
―― *The World Religions in the Global Public Sphere: Towards Concrete Freedom and Material Democracy*. New Delhi: Sanbun, 2013.
―― *Early Critical Theory of Religion: The Island of Happiness*. New Delhi: Sanbun Publisher, 2014.
Siebert, Rudolf J. and Michael R. Ott and Dustin J. Byrd. "The Critical Theory of Religion: From Having to Being." *Critical Research on Religion* 1, no. 1 (2013).
Tillich, Paul. *Systematic Theology: Volume 3*. Chicago: The University of Chicago Press, 1963a.
―― *Morality and Beyond*. New York: Harper and Row, 1963b.
―― *On the Boundary*. New York: Charles Scribner's Sons, 1966.
―― *The Courage to Be*. New Haven, CT: Yale University Press, 1972.
―― *The Socialist Decision*. New York: Harper and Row, 1977.
Waldschmidt-Nelson, Britta. *Dreams and Nightmares: Martin Luther King Jr., Malcolm X and the Struggle for Black Equality in America*. Gainesville: University Press of Florida, 2012.

CHAPTER 7

"The Enemy of My Enemy": Malcolm X and the Legacy of John Brown

Louis A. DeCaro, Jr.

Allies, Not Brothers

In recent years it has become somewhat fashionable to cite Malcolm X as an admirer of John Brown the controversial 19th century abolitionist, particularly by those who have advanced the latter as a forerunner of the contemporary black struggle for freedom or an example of black-white unity. Perhaps the most notable in this regard is David Reynolds's *John Brown Abolitionist* (2005), who mentions Malcolm X several times in conjunction with the militant black struggle. In his proposal that Brown seeded the Civil Rights movement, Reynolds points out that some of Brown's Harper's Ferry raiders had envisioned a revolutionary black state and even contrived a logo of a black warrior bearing a sword. Reynolds writes: "To make an angry, armed black man the state symbol was more than daring or progressive; it was revolutionary. It looked forward not to liberal legislation but to militant pronouncements by the likes of Robert F. Williams and Malcolm X" (Reynolds, 2005: 247). Reynolds also quotes Malcolm referring to John Brown in January 1965, although he uses only the brief excerpt of Malcolm's words quoted by Benjamin Quarles in *Blacks on John Brown* (1972): "I don't go for non-violent white liberals. If you are for me and my problems – when I say me I mean us, our people – then you have to be willing to do as old John Brown did" (Reynolds, 2005: 498; Quarles, 2001: 107).[1]

As the first to prepare a full-fledged biography of Brown in the 21st century, perhaps I must also bear some of the responsibility for promoting the Malcolm-Brown theme, which at times has been taken too far. On the dust jacket of my book, *"Fire from the Midst of You": A Religious Life of John Brown* (2002), it is stated that Malcolm called Brown "a real white liberal" – really an editorial error since Malcolm's actual phrasing was simply "a white liberal." However, when I was writing *"Fire from the Midst of You,"* I was still quite mindful of Malcolm since this was the first major point of transition in my biographical

---

1 Reynolds quotes from Benjamin Quarles, *Blacks on John Brown* (1972), reprinted with his other monumental work, *Allies for Freedom* (1974) as *Allies for Freedom & Blacks on John Brown*, New York DaCapo Press, 2001.

labors from the Muslim activist to the Christian abolitionist. Although I did not make some of the explicit claims that Reynolds does in his preeminent work, perhaps my biography is equally graphic in illustrating the extent to which Brown himself was both involved with and committed to black people. This was what I had in mind in my introduction, where I quote Malcolm's words before his Organization of Afro-American Unity (OAAU) in New York City on July 5, 1964,

> You know what John Brown did? He went to war. He was a white man who went to war against white people to help free slaves. White people call John Brown a nut. Go read the history, go read what all of them say about John Brown. They're trying to make it look like he was a nut, a fanatic. They made a movie on it, I saw movie on the screen one night. Why, I would be afraid to get near John Brown if I go by what other white folks say about him. But they depict him in this image because he was willing to shed blood to free the slaves. And any white man who is ready and willing to shed blood for your freedom – in the sight of other whites, he's nuts... So when you want to know good white folks in history where black people are concerned, go read the history of John Brown. That was what I call a white liberal. But those other kind, they are questionable.
> MALCOLM X, 1970: 81–82

Although there is undoubted appreciation for Brown in Malcolm's public expressions, I have come to reflect somewhat differently upon his intentions in such remarks. Certainly, it is incorrect to portray Malcolm's words as being a reference to Brown's strategic value to black resistance. Reynolds is mistaken in concluding that Malcolm X believed Brown's "violent response to injustice was a paradigm modern blacks must follow" (Reynolds, 2005: 498). Quite to the contrary, Malcolm X never used John Brown's militant example as a paradigm for blacks, but rather as a challenge to white liberals. This would have been clearer had closer attention been paid to the context of Malcolm's words as found in the edited transcription by George Breitman in his essential collection, *Malcolm X Speaks*. In fact, this reference to Brown was made during a post-speech question-and-answer session before the Militant Labor Forum, a socialist group, on January 7, 1965. "There are many white people in this country," Malcolm declared, "especially the younger generation," who had come to realize that the injustices committed against black people would result in negative consequences for whites, "the chickens coming home to roost eventually." Malcolm continued that even if these whites were not morally motivated, at least intelligence "obligated them to see that something had to be done," and many would be willing to involve themselves in militancy. Then, to the point, Malcolm added,

> For one, when a white man comes to me and tells me how liberal he is, the first thing I want to know, is he a nonviolent liberal, or the other kind. I don't go for any nonviolent white liberals. If you are for me and my problems – when I say me, I mean us, our people – then you have to be willing to do as old John Brown did. And if you're not of the John Brown school of liberals, we'll get you later – later.
> MALCOLM X, 1970: 224–225

It is important to point out that Malcolm was speaking to a largely white leftist group in criticism of the prominent 'nonviolent resistance' philosophy of the Civil Rights movement. His point was to challenge white 'nonviolent resistance' as the best means of supporting the black struggle. As far as black resistance was concerned, however, Malcolm did not derive any ideology or example from white radicals like Brown. For this theme he always drew from the context of black resistance. Historically speaking, Malcolm would have preferred Toussaint L'Ouverture, Nat Turner, Denmark Vesey, and other militant black freedom fighters, most of whose strategies actually were far more 'violent' than John Brown's actual conduct at Harper's Ferry.

As I have shown elsewhere, Brown's intentions in his 1859 invasion of Virginia were not insurrectionary, as he was charged by the slaveholders' court that condemned him to death. Rather, Brown intended his assault on the Virginia armory as a kind of armed demonstration whereby he fought only defensively while leading off as many enslaved people as possible into the mountains of the South (DeCaro, 2015: 54–57). Notwithstanding history and its lessons, Malcolm X was much more focused on contemporary black liberation movements in presenting a 'violent' paradigm for black people – often using anticolonialist movements from his own era as examples of black resistance, such as the Mau Mau of Kenya. So the point of Malcolm's public references to 'the John Brown school' was for the sake of white liberals, whom he believed to have been misled by the nonviolent philosophy espoused by Martin Luther King Jr. and the other Civil Rights leaders.

Closely related to the first error is the mistaken notion that Malcolm X openly exalted Brown for the sake of praising him as a good white man. As noted above in the quote from July 5, 1964, Malcolm had a specific reason for highlighting the white abolitionist. Besides using him as a historical lesson for white liberals, he specifically mentioned him with the intention of setting a standard or high bar for racial rapprochement. In other words, Malcolm understood precisely the danger of praising John Brown too much, believing that the psychology of the white liberal would allow him to find 'racial' consolation and affirmation in his words, while yet obfuscating the political realities that demanded a white militant revolt against white supremacy.

One of the most powerful aspects of Malcolm's role in his generation was his ability to articulate the unbridled indignation of the black community in terms both clear and 'intelligent,' a term that he stressed in his discourse. As such, Malcolm's criticisms were upsetting to white and black liberals alike. As far as whites were concerned, however, his impact elicited two responses: either vociferous denial of his claims and countercharges of hatemongering, or a kind of frustrated yearning to win his approval and prove themselves 'good whites.' The famous scene of Malcolm spurning the appeals of a white college woman is preserved in both his autobiography and the movie based upon it, although it is often only remembered as a point of Malcolm's regret in retrospect (Malcolm X, 1965: 286). However, she was among many young whites who found Malcolm both magnetic and convicting, and who doubtless wished they could prove to him that they were different from the rest of white society.

The white journalist George Plimpton, who had a rigorous interview with Malcolm in 1964, similarly wanted to prove himself a 'good white man' to the Muslim activist, somewhat inadvertently revealing these feelings in a piece he did for *Harper's Magazine*. Following his interview with Malcolm at the Hampton House Hotel in Miami, Plimpton wrote, he had chanced to meet Richard 'Night Train' Lane of the Detroit Lions. Plimpton wrote that he shouted so warmly in greeting Lane that he startled the football player – an overcompensation that apparently was spurred by Plimpton's private hopes that Malcolm X had somehow seen that he had black friends (Plimpton, 1964: 59).[2] It is amazing today to think that one man had such evident impact upon his generation; it was one of his marks as a cultural prophet, not unlike the kind of moral influence that John Brown brought to bear upon his own generation, even as a doomed prisoner of Virginia in 1859.

One should recall likewise how white liberals were so hopeful at the time of Malcolm's famous hajj, or pilgrimage, to Mecca in the spring of 1964. Recall that his letters to white associates in the United States made quite a splash in the press, especially when journalist M.S. 'Mike' Handler published them

---

2 Plimpton interviewed Malcolm on or about February 25, 1964, toward the end of Malcolm's alleged ninety-day silencing by Elijah Muhammad of the Nation of Islam. Of course, by this time Muhammad had no intention of restoring Malcolm to active duty, and Malcolm was violating the silencing by giving the interview.

in *The New York Times*.³ Malcolm's famous letters to Handler, describing his fellowship with blue-eyed, blond-haired Muslims really excited white liberals back in the United States, all of which were hoping that the Muslim leader had finally 'changed.' This showed no small measure of narcissism, since they assumed that it was Malcolm who had needed to change instead of white society.

Observing that Malcolm did renounce the 'Black Muslim' view of white people as devils, Peter Goldman writes that he had even "squared with his conscience the uncomfortable fact that there were possibly a half-dozen or so white journalists and a generation of white college kids that he actually rather liked." Still, Mecca had not 'changed' Malcolm's politics or conviction, Goldman concludes. After his pilgrimage, Malcolm perceived that "white people were evil *de facto* rather than *de jure*." Now, "whites were merely his enemy." Malcolm himself renounced any notion that he had changed as a result of his conversion to traditional Islam: "There has been no metamorphosis. Travel broadens your scope… I think that my scope was broadened sufficiently to enable me to work with anybody for a solution to the problem" (Goldman, 1973: 171–172; DeCaro, 1995: 250).⁴ In other words, the fact that individual whites like John Brown might yet prove to be allies did not mitigate the fact that white society as a whole remained inimical toward black freedom in Malcolm's understanding. Under such circumstances, he naturally did not want his words about Brown to be misconstrued by whites either as conciliatory or consolation before they had properly demonstrated the same radical commitment to black liberation that they would express for their own freedom.

This is further clarified in the question-and-answer session that followed Malcolm's speech before the OAAU, an all-black organization, on July 5, 1964. According to the transcript published by George Breitman, one person in the audience raised a question prompted by Malcolm's remarks on Brown in the same speech. Malcolm responded,

> Brother, yes, I understand what you're saying, I think. There's an old African proverb which I find most enlightening, which says that the enemy of my enemy is my friend. … This doesn't mean that you always trust your allies. But as long as they want to ally themselves against the same one that you're fighting against, attach them and let them go ahead and fight against it.
> MALCOLM X, 1970: 97–98

---

3   A sampling of Malcolm's hajj letters is found in *Malcolm X Speaks*, 58–60.
4   Malcolm X, telephone interview with Art Sears, May 26, 1964.

The point of Malcolm's words in relation to Brown is that the abolitionist was not so much to be viewed as a beloved friend and brother, but rather as the enemy of black people's enemy. As such, John Brown's political offspring could be provisionally embraced as an allies, but only as long as they took his struggle to the point of militancy. This was underscored in Malcolm's answer to a second question relating directly to the abolitionist: "Brother teacher, must we utilize John Brown as a friend of the black man?" Malcolm's response is revealing: "No, I don't say he was a friend of the black man. I use it to give you an example of how to test the white man who says he's your friend. Let him go down with some action similar to John Brown's. If he's willing to die for you and all of that, then let him go ahead and do it" (Malcolm X, 1970: 97–98).

Writing in the 1970's, Benjamin Quarles read these words somewhat critically, concluding that "from the black militant's point of view, even if an unusual white warranted absolution, he could hardly be worthy of commendation by blacks, such an accolade being reserved exclusively for their own" (Quarles, 2001: 196–197). To what degree Quarles was correct in assessing Malcolm's words is a question open to discussion, although it seems the leader's statements must be properly contextualized as political rhetoric. This was certainly the case when asked by a reporter if whites could join his newly founded OAAU. "If John Brown were alive," Malcolm replied, "maybe him" (Alex Haley in Malcolm X, 1965: 416).

As a black revolutionary ideologue, Malcolm X was critical of both white supremacy and conformist nonviolent strategies that he perceived as undermining black liberation. He was well aware that declaring a posthumous alliance with John Brown was a kind of finger in the eye of white supremacy. Yet it seems that Malcolm's real motivation for invoking Brown at that moment was more or less a swipe at nonviolent white liberals. Yet it would be an error to conclude that these public comments represent the fullest scope of Malcolm's personal historical and political reading of the Old Man of Harper's Ferry.

"Somewhere I Have Read"

Unlike black scholars such as Vincent Harding, who has dismissed Brown as a condescending paternalist, or James Smalls, who has castigated him quite harshly as a racial hypocrite, Malcolm X suffered from neither Harding's political parochialism nor Smalls' debilitating prejudice.[5] And while there is no

---

5 In his memorable narrative of the black struggle against slavery, Harding completely misreads John Brown as a rebel "with a strong streak of paternalism" rather than "an exemplary

substantial historical evidence of Malcolm's personal thoughts on John Brown, there are some interesting points that may at least convey a context for understanding Malcolm's personal appreciation for the radical abolitionist.

The logical starting point is to discern Malcolm's background as the son of activists in the Universal Negro Improvement Association (UNIA) of Marcus Garvey. As I have discussed elsewhere, Malcolm's parents, Earl and Louise Little were devout Garveyites (DeCaro, 1995: 67–68). Having been reared in a Garveyite home, it is reasonable to assume that Malcolm and the rest of his siblings absorbed a political and historical view of the United States that entailed a favorable assessment of John Brown vis-à-vis the teachings of Marcus Garvey. Garveyite authority Tony Martin writes that the Caribbean Black Nationalist leader "often had a good word for historical figures such as John Brown, Elijah Lovejoy, and others of abolitionist inclination" (Martin, 1976: 31). While this is not precise historical evidence, it is arguably strong in favor of a positive sentiment toward Brown being seeded in Malcolm's early life and thinking.

I have argued likewise that Malcolm's political and social understanding was far more mature and sophisticated in his youth than he portrays in his famous autobiography. We must remember that *The Autobiography of Malcolm X* originally was undertaken to glorify Elijah Muhammad at a point when Malcolm felt his security in the "Black Muslim" movement slipping away. Malcolm acknowledged the role of his parents, but he tended to attribute his political, social, and spiritual redemption almost exclusively to Elijah Muhammad. In fact, even as a Harlem hustler, Malcolm had not forgotten his Garveyite sensibilities, nor his early home training as a reader and observer of white society (DeCaro, 1995: 63–64).

To no surprise, shortly after his incarceration in the Massachusetts prison system in the 1940's, he was already taking classes and reading extensively at the time he was 'saved' by Elijah Muhammad's cultic message. While there is no doubt that Muhammad's 'Muslim' movement gave Malcolm his raison d'être for many years, it is important to acknowledge that actually he brought a

---

white hero of the struggle for black freedom." My sense is that Harding was misinformed about Brown when he wrote his book; furthermore, given his personal history as a non-violent civil rights activist, he may also have an ideological bias against Brown. See Vincent Harding, *There is a River: The Black Struggle for Freedom in America* (New York: Vintage, 1981, 1983), 206. James Smalls (whose reputation as a great scholar in the Harlem community is perhaps exaggerated) is even more dismissive of Brown. In a New York City cable television interview on "The Gilchrist Experience" (originally recorded in 2000), Smalls seemed to be guided more by resentment than scholarly understanding. See "History Black and Blurred: John Brown and Malcolm X According to James Smalls" (8 February 2007), in *John Brown the Abolitionist: A Biographer's Blog* (http://goo.gl/2kJu9t).

good deal more understanding and insight concerning black history and Black Nationalism into Muhammad's Nation of Islam than he acknowledged in his autobiography. Even his famously portrayed 'discovery' of the dictionary is a stylization, since his mother had trained him and his siblings always to look up words in the dictionary, and this gave him the initial impetus for research in the prison library (DeCaro, 1995: 63, 78–79; DeCaro, 1998: 74).

In discussing his extensive readings in the Norfolk Prison Colony's library, Malcolm afterward devoted several pages recounting the books he had read and the critical reflections on history related to them, from linguistics to religion, and from ancient history to the history of slavery in the United States. "I never will forget how shocked I was when I began reading about slavery's total horror," he wrote (Malcolm X, 1965: 175). Interestingly, Malcolm had access to the Parkhurst Collection, a vast library particularly inclusive of history and religious texts, donated to the prison and richly endowed with 19th century abolitionist materials, including anti-slavery pamphlets and books.

In this light, Lewis Parkhurst is an important figure to understand. Born in 1856, he was a successful New England Unitarian and Republican who served as a bank president, secondary school principal, and as a trustee of Dartmouth College (a building on the Dartmouth campus bears his name), where Malcolm would make a notable speech in 1965. Parkhurst likewise served in the Massachusetts State Legislature in the early 20th century and was an executive in a number of publishing companies, especially Ginn & Company in Boston (Catalogue of the Delta Kappa Epsilon Fraternity, 1910: 632; Parker, 1906: 584). Given his religious, social, and political roots, Parkhurst would quite likely have held Brown in high esteem and included all of the notable works on the abolitionist from the 19th and early 20th centuries.

Parkhurst's massive library probably had been donated sometime before Malcolm arrived at Norfolk, although there were still unopened crates of books during his time of incarceration. He specifically recalled that the Parkhurst collection included a significant portion of anti-slavery literature, including abolitionist pamphlets. He specifically mentions having read Harriet Beecher Stowe's *Uncle Tom's Cabin*, the writings of Frederick Law Olmstead – probably *The Cotton Kingdom: A Traveller's Observations on Cotton and Slavery in the American Slave States* (1862), and Frances 'Fanny' Kemble's *Journal of A Residence on a Georgian Plantation in 1838–1839* (1863). These works horrified him as he read about the realities of chattel slavery in the antebellum era. To no surprise, Malcolm mentioned both Nat Turner's revolt and John Brown's raid in his autobiography, but it is Turner that receives the priority: the black rebel was the antidote to what he calls the 'pie-in-the-sky and non-violent' message so prevalent in the black community (Malcolm X, 1965: 175–176).

In the same context, Malcolm likewise wrote: "Somewhere I have read where Nat Turner's example is said to have inspired John Brown to invade Virginia and attack Harper's Ferry nearly thirty years later, with thirteen white men and five Negroes" (Malcolm X, 1965: 176). Contrary to the portrayal by David Reynolds, Malcolm saw Nat Turner as the archetype and John Brown as the derivative. To put it another way, without diminishing the importance of Brown in the broader context of United States history, Brown is a figure complementary to – not a personification of – the militant black struggle.

Without setting aside Reynolds' thesis that John Brown seeded the Civil Rights movement, nevertheless this observation bears correction. Despite Brown's apparent attraction to and friendly rapport with the forerunners of black militancy in the 19th century, he was himself seeded by black resistance, not the other way around. This explains to some degree why the first intention of W.E.B. DuBois in the early 1900s actually was to write a biography of Nat Turner. After his white publisher nixed his plans, DuBois turned to his second choice, the writing of a Frederick Douglass biography. However, he was once more thwarted by the overreaching influence of Booker T. Washington, whose own aspirations pertained to a work on the famous black abolitionist. Only as a third choice, then, did DuBois thankfully take up the writing of his lyrical 1909 biography of John Brown (DeCaro, 2005: 19).

As far as young Malcolm and the Parkhurst collection are concerned, we cannot be certain what particular reference to Brown he later remembered reading. However, it is likely that the Parkhurst collection included James Redpath's authorized 1860 biography, *The Public Life of Capt. John Brown* (1860), and at least one edition of Franklin B. Sanborn's *Life and Letters* (1885). It is also possible that Malcolm had access to the notable biography of Brown by Oswald Garrison Villard, which was published twice before Malcolm's rise (1910, 1929). Of course, we should assume that Malcolm became especially acquainted with the DuBois biography, and that he would have been interested in reading it after having reading DuBois's classic, *The Souls of Black Folks*. To be sure, we can only say with confidence that prisoner Malcolm Little read 'somewhere' about John Brown, and it is reasonable to assume that the available texts only reinforced the Garveyite son's favorable assessment of the martyred abolitionist.

"Not Even Elijah Muhammad Could Have Been More Eloquent"

When writing his autobiography with Alex Haley almost two decades later, Malcolm looked back at the Parkhurst anti-slavery collection as having had a profound impact upon him. Indeed, he went so far as to say, "Not even Elijah

Muhammad could have been more eloquent than those books were in providing indisputable proof that the collective white man had acted like a devil in virtually every contact he had with the world's collective non-white man" (Malcolm X, 1965: 177). This is a significant statement that either was a slip-of-the-tongue, or possibly an editorial revision – the voice of the post-Nation of Islam Malcolm X, still laboring over his autobiography after Elijah Muhammad had mercilessly ousted him from the 'Black Muslim' movement in early 1964. Either way, the remark demonstrates the primacy of reading history as a fundamental aspect of Malcolm's ideological and personal development as a spokesman for black liberation.

Yet the statement may also hint at the internal incongruities of the Nation of Islam, at least at the point where flesh-and-blood met ideology. We know that the more that Malcolm X interacted with whites in the public arena, the more he likely was struggling with the absolutes of Elijah Muhammad's 'white devil' doctrine. As noted above, anyone familiar with Malcolm's autobiography is aware that his religious pilgrimage to Mecca allowed Malcolm to divest himself of Muhammad's comprehensive demonization of whites. However, only few have considered to what extent Elijah Muhammad himself could consistently live within what Malcolm later called the 'straitjacket' teachings of the Nation of Islam. Interestingly, Peter Goldman, who remains the foremost biographer of Malcolm X (more so, even now that Manning Marable's dishing, dilettante biography has been published), has an interesting vignette of a little known conversation between Elijah Muhammad and Martin Luther King, Jr.,

> "Do you really believe that all white folks are devils? I know a lot of white people have a lot of devil in them, but are you going to say that all of them are devils?" Mr. Muhammad smiled. "Dr. King," he said, "you and me both grew up in Georgia, and we know there are many different kind of snakes. The rattlesnake was poisonous and the king snake was friendly. But they both snakes, Dr. King." And the two of them, the Messenger of Allah and the apostle of Christian love, had a hearty laugh.
> GOLDMAN, 1973: 65

Elijah Muhammad's concession that some whites might be 'friendly snakes' indicated awareness that perhaps some whites were good enough to befriend – although in public discourse the Nation of Islam characteristically refused even to admit the existence of 'good' whites, or at least refused to acknowledge that a handful of well-meaning whites had made any significant contribution to the struggle for justice.

Still, if one were to have asked Elijah Muhammad which whites were the most-friendly 'snakes' in history; probably even he would have included John Brown. This is not entirely speculation. In March 1963, even before Malcolm X was silenced and put out of the Nation of Islam, the organization's newspaper, *Muhammad Speaks*, featured an article written by 'Black Muslim' author, Robert 18X.[6] The article, "Another Look at John Brown; Believed Only Black Militia Could Destroy Slave System," is a salutary remembrance of the Old Man (Robert 18X, 1963: 19). Interestingly, the article is prefaced by an editor's note, observing the centennial year of the Emancipation Proclamation, and recalling "many events in the history of the abolition movement in the United States, including the saga of John Brown, [the] man who gave his life and the lives of his sons to the cause of the slaves." The author was perhaps influenced by DuBois's *John Brown*, not only in his appreciative reference to the abolitionist, but also in another reference to Harper's Ferry as "the safest natural entrance to the Great Black Way," a term directly taken from the DuBois biography. Indeed, the article seems to have been prompted by the publication of the 'Centennial Edition' of the DuBois biography by International Publishers in December 1962. The book not only celebrated the hundredth anniversary of Lincoln's Emancipation Proclamation, but also included a new preface and an expanded closing summation of Brown's legacy, written by the aged DuBois himself (DuBois, 1962).

It is not clear whether Robert 18X was part of the *Muhammad Speaks* staff or whether his article was submitted to the editor for publication. Malcolm X founded the publication (as *Mr. Muhammad Speaks*) in 1960, and published it in New York City until jealousy in Muhammad's family forced its relocation to the organization's headquarters in Chicago in 1961 (Malcolm X, 1965: 238). Certainly, thanks to Malcolm's leadership, the 'Black Muslims' in New York City tended to be the most progressive and entrepreneurially successful in the movement.[7] Documentary scholar Paul Lee credits the overall contributions

---

6   For those unacquainted with Nation of Islam protocol, '18' signified that he was the eighteenth person named Robert in his particular mosque or congregation. Charles Morris (Kenyatta), one of Malcolm's drivers in the Nation of Islam, was known as Charles 37X while in the movement, meaning that thirty-six 'Black Muslims' named Charles preceded him in joining Harlem's famous 'Temple No. 7.' There is a certain irony in the Nation of Islam's system of differentiating people in this way. Numbers were utilized because 'Black Muslims' rejected their European family names as 'slave names' inherited from the days of chattel slavery. Yet by using number-names, the Nation of Islam actually revived a practice in ancient Rome wherein slaves were often given numbers as names.

7   The sophistication and progressiveness of the New York City Nation of Islam mosques beyond the rest of the movement certainly was Malcolm's own understanding after the fact.

of the Little family, especially Malcolm, with advancing the Nation of Islam by means of a number of progressive innovations, especially in media and communication. One earmark of Malcolm's impact was to feature 'non-[Nation of Islam] news and commentary,' including international news emanating from what Malcolm liked to call the 'Dark World.' Lee concludes that this "was the secret of its great success, a pattern that was continued after Mr. Muhammad moved the paper to Chicago in 1961 under the shortened title, Muhammad Speaks" (Lee, 2010).

In his autobiography, Malcolm likewise wrote that the appropriation of his newspaper by Muhammad's leaders in Chicago resulted from jealousy in the hierarchy of the cult, assuring that "nothing about me would be printed in the paper I had founded." Malcolm recalled that this censoring of his name and activities became apparent in 1962 (Malcolm X, 1965: 292). This may have been the case in large part, but in the March 1963 issue in which Robert 18X's article was published, Malcolm was not yet omitted from the pages of *Muhammad Speaks*; it is also possible that his wilting influence in the movement yet allowed him to have introduced the John Brown piece for publication. One may but speculate further that the Brown article emanated from New York's Muslims since it appears on a page replete with advertisements exclusively pertaining to 'Black Muslim' businesses and functions in New York City, including an advertisement for Muhammad's Mosque No. 7, Malcolm's primary congregation in the city. If this is the case, then the only feature on the entire page that was produced in Chicago was the fascinating illustration of a friendly, dark-bearded John Brown arming a black man with a weapon. The illustration, signed by Eugene xxx, was the work of Eugene Majied, who would later turn his pen like a Brutus dagger against Malcolm, portraying him as a traitor worthy of death in the same publication (Goldman, 1973: 192).

That the Nation of Islam's central publication would feature a warmly appreciative article about John Brown may have illustrated the impact of Malcolm's maturing political outlook upon the movement. But Brown was not the only white person to be recognized in the pages of *Muhammad Speaks* in

---

Shortly before his assassination, he told an interviewer, "the only [Nation of Islam] Muslims in business, who operated businesses in the black, were the Muslims in the New York area. And one of the bones of contention that developed between the factions in the Black Muslim movement was the jealousy that developed in Chicago toward the New York Muslims because they were more successful than the ones there in Chicago." Malcolm X interview on "Stan Bernard's Contact," 18 February 1965 (New York: WINS Radio). Transcribed in *Malcolm X: February 1965, The Final Speeches* (New York: Pathfinder Press, 1992), 202.

the last phase of Malcolm's tenure in the Nation of Islam. In the same issue, an anti-racist booklet by author Truman Nelson is also featured; and at least one white writer, a student named Charles Keil, was befriended by Malcolm, and even wrote some articles for publication in the 'Black Muslim' paper (Keil, 1990; DeCaro, 1995: 175–176).

Yet the influence of Malcolm X is not sufficient to explain these uncharacteristic features. In order for any article pertaining to white subjects or featuring white writers to reach publication in *Muhammad Speaks*, it is likely that Elijah Muhammad himself would have to have approved them. Although Malcolm was far more internationally oriented and politically astute than the culturally provincial Muhammad, both men ultimately made room for the memory of John Brown – perhaps reflective both of Marcus Garvey's appreciation as well as Elijah Muhammad's old school sensibility as a black man from Georgia, where Brown's name would likely have been recalled with respect and sympathy. Even at worst, perhaps 'Captain Brown' (as he was affectionately called by blacks throughout the 19th century) was the friendly 'king snake' in the garden of Elijah's political memory. Beyond even 'the enemy of my enemy,' Brown thus appears in the pages of *Muhammad Speaks* as an admired ally, no doubt with the oversight and approval of Elijah Muhammad.

More like Echoes than Voices

While the nature of historical research involves seeking evidence, there are times when the pages of our work are haunted by curious themes that resonate more like echoes than voices, more like shadows than figures. Yet these themes nevertheless are aligned with the evidence in such a way that they too seem worth mentioning, if only in closing reflection. One such shadow is the use of 'God's Angry Men' by Malcolm X as the title of a newspaper column that he wrote for the Nation of Islam prior to the founding of *Muhammad Speaks*. 'God's Angry Men' was featured in African American newspapers like the *New York Amsterdam News*, *Los Angeles Herald Dispatch*, and *The Westchester* [NY] *Observer*.

It is not clear how Malcolm came to adopt this title for his column, but it is fascinating that 'God's Angry Man' was a term twice applied to John Brown quite notably in literature. The most prominent use, roughly equivalent to Malcolm's time, was the title of Leonard Erlich's award winning historical work of fiction, *God's Angry Man* (1932). In turn, Erlich probably derived the paradigmatic title from a famous poem by the Christian devotional author, Charles

Sheldon, which was published in 1910. Sheldon's poetic tribute to Brown is premised on a comparison with the biblical character Moses, the liberator of the children of Israel,

> John Brown! Thy soul is marching boldly yet
> Across the path of cold indifferent men.
> The world cannot and will not soon forget
> That soul that counted not the cost again.
> God give us angry men in every age,
> Men with indignant souls at sight of wrong,
> Men whose whole being glows with righteous rage,
> Men who are strong for those who need the strong.
> SHELDON, 1910: 113

Whether or not Malcolm drew his 'God's Angry Men' title from the Sheldon-Erlich tradition is not clear. Yet if there is a figure cut from the pattern of Sheldon's "men with indignant souls at sight of wrong...whose whole being glows with righteous rage" in the era of the Civil Rights movement, it was Malcolm X. Indeed, in his own day, Malcolm manifested an alternative to the liberal, nonviolent Civil Rights crusade, even as Brown had represented a militant alternative to the pacifist 'moral suasion' ideology that so permeated the abolitionist movement in the antebellum era. Both men displayed a deeply religious sensibility, belief in the authority of a sacred text, and expressed some sense of impending divine judgment upon the nation for the evils of white supremacy. Yet neither man was embraced by the status quo of their putative liberal allies, Brown being perceived as a fanatic and 'monomaniac,' and Malcolm as 'violent.'

In turn, both men were frustrated by the nonviolent philosophies that prevailed among the liberals of their respective periods. Before and after his ouster from the Nation of Islam, Malcolm X consistently upheld the right of black people to self-defense against racist violence, and decried the nonviolent philosophy of the Civil Rights leadership. Brown, too, believed that it was a mistake for the established abolitionist leadership to insist on pacifist 'moral suasion' in the face of slavery's violent and unrelenting program of expansion and conquest. Malcolm considered the rhetoric of nonviolent resistance as coming from 'mealy-mouth' activists; Brown once opined that were the abolitionist orators to have their tongues cut out, perhaps they might finally stop talking and take real action (Goldman, 1973: 6; Redpath, 1886: 2). Despite the historical distance between the two leaders, John Brown and Malcolm X finally surrendered their lives in common cause on behalf of the oppressed, likewise trusting that the Almighty would somehow use their deaths for the betterment of humanity. And in this finally they were more than allies.

Bibliography

DeCaro, Louis A. Jr. "Black People's Ally, White People's Bogeyman." In *The Afterlife of John Brown*, edited by Andrew Taylor and Eldrid Herrington. New York: Palgrave Macmillan, 2005.

——— *Freedom's Dawn: The Last Days of John Brown in Virginia*. Lanham, Md.: Rowman & Littlefield Publishers, 2015.

——— "History Black and Blurred: John Brown and Malcolm X According to James Smalls" (8 February 2007), in John Brown the Abolitionist: A Biographer's Blog (http://goo.gl/2kJu9t).

——— *Malcolm and the Cross: The Nation of Islam, Malcolm X, and Christianity*. New York: New York University Press, 1998.

——— *On the Side of My People: A Religious Life of Malcolm X*. New York: New York University Press, 1995.

DuBois, W.E.B. *John Brown: Centennial Edition*. New York: International Publishers, 1962.

Goldman, Peter Goldman. *The Death and Life of Malcolm X*. Urbana: University of Illinois, 1973.

Harding, Vincent. *There is a River: The Black Struggle for Freedom in America*. New York: Vintage, 1981.

Keil, Charles. "Remembering Malcolm," *MS*, 28 February 28, 1990.

Lee, Paul and Best Efforts, Inc. "'A World of Negatives and Positives' (With Thanx to Wilfred Little)." 8 March 2010. Personal e-mail (8 March 2010).

Malcolm X. *The Autobiography of Malcolm X, as told to Alex Haley*. New York: Ballentine, 1965.

——— *By Any Means Necessary: Speeches, Interviews and a Letter*. Edited by George Breitman. New York: Pathfinder Press, 1970.

Martin, Tony. *Race First: The Ideological and Organizational Struggles of Marcus Garvey and the Universal Negro Improvement Association*. Dover, MA: The Majority Press, 1976.

Parker, Edward E. *History of the Town of Brookline*. Town of Brookline: MA, 1906.

Plimpton, George. "Miami Notebook: Cassius Clay and Malcolm X," *Harper's Magazine* (June, 1964): 59.

Quarles, Benjamin. *Allies for Freedom & Blacks on John Brown*. New York: DaCapo Press, 2001.

Redpath, James. "John Brown's Oratory," *John Swinton's Paper* [NY], Feb. 7, 1886, p. 2.

Reynolds, David S. *John Brown Abolitionist*. New York: Alfred A. Knopf, 2005.
Robert 18X. "Another Look at John Brown; Believed Only Black Militia Could Destroy Slave System," *Muhammad Speaks*. March 18, (1963), 19.
Sheldon, Charles. "God's Angry Man." *The Independent* [NY] (July, 1910): 113.
Catalogue of the Delta Kappa Epsilon Fraternity. New York: DKE Council, 1910.

CHAPTER 8

Malcolm X, Alatas and Critical Theory

Syed Farid Alatas

The Meaning of Critical Theory

The objective of this chapter is to examine the thought of Malcolm X as critical theory and to draw parallels with the tradition of critical theory in the field of Malay Studies that was begun by the late Syed Hussein Alatas (1928–2007).[1] By presenting the views of these thinkers I hope it will be readily seen that both can be seen as points of departure and resources for Malay Studies to develop critical theories of history and society. This chapter proceeds as follows: in the first section, I provide a brief discussion on the meaning of critical theory. The sections that follow discuss three aspects of critical theory with reference to the thought of Malcolm X and Alatas. These aspects are the critique of history, the diagnosis of the uncritical mind, and the role of the intellectual in dealing with the aforementioned.

Critical theory refers to theory that is critical of domination and inequality in history and contemporary society. It not only theorizes these problems but also advocates for the transformation of society and the emancipation of the dominated. This separates critical theory from traditional theory. As stated by Reiland Rabaka, critical theory is to be distinguished from traditional theory in that the latter merely describes or explains certain phenomena. Critical

---

1 Syed Hussein Alatas was a Malaysian but was born in the town of Bogor, in West Java, Indonesia. He completed his primary education in Johor Bahru, then part of British Malaya, and went on to graduate with degrees in the political and social sciences from the University of Amsterdam. His doctoral thesis, defended in 1963, was a sociological study on religion entitled, *Reflections on the Theories of Religion*. He then returned to Malaysia and took up a position of lecturer in the Department of Malay Studies at the University of Malaya, Kuala Lumpur. In 1967 he moved to Singapore to become Professor and Head of the Department of Malay Studies at the National University of Singapore, a post that he held till 1988. In the late 1960's and early 1970's Alatas was active in Malaysian politics, despite living in Singapore. He was a founding member of the then opposition party, Gerakan Rakyat Malaysia (Malaysian Peoples' Movement) and was a Member of Senate, Parliament of Malaysia, elected by the State of Penang. In 1988 he returned to Malaysia to become the Vice-Chancellor of the University of Malaya. He left this post in 1991. His last position was Professor at the Institute of Malay World Civilizations (ATMA – Institut Alam dan Tamadun Melayu), National University of Malaysia. Syed Hussein Alatas passed away on January 23, 2007.

theory, on the other hand, not only does this but goes further by critiquing and correcting conventional constructions of history and society, and calling for a transformation of the established order (Rabaka, 2002: 147–148).

Critical theorists like Alatas and Malcolm X are in the company of postcolonial thinkers such as Franz Fanon, Ali Shariati, Mahatma Gandhi, Martin Luther King Jr., Fidel Castro, Desmond Tutu, A.L. Tibawi, Edward Said, and others. These thinkers were not only critical of oppression and injustice but also provided alternative analyses of the problems as they saw them, and labored hard to raise consciousness in their respective societies about the nature, causes and functions of domination, control and inequality.

Malcolm X is a crucial resource for an African American or even pan-African critical theory while the work of Alatas can be considered as the start of a tradition of critical theory for the field of Malay Studies. The next three sections discuss these aspects, that is, the critique of history, the recognition and conceptualization of the uncritical mind, and the role of the intellectual in the development of a critical approach to the study of history and contemporary society.

The Critique of History

It was in 1948 while in prison at the Norfolk Prison Colony that Malcolm X was introduced to the Nation of Islam and the teachings of Elijah Muhammad. His brother Reginald, who visited him in prison, encouraged Malcolm to avoid consuming pork, alcohol and narcotics (Malcolm X, 1965: 161). These were to be the first steps towards Malcolm's conversion to the creed of the National of Islam (NOI). It was also in prison that Malcolm received his first lessons about the problem of history, in the form of letters that he received from family members such as his brothers Wilfred, Philbert and Reginald. They were able to persuade Malcolm to accept the controversial teachings of Elijah Muhammad:

> 'The true knowledge,' reconstructed much more briefly than I received it, was that history had been 'whitened' in the white man's history books, and that the black man had been 'brainwashed for hundreds of years.' Original Man was black, in the continent called Africa where the human race had emerged on the planet Earth. The black man, original man, built great empires and civilizations and cultures while the white man was still living on all fours in caves. 'The devil white man,' down through history, out of his devilish nature, had pillaged, murdered, raped, and exploited every race of man not white.
> MALCOLM X, 1965: 162

While this critical view of history was equally distorted as the one the members of the Nation of Islam and Malcolm sought to replace, it instilled in Malcolm consciousness the need for African Americans to have an alternative view of their history. While some aspects of Malcolm's revisionist history are clearly problematic, others were reasonable and compelling and did not require rejection even after Malcolm was to leave the Nation of Islam and become a Sunni Muslim.

An example is Malcolm's views on the impact of slavery on the consciousness of African Americans. In an interview on City Desk in Chicago in 1963, Malcolm said that the African Americans should not accept their current names as they were not their real names. Rather, they were gifted names by the slave owners. Their original names were displaced. The gifting of names is symbolic of the distorted history that African Americans had been taught by the white man. Malcolm goes on to say that Master W.F. Muhammad had taught Elijah Muhammad the true history of the Negroes and made him aware of the origins of his English name (Malcolm X, 1963a). Malcolm went on to stress the need for African Americans to study their own history in order to know themselves and to instill racial dignity and pride. This was necessary in order to counter "the subservient inferiority complex that most Negroes have or that is instilled within most Negroes who have received this sort of integrated education" (Malcolm X, 1963a). A famous example of the inferiority complex that Malcolm referred to was the habit of African Americans straightening their hair. On this Malcolm asks, "Who taught you to hate the texture of your hair... who taught you to hate yourself" (Malcolm X, 1960–1965).

Malcolm stressed that it was important for African Americans to know their past in order to know the reasons for which they were crippled in American society. African Americans differ from other people in that they lack the knowledge of their past. The proof of this is that

> almost anyone else can come into this country and get around barriers and obstacles that we cannot get around; and the only difference between them and us, they know something about the past, and in knowing something about the past, they know something about themselves, they have an identity. But wherein you and I differ from them is primarily revolved around our lack of knowledge concerning the past.
> MALCOLM X, 1990: 11–12

History was important because it dealt with the past, with the origin of a thing, a person and nation. Knowing the origin means acquiring a better understanding of the phenomenon in question. Going back to the past would result in African Americans knowing that they were not always at the level they were in contemporary America, and that they had once attained a higher level (Malcolm X, 1990: 12). This is not only a matter of knowledge but also inspiration. As Malcolm said:

> And you know that if you once did it, you can do it again; you automatically get the incentive, the inspiration, and the energy necessary to duplicate what our forefathers formerly did. But by keeping us completely cut off from our past, it is easy for the man who has power over us to make us willing to stay at this level because we will feel that we were always at this level, a low level. That's why I say it is so important for you and me to spend time today learning something about the past so that we can better understand the present, analyze it, and then do something about it.
> MALCOLM X, 1990: 12–13

Furthermore, it is necessary to study history because the history of African Americans that had been presented to African Americans was a distorted one. Malcolm gives the example of the annual Negro History Week as a trick in which selective information was imparted:

> And during this one week they drown us with propaganda about Negro history in Georgia and Mississippi and Alabama. Never do they take us back across the water, back home. They take us down home, but they never give us a history of back home. They never give us enough information to let us know what we were doing before we ended up in Mississippi, Alabama, Georgia, Texas, and some of those other prison states. They give us the impression with Negro History Week that we were cotton pickers all of our lives. Cotton pickers, orange growers, mammies, and uncles for the white man in this country – this is our history when you talk in terms of Negro History Week.
> MALCOLM X, 1990: 22–23

It is through the writing of history that the white man constructed a certain image of the Negro that Malcolm is calling into question:

> The worst trick of all is when he names us Negro and calls us Negro. And when we call ourselves that, we end up tricking ourselves. My brother Cassius [Clay] was on the screen the other night talking with Les Crane about the word *Negro*. I wish he wouldn't have gone so fast, because he was in a position to have done a very good job. But he was right in saying that we're not Negroes, and have never been, until we were brought here

and made into that. We were scientifically produced by the white man. Whenever you see somebody who calls himself a Negro, he's a product of Western civilization – not only Western civilization, but Western crime. The Negro, as he is called or calls himself in the West, is the best evidence that can be used against Western civilization today.

One of the main reasons we are called Negro is so we won't know who we really are. And when you call yourself that, you don't know who you really are. You don't know what you are, you don't know where you came from, you don't know what is yours. As long as you call yourself a Negro, nothing is yours. No languages – you can't lay claim to any language, not even English; you mess it up. You can't lay claim to any name, any type of name, that will identify you as something that you should be. You can't lay claim to any culture as long as you use the word *Negro* to identify yourself. It attaches you to nothing. It doesn't even identify your color.

MALCOLM X, 1990: 24

This construction of the Negro does not allow the Negro to know who he really is, who he was in history and is unable to lay claim to an identity that will allow him to love rather than hate himself.

The need to critique history as well as recover an alternative reading of history in order to correct problematic images of the oppressed was also stressed by Syed Hussein Alatas. Alatas' work on revisionist history focused on colonial ideology, specifically on the political philosophy of Raffles, the British colonial administrator of Singapore (Alatas, 1971), and on the myth of Malay, Javanese and Filipino laziness (Alatas, 1977). Such reinterpretation of history was what Edward Said called 'revisionist' scholarship, that is, works that "set themselves the revisionist, critical task of dealing frontally with the metropolitan culture, using the techniques, discourses, and weapons of scholarship and criticism once reserved exclusively for the European" (Said, 1993: 293). Two examples of Syed Hussein Alatas' works that come under this category are *Thomas Stamford Raffles: Schemer of Reformer* (1971) and *The Myth of the Lazy Native* (1977). In the latter work, Alatas exposes and critiques the ideological function of the colonial view of native indolence in colonial Southeast Asia, and the continuity of this ideology among the native elite themselves.

In his work on Raffles, Alatas presents a critique of the philosophy of the colonial administrator at a time in Singapore scholarship when there was hardly any critical assessment of the man. In fact, Raffles had been presented by the independent Singapore state as a hero of sorts, one of the rare instances in history of a colonial administrator serving as a national icon. Alatas' task was to present a critical and not Eurocentric account of the thinking and deeds of

Raffles. Specifically, he had set out to examine the status of Raffles as a hero through an assessment of his political philosophy and his conduct. Alatas concluded that the silence among scholars about Raffles questionable political philosophy and conduct was strange in that even by colonial standards he fell short of the humanitarianism that was attributed to him (Alatas, 1971: 50–51).

Understanding the Uncritical Mind

The failure of the contemporaries of Malcolm X and Alatas to be critical of the dominant ideas of their times impressed upon them the need to engage in the critical reflection on the history of their respective societies. Beyond that, they were also interested in understanding the nature of the uncritical mind that they opposed. Malcolm suggested the distinction between house and field negroes as a means to achieve this while Alatas spoke of the captive mind.

> During the time of slavery in the American south, the house negro was the slave who lived in the master's house, in the attic or basement. He ate the same food as the master, loved him, and protected him. The field negro, on the other hand, lived in a hut and hated his master. Malcolm stated that in his time there were still house and field Negroes. He referred to himself as a field Negro.
> MALCOLM X, 1960–1965

Malcolm was critical of Dr. Martin Luther King Jr., likening him to a modern Uncle Tom. Uncle Tom was taught by the white man to teach negroes to love thine enemy and to keep them from resisting the bloodhounds against the negroes (Malcolm X, 1963b; Malcolm, 1990: 75–76). On Uncle Tom, Malcolm said:

> So now you have a twentieth-century-type of house Negro. A twentieth-century Uncle Tom. He's just as much an Uncle Tom today as Uncle Tom was 100 and 200 years ago. Only he's a modern Uncle Tom. That Uncle Tom wore a handkerchief around his head. This Uncle Tom wears a top hat. He's sharp. He dresses just like you do. He speaks the same phraseology, the same language. He tries to speak it better than you do. He speaks with the same accents, same diction. And when you say, "your army," he says, "our army." He hasn't got anybody to defend him, but anytime you say "we" he says "we." "Our president," "our government," "our Senate," "our congressmen," "our this and our that." And he hasn't even got a seat in that "our" even at the end of the line. So this is the twentieth-century

Negro. Whenever you say "you," the personal pronoun in the singular or in the plural, he uses it right along with you. When you say you're in trouble, he says, "Yes, we're in trouble."

MALCOLM X, 1963C

The mentality of the house Negro can be further understood in terms of Alatas' concept of the captive mind. Alatas originated and developed the concept of the captive mind to conceptualize the nature of scholarship in the developing world, particularly in relation to Western dominance in the social sciences and humanities. The captive mind is defined as an "uncritical and imitative mind dominated by an external source, whose thinking is deflected from an independent perspective" (Alatas, 1974: 692). The external source is Western social science and humanities and the uncritical imitation influences all the constituents of scientific activity such as problem-selection, conceptualization, analysis, generalization, description, explanation, and interpretation (Alatas, 1972: 11). Among the characteristics of the captive mind are the inability to be creative and raise original problems, the inability to devise original analytical methods, and alienation from the main issues of indigenous society. The captive mind is trained almost entirely in the Western sciences, reads the works of Western authors, and is taught predominantly by Western teachers, whether in the West itself or through their works available in local centers of education. Mental captivity is also found in the suggestion of solutions and policies. Furthermore, it reveals itself at the levels of theoretical as well as empirical work.

Earlier, in the 1950's, Alatas referred to the "wholesale importation of ideas from the Western world to eastern societies" without due consideration of their socio-historical context, as a fundamental problem of colonialism (Alatas, 1956). He had also suggested that the mode of thinking of colonized peoples paralleled political and economic imperialism. Hence, the expression *academic imperialism*,[2] the context within which the captive mind appears.

The consumption of social science knowledge from the West arises from the belief in the superiority of such knowledge. Among the traits of this consumption that parallel the economic demonstration effect are: (a) the frequency of contact with Western knowledge; (b) the weakening or erosion of local or indigenous knowledge; (c) the prestige attached to imported knowledge; and (d) that such consumption is not necessarily rational and utilitarian (Alatas, 1972: 10–11).

---

2   This was first elaborated in a lecture in 1969 on academic imperialism. See Alatas (1969). This was expanded and published about 30 years later (Alatas, 2000).

Alatas provides illustrations of the workings of the captive mind from development studies. The example given is Hagen's view that digging with the Southeast Asian hoe is an "awkward process," but the spade, which is a better instrument, can only be of limited use in low-income societies to the extent that shoes are not widely used (Hagen, 1962: 31–32, cited in Alatas, 1972: 15). Alatas suggested that Hagen did not comprehend the function of the hoe in its proper, that is, the Southeast Asian context. The geography of Southeast Asia is such that the hoe would actually be the more efficient instrument because of terrace cultivation on mountain slopes. Hagen's failure to judge the efficiency and utility of the hoe by reference to its context is a violation of an important anthropological principle (Alatas, 1972: 15).

It is problems such as these in development studies as well as the social sciences in general that are imitated and assimilated by the captive mind and resulting in ill-conceived development plans. Dominated by Western thought in a mimetic and uncritical way, the captive mind lacks creativity and the ability to raise original problems, is characterized by a fragmented outlook, is alienated both from major societal issues as well as its own national tradition, and is a consequence of Western dominance over the rest of the world (Alatas, 1974: 691). The problem of the captive mind is unique to the non-Western world. While uncreative, imitative, fragmented and alienated minds are to be found in the West as well, the context in which these occur is not the same. Alatas argues that the counterpart of the captive mind does not exist in the West because in the West we do not find people who are trained in non-Western sciences, in non-Western universities, trained by non-Western professors, and assigned works of non-Western scholars in non-Western languages (Alatas, 1974: 692). The captive mind is a phenomenon peculiar to the developing world in that the uncritical and imitative thought exists in the context of the domination by an external civilization, the West (Alatas, 1976).

The Role of Intellectuals

According to Alatas, the presence of the captive mind is a central problem of developing societies and affects practically all areas of economic, political, social and cultural life. The main factor accounting for the perversity of the captive mind is the lack of intellectual leadership. Since the 1950's, Alatas had devoted a great deal of his attention to the absence of an effective group of intellectuals in Malaysia and other developing societies. The task of the intellectual is to think creatively and in a non-captive manner, consider the specific problems of his or her society, and attempt to arrive at their solutions. Alatas' attention to the various problems surrounding intellectuals resulted in the appearance of a book entitled *Intellectuals in Developing Societies* (Alatas, 1977b). In this work he defines the intellectual as a "person who is engaged in thinking about ideas and non-material problems using the faculty of reason." Furthermore, "knowledge of a certain subject or the possession of a degree does not make a person an intellectual although these often coincide. There are many degree holders and professors who do not engage in developing their field or trying to find the solution to specific problems within it. On the other hand, a person with no academic qualifications can be an intellectual if he utilizes his thinking capacity and possesses sufficient knowledge of his subject of interest" (Alatas, 1977b: 8).

One of the roles of intellectuals is to think about the direction a society should take. Alatas promoted the idea of a form of socialism that was compatible with Islam. In 1956, while a student at the University of Amsterdam, he published small monograph entitled *The Democracy of Islam*, which contains among other things a discussion on socialism, including Scientific Socialism and its philosophical basis, historical materialism. He attacked some aspects of socialism for the "shallowness of its doctrines" (Alatas, 1956: 33). For example, Alatas suggested that the view that man was merely a product of institutions had been proven to be wrong (Alatas, 1956: 33). Many years later, while teaching at the University of Singapore, Alatas worked out in greater detail the relationship between Islam and socialism. This was in response to a number of anti-socialist statements among Islamic circles in Malaysia that he felt required correction. He expressed agreement with Seyyed Jamaluddin Afghani and Haji Omar Said Tjokroaminoto that there were certain characteristics of socialism that can be found in Islam (Alatas, 1977c). These can be enumerated as follows (Alatas, 1977c: 2–4):

1. The vital means of production should be owned by the state.
2. The working class and consumers are to be protected from being exploited.
3. The state should ensure the just and equitable distribution of commodities.
4. The environment influences the individual and the emergence of social problems.
5. Society is influenced by class interests.
6. Socialism strives to eradicate injustices that arise from the capitalist system.
7. Every healthy person of age should work.

8. All aspects of society such as culture, religion, and the educational system must be such that they do not obstruct but encourage economic growth, the development of science, justice, health, and general satisfaction.
9. Socialism considers the good of the majority and the underprivileged on the basis of justice.
10. Socialism utilizes scientific knowledge to the greatest possible degree in the formulation of problems, the interpretation of history, and in the construction of an edifice for belief.

Alatas stressed that Muslims have to make a distinction between those aspects of socialism that are contrary to Islam and those that are not. For example, the Marx's outlook on religion is clearly incompatible with Islam. This is to be contrasted with the socialisms of Tolstoy, Gandhi, Jayaprakash Narayan, Iqbal and others which give a central role to religion (Alatas, 1977c: 4).

On Marxism, Alatas said that "what is rejected is not the complete outlook of dialectical materialism but only specific elements such as those concerning the origins of and role of religion, the dictatorship of the proletariat, class struggle as the motor of history, moral relativism, and other" (Alatas, 1977c: 7). Dialectical materialism's stance on the role of ideology, false consciousness, and the problems of colonialism is valid (Alatas, 1977c: 7–8). To support his view, Alatas also makes extensive references to the Qur'an, the *hadith* of the Prophet Muhammad (peace be upon him), the *Nahj al-Balagha* of Sayyidina Ali, and scholars such as al-Ghazzali, Ibn Khaldun, and Allamah Iqbal.

The elaboration of an ideology or a system, such as that attempted by Alatas with regard to Islam and socialism, can only be done by a non-captive mind. For such a mind to emerge, Alatas advocated the development of an autonomous social science tradition. The call for an autonomous approach in the social sciences and humanities refers to the development of social sciences whose practitioners would raise and deal with original problems and devise new research questions. They are also engaged in original concept formation (Alatas, 1979: 265). What is required for this task is endogenous intellectual creativity.

Alatas discussed the topic of endogenous intellectual creativity at the Asian Symposium on Intellectual Creativity in Endogenous Culture which was jointly sponsored by the United Nations University and Kyoto University, which was held in Kyoto, Japan on 13–17 of November, 1981. Endogenization refers to the effort at intellectual creativity in the context of original problem-raising, the generation of new concepts and theories, and the synthesis between Western and non-Western knowledge. The 'endogenous' here is "understood as referring to the effort at intellectual creativity rather than to the constituent elements of the accomplished result" or the material used (Alatas, 1981: 462). The selective assimilation of exogenous elements should be considered as a part of endogenous activity (Alatas, 1981: 462) as both the exogenous and the endogenous are required in the effort to address the problem of irrelevancy.

The approach to all knowledge is therefore based on criteria of selection that have not to do with the cultural origins of concepts, but rather their compatibility with Islam, as far as normative questions are concerned, and their interpretive value. In a work that is properly speaking, revisionary history, Alatas demonstrates this outlook in no uncertain terms (Alatas, 1977a). Said refers to revisionary history as works that reject dominant discourses and goes "beyond the reified polarities of East versus West, and in an intelligent and concrete way attempts to understand the heterogeneous and often odd developments that used to elude the so-called world historians as well as the colonial Orientalists..." (Said, 1993: 48). It is precisely this awareness of the need to transcend the Orientalist-Occidentalist divide that would lead to a fair assessment of socialism, Marxism and other Western idea systems.

Malcolm X advocated a critical theory as an alternative to the dominant Eurocentric narrative that informed even the African American self-understanding, a critical theory that resonates with the autonomous social science advocated by Alatas. One of Malcolm's important contributions in this effort was to call for an Afrocentric ideology as a response to the ideology of White supremacy. To this end, Malcolm urged the youth among civil right fighters to see, listen and think for themselves (Malcolm X, 1991: 49, cited in Rabaka, 2002: 153). Furthermore, he called on African Americans to adopt Black Nationalism for their liberation. If Alatas advocated an Islamic interpretation of Socialism, Malcolm called for Black Nationalism.

> I mean by Black Nationalism that the Black man must control the radio, the newspapers and the television for our communities. I also mean that we must do these things necessary to elevate ourselves, socially, culturally, and to restore racial dignity.
> RUSSELL, 1964, cited in Sales, 1994: 79–80

Malcolm would have probably shared Alatas' views on the compatibility between Islam and socialism as he was himself very critical of capitalism:

> It is impossible for capitalism to survive, primarily because the system of capitalism needs some blood to suck. Capitalism used to be like an eagle, but now it's more like a vulture. It used to be strong enough to go and suck anybody's blood whether they were strong or not. But now it has

become more cowardly, like the vulture, and it can only suck the blood of the helpless. As the nations of the world free themselves, then capitalism has fewer victims, less to suck, and it becomes weaker and weaker. It's only a matter of time in my opinion before it will collapse completely.

MALCOLM X, 1990:199

Malcolm also said:

> The economic exploitation in the Afro-American community is the most vicious form practiced on any people in America. In fact, it is the most vicious practiced on any people on this earth. No one is exploited economically as thoroughly as you and I, because in most countries where people are exploited, they know it. You and I are in this country being exploited and sometimes we don't know it...
>
> The Afro-American pays more for food, pays more for clothing, pays more for insurance than anybody else, and we do. It costs you and me more for insurance than it does the white man in the Bronx or somewhere else. It costs you and me more for food than it does them. It costs you and me more to live in America than it does anybody else, and yet we make the greatest contribution.
>
> You tell me what kind of country this is? Why should we do the dirtiest jobs for the lowest pay? Why should we do the hardest work for the lowest pay? What should we pay the most money for the worst kind of food and the most money for the worst kind of place to live in? I'm telling you we do it because we live in one of the rottenest countries that has ever existed on this earth. It's the system that is rotten, we have a rotten system. It's a system of exploitation, a political and economic system of exploitation, of outright humiliation, degradation, discrimination....

MALCOLM X, 1992: 47

For Malcolm, the problem was not just class but race as well. According to a famous statement by Marx and Engels

> The ideas of the ruling class are in every epoch the ruling ideas, i.e. the class which is the ruling *material* force of society, is at the same time its ruling *intellectual* force. The class which has the means of material production at its disposal, has control at the same time over the means of mental production, so that thereby, generally speaking, the ideas of those who lack the means of mental production are subject to it.

MARX & ENGELS, 1970: 64

Malcolm would undoubtedly agree with this but would substitute race/class for class and would refer to the American ruling race/class. Malcolm differs from many Black Nationalist who operate within a Marxist framework tend to emphasise class at the expense of race and racism (Rabaka, 2002: 154, 156). Furthermore, Malcolm's thought was evolving and he had referred to the need to reappraise his views on Black Nationalism (Rabaka, 2002: 157).

This he did when he began to think about pan-Africanism and socialism. In his earlier days as a member of the Nation of Islam, Malcolm advocated the physical return of African Americans to Africa. Later he suggested that the solution for Afro-Americans was twofold. There were the long-range and short-range solutions. He referred to the need for a psychological, cultural and philosophical rather than physical migration to Africa. By this he meant the strengthening of the common bond between Afro-Americans and Africans that would serve to develop greater spiritual resolve and incentive for the improvement of the situation of Afro-Americans in America. During this process, Malcolm believed that many Afro-Americans would be motivated to visit and even migrate to Africa and that "those who stay here can help those who go back and those who go back can help those who stay here" (Malcolm X, 1992: 152, cited in Rabaka, 2002: 157). The appreciation of African culture and traditions and migration to Africa were the long-range goals. Before this could happen, Afro-Americans had to be educated, particularly about politics so that they would understand what politics is supposed to produce and what their responsibilities were (Malcolm X, 1992: 152, cited in Rabaka, 2002: 158). Malcolm called upon Afro-Americans to adopt an oppositional ideology, an alternative thought-style, and to be 'Black-minded' such that they would be able to understand their state of oppression and the ideology of their oppressors (Malcolm X, 1992: 104, cited in Rabaka, 2002: 158).

Malcolm placed a great deal of importance upon critique, stating that:

> I think all of us should be critics of each other. Whenever you can't stand criticism you can never grow. I don't think that it serves any purpose for the leader of our people to waste their time fighting each other needlessly. I think that we accomplish more when we sit down in private and iron out whatever differences that may exist and try and then do something constructive for the benefit of our people.
> MALCOLM X, 1964A

While Malcolm was very critical of the racism of White America, of capitalism and of democracy, he also called upon Afro-Americans to be self-critical, and that they should not be above criticism (Malcolm X, 1964a).

Conclusion

While Dr. Martin Luther King Jr. dreamt of a united America freed from legal segregation, Malcolm X saw life as a nightmare even where legal segregation was no more. In the *The Autobiography of Malcolm X*, his first twelve years of life is described as a nightmare. Malcolm experienced and endured events such as the burning of his family's home in Lansing, Michigan, the friction between his parents and their tough treatment of the children; the violent death of his father; continuous harassment by welfare officials; and the mental breakdown of Malcolm's mother Louise. The "nightmare" was to become a metaphor for Malcolm's understanding of the plight of Afro-Americans (Cone, 1991).

Alatas' fear on the other hand was that society was being taken over by fools. The traits of the fool include (i) the inability to recognize a problem; (ii) the inability to solve a problem if told to him; (iii) the inability to learn what is required; (iv) the inability to learn the art of learning; and (v) not admitting that he is a fool (Alatas, 1977b: 45). Furthermore,

> The revolution of the fools which had occurred in many developing societies was to a great extent due to the colonial period. The colonial government did not pay much attention to the creation of high-caliber administrators in the colonies. During that time all the thinking at national levels was done by the colonial government abroad... After independence following the Second World War, there was a sudden increase in the volume and intensity of administration and other decision-making centres covering diverse projects which were introduced in increasing number by the newly independent states. During this period there was a shortage of intelligent manpower to deal with the sudden increase of planning and administration, both in the official and in private realms, in the newly independent states. Hence the rise to power of the fools. Once the fools came to power, they perpetuate their own breed. With the fools came nepotism, provincialism, parochial party politics, to condition selection and ascent in the hierarchy of administrative power. Fools cannot cope with a situation where merit and hard work are the criteria of success, and so corruption is the hallmark of the rise to power of the fools, making a farce of government tenders and leading to bureaucratic intrigues to gain office or promotion. Where fools dominate it is their values which become society's values, their consciousness which becomes society's consciousness.
>
> ALATAS, 1977B: 45–46

Malcolm would likely agree with this assessment and call for the study and adoption of those universalistic aspects of African culture and traditions that would help to strengthen the moral integrity of Afro-Americans, even as the struggle to "bring about the freedom of these people by any means necessary" (Malcolm X, 1964b) is carried out.

Bibliography

Alatas, Syed Hussein. "Some Fundamental Problems of Colonialism," *Eastern World* November 1956.

―――― "Academic Imperialism," Lecture delivered to the History Society, University of Singapore. September 26, 1969.

―――― *Thomas Stamford Raffles 1781–1826: Schemer or Reformer*, Sydney: Angus and Robertson, 1971.

―――― "The Captive Mind in Development Studies," *International Social Science Journal* 24, no. 1 (1972): 9–25.

―――― "The Captive Mind and Creative Development," *International Social Science Journal* 26, no. 4 (1974): 691–700.

―――― "Intellectual Captivity and the Developing Societies." Paper presented at the 30th International Congress of Human Sciences in Asia and North Africa, Mexico, August 3–8, 1976.

―――― *The Myth of the Lazy Native: A Study of the Image of the Malays, Filipinos, and Javanese from the Sixteenth to the Twentieth Century and its Functions in the Ideology of Colonial Capitalism*. London: Frank Cass, 1977a.

―――― *Intellectuals in Developing Societies*. London: Frank Cass, 1977b.

―――― *Islam dan Sosialisma (Islam and Socialism)*. Penang: Seruan Masa, 1977c.

―――― "Towards an Asian Social Science Tradition," *New Quest* 17 (1979): 265–269.

―――― "Social Aspects of Endogenous Intellectual Creativity: The Problem of Obstacles – Guidelines for Research," ed. A. Abdel-Malek & A.N. Pandeya, *Intellectual Creativity in Endogenous Culture*, Tokyo: United Nations University, 1981.

―――― "Intellectual Imperialism: Definition, Traits and Problems," *Southeast Asian Journal of Social Science* 28, no. 1 (2000): 23–45.

Cone, James H. *Martin and Malcolm and America: A Dream or a Nightmare*. Maryknoll, New York: Orbis, 1991.

Hagen, E.E. *On the Theory of Social Change*. Homewood: Dorsey Press, 1962.

Malcolm X. 1960–1965. Malcolm X: Speeches and Interviews (1960–1965). www.youtube.com/watch?v=2TykiC4GfxU.

―――― Interview on *City Desk*, Chicago, March 17, 1963a. https://www.youtube.com/watch?v=XqcsAygHAhA.

———— Interview at the University of California, Berkeley, October 11, 1963b.

———— "The Race Problem." Speech to the African Students Association and NAACP Campus Chapter. Michigan State University, East Lansing, Michigan. January 23, 1963c. http://www.brothermalcolm.net/mxwords/whathesaid7.html.

———— Necessary to Protect Ourselves, Interview with by Les Crane, 1964a. https://www.wuhsd.org/cms/lib/CA01000258/Centricity/Domain/18/assignment_e11.pdf.

———— By Any Means Necessary – Organization of Afro American Unity, June, 1964b. https://www.youtube.com/watch?v=WBS416EZsKM.

———— *The Autobiography of Malcolm X as told to Alex Haley*. New York: Ballantine Books, 1965.

———— *Malcolm X on Afro-American History*. New York: Pathfinder, 1990.

———— *Malcolm X Speeches at Harvard*. Archie Epps, ed., New York: Paragon House, 1991.

———— *By Any Means Necessary*. New York: Pathfinder, 1992.

Marx, Karl & Engels, Frederick. *The German Ideology*. New York: International Publishers, 1970.

Rabaka, Reiland. "Malcolm X and/as Critical Theory: Philosophy, Radical Politics, and the African American Search for Social Justice," *Journal of Black Studies* 31, no. 2 (1964): 145–165.

Russell, Carlos E. "Exclusive Interview with Brother Malcolm X," *Liberator* 4, no. 5 (1964): 12–13.

Said, Edward. *Culture and Imperialism*. London: Chatto & Windus, 1993.

Sales, William W. *From Civil Rights to Black Liberation: Malcolm X and the Organization of Afro-American Unity*. Boston: South End Press, 1994.

CHAPTER 9

Malcolm X: Message to Humanity

John Andrew Morrow

As we mark the fiftieth anniversary of the martyrdom of El-Hajj Malik El-Shabazz, it is important that we remember his message, preserve it, and disseminate it. But what exactly was his message? For many, unfortunately, Malcolm X remains renowned for his vitriolic attacks against whites as a whole. While there is no doubt that Malcolm believed in the teachings of Elijah Muhammad with all his heart and all his soul for most of his adult life, namely, the belief that all whites were devils, it cannot be denied that his views about Caucasians evolved and that he eventually rejected them wholeheartedly. By focusing on his pre-Mecca phase as opposed to his final post-Mecca phase, Muslims and non-Muslims do a great disservice to the memory of Malik Shabazz and the true teachings of traditional Islam. As Malcolm came to realize, Islam was a universal religion based on fraternity and sorority. It was an inclusive as opposed to exclusive faith which was open to all believers regardless of race. It is important, then, to remind readers that while Malcolm X was determined to bring Islam to African-Americans, he was also committed to delivering this very same message to all Americans regardless of race.

An obligation upon all adult Muslims who are healthy and wealthy enough to undertake it, the *hajj* is saturated with spiritual lessons of all sorts. Upon the completion of a successful pilgrimage to Mecca, a Muslim is said to return home as pure as a new-born baby, purified of sins, and provided with a soul like a shinny blank slate. If ever there was a transformative *hajj*, it was the pilgrimage of Malcolm X, a man torn between the teachings of Elijah Muhammad, the self-proclaimed Messenger of Allah, and the teachings of Muhammad ibn 'Abd Allah, the final Messenger of Allah according to all orthodox Muslims. In fact, Malcolm had, for years, struggled between heterodoxy and orthodoxy. In fact, as early as October 10, 1963, Malcolm X remarked that "When you become a Muslim, you don't look at a man as being black, brown, red, or white. You look upon him as being a man" (Marable, 2011: 262). While he had been gradually drawing closer to mainstream Islam for over a decade, being gently groomed by Sunni and Shi'ite Muslims, Malcolm X had yet to take the final step: namely, to reject the racist and heretical doctrines of the Nation of Islam and enter fully into the fold of the Muslim Ummah. This step would come as a result of interaction with a myriad of Muslims from all over the world during the course of the *hajj*, the impact of which can only be described by Malcolm himself: Jedda, Saudi Arabia, April 20, 1964

> Never have I witnessed such sincere hospitality and overwhelming spirit of true brotherhood as is practiced by people *of all colors and races* here in this ancient holy land, the home of Abraham, Muhammad and all the other Prophets of the holy scriptures. For the past week, I have been utterly speechless and spellbound by the graciousness I see displayed all around me by people *of all colors*.
>
> I have been blessed to visit the holy city of Mecca; I have made my seven circuits around the Ka'aba, led by a young Mutawwaf (guide) named Muhammad; I drank water from the well of the Zamzam. I ran seven times back and forth between the hills of mount al-Safa and al-Marwa. I have prayed in the ancient city of Mina, and I have prayed on mount Arafat.
>
> There were tens of thousands of pilgrims, from all over the world. They were *of all colors*, from blue-eyed blondes to black-skinned Africans. But we were all participating in the same ritual, displaying a spirit of unity and brotherhood that my experiences in America had led me to believe never could exist between the white and non-white.
>
> America needs to understand Islam, because this is the one religion that erases from its society the race problem. Throughout my travels in the Muslim world, I have met, talked to, and even eaten with people who in America would have been considered white – but the white attitude was removed from their minds by the religion of Islam. I have never before seen sincere and true brotherhood practiced by all colors together, irrespective of their color.
>
> You may be shocked by these words coming from me. But on this pilgrimage, what I have seen, and experienced, has forced me to rearrange much of my thought-patterns previously held, and to toss aside some of my previous conclusions. This was not too difficult for me. Despite my firm convictions, I have always been a man who tries to face facts, and to accept the reality of life as new experience and new knowledge unfolds it. I have always kept an open mind, which is necessary to the flexibility that must go hand in hand with every form of intelligent search for truth.
>
> During the past eleven days here in the Muslim world, I have eaten from the same plate, drunk from the same glass, and slept on the same rug – while praying to the same God – with fellow Muslims, whose eyes were the bluest of blue, whose hair was the blondest of blond, and whose skin was the whitest of white. And in the words and in the deeds of the

white Muslims, I felt the same sincerity that I felt among the black African Muslims of Nigeria, Sudan and Ghana.

We were truly all the same (brothers) – because their belief in one God had removed the white from their minds, the white from their behavior, and the white from their attitude.

I could see from this, that perhaps if white Americans could accept the Oneness of God, then perhaps, too, they could accept in reality the Oneness of Man – and cease to measure, and hinder, and harm others in terms of their 'differences' in color.

With racism plaguing America like an incurable cancer, the so-called 'Christian' white American heart should be more receptive to a proven solution to such a destructive problem. Perhaps it could be in time to save America from imminent disaster – the same destruction brought upon Germany by racism that eventually destroyed the Germans themselves.

Each hour here in the holy land enables me to have greater spiritual insights into what is happening in America between black and white. The American Negro never can be blamed for his racial animosities – he is only reacting to four hundred years of the conscious racism of the American whites. But as racism leads America up the suicide path, I do believe, from the experiences that I have had with them, that the whites of the younger generation, in the colleges and universities, will see the handwriting on the walls and many of them will turn to the spiritual path of truth – the only way left to America to ward off the disaster that racism inevitably must lead to.

Never have I been so highly honored. Never have I been made to feel more humble and unworthy. Who would believe the blessings that have been heaped upon an American Negro? A few nights ago, a man who would be called in America a white man, a United Nations diplomat, an ambassador, a companion of kings, gave me his hotel suite, his bed. Never would I have even thought of dreaming that I would ever be a recipient of such honors – honors that in America would be bestowed upon a King – not a Negro.

All praise is due to Allah, the Lord of all the worlds.

Sincerely,

EL-HAJJ, MALIK EL-*SHABAZZ* (MALCOLM X) (*MALCOLM X Speaks* 59–60)

"The publication of his letter from Mecca," wrote Malcolm "Shorty" Jarvis, "did cause a lot of controversy" (Jarvis, 130). "Most people," he continues, "didn't believe he had experienced a change of heart... The mutual feeling among the general public was, the letter was a camouflage, a fake – indeed a con or a hustle" (Jarvis, 130). Jarvis, however, was perspicacious enough to see the truth for what it was: "I believe Malcolm said it all when he said, 'I learned the truth in Mecca'" (Jarvis, 130). For Jarvis, it was an admission of guilt in the form of an explanation (Jarvis, 130). According to Jarvis, Malcolm X had been previously incapable of seeing through deceitfulness (Jarvis, 130). As he explains,

> The Supreme Power knows I tried relentlessly to make him see a different point of view about people being people, regardless of race, creed or color. Once again, he flatly refused to hear this saying, 'Black is black and white is white, and the two will never mix.'
> JARVIS, 131

The irony of this statement is that it came from a green-eyed, red-headed, man whose mother easily passed for white and who was derided by black Africans for being an 'albino.' Genetically-speaking, Malcolm was one quarter Caucasian. Culturally and educationally he was completely Westernized. It was only intellectually and spiritually that he expressed his independence. As Malcolm Jarvis has explained to him time and again, "Let's not follow the white man's ways of evil, hatred, hypocrisy and deceitfulness. Let's find another way" (Jarvis, 131). That way, Malcolm would finally find in Mecca.

Although Malcolm X had been exposed to mainstream Islam from the time he was a teen, while he was in prison, and during his ministry with the Nation of Islam, it was not so much the theology of Islam that made him reconsider his mode of thinking, but rather the practice of Islam. In Mecca, Malcolm met Muslims from all over the world, and while they hailed from different countries, came from different cultures, and expressed themselves in different languages, they were all united by their common creed. As a black man coming from the United States, a country with a shameful history of racism, Malcolm could scarcely conceive that whites and blacks could get along as brothers and sisters. This was certainly not the first time that Malcolm had met white Muslims. In fact, he had visited Egypt, Palestine, Syria, Iran, the United Arab Republic, and Saudi Arabia in 1959 as the emissary of Elijah Muhammad (Gomez, 2005: 350; Ambar, 2014: ix, 66). Malcolm X could not have helped but notice that Muslims were not all black, as W.D. Fard and Elijah Muhammad had taught, and that many whites were actually devout Muslims. As I revealed in "Malcolm X and Mohammad Mehdi: The Shi'ite Connection", Malcolm's relationship with Dr. Mehdi, which commenced in 1958 and would last until his martyrdom in 1965, had already obliged him to do some introspection:

> Since Dr. Mehdi was very much a white man according to American standards, Malcolm X was forced to confront his own prejudices and stereotypes. In fact, Malcolm's meeting with this white Arab Muslim activist of Persian origin seems to have started the process of self-reflection and study which culminated in his conversion to universal Islam during his pilgrimage to Mecca in 1964 and his rejection of racism. Although he was Caucasian, Dr. Mehdi always insisted that he was neither white nor black but a human being. Dr. Mehdi was very much one of those Muslims who, although white on the outside, were certainly not white on the inside, if by white we refer to the mentality associated with racist Americans. When Malcolm X spoke of his experience in Mecca, where he mingled with Muslims of every colour and complexion, as well as his newfound appreciation for human diversity, he expressed himself in terms that were regularly employed by Dr. Mehdi.
> MORROW, 2012: 18–19

If Malcolm X had seen Egyptians in Egypt, Palestinians in Palestine, Syrians in Syria, and Saudis in Saudi Arabia, they were all, very much, birds of a feather. What was unique about the pilgrimage to Mecca was that Muslims of every imaginable color came together in one place, at one time, in a spirit of fraternity and sorority. By 1964, Malcolm had read the Qur'an, he knew that all human beings descended from Adam (4:1); and he knew that God created diversity to enrich humanity (49:13). He was most certainly familiar with the Prophet Muhammad's "Final Sermon" in which he stated that there was no difference between Arabs and non-Arabs and between whites and blacks. What Malcolm lacked was experiential knowledge of this reality. This he found during his 1964 *hajj* to Mecca.

In a letter directed to Alex Haley, authored on April 25, 1964, Malcolm X explained that he "began to perceive that 'white man,' as commonly used, means complexion only secondarily; primarily it describes attitudes and actions" (Marable, 2011: 310). He also observed that the white Muslims he had encountered during the pilgrimage "were more genuinely brotherly than anyone else had ever been" (Marable, 2011: 310). He realized that, in Islam, faith comes before color. He came to comprehend that people in other parts of the world identified themselves on the basis of religion, language, culture, and nationality, and not pigmentation which they cannot possibly control. "In his diary," writes Ambar, "Malcolm described the symbiotic relationship between his religious awakening and the possibilities for racial brotherhood" (Ambar, 2014: 66). Speaking of his pilgrimage, he wrote:

> Never in America have I received such respect + honor as here in the Muslim world, just upon learning I am a Muslim. People: white, black, brown, red [and] yellow – all act alike as one, as *Bros*. People with blue eyes + blonde hair, bowing in complete submission to Allah, beside those with black skin + kinky hair. As they give the *same* honor to the same God, they in turn give some (equal) honor to each other.
>
> AMBAR, 2014: 66

As Ambar explains, "Malcolm's conversion to Orthodox Islam enlivened in him a broader hopefulness for humanity, and specifically relations between blacks and whites, than was previously conceivable" (Ambar, 2014: 66). "Nothing," continues Ambar, "surpassed his excitement about Islam's potential to transcend racial and socioeconomic differences during the hajj" (Ambar, 2014: 66).

Since he had marked his conversion from criminal atheist to Black Muslim by dropping his family name, Little, and replacing it by X, he formally changed his name to El-Hajj Malik El-Shabazz to mark his religious conversion to traditional Islam. As Ambar puts it

> Becoming *El-Hajj Malik El-Shabazz* was freedom from organizational orthodoxy within the NOI and its deviation from acceptable Islamic teachings. And yet, by remaining X and Malik El-Shabazz, Malcolm was holding on to two visions of himself and his politics. He was linking himself to the black diaspora in the 'Western hemisphere,' as he responded to Berkeley at Oxford; and he was forging ties to the broader *Dar al-Islam* – the Muslim world that he had already joined to great personal satisfaction. In reaching out in this way, Malcolm also sought to project himself as someone whose extremism was within the bounds of moral conduct – despite whatever images of himself were formed in the minds of his worldwide audience.
>
> AMBAR, 2014: 73

In an interview conducted with CBS's Mike Wallace after his return from Mecca, the following exchange took place:

Wallace: Then the white man is no longer the devil and evil?
Malcolm X: The Holy Koran teaches us to judge a man by his conscious behavior, his intentions. So I judge a man by his conscious behavior, his deeds. I am not a racist. I do not subscribe to any of the tenets of racism.
Wallace: And so you feel that there are good whites and good blacks and bad whites and bad blacks?

> Malcolm X: It's not a case of being good or bad blacks and whites. It's a case of being good or bad human beings.
>
> AMBAR, 2014: 86

On August 25, 1964, four months after his life-altering hajj, Malcolm was humble enough to recognize the error of his ways and publicly repented for his wrong-doing:

> In the past I permitted myself to be used by Elijah Muhammad, the leader of the sect known as the Black Muslims, to make sweeping indictments of all white people, the entire white race, and these generalizations have caused injuries to some whites who perhaps did not deserve to be hurt. Because of the spiritual enlightenment which I was blessed to receive as a result of my recent pilgrimage to the Holy City of Mecca, I no longer subscribe to sweeping indictments of any one race.
>
> My religious pilgrimage (hajj) to Mecca has given me a new insight into the true brotherhood of Islam, which encompasses all the races of mankind. The pilgrimage broadened my scope, my mind, my outlook, and made me more flexible in approaching life's many complexities and in my reactions to its paradoxes.
>
> At Mecca I saw the spirit of unity and true brotherhood displayed by tens of thousands of people from all over the world, from blue-eyed blonds to black-skinned Africans. This served to convince me that perhaps some American whites can also be cured of the rampant racism which is consuming them and about to destroy that country.
>
> I am now striving to live the life of a true Sun[n]i Muslim. In the future I intend to be careful not to sentence anyone who has not first been proven guilty. I must repeat that I am not a racist nor do I subscribe to the tenets of racism. I can state in all sincerity that I wish nothing but freedom, justice, and equality, life, liberty, and the pursuit of happiness for all people.
>
> MALCOLM X, 1969: 302–303

From a Black Nationalist or supremacist, Malcolm X had become an internationalist and a humanist committed to social justice for all. Malcolm no longer viewed the world or socio-economic and political matters as black and white. Elijah Muhammad's Manichaeism and pessimism was replaced with critical thinking and optimism. Islam, besides being a source of spiritual salvation, could facilitate the elevation, not only of blacks, but of whites as well. If converting blacks to Islam was beneficial to blacks, Malcolm X realized that the conversion of whites, particularly those in positions of power and influence, could contribute to the betterment of life for people of color. Even the conversion of ordinary Caucasians to Islam would exponentially improve socio-economic conditions for African Americans. If Malcolm X said that he was committed to spreading orthodox Islam and undoing the damage done by Elijah Muhammad, this time the message would be directed to all human beings even though the oppressed took obvious priority.

In a letter to M.S. Handler dated September 22, 1964, Malcolm admitted that he had lived within the narrow-minded confines of the 'straight-jacketed' world of Elijah Muhammad, a man whom he represented and defended beyond the level of intellect and reason (Marable, 2011: 369). He vowed that he would never rest until he could undo the harm he did to so many innocent blacks and affirmed that he was now "a Muslim in the most orthodox sense; my religion is Islam as it is believed in and practiced by the Muslims here in the Holy City of Mecca" (Marable, 2011: 369). Demonstrating a remarkable degree of tolerance and acceptance for diversity, he wrote that:

> I am a Muslim who believes whole heartily that there is no God but Allah and that Muhammad ibn Abdullah...is the Last Messenger of Allah – yet some of my dearest friends are Christians, Jews, Buddhists, Hindus, agnostics and even atheists – some are capitalists, socialists, conservatives, extremists...some are black, brown, red, yellow and some are even white. It takes all of these religious, political, economic, psychological and racial ingredients (characteristics) to make the Human Family and the Human Society complete.
> MARABLE, 2011: 369–70

Categorically rejecting the racist doctrines of the Nation of Islam, Malcolm Shabazz professed on December 12, 1964, that he was "against any form of racism" (Malcolm X, 1969: 311). He was no longer a Black Muslim, namely, a follower of Elijah Muhammad's movement, but simply a Muslim:

> I'm a Muslim, which means my religion is Islam. I believe in Allah. I believe in all of the prophets, whoever represented God on this earth. I believe what Muslims believe: prayer, fasting, charity, and the pilgrimage to the Holy Land, Mecca, which I've been fortunate to have made four or five times. I believe in the brotherhood of man, all men, but I don't believe in brotherhood with anybody who doesn't want brotherhood with me.
> MALCOLM X, 1969: 311–312

As a mainstream Muslim, Malik Shabazz had realized that people were people, namely, that there were righteous people and that there were evil people of all colors and creeds. As such, he was prepared to be a brother to anyone who wished to be his brother, whether such a person was black, brown, red, yellow or white. Understandably, there was no place in his heart for racists and bigots of any ilk. Still, he observed that while racism was deeply rooted among the older generations of white Americans, many of the younger whites were opposed to segregation, discrimination, and racism. They were thus a fertile ground for planting the seeds of Islam, or, at the very least, sentiments of humanity. As Malik remarked on January 7, 1965:

> There are many white people in this country, especially the younger generation, who realize that the injustice that has been done and is being done to black people cannot go on without the chickens coming home to roost eventually. And those white people, even if they're not morally motivated, their intelligence forces them to see that something must be done. And many of them would be willing to involve themselves in the type of operation that you were just talking about. For one, when a white man comes to me and tells me how liberal he is, the first thing I want to know; is he a nonviolent liberal, or the other kind? I don't go for any nonviolent white liberals. If you are for me and my problem – when I say me, I mean *us*, our people – then you have to be willing to do as old John Brown did. And if you're not of the John Brown School of liberals, we'll get you later – later.
> MALCOLM X, 1989: 225

As radical and revolutionary as ever, Malik Shabazz continued to espouse direct action as opposed to sitting still in the face of civil and human rights violations; only now, he was willing to join ranks with militants of all backgrounds. Unlike the apolitical and non-interventionist views of the Nation of Islam, orthodox Islam had provided Malcolm with ample support for revolutionary tactics against oppression (Ambar, 2014: 108). Consequently, he was to collaborate with sympathetic revolutionaries. As he made clear in an interview conducted on January 18, 1965: "I'm not a racist. I'm against every form of racism and segregation, every form of discrimination. I believe in human beings and that all human beings should be respected as such, regardless of their color" (Malcolm X, 1991: 83).

No longer did Malcolm judge people on the basis of something they could not control, namely, the pigment of their skin or their facial features, and no longer did he espouse the separation of the races and object to mixed marriages. When asked whether he was opposed to interracial marriages after the speech he delivered in Paris in late 1964, he compared it to a matter of faith, saying: 'How can anyone be against love? Whoever a person wants to love that's their business - that's like their religion' (Ambar, 2014: 29–30). For those who believe that he was pandering to French liberals, Malcolm made the same statement when he returned to the United States. As he put it plain and clear on January 19, 1965:

> I believe in recognizing every human being as a human being – either white, black, brown or red – and when you are dealing with humanity as a family there's no question of integration or intermarriage. It's just one human being marrying another human being, or one human being living around and with another human being.
> MALCOLM X, 1989: 197

It is therefore sad that some African-Canadian, African-American, and Afro-Caribbean Malcolmites, both Sunni and Shi'i, raise objections when a Muslim of African ancestry wishes to marry a Muslim from a different background. While they claim to follow Malcolm X, they continue to maintain beliefs that belong to Elijah Muhammad and W.D. Fard. Malcolm did indeed change; however, some of those who claim to follow him most certainly have not. In fact, many activists still describe Malcolm X as a proponent of Black Nationalism. However, after a thought-provoking exchange with Taher Kaid in May of 1964, he had a change of heart. In the words of Malcolm:

> When I was in Africa in May, in Ghana, I was speaking with the Algerian ambassador who is extremely militant and is a revolutionary in the true sense of the world (and has his credentials as such for having carried on a successful revolution against oppression in his country). When I told him that my political, social, and economic philosophy was Black nationalism, he asked my very frankly: Well, where did that leave him? Because he was white. He was an African, but he was an Algerian, and to all appearances, he was a white man. And he said if I will define my objective as the victory of Black nationalism, where does that leave him? Where does that leave revolutionaries in Morocco, Egypt, Iraq, Mauritania? So he showed me where I was alienating people who were true revolutionaries dedicated to overturning the system of exploitation on this earth by any means necessary.
>
> So I had to do a lot of thinking and reappraising of my definition of Black Nationalism. Can we sum up the solution to the problems

> confronting our people as Black Nationalism? And if you notice, I haven't been using the expression for several months. But I still would be hard pressed to give a specific definition to the overall philosophy which I think is necessary for the liberation of the Black people in this country.
> MALCOLM X, 1991: 85; AMBAR, 2014: 119–120

From a political perspective, Malcolm X realized that Black Nationalism was too narrow. During his December 3rd, 1964, debate at Oxford Union, Malcolm "rejected both the lure of 'colorblindness' as well as the exclusivity of Black Nationalism" (Ambar, 2014: 71). What he was articulating was *internationalist humanism*. As such, Malcolm X cannot be considered the sole possession of Black people. As a man of global proportions, who stood up for human dignity, freedom, liberty, and justice, he belongs to humanity as a whole. The dichotomy of black versus white was replaced with the struggle between right and wrong and good versus evil. To him, black liberation, human dignity, and Islam, were all connected (Ambar, 2014: 108). There is no doubt that Malcolm X was a proud African American and a committed Muslim; however he was a human being first and foremost. As Malcolm noted in his diary, "I feel it is detrimental to our cause to reject whites from the benefits of nationalism or reject help from them that would safely help our cause" (Ambar, 2014: 139). Struggling with the term 'nationalist,' he stressed that "We don't want to be integrationists, nor separatists. We want to be human beings" (Ambar, 2014: 139). "We are fighting for the right to live as free human beings," he wrote (Ambar, 2014: 139). "In fact," he continues, "we are actually fighting for rights even greater than civil rights. We are fighting for human rights" (Ambar, 2014: 139). Malcolm had finally found the term that truly encompassed the scale of his struggle.

During the course of his interview with Pierre Berton in Toronto, Canada, Malcolm demonstrated how cosmopolitan he had become. He insisted that God embraced Jews, Christians, and Muslims alike, rejected the notion that whites were devils as taught by Elijah Muhammad, and stressed that "a man should not be judged by the color of his skin but rather by his conscious behavior, by his actions" (Marable, 2011: 407). He no longer believed in black supremacy but in equality (Marable, 2011: 407). As for the Nation of Islam's belief in a racial Armageddon, Malcolm X spoke instead of a conflict between the oppressed and the oppressors:

> I do believe that there will be a clash between East and West. I believe that there will ultimately be a clash between the oppressed and those that do the oppressing. I believe that there will be clash between those who want freedom, justice, and equality for everyone, and those who

want to continue the systems of exploitation. I believe that there will be that kind of clash, but I don't think that it will be based upon the color of the skin, as Elijah Muhammad has taught it.
MARABLE, 2011: 407

For Malik Shabazz, the world was divided between oppressors and the oppressed and between the exploiters and exploited. Issues came first and race, ethnicity, culture, and other components came second. "We must approach the problem as humans first," he said on January 26, 1965, "and whatever else we are second" (Marable, 2011: 408). Malcolm's concerns were no longer national; they were international. His scope was now global in reach. On January 30, the FBI recorded him as saying that "As a Muslim whose religion is Islam, as it is practiced and taught in the Muslim world, I realize that it is impossible to call oneself a Muslim, to call one's religion Islam and at the same time to judge a man by the color of his skin" (Carson, 1991: 345). He also noted that millions of Muslims, be they Arabs, Berbers, Bosnians, Albanians, Turks, and others, were white: "If Elijah Muhammad says that all white men are devils, then you have the King of Arabia, King Faisal, who is white. He is the keeper of the Holy City of Mecca and many other Arabs, in Egypt, in Algeria, and in other places. They are from all appearances white" (Carson, 1991: 345). This appraisal stands in stark contrast to claims made by certain Malcolmites who claim that real Arabs are black. This is, yet again, another myth of Elijah Muhammad and W.D. Fard that Malcolm X had duly dismissed.

Following in the example of the Prophet Muhammad, who prohibited Muslims from oppressing and remaining oppressed, Malik Shabazz confronted his critics on February 9, 1965, reassuring them that he was not the violent racist that he was made out to be in the media:

> I don't advocate violence and I'm not a racist, and I'm against racism and against segregation. I'm against anything that is immoral and unjust. I don't judge a person according to the color of their skin, I judge a person according to what he believes, according to his deeds and his intentions.
> MALCOLM X, 1969: 206

Rather than echo the teachings of Elijah Muhammad, Malcolm X was echoing the teachings of the Qur'an which commands Muslims to oppose racism (49:13), promote the good and forbid the wrong (3:110; 9:71; 3:104), stand out firmly for justice (4:135), and judge people on the basis of their actions and intentions (2:225). He further added that: "I believe in taking an uncompromising stand against any forms of segregation and discrimination that are based on race. I myself do not judge a man by the color of his skin" (Marable, 2011: 413). As he expressed during his debate at Oxford Union in late 1964, "I don't believe in any form of apartheid. I don't believe in any form of segregation. I don't believe in any form of racialism" (Ambar, 2014: 37–38).

In a letter to Dean Rusk, in which he protested being barred from France, Malik Shabazz disavowed any identification as a 'racialist' stating that "I adopt a judgment of deeds, not of color" (Marable, 2011: 413). Not only was Malcolm X objecting to the segregation of blacks by whites, he was evidently opposing the separation of blacks from whites espoused by the Nation of Islam. He realized that the cure to racism was not segregation and separation but rather unity.

In his last meeting with Gordon Parks, Malik Shabazz made some moving comments which showed his remorse for having rejected the solidarity of socially-conscious and committed whites who could have made important contributions to his cause:

> Remember the time that white college girl came into the restaurant – the one who wanted to help the Muslims and the whites get together – and I told her there wasn't a ghost of a chance and she went away crying? Well, I've lived to regret that incident. In many parts of the African continent I saw white students helping black people. Something like this kills a lot of argument. I did many things as a Muslim that I'm sorry for now. I was a zombie then – like all [Black] Muslims – I was hypnotized, pointed in a certain direction, and told to march. Well, I guess a man's entitled to make a fool of himself if he's ready to pay the cost. It cost me twelve years.
> MALCOLM X, 1969: 122

Malik Shabazz realized that any social, cultural, economic, and spiritual revolution would require the support of people from all ethnic, racial, cultural, religious, and linguistic backgrounds, and that peace, equality, justice, and liberty could only come about through unity. In short, Malik Shabazz had realized that he had been wrong to generalize about all whites as experience had showed him that white Muslims, along with some whites who were not Muslims, rejected racism as strongly as he did (Haskins, 1996: 61). During his debate at Oxford Union in late 1964, "Malcolm sought to enlist whites in the cause of extremism in the defense of liberty for African Americans" (Haskins, 1996: 56). Casting off the coil of the Nation of Islam and affirming his spiritual independence, Malcolm called upon young people of all races to unite in revolution:

> And in my opinion the young generation of whites, Blacks, browns, whatever else there is – you're living at a time of extremism, a time of

> revolution, a time when there's got to be a change. People in power have misused it, and now there has to be a change and a better world has to be built, and the only way it's going to be built is with extreme methods. And I for one will join in with anyone, I don't care what color you are, as long as you want to change this miserable condition on this earth. Thank you.
>
> AMBAR, 2014: 118

While Malik Shabazz was man enough to make this change from racialist to internationalist, some of his friends, associates, and followers failed to make the same transition and continued, for decades, to insist that Malcolm had not changed his views about whites as a whole, remained loyal to Elijah Muhammad until his death, hoped for a reconciliation, and would have returned to him in a heart-beat. Not only does this fly in the face of the evidence itself, all of it drawn directly from the mouth and pen of Malik Shabazz, it speaks much about the intellectual and spiritual state of these deniers who actually prefer the pre-Mecca Malcolm to the post-Mecca Malcolm. And since many of these deniers maintained such beliefs while professing to be Sunni or Shi'ite Muslims, it demonstrates that, unlike Malcolm, they were never able to heal their hearts from the disease of racism.

If such a disproportionate amount of emphasis has been placed on the pre-Mecca Malcolm as opposed to the post-Mecca Malcolm, it is also the result of reasons of state. As a result of the Cold War, the United States established the United States Information Agency, "to explain and advocate U.S. policies," which, in reality, meant, to engage in propaganda activities. In 1964, the director of this agency was Carl T. Rowan, "a long-standing ideological nemesis of Malcolm's" (Ambar, 2014: 133). The comments he submitted after Malcolm's death were closely scrutinized by the US government (Ambar, 2014: 133). According to his assessment, Malcolm X was a proponent of black supremacy and separatism (Ambar, 2014: 144). Rowan asked his colleagues in the agency "to do an extra-zealous job of getting out the facts, of informing the world" (Ambar, 2014: 144). As Ambar elaborates,

> Rowan's sentiments were squarely in line with US Cold War imperatives. They captured US foreign policy interests better than the more comprehensive but more complicated analysis of where Malcolm stood intellectually in the last months of his life. There is nothing in the Oxford address, for example, to confirm Rowan's 'black supremacist' view of Malcolm. The 'image-making' of the West that Malcolm had so skillfully exposed throughout his Oxford talk was very much at hand with respect to his death. The United States ultimately had a vested interest

> in ignoring any changes in Malcolm, change that would make his views more, rather than less, transferable on the international stage.
>
> AMBAR, 2014: 134

There is no doubt whatsoever that the powers that be have deployed all of their efforts into disseminating the image of Malcolm X as some sort of racist, black supremacist, separatist. The speeches that are spread, the citations that are selected, the images that are circulated, all portray a parochial, localized, time-bound, Malcolm X, whose extreme views are expired, and which have no global resonance. With the exception of a small circle of scholars, most people, including Americans and non-Americans of all religious and racial backgrounds, have been presented a myopic, reductionist, and unrepresentative, vision of Malcolm X. In film, documentaries, publications, and popular culture, Malcolm X is an angry ghetto preacher whose words are ironically echoed by Louis Farrakhan. The pre-Mecca Malcolm actually keeps the black man down. This is the real reason that so much energy has been invested in maintaining this mythical representation. The few words of Malcolm that have reached the masses are those from his Nation of Islam days and those which precede his pilgrimage to Mecca. Most lay people and even many Western scholars have completely ignored the speeches and interviews that Malcolm X gave in Africa and Europe during the last months of his life and which exemplify his ideological growth and development. As such, it will take the concerted effort of colleagues from various fields of study to help redirect attention to the real Malcolm X: the cosmopolitan, orthodox Muslim, who was concerned with humanity as a whole and committed to justice for all.

Conclusions

Since only God is immutable, it is in the nature of human beings to evolve and to pass through stages of intellectual and spiritual development. The identity of a man is his current state. Just like it would be unfair to portray Malcolm X as Detroit Red, the drug-addicted criminal and whore-monger, or Satan, the blasphemous atheist prisoner, it is equally unjust to present him as Minister Malcolm X, the white-loathing spokesman from the Nation of Islam. As Betty Shabazz would tell scholars and authors after they surveyed Malcolm's life during commemorative events: "Your speech was very beautiful...but you left my husband in the Nation" (Rickford, 2003: 67). Malcolm, it must always be remembered, left, rejected, and repudiated the Nation of Islam. It is therefore dishonorable for people who profess to follow in his footsteps to continue to cite statements that he himself regretted at having uttered. As Thomas Peele has expressed, "in his brief, bright moment of enlightenment before his assassination, he would quote Hamlet and say, 'I don't care what color you are as long as you want to change this miserable condition that exists on this earth'" (Peele, 2012: 102). Who exactly then was Malcolm X? Malcolm X was his final manifestation in physical form: El-Hajj Malik El-Shabazz, the mainstream Muslim who was martyred for traditional Islam on February 21st, 1965, the man who rejected racism and embraced not only the oneness of God but the oneness of humanity as its natural consequence.

Bibliography

Ali, Abdullah Yusuf. *The Holy Qur'an*. Brentwood: Amana Corporation, 1983.
Ambar, Saladin. *Malcolm X at Oxford Union*. Oxford: Oxford University Press, 2014.
Carson, Clayborne. *Malcolm X: The FBI File*. New York: Carroll & Graf, 1991.
Gomez, Michael A. *Black Crescent: The Experience and Legacy of African Muslims in the Americas*. Cambridge: Cambridge University Press, 2005.
Haskins, Jim. *Louis Farrakhan and the Nation of Islam*. New York: Walker and Company, 1996.
Jarvis, Malcolm "Shorty." *The Other Malcolm, "Shorty," Jarvis: His Memoir*. Jefferson, NC: McFarland, 2001.
Marable, Manning. *Malcolm X: A Life of Reinvention*, New York: Viking, 2011.
Morrow, John Andrew. "Malcolm X and Mohammad Mehdi: The Shi'a Connection?" *Journal of Shi'a Islamic Studies* 5, no. 1 (Winter, 2012): 5–24.
Peele, Thomas. *Killing the Messenger: A Story of Radical Faith, Racism's Backlash, and the Assassination of a Journalist*. New York: Crown Publishers, 2012.
Rickford, Russell J. *Betty Shabazz*. Naperville, IL: Sourcebooks, Inc., 2003.
Malcolm X, and Alex Haley. *The Autobiography of Malcolm X*. New York: Grove, 1966.
Malcolm X. *Malcolm X: The Man and His Times*. Ed. John Henrik Clarke, New York: MacMillan Publishing, 1969.
────── *Malcolm X Speaks: Selected Speeches and Statements*, ed. George Breitman, New York: Pathfinder, 1989.
────── *Malcolm X Talks to Young People: Speeches in the U.S., Britain & Africa*. New York: Pathfinder Press, 1991.

CHAPTER 10

Malik al-Shabazz's Practice of Self-Liberation

Emin Poljarevic

Introduction

Malik al-Shabazz's last year of life presents an enthralling example of an individual's ability to transcend one's ideological belligerency without relinquishing one's sense of moral purpose. His religious commitment to Islam and revolutionary dedication to improving socio-political conditions for Blackamericans[1] were arguably the primary forces that drove his activism (Dyson, 1995: 15ff.; Dabashi, 2008: 243ff.). Throughout his period within the Nation of Islam (hereinafter the Nation), he maintained that his two primary motivational forces were inseparable and therefore inherently dependent on attaining equal rights for the U.S.'s black population. Some appropriately argue that after his break with the Nation and conversion to Sunni Islam, he sought to distinguish more clearly the religious and political sides of his social activism (Dyson, 1995; Curtis, 2009; Marable, 2011). In fact, we could separate these two dimensions of his struggle for freedom, but this would risk a more coherent understanding of the direction of his ideological and spiritual evolution. In this chapter I argue that al-Shabazz's radical claim on freedom has stimulated consciousness and search for freedom of ethnic minorities beyond the U.S. socio-political context. What is more, the effects of this stimulus are greater than what the scholarship on Malcolm X has been willing to recognize hitherto. Before going into more details about some of the elements of this inspiration, I will contextualize, frame, and explain the more dominant element of his activism, namely, its socio-political dimension.

A number of contemporary scholars have chosen to focus on exploring the impact of al-Shabazz's ideas and activism on various elements of contemporary Blackamerican culture (see for instance Barboza, 1994; Dyson, 1995; DeCaro, 1996; Hart, 2008; Curtis, 2009; Leak, 2010; Smethurst, 2010; Turner, 2010). Others have investigated his message's influence on the evolution of the civil rights movement in general and on Blackamerican militancy in particular (Harper, 1971; Martin, 1991). Nevertheless, despite a serious amount of research on 'Malcolm X,' few if any have explored Islam's role in al-Shabazz's idea of liberation beyond the U.S. context. For example, in the recently published *Cambridge*

---

1 The term "Blackamericans" derives from the work of Sherman Jackson (2005, 70).

Companion to Malcolm X (Terrill, 2010), none of the 15 contributing scholars discuss at any length how the broader Islamic tradition affected the evolution of al-Shabazz's struggle for liberation of Blackamerican identity from the dominance of the popular (read: white) American culture. The absence of such analysis reminds me of 'epistemic violence' (Spivak, 1998: 280–281; 2006: 118ff.), or is at least indicative of *epistemic bias*, for it reveals how contemporary scholarly analyses sidestep an Islamic dimension of an iconic civil rights leader.

As an extension of this supposed bias, we find that little has been said about the impact of Malcolm X's thought and activism for Muslim minorities living outside the U.S. context. This chapter seeks therefore to contribute to widening the analysis and thereby complementing the field of 'Malcolm X studies' through an innovative analysis of al-Shabazz's religious significance for Muslims in a European social context.[2] However, it is limited to a single case study and based on an analysis of a selected number of his speeches, a review of the secondary literature, and the autoethnographical methodology through which I critically scrutinize my own understanding of his thought. The chapter is therefore an attempt to explore the impact of al-Shabazz's activism on a non-Blackamerican Muslim's experience.

In the first instance, the analysis explores his religious and political transformation through a critical study of several public and private statements related to his conversion to Sunni orthodoxy. Moreover, by tracing my own experiences with parts of the African-American culture while pursuing my education in the U.S., I will become part of the case study. But I consider this is a methodological risk well worth taking, as it narrows the gap between the analytical constructs of what is usually described as the 'subject' and the 'object' of research project. In a way, autoethnography enables the two research dimensions to merge together through a process of "rigorous, [and] multi-layered levels of researcher reflexivity" (Grant et al., 2013).

More clearly, autoethnography is "[a] form of self-narrative that places the self within a social context [...] The term has a dual sense and can refer either to the ethnographic study of one's own group(s) or to autobiographical reflections that include ethnographic observations and analysis" (Jupp, 2006: 15; also Jones, 2005). Such reflections presented through a personal narrative based on ethnographic observations of Blackamerican experiences will reveal some important insights about the *living legacy* of al-Shabazz's civil rights struggle and, most importantly, its Islamic dimension. In brief, the following narrative seeks to present a well-rounded argument of a relatively underdeveloped component of Malcolm X studies. There are, however, exceptions worth mentioning.

---

2   See "Malcolmology" (*Democracynow.org*, 2011).

Steven Barboza (1994), Luis A. DeCaro (1996), Amiri al-Hadid (2002), William Hart (2008), Abdin Chande (2008) are some of the scholars who have attempted to understand this religious dimension and its motivational strength. I have gained many insights from their works something that will become more apparent below.

Throughout the chapter I refer to Malcolm X as Malik al-Shabazz primarily due to my belief that his search for cultural authenticity and personal liberation through developing an Afro-Islamic identity both symbolizes and reflects why he chose to rename himself (see Al-Hadid, 2002: 51).

Boundaries of Otherness

As a Muslim outsider to the broader U.S. cultural and socio-political context, one might be confounded by the characteristics of its race relations, particularly in the South. As an international college student in a small central Georgian liberal arts college at the turn of the century, I found myself surrounded by subtle racial confines that, at least on the college campus, initially appeared elusive and inconspicuous. However, as my first semester came to the end, the boundaries became more lucid and apparent. Being a basketball player and clearly white, I ended up interacting with black college students both on and off the court. This sentence is rather interesting, as it summarizes an assertion of situational strangeness where, as a white basketball player, I found myself in a minority position vis-à-vis a Blackamerican majority and therefore outside of my own cultural comfort zone. For me, this strangeness went beyond the 'color' boundaries, for was an international student from Sweden and a part of ethnic minority therein, and therefore every interaction with American students (regardless of race) *is* inter-cultural communication.

As the school year progressed, I started to probe into the nature of what I perceived to be radical serious boundaries. Many of the Blackamerican college students whom I met came from Georgia and the neighboring states. They had been brought up and lived in a social context where informational racial boundaries were the norm and regarded my constant inquiries as outlandish. Nevertheless, some of them took the time to explain that what I described as 'boundaries' were actually mere 'expressions of cultural differences' between American blacks and whites. One of my teammates in particular explained that "African-Americans" simply "did things differently" from whites, but that this was also true for other ethnic groups in the U.S. (e.g. Latinos, Asians, etc.). This strong emphasis on race-based cultural differences is perhaps not unreasonable after all (see Aja, 2012). Still it is also a deeply unsettling idea or reality

– depending upon the understanding of a discussion interlocutor. This eventually led me to a naïve question: Why should race be one of the primal defining elements of a culture?

Part of the answer to this question can be found in the country's racial history. Herein we can find references to the injustices of slavery (Weld, 2011), the socio-political dynamics that had led to the civil war and the subsequent civil rights struggle (Blight, 2011), the continued processes of segregation and urban gentrification (Perry, 2013), and similar historical processes that have shaped its racial polity. Whatever readings the answer might contain, it is clear that those (in)visible "frames of color" remain pervasive in many parts of U.S. society (see Pendergrass, 2013). And yet these frames are not fixed, because if they were it would have been impossible for bi-racial Barack Obama to be elected and then re-elected as the country's president. Thus it seems that race is a 'floating signifier' that loosely represents the boundaries of the imagined frame of color (Levi-Strauss, 1987: 67ff.; Hall, 1997). The frame, regardless of how we imagine or experience it, has been at the core of society's public debate and history since the country's inception (Ehlers, 2012). What seems to have shifted in terms of its recent race history is the perforation of the color frame (see Cohen, 2010; Merolla and Jackson, 2014). Race has not evaporated from the national debate on public relations; it has only been reformulated, redefined, and reshaped through a new discursive emphasis on class and the functionality of the idea behind perpetual accumulation of economic and cultural capital (Weitzer and Tuch 2006: 30ff, 74ff; Alexander, 2010: 44ff, 190–195).

In a way, the 'floating' property of otherness enables perpetuity of social stratification (Kao and Thompson, 2003: 421, 432). The process of differentiation has gradually developed into each state's politics of how cultural and ethnic differences are represented and identified (see Leung et al. 2008). Such politics tend to highlight socio-cultural fissures out of which fear, suspicion, hatred, discrimination, and sometimes violence can emerge creating enduring harm (see Sacerdote, 2005). This is not to say that I equate the effects of social stratification in Sweden and the U.S. Clearly, the power differentials, magnitudes of experienced social injustices, cultural and social structures and countless other elements of political system are different. Nevertheless, I do consider some of the important effects of power differentials between the dominant culture (i.e. ethnic Swedes or white Anglo-Saxon Protestants) and various minorities (e.g. Blackamericans and various types of *invandrare*, see below) unrelated. Rather, I do see the effects of social stratification in these two contexts, apart from their different historical trajectories, as related when one considers the socio-economic alienation of ethnic, religious and cultural minorities in particular.

As I listen to hours of al-Shabazz's 1960's speeches, it is remarkable how contemporary he sounds. Many, if not a majority, of his recorded talks evaluate and discuss the race issue by identifying the blatant injustice and discrimination against Blackamericans. His rhetoric is strident and seemingly angry; but not careless, for he makes constructive recommendations to his audiences about how they can empower themselves. For instance, in his 1964 New Year's Eve speech he advised Mississippi youth

> see for yourself and listen for yourself and think for yourself. Then you can come to an intelligent decision for yourself. But if you form the habit of going by what you hear others say about someone, or going by what others think about someone, instead of going and searching that thing out for yourself and seeing for yourself, you'll be walking west when you think you're going east, and you'll be walking east when you think you're going west. So this generation, especially of our people, have a burden upon themselves, more so than at any other time in history. The most important thing we can learn how to do today is think for ourselves.
> MALCOLM X, 1965: 137

This intuitive advice is arguably relevant even today; especially if we consider the deepening social effects of contemporary culture of mass distraction (see Halnon, 2013). The advice to think critically, to be aware of one's environment and its power components, is significant. To be able to 'see and think for yourself' *en masse* is difficult primarily due to the complexity of the processes involved within the context of independent change within a collective. After all, being 'yourself' means diverging from your in-group in a way that meaningfully separates you from other members. On the other hand, the mode of separation needs to be sufficiently small in order for one to remain a member of the group. This means that we, as social actors, retain a level of agency to act independently. At the same time, we are simultaneously surrounded by the confines of a specific social (and host of other cultural, economic, institutional structural elements etc.) structure (see Bourdieu, 1990: 52ff.). The sense of confinement, boundaries, and differences becomes remarkably clear if a person is a visible minority of some sort. Stuart Hall draws on Foucault and Butler when he argues that a person's body contains all the elements of a socially constructed and contingent signifier through which an individual forms his/her identity, sense of belonging to one group of people as opposed to another, and by which self-perception is shaped and re-shaped (2003: 12–16; Derrida, 1978: 112–114). This consideration is helpful, as it places al-Shabazz in a context that both defined his social critique and prompted him to broaden his own social mobilization beyond the boundaries of color. It is here that his rediscovery of Islam played its decisive role.

The Dynamics of Subaltern Identity Claims

In an interview on May 21, 1964, his first broadcast interview after returning from the *hajj*, al-Shabazz told the present journalists and supporters:

> When I was at Mecca making the pilgrimage, I spoke about the brotherhood that existed at all levels and among all people who were there on that hajj and who have accepted the religion of Islam. And I pointed out that, for what it had done, for what religion of Islam had done for those people over there, despite of their complexion differences, that it would probably do America well to study the religion of Islam, and it perhaps it could drive some of the racism from this society, as it had driven racism from Muslim society [...] When I was on the pilgrimage I had close contact with Muslim whose skin in America would be classified as white [...] but these particular Muslims didn't call themselves white. They looked upon themselves as *human beings*, as a part of human family, and therefore they looked upon other human beings, as part of that same human family, and therefore they looked upon all other segments of human family as part of that same family [...] They had a *different* look, or a *different* air, or a *different* attitude than that which is reflected in the attitude of the men in America who call themselves white. So I'd said, if Islam had done that for them, perhaps if the white man in America had studied Islam, *perhaps* it could do the same thing for him.
>
> MALCOLM X NETWORK, 2014; see also MARABLE, 2011: 650–651

These and similar statements before his assassination (February 25, 1965) suggest a general outline of his political theology, an outline grounded in including *all* activists who are ready to mobilize for realizing racial equality on all levels of society. The idea of equality subsumes various processes of liberation. In one interview, al-Shabazz talks about liberating Blackamericans from material, mental, and cultural colonialism, which he sees as necessary if the people are to achieve both intellectual and cultural equality (Malcolm X, 1965: 50ff.). He seems to argue that Islam has a great deal to offer if the end goal of the attempt to liberate ethnic minorities, both individually and communally, is to reach the aforementioned scale of equality in the U.S. (Dabashi, 2008: 242ff.). In other words, his experiences within the Nation and his travels in Muslim-majority societies inspired him to develop a theology of cultural identity. This is an idea that clearly resonates with many Muslims living beyond the American context (see Esack, 1997).[3]

As an outsider to Georgia's cultural context and its deep race-relation convolutions, I felt unsettled in a number of social situations. For instance, this was obvious whenever I played an intramural basketball series on an all-black team against several exclusively white college fraternity teams. The initially subtle surprise and seeming disapproval for my 'daring' to do so was clearly voiced by some members of the opposing teams. This news was later conveyed to me by my (white) roommate who overheard conversations on the other side of the basketball court. This negative attitude became more apparent when I was deliberately and flagrantly fouled in the final moments of the game. What followed after that can be described as a full-scale brawl between the two teams and a number of spectators.

In retrospect, what I considered as an exciting basketball tournament turned into an unanticipated social experiment. In the aftermath my teammates, many of whom I had become friends with off the basketball court, tried to explain why the white players were so upset that I was 'playing' for the 'black team.' Their explanation can be summarized as follows: The 'frat-boys' were 'most likely' provoked by my unconventional social behavior and expressing their feelings through a 'knee-jerk reaction' to the same behavior. So I asked them: "If this was so out of the ordinary, how come you haven't had this reaction?" A couple of them replied that they thought I was strange for 'daring' to play 'ball' with them in the first place and also for wanting to 'hang out' with them. This arguably meant that the threat of unsettlement of the color boundaries was directly threatening the racial 'order.'

It later became obvious that I, as an international student and a Muslim, did not fit the Blackamerican students' stereotypical template of a 'white boy' (see Jackson, 2009: 34ff.). This was indeed intriguing, but at the same time familiar. As a teenager growing up in Sweden during the 1990s, I was a part of an ethnic and religious minority. In fact, I am still categorized primarily as a part of a loosely defined social stratum of 'immigrants' (*invandrare*). This and similar informal stratifications of citizenry is common in other European countries with significant ethnic and religious minorities (Dahlstedt, 2009; Bisin et al., 2011; Burgoon, 2014). But in Sweden it is difficult to find an official definition for this term (see Hermansson and Friberg, 2000). In social and political contexts, *invandrare* is a floating signifier used to differentiate 'native ethnic populations'

---

3   An interesting case of Malcolm X's influences on the idea of liberation can be observed on the left-wing blog "Sons of Malcolm": http://sonsofmalcolm.blogspot.se.

from 'others' (Sandberg, 2005: 83ff.). In the official Swedish census statistics, skin color is not considered an explicit marker of differentiation (i.e. 'native,' 'of Swedish background' or 'of immigrant background'). Nevertheless, much like Blackamericans, the category of *invandrare* is usually loaded with negative imageries in popular perception that is generally associated with a negative socio-economic status (Borevi and Strömblad, 2004: 46, 88; Alm et al., 2010: 16ff.; Hübinette et al., 2012; for the U.S. case see Hetey and Eberhardt 2014). In addition, being a Muslim causes one's social status to decline even further (See Gardell, 2010).

It might be too conceptually audacious to invoke the term *subaltern* when speaking of the socio-political minorities in the contexts of the U.S. and Sweden. Since we can recognize the diversity of socio-structural power mechanisms that by and large marginalize the 'other,' we can consider subaltern people in the two contexts. Such people are surely diverse enough in their composition that it is impossible and undesirable to define either Blackamericans or *invandrare*s as coherent groups. Nevertheless, the commonality of being marginalized, even culturally ostracized, by the dominant socio-political groups, as well as the mainstream modes of social and political communication and participation, marks the common features of their experiences (Malcolm X, 1965: 50ff.). Spivak would most probably dismiss my over-stretching the concept of subaltern to this extent (see de Kock, 1997); nevertheless, I argue that the socio-political marginalization of minorities in these two particular democratic contexts echoes important components of her concept of the subaltern (see Spivak, 1998).

What ostensibly sets the Blackamericans and *invandrare* apart within this framework is their different forms of cultural communication, for they are separated by particular social cues and symbols recognized by its members. As an *invandrare*, a person is socially compartmentalized into a group that is seen as disempowered in a social system (see Dahlstedt, 2009). The feeling of being disempowered and set apart from the majority has produced my sense of familiarity with the everyday experiences of my Blackamerican peers. But this does not, by any means, equate our specific particularities, histories, and depth of disenfranchisement in our respective socio-historical contexts. Although the content of emotional experiences of (political and social) minorities in various contexts might be similar, the intensity, structure, and emphasis on various parts of that content bear little, if any resemblance, to each other.

This consideration presents multicultural societies with inevitable tensions that tend to produce a string of difficulties (for an overview see Wise and Velayutham, 2009: Chapter 1), some of which clearly affect minorities more intensely than any other group in that particular society. The important issues that shape and express group identity, which have been noted earlier, frequently create tensions between the dominant majority and the disempowered minority. For instance, it is reasonable to assume that social systems are dedicated to preserving order and stability for those living there and thus are built on a particular power distribution framework. Any disruption to the power-distribution paradigm is seen as a threat to that 'power' order, and consequently disruptive and undesirable by the power-holders (see Carson, 2012: 19–23, 86ff.; also Hall, 1997; Hetey and Eberhardt 2014).

The assortment of characteristics that are habitually associated with disempowered groups in multi-ethnic societies (e.g. Blackamericans and Chicanos in the U.S., Asians and Afro-Caribbean peoples in the UK, *invadrare* in Sweden etc.) offer mind-maps by which citizens navigate their social environment. As a keen observer of these processes back in the 1960's, al-Shabazz could effectively articulate the Blackamericans' socio-economic and political grievances (Malcolm X, 1971: 201–209). A significant part of the Blackamerican masses could recognize the mainstream society's important landmarks as presented by him, and his ability to 'connect the dots' identified him as a threat to the state's security (Rummel, 2005: 62–63, 64ff.).

In effect, what al-Shabazz offered through his life example is the multi-layered liberation, both personal and communal. Firstly, he demonstrated an idea of radical empowerment through the disciplined routines of his everyday life. For instance, he initially transformed his life by internalizing the doctrines and methods of the Nation. In his own words, this transformation was a process of personal change: "Once you change your philosophy, you change your thought pattern. Once you change your thought pattern, you change your attitude. Once you change your attitude, it changes your behavior pattern and then you go on into some action" (Malcolm X, 1964). This seems to suggest that the process of change starts by changing the dominant epistemic framework of one's consciousness. Changing 'your philosophy' suggests breaking out of the framework of white cultural domination, where white skin implies socio-economic, political, and even intellectual superiority over non-whites. Numerous post-colonial and subaltern studies' scholars have demonstrated this paradigm elsewhere (see Fanon, 1967; Said, 1985; Mazrui and Mazrui, 1998; Spivak, 1999; Chakrabarty, 2000; Roy, 2002).

Secondly, al-Shabazz's mental emancipation began with his contact with the Nation and the teachings of Elijah Mohammad. But it did not end there, for he pursued it by adopting and developing the secular doctrine of Black Nationalism and reforming his religious beliefs, which allowed him to develop a more inclusionary worldview. Thirdly, and notwithstanding his socio-religious conservatism based on a broader reading of Islamic texts, his political sympathies were, for the lack of better term, progressive.[4] For instance, Rabaka posits that al-Shabazz can be understood better if placed within the intellectual context of critical theory: "Drawing from the critical nationalist tradition of Martin Delany and Marcus Garvey, Carlos Cooks and Robert Williams, Malcolm X sought consistently to combine his analysis of the present, 'what is,' with the possibilities and prospects of the future, 'what ought to be'" (Rabaka, 2002: 160). This is indeed reminiscent of the aim of the Frankfurt School's neo-Marxist intellectual project, wherein constant attempts to deepen the analysis of the patterns of contemporary life are driven by ambitions of what life could be (see Marcuse, 2001). Al-Shabazz's message and life-work have shown, at least in part, that imagination and ambition of achieving 'what life could be' offers inspiration to a number of ethnic minorities even today.

My interaction with Blackamericans during my student days suggests similar, yet distinct, conclusions. Our respective experiences as members of ethnic and cultural minorities produced distinctive paths toward a similar understanding of socio-political power-differentials. This process of understanding has allowed al-Shabazz's message to Blackamericans during the early 1960's to resonate with members of a minority community who live in vastly different historical, socio-political, and cultural contexts (see Svensson, 2005; Sörberg, 2011; Lundén, 2014; Sohl, 2014). In other words, the connection between the experiences of Blackamericans and '*invandrare*', and, for that matter, other socio-economic and political minorities, is defined through the rhetorical imagery of minority identities (Pantrarna, 2012; Trindvy, 2012; Hamad, 2015).

So where does this leave the important religious dimension of al-Shabazz's message? To address that question properly, one must look at his search for cultural and religious authenticity, for this search prompts an individual to develop a high level of self-awareness, a state that is often linked to one's cognizance of his/her collective identity (see Poljarevic, 2012). It is safe to claim, therefore, that al-Shabazz's constant search for religious and cultural authenticity enabled him to develop a hyperawareness of the Blackamerican community's collective past (Clark, 1991: 86; see also Rabaka, 2002: 151).

Religious Identity

Al-Shabazz's religious transformation from the Nation to Sunni orthodoxy, profound and genuine as it were, allowed him to more readily separate re-

---

4   Al-Shabazz's New York lectures, at least in the early 1960's, were frequented by a number of international Sunni-Muslim students who oftentimes confronted Elijah Mohammad's religious doctrines, and who frequently supplied al-Shabazz with religious literature.

ligion from politics (Curtis, 2009: 55ff.; al-Hadid, 2002: 74). This decision increased his independence, for he had rid himself from the control of a patriarch (i.e. Elijah Mohammad) and the narrow framework of the Nation's political theology. During this new stage of his life, he consciously channeled his activist voice in a way designed to include the widest possible base of supporters in order to achieve the deepest political impact. Nevertheless, Islam remained a vital source of his ideas when it came to both individual and social liberation (Curtis, 2002: 100–101; Barboza, 1994: 40ff., 273–274, 289–291; see also Perry, 1991). In early 1965, he proclaimed: "I believe in Islam. I am a Muslim and there is nothing wrong with being a Muslim, nothing wrong with the religion of Islam. It just teaches us to believe in Allah as the God. Those of you who are Christians probably believe in the same God, because I think you believe in the God who created the universe. That's the one we believe in, the one who created the universe – the only difference being you call him God and we call him Allah" (Malcolm X, 1965: 167). This religious outlook was a result of a long process of religious transformation.

What became clear throughout this process is that his personal commitment to *the search* for authenticity was consistent with his previous decision to transform himself: he consciously decided to end his life as a criminal and adopt the life of a Muslim. In other words, his search for authenticity was directly linked to an idea of both personal and communal liberation – something that is not uncommon even today. While in Georgia, I developed a close relationship with a military college graduate, a young Blackamerican from North Carolina. After sometime he had become curious about my religious affiliation and my personal experiences with prejudice and discrimination in Sweden. On top of that, my insistence on showing up on the basketball court every afternoon, when white students rarely came, at first seemed unexpected to him. A year into our friendship, he became interested in a fellow student whose parents were members of the Nation from Macon, GA. This meant that if his pursuit of her were to succeed, he would eventually need to become a Muslim.

Initially, I became an obvious source of religious information; however, the Nation's doctrine stood in stark contrast to my own mainstream Sunni doctrine of the omnipotent God and the finality of prophethood in the personhood of the Prophet Muhammad. This divergence in religious doctrines did not hinder our friendship; to the contrary, our discussions became more frequent and stimulating. On one occasion I was invited to visit the Nation's Macon temple during a Friday sermon and talk with the Minister, at my friend's request. My insensitive questions about the Nation's relation to non-Black Muslims and the experiences of al-Shabazz and Warith Deen Mohammed (1933–2008), a son of Elijah Mohammad, the leader of the Nation (1975–1976), 'entering the fold of

Islam' were largely disregarded during our brief conversation, as was my presence in the temple.

My friend's plans to marry a fellow student were soon suspended, due to her decision to end their relationship. Thus he stopped his weekly visits to the temple. But what seem to have remained with him is the heightened sense of pride, as well as the heightened level of awareness of the existing power disparities between the races. In other words, race mattered to him more than he had admitted to himself previously (see West, 1994). His shared reflections about institutional injustice, primarily related to his experiences in high school, military college/service, and his life on welfare in Fayetteville, NC, indicated a change in his consciousness. "Malcolm X was 'dead on' regarding the injustices of the white man upon us [Blackamericans]," he once lashed out. "We [Blackamericans] are still trapped in that game of materialism, we simply don't have enough education and sense of community to work together and free ourselves from the spiritual poverty of Christianity." He seemed to be rephrasing his earlier social criticism into a more abstract set of ideas that included a critique of institutionalized Christianity.

It became clear that during that brief exposure to the Nation, my friend was able to adopt and build upon a view on social and political power differentials in the U.S. We frequently talked about the role of al-Shabazz and the Nation in shaping the contemporary Blackamerican (and also *invandrare*'s) consciousness of its collective potential to transcend, real or imagined, structural boundaries in diverse and multicultural polities. 'Transcending' here does not mean to eradicate cultural or even class boundaries, for what my friend and I came to agree upon was the constructive intellectual direction toward which we understood al-Shabazz to have been working. Despite our different ways of explaining what he meant to us, we clearly articulated that in the end he was trying to minimize the negative effects of cultural differences in the U.S.

Years later, during my time as a Visiting Scholar at the University of Edinburgh, Scotland, I came in contact with a Blackamerican post-graduate student. As I told him about my experiences in the U.S., he related about his life as a Sunni Muslim in his native Philadelphia. The main focus of our conversations was the current situation of Blackamerican Muslim communities in the U.S. in which as Elijah Mohammad, Malik al-Shabazz, Warith Deen Mohammad, Imam Siraj Wahhaj,[5] and other personalities were the main topics. During the course of our conversations, what had surprised me the most were his overwhelming positive opinions about Elijah Muhammad and his contribution to

---

5 Siraj Wahhaj b. 1950 is an American Muslim leader (Muslim Alliance in North America) and a former member of the Nation of Islam.

the country's present Sunni community. This reaction was a rather telling of my own narrow and partisan reading of the history of Blackamerican Muslim community, for I had always seen Elijah as just another false prophet and the Nation as a marginal and renegade Muslim group.

I had clearly failed to appreciate the Nation's impact upon the contemporary Blackamerican Muslim community and shaping of its collective identity. It's likely that Warith Deen Mohammad's reconciliatory leadership style and his affection toward his father are some of the factors that have shaped Blackamerican Sunni Muslims' positive outlook on Elijah's historical role. Even if we consider that there were other Blackamerican Muslims proselytizing right along with the Nation during the 1950's and 1960's, they were politically reclusive, often socially isolated, and thus far less influential in shaping the Blackamericans' religious dynamics (see Chande, 2008; Lo and Nadhiri, 2010).

The Catharsis of Redefining the Self

The Nation's influence on Blackamerican Muslims comes from its ability to 'clean up' culturally and spiritually downtrodden individuals. Its message of cultural and historical authenticity and claims of superiority over whites resonated well with a substantial number of Blackamericans during the 20th century – especially with Elijah Mohammad himself. Wali Farad Muhammad, one of Elijah's grandchildren, relates that his mother had told him that she remembered seeing her father (Elijah) drunk nearly every Friday during the early 1930's. But after the mysterious and historically controversial figure Farad Muhammad introduced Elijah to the teachings of Islam, all of that changed. Elijah was impressed enough to quickly embrace Farad's message and shortly thereafter becoming his prophet and the leader of the emerging Nation (Muhammad, 1994: 272ff.). This and similar experiences of transformation and spiritual awakening through the belief in what was said to be the original religion of the African ancestors offered Blackamerican Muslims a powerful sense of collective identity that was rarely encountered elsewhere (see Barboza, 1994; Korb, 2012).[6]

These individual experiences of spiritual transformation were cemented through a strict personal and group discipline that was promoted as the basis for a healthy and strong Blackamerican community (Saldaña-Portillo 2008, 145–148). As al-Shabazz noted in his autobiography: "I knew that our strict

---

6 Such feelings of religious community among Blackamericans could in fact be compared to collective spiritual experiences in many "black" churches (see Lincoln and Mamiya 1990, 164ff).

moral code and discipline was what repelled them whites most. I fired at this point, at the reason for our code. 'The white man wants black men to stay immoral, unclean and ignorant. As long as we stay in these conditions we will keep on begging him and he will control us. We never can win freedom and justice and equality until we are doing something for ourselves!'" (Malcolm X, 1992: 252). This is another manifestation of the evolving theology of identity. In effect, the sense of cultural and religious distinctiveness from the majority society was deeply entrenched in his thought. For instance, even when he broke with Elijah Mohammad he made sure to reaffirm his identity as a Muslim during a press conference held on March 12, 1964:

> I am and always will be a Muslim. My religion is Islam. I still believe that Mr. Muhammad's analysis of the problem is the most realistic, and that his solution is the best one. This means that I too believe the best solution is complete separation, with our people going back home, to our own African homeland [...] I am going to organize and head a new mosque in New York City, known as the Muslim Mosque, Inc. This gives us a religious base, and the spiritual force necessary to rid our people of the vices that destroy the moral fiber of our community.
> MALCOLM X, 1965: 20–21

This brings up the issue of the 'Islamic' content of his message. It is fairly clear that al-Shabazz had expressed an interest in and developed important contacts with Sunni Muslims as early as 1959 (Rickford, 2003: 177–178; Curtis, 2007: 693ff.; Marable, 2011: 301, 308ff.). In other words, he had at least several years of (unspecified) contact with Sunni Muslims. For example, in Saudi Arabia and Egypt he was questioned and taught about the basic tents of Islam, and thus acquired a more traditional understanding of the doctrine and religious practices (see Curtis, 2007; Marable, 2011: 365). The fact that Ahmed Hassoun, a Sudanese imam, accompanied him to the U.S. and assumed the responsibility of educating the members of al-Shabazz's newly created Muslim Mosque Incorporated gives additional credence to the 'sunnification' of al-Shabazz and his followers (Marable, 2011: 390ff.; Clark, 1992: 226–227). This religious transformation was thorough; however, it was limited to a small group of followers.

In comparison to Warith Deen Mohammad's religious life, al-Shabazz's religious credentials are limited for many reasons. Yet, the importance of his legacy as a political activist has amplified all aspects of his life, not least its religious dimension. It is here that we find the source of many contemporary

Muslims' fascination with his life and message. After all and as I learned from my Blackamerican friend in Edinburgh, Imam Warith, as he was referred to, focused on developing the Blackamerican Muslims' "solid and sound" religious consciousness. Understanding and adopting these specific religious doctrines and practices were therefore at the center of his mission. He had started his transformation earlier than al-Shabazz did, while serving as a minister of Temple No. 11 in Philadelphia during 1958 (Terry, 2002; Linson, 2007).

Al-Shabazz, a close friend of Imam Warith, was far more secular in his approach to social mobilization. As previously noted, his political mission to renew and redefine Black Nationalism needed as designed to secure a wider appeal among Blackamericans. From a political activist point of view, focusing on Islamizing all Blackamericans would have distracted a great deal of attention from the immediate problems of millions of people who had already been spiritually assimilated into the majority society's religious framework. The central purpose of al-Shabazz's mobilization efforts, therefore, was to widen the political awareness of Blackamerican population, wherein religion (Christianity and Islam) played a supporting role in terms of the general struggle for civil rights. In his *Ballot or the Bullet* speech in Detroit, where he favored separation between his religious and political life, he stated,

> Islam is my religion, but I believe my religion is my personal business. It governs my personal life, my personal morals. And my religious philosophy is personal between me and the God in whom I believe; just as the religious philosophy of these others is between them and the God in whom they believe.
> MALCOLM X, 1964

In the same speech delivered in Cleveland in April, 1964, he rephrased it:

> I would like to say, in closing, a few things concerning the Muslim Mosque, Inc., which we established recently in New York City. It's true we're Muslims and our religion is Islam, but we don't mix our religion with our politics and our economics and our social and civil activities not any more. We keep our religion in our mosque, After our religious services are over, then as Muslims we become involved in political action, economic action and social and civic action. We become involved with anybody, anywhere, any time and in any manner that's designed to eliminate the evils, the political, economic and social evils that are afflicting the people of our community.
> MALCOLM X, 1965: 38

Talking to socialist youth, he elaborated on his ideas even further:

> See, as a Muslim, I don't get my religion involved in my politics, because they clash. They don't clash, but when you go into something as a Muslim, you've got a whole lot of Negroes who are Christians, who aren't broad-minded enough, so you get into a religious argument, and it doesn't pay.
> CLARK, 1991: 64

But is it really possible to separate one's deepest moral framework and deeply held religious beliefs from one's political views and doctrines? It is perhaps simplistic to answer this question with a simple 'no,' but it seems to me that a person's moral framework has an important bearing upon one's political activism. During a January 1965 interview right after his return from Mecca, the seemingly exhausted al-Shabazz remarked, "I want to talk about what is sacred, how in the Holy Land I pulled the breath of Allah into my own lungs, how this made me want to laugh and embrace anyone, how I want my people to know their skin unbruised as it had been once early in the world" (Seibles 1993, 501). This indicates that he, perhaps in a moment of fatigue, felt uplifted, tranquil, and safe in a social environment where he could experience a moment of universal human unity. But at the same time, he was aware of what we can today describe as Islamophobia, for even at that time Americans had (and still have) an overwhelmingly negative view of Islam even if they respected 'Malcolm X' (Hart, 2008: ix).

Warith D. Mohammad, on the other hand, sought to Islamize the Blackamerican community by bringing it closer to mainstream Sunni Islam, thereby creating a powerful synergy effect of transformative processes that many Blackamericans experienced throughout the early and mid-20th century.[7] The two distinct directions of this community's improvement rested solidly on the legacy of Elijah Mohammad and the Nation. Elijah's activism, although rooted in the Nation's theology of Yakub's story and the attached idea of Black supremacy, was essentially focused on the Blackamericans' collective transformation through reorientation of the identity of their theological framework (see Ansari 1981, 146ff).

The three components of Blackamerican liberation within the American context are interwoven and cannot be fully disconnected. Al-Shabazz's activism, although primarily focused on making political claims during the last year of his life, is well rooted in his religious conviction concerning the universality

---

7   By many, I mean Muslims from Nation of Islam, pockets of Sunni Blackamericans in urban areas on the East Coast.

of human experience. Curtis shows that he went through several stages of religious (re)education, the end result of which was his embrace of mainstream Sunni Islam. Throughout the 1950's, al-Shabazz was in contact with foreign Muslim missionaries, students, and diplomats who, in different ways, criticized the Nation by promoting Sunni religious doctrine (Curtis, 2007: 693–694; see also Ansari 1981). The example of an international student (Ahmed Osman), who came to New York to confront al-Shabazz with the theological principles of Sunni Islam, is one of many mentioned in the relevant literature (see Marable, 2011; DeCaro, 1996; Curtis, 2007). These experiences certainly complicated al-Shabazz's understanding of Islam and Blackamerican cultural history, which pushed him to develop a distinct internationalist outlook on the American race problem.

In an interview published four days after his assassination, al-Shabazz is recorded to have said:

> The greatest mistake of the movement has been trying to organize a sleeping people around specific goals. You have to wake the people up first, then you'll get action.
> *Miss Nadle*: Wake them up to their exploitation?
> *Malcolm*: No, to their humanity, to their own worth, and to their heritage. The biggest difference between the parallel oppression of the Jew and the Negro is that the Jew never lost his pride in being a Jew. He never ceased to be a man. He knew he had made a significant contribution to the world, and his sense of his own value gave him the courage to fight back. It enabled him to act and think independently, unlike our people and our leaders.
> MALCOLM X, 1965: 198

Such reasoning was supported by his new understanding of religious consciousness and moral duty, both of which were tied with his socio-political vision:

> [T]he thing about the Egyptian revolution [1952] was that it never de-emphasized the importance of religion. In these new cities, the first thing they build is a mosque, so people can practice their religion. Then they build schools so the people can be educated free; and then they build hospitals. They believe that the religious aspect keeps the people spiritually and morally balanced, and then everyone should have the best education and free hospitalization.
> MALCOLM X, 1965: 126–127

Based on these statements, it is reasonable to claim that his version of liberation theology was based on the idea of an elevated sense of human dignity (and for Blackamericans in particular), social empowerment, and cultural transformation (see al-Hadid, 2002). Dyson explains this theology as a "project to reclaim the dignity of black identity from the chaotic dissemblances and self-deceptions instigated by racist oppression" (Dyson, 1995: 15). This and similar tropes are reminiscent of the basic claim of the Black Power movement that developed in the wake of Blackamerican upheavals during the mid 1960's (see Cone, 1997: preface; Rummel, 2005).

In his search for self-worth, cultural pride, and increased freedom for Blackamericans, al-Shabazz translated his social experiences into a framework of collective claim-making arguments that he could then link to the global struggle of disenfranchised peoples the subaltern, if you like. His ethos, captured in many mythicized versions of his life and rhetoric, popularized his theology of identity to such a degree that we find ethnic and religious minorities in Europe referring to 'Malcolm X' as a source of inspiration (see Horne, 1993; Urla, 2001; Saeed, 2007). The process of universalizing and popularizing al-Shabazz's life is intrinsic to how our popular culture works today (see Street, 1997). Be that as it may, without the important content of his message and its, still insufficiently explored, connection to the marginalized ethnic and religious minorities' wide-ranging desires and search for authenticity, freedom and independence, his ideas and activism would be of far less value and consideration to international audiences.

Conclusion

Al-Shabazz's life story, its transformative undertones, his idea of freedom and identity as well as his social activism continue to inspire marginalized minority groups around the world. I have partly discussed how this inspiration is manifested in the thinking of some Muslims in Sweden. Although al-Shabazz attempted to separate his religious and political activism, we find his life being guided by a sense of Islamic ethics because this is the bedrock upon which his everyday discipline activism and heightened awareness of cultural distinctiveness were built. The influences of the Nation's code of behavior, the idea of Black pride, and his own rhetorical and mobilizing skills helped him develop an original mode of activism through which he, much like a skilled musical soloist, could communicate collective Blackamerican experiences in a highly contentious and evidently dangerous socio-political context. It is his rhetorical skills, intellectual ability to organize his thoughts, and his charisma that has allowed his message to affect generations of young people long after his assassination in Manhattan, NY on that cold afternoon, February 21, 1965 (see Daulatzai, 2014).

As a member of a visible religious and ethnic minority (i.e. the generic term, *invandrare*), although in a much less contentious environment, I can sympathize with and relate to his quest for self liberation. More importantly, however, I consider al-Shabazz's concern for the underprivileged ethnic groups, his vocation as an activist, and his method of delivering his message as particularly inspiring and purpose-driven. Today, these elements are fused in such a way that they have become indistinguishable from his complex persona. For instance, I have seen popularized images of him in the most unexpected places, such as the controversial Nicki Minaj's album cover alluding to the famous 'riffle photo' portraying him in his living room looking through the window (Coleman 2014).

My reading of al-Shabazz's lifework and its religious dimension may seem yet another attempt to reinvent or re-construct this iconic personage (see Marable, 2011); however, my intention has been to highlight the importance of his thought even today. In fact, this entire volume is evidence of the continuing relevance of al-Shabazz's thought in terms of understanding the contemporary struggles of underprivileged people in the United States and elsewhere around the globe. Much like David Henry Thoreau's idea of civil disobedience, al-Shabazz's radicalism and framing of socio-political injustices have endured the test of time. Not only is this telling of their well-placed intellectual foresight, but it also includes the durability of the structures that uphold social, economic, cultural and political inequality. Al-Shabazz's unapologetic response to the extremes of the socio-political situation elevated him above the most of the Blackamerican leadership. For instance, while replying to an audience member after one of his public lectures, he described nonviolent activism in Mississippi (1964) as a person going in the ring to fight "Cassius Clay, or Sonny Liston" with handcuffs on. Statements like these showed just how in tune he was with contemporary events. He had framed his thoughts in such a way that those who listened to him could understand him.

In the end, framing al-Shabazz's activism through an analysis of his theology of identity is useful only if we are willing to consider the spiritual underpinnings of his mobilization. I have tried to link my understanding of his activist life by relating its social dimension to my own experiences as a member of a minority community in Sweden along with my impressions of contemporary Blackamerican experiences. This is a strained comparison, no doubt; however, it offers an important insight into how his legacy remains evermore relevant in the 21st century. His fearless commitment to justice and equality are still great moral resources for contemporary minority populations in the U.S. and, potentially, in Europe as well. As such, his ideas are empowering as we are alerted to our lived realities (persistent marginalization, discrimination, foreign occupation etc.) in combination with un-lived abstractions (official narratives of liberalism, human rights, economic equability etc.), both of which allow us to envisage new, and potentially radical, solutions to the contemporary ills in our respective societies.

Bibliography

Aja, Alan A. "Anyone But Blacks Latinos, El Nuevo Blanqueamiento (Neo-Whitening), and Implications for Black-Brown Alliances," *SOULS* 14, no. 1–2 (2012): 88–116.

Alexander, M. *The new Jim Crow: Mass incarceration in the age of colorblindness.* New York: The New Press, 2010.

Al-Hadid, Amiri YaSin. "Al-Qur'an and Sunnah: From Malcolm X to El-Hajj Malik al-Shabazz." In *Between Cross and Crescent The History of African-American Religions*, edited by Lewis V. Baldwin and Amiri YaSin Al-Hadid. Gainesville, FL: University Press of Florida, 2012.

Alm, Susanne et al. "Utsatthetens olika ansikten: Begreppsöversikt och analys Arbetsrapport/Institutet för Framtidsstudier." (Different faces of vulnerability: overview of the concepåt and analysis). 2010. http://www.iffs.se/wpcontent/uploads/2011/01/20101208132445fildyxF9W9whKiTU1N0Bx1q.pdf (Accessed October 30, 2014).

Barboza, Steven. *American Jihad: Islam after Malcolm X.* New York: Double Day. 1994.

Bisin, Alberto et al "Ethnic identity and labour market outcomes of immigrants in Europe." *Economic Policy* 26, no. 65 (2011): 57–92.

Blight, David W. *American Oracle: The Civil War in the Civil Rights Era.* Cumberland, RI: Harvard University Press, 2011.

Borevi, Karin and Per Strömblad. *Kategorisering och integration. Om föreställda identiteter i politik, forskning, media och vardag* (Categorization and integration. About envisaged identities in politics, research, media and everyday life). Stockholm: Fritzes Offentliga Publikationer, 2004. http://www.regeringen.se/content/1/c6/04/74/92/9048b3fd.pdf (Accessed October 17, 2014).

Bourdieu, Pierre. *The Logic of Practice*, Translated by R. Nice. Stanford, CA: Stanford University Press, 1990.

Burgoon, Brian. "Immigration, Integration, and Support for Redistribution in Europe." *World Politics* 66, no. 3 (2014): 365–405.

Carson, Clayborne. *Malcolm X: The FBI File.* New York: Skyhorse Publishing, 2012.

Chakrabarty, Dipesh. *Provincializing Europe. Postcolonial Thought and Historical Difference.* Princeton: Princeton University Press, 2000.

Chande, Abdin. "Islam in the African American Community: Negotiating between Black Nationalism and Historical Islam." *Islamic Studies* 47, no. 2 (2008): 221–241.

Clark, Steve, ed. *February 1965: The Final Speeches*. New York: Pathfinder, 1992.

Clark, Steven. *Malcolm X Talks to Young People*, New York: Pathfinder. 1991.

Cohen, Cathy. *Democracy Remixed: Black Youth and the Future of American Politics*. Cary, NC: Oxford University Press, 2010.

Coleman, Miriam. "Nicki Minaj Apologizes for Using Malcolm X Photo in Single Artwork." *RollingStone*, February 16 2014. http://www.rollingstone.com/music/news/nicki-minaj-apologizes-for-using-malcolm-x-photo-in-single-artwork-20140216.

Cone, James H. *Black Theology and Black Power*. Maryknoll, NY: Orbis Books, 1997.

Curtis IV, Edward E. *Islam in Black America, Identity, Liberation, and Difference in African-American Islamic Thought*. Albany: State University of New York Press, 2002.

———. "Islamism and Its African American Muslim Critics: Black Muslims in the Era of the Arab Cold War." *American Quarterly* 59, no. 3 (2007): 683–709.

———. "Islamism and Its African American Muslim Critics: Black Muslims in the Era of the Arab Cold War." In *Black Routes to Islam*, edited by Manning Marable and Hishaam D. Aidi, New York: Palgrave Macmillan, 2009.

Dabashi, Hamid. *Islamic Liberation Theology: Resisting the empire*. Oxon: Routledge, 2008.

Dahlstedt, Magnus. "The Swedish Road to Democracy? Governmentality, Technologies of Citizenship and Popular Movements." *TheMES – Themes on Migration and Ethnic Studies, Occasional Papers* 30. Norrköping: Institute for Research on Migration, Ethnicity and Society (REMESO), 2009. https://www.academia.edu/214588/The_Swedish_Road_to_Democracy_Governmentality_Technologies_of_Citizenship_and_Popular_Movements (Accessed September 2, 2014).

Daulatzai, Sohail. *The Return of the Mecca: The Art of Islam and Hip Hop*. Los Angeles: Razor Step Media, 2014.

DeCaro Jr., Louis. *On the Side of My People: A Religious Life of Malcolm X*. New York: New York University Press, 1996.

de Kock, Leon. "Interview With Gayatri Chakravorty Spivak: New Nation Writers Conference in South Africa." *ARIEL: A Review of International English Literature* 23, no. 3 (1997): 29–47.

Democracynow.org. "'Malcolmology': The Late Dr. Manning Marable's Last Video Recordings on Malcolm X," July 12, 2011. http://www.democracynow.org/blog/2011/7/12/malcomology_dr_manning_marables_last_video_recordings.

Derrida, Jacques. *Writing and Difference*. Translated by Alan Bass. London: Routledge & Kegan Paul, 1978.

Ehlers, Nadine. *Racial Imperatives: Discipline, Performativity, and Struggles Against Subjection*, Bloomington, IN: Indiana University Press, 2012.

Esack, Farid. *Qur'an, Liberation and Pluralism*. Oxford: Oneworld, 1997.

Fanon, Frantz. *Toward the African Revolution.* Translated by Haakon Chevalier. New York: Monthly Review Press. 1967.

Gardell, Mattias. *Islamofobi,* (Islamophobia). Stockholm: Leopard, 2011.

Grant, Alec et al. "Introduction: Storying Life and Lives." In *Contemporary British Autoethnography,* edited by Nigel P. Short, Lydia Turner, and Alec Grant. Amsterdam: Sense Publishers, 2013.

Haley, Alex. *The Autobiography of Malcolm X.* New York: Ballantine Books, 1973.

Hall, Stuart. "Who Needs 'Identity'?" In *Questions of Cultural Identity,* edited by Stuart Hall and Paul du Gay. London: Sage Publications, 2003.

——— "Race, the Floating Signifier." St. Northamptin, MA.: Media Education Foundation. http://www.mediaed.org/assets/products/407/transcript_407.pdf (Accessed August 20, 2014).

Halnon, Karen Bettez. *The Consumption of Inequality: Weapons of Mass Distraction.* New York: Palgrave Macmillan, 2013.

Hamad, Husein. "Giganternas sammandrabbning – Malcolm X och Muhammad Ali" (Encounter of the Giants: Malcolm X and Muhammad Ali), 2015 www.nyansmuslim.se/2015/02/21/giganternas-sammandrabbning-malcolm-x-och-muhammad-ali/ (Accessed February 21, 2015).

Harper, Frederick D. "The Influence of Malcolm X on Black Militancy." *Journal of Black Studies* 1, no. 4 (1971): 387–402.

Hart, William David. *Black religion: Malcolm X, Julius Lester, and Jan Willis.* Basingstoke: Palgrave Macmillan, 2008.

Hermanson, Gunnar and Annika Friberg. "Begreppet invandrare – användningen i myndigheters verksamhet," (Swedish Government Report: "The concept of Immigrant – its usage in state institutions"). *Ds* 43. Stockholm: 2000. http://www.regeringen.se/content/1/c4/18/78/6e54e14b.pdf (Accessed October 4, 2014).

Hetey, Rebecca C. and Eberhardt, Jennifer L. "Racial Disparities in Incarceration Increase Acceptance of Punitive Policies." *Psychological Science* 25, no. 10 (2014): 1949–1954.

Horne, Gerald. "'Myth' and the Making of 'Malcolm X.'" *The American Historical Review* 98, no. 2 (1993): 440–450.

Hübinette, Tobias et al. *Om ras och vithet i det samtida Sverige* (About Race and Whiteness in Contemporary Sweden), Stockholm: Mångkulturellt centrum, 2012.

Jackson, Sherman A. *Islam and the Blackamerican: Looking toward the Third Resurrection.* New York: Oxford University Press, 2005.

——— "Black Orientalism: Its Genesis, Aims, and Significance for American Islam." In *Black Routes to Islam,* edited by Manning Marable and Hishaam D. Aidi. New York: Palgrave Macmillan, 2009.

Jones, Stacey Holman. "Autoethnography: Making the Personal Political." In *The Sage Handbook of Qualitative Research,* (3rd ed.), edited by Norman K. Denzin and Yvonna S. Lincoln. Thousand Oaks, CA: Sage Publications Ltd., 2005.

Jupp, Victor, ed. *The Sage Dictionary of Social Research Methods*. London: SAGE Publications Ltd., 2006.

Kao, Grace and Jennifer S. Thompson. "Racial and Ethnic Stratification in Educational Achievement and Attainment." *Annual Review of Sociology* 29 (2003): 417–442.

Korb, Scott. "Yasiin Bey Would Like You To Quit Calling Him Mos Def." *The Awl*, June 26, 2012. www.theawl.com/2012/06/mos-def-yasiin-bey.

Leak, Jeffrey. "Malcolm X and black masculinity in process." In *The Cambridge Companion to Malcolm X*, edited by Ronert E. Terril. Cambridge: Cambridge University Press, 2010.

Leung Angela Ka-yee et al "Multicultural Experience Enhances Creativity: The When and How." *American Psychologist* 63, no. 3 (2008): 169–181.

Levi-Strauss, Claude. *Introduction to the Work of Marcel Mauss*. Translated by Felicity Baker. London: Routledge & Kegan Paul, 1987.

Lincoln, C. Eric and Lawrence H. Mamiya. *The Black Church in the African American Experience*. Durham NC: Duke University Press, 1990.

Linson, Valerie. *This Far By Faith: African American Spiritual Journeys*, DVD. Arlington, VA: Public Broadcast Service, 2003.

Lo, Mbaye and Aman Nadhiri. "Contextualizing 'Muridiyyah' within the American Muslim community: Perspectives on the past, present and future." *African Journal of Political Science and International Relations* 4, no. 6 (2010): 231–240.

Lundén, Ulf. "Osminkat porträtt av Malcolm X" (Un-masked portrait of Malcolm X). *Da-la-Demokraten* (Kultur), August 25, 2014. www.dalademokraten.se/kultur/bocker/osminkat-portratt-av-malcolm-x (Accessed September 30, 2014).

Malcolm X. "The Ballot or the Bullet," April 12, Detroit, Michigan. Digital History, ID 3624, University of Huston, 1964. www.digitalhistory.uh.edu/disp_textbook.cfm?smtid=3&psid=3624 (Accessed September 1, 2014).

―――― *Malcolm X Speaks: Selected Speeches and Statements*. Edited by George Breitman. London: Secker and Warburg, 1965.

―――― *The End of White World Supremacy: Four Speeches*. Edited by Imam Benjamin Karim. New York: Arcade Publishing, 1971.

Malcolm X Network (YouTube Channel): "Malcolm X: Americans should Study Islam." 2014 http://www.youtube.com/watch?v=NownVoEsmqA (Accessed September 15, 2014).

Marable, Manning. *Malcolm X: A Life of Reinvention*. London: Viking Penguin, 2011.

Marcuse, Herbert. *Towards a Critical Theory of Society: Collected Papers, Vol. 2*. Edited by Douglas Kellner. London: Routledge, 2001.

Martin, Ben L. "From Negro to Black to African American: The power of names and naming." *Political Science Quarterly* 106, no. 1 (1991): 83–107.

Mazrui, A. and Alamin Mazrui. *The Power of Babel. Language and Governance in the African Experience*. Oxford: James Currey, 1998.

Merolla, David and Omari Jackson. "Understanding Differences in College Enrollment: Race, Class and Cultural Capital." *Race and Social Problems* 6 (2014): 280–292.

Muhammad, Wali Farad. "The Communicator." In *American Jihad: Islam after Malcolm X*, edited by Steven Barboza. New York: Double Day, 1994.

Pantrarna. "47 År sedan Malcolm X blev mördad-By Any Means Necessary," 21 February, *Pantrarna För Upprustning Av Förorten* (The Panthers for the Advancement of the Projects) http://pantrarna.wordpress.com/2012/02/21/47-ar-sedan-malcolm-x-blev-mordad-by-any-means-necessary/ (Accessed October 10, 2014).

Pendergrass, Sabrina. "Perceptions of Race and Gegion in the Black Reverse Migration to the South." *Du Bois Review – Social Science Research on Race* 10, no. 1 (2013): 155–178.

Perry, Bruce. *Malcolm: The Life of a Man Who Changed Black America*. Barrytown, NY: Station Hill Press, 1991.

Perry, Ravi K. ed. *Research in Race and Ethnic Relations*, Vol. 18. Bradford, GBR: Emerald Group Publishing Ltd., 2013.

Rabaka, Reiland. "Malcolm X and/as Critical Theory: Philosophy, Radical Politics, and the African American Search for Social Justice." *Journal of Black Studies* 33, no. 2 (2002): 145–165.

Rickford, Russell J. *Betty Shabazz: A Remarkable Story of Survival and Faith Before and After Malcolm X*. Naperville, IL: Sourcebooks, 2003.

Rummel, Jack. *Malcolm X: Militant Black Leader*. Philadelphia: Chelsea House Publishers, 2005.

Sacerdote, Bruce. "Slavery and the intergenerational transmission of human capital." *The Review of Economics and Statistics* 87, no. 2 (2005): 217–234.

Saeed, Amir. "Malcolm X and British Muslims: A Personal Reflection." *Journal of Religion and Popular Culture* 16, no. 1 (2007).

Said, Edward W. *Orientalism: Western Representations of the Orient*. Harmondsworth: Penguin, 1985.

Saldaña-Portillo, Maria Josefina. "On Male Black Muslim Identity." In *Bloom's Guides: The Autobiography of Malcolm X*, edited by Harold Bloom. New York: Infobase Publishing, 2008.

Sandberg, Greta. "Institutionella praktiker och »den Andre«," (Instetutional practices and "the Other"), Norrköping: Integrationsverket, 2005. Web. October 15, 2014. http://www.mkc.botkyrka.se/biblioteket/Publikationer/ri2005/bilagor/2006-509.pdf (Accessed October 15, 2014).

Seibles, Tim. "Outtakes From an Interview With Malcolm X after Mecca: January 1965." *Callaloo* 16, no. 3 (1993): 501–505.

Smethurst, James. "Malcolm X and the Black Arts Movement." In *The Cambridge Companion to Malcolm X*, edited by Ronert E. Terril. Cambridge: Cambridge University Press, 2010.

Sohl, Lena. "Malcolm X's kamp är inte over" (Malcolm X's struggle is not over), *Upsala Nya Tidning* (Kultur-Litteratur), August 30, 2014. www.unt.se/kultur-noje/litteratur/malcolm-xs-kamp-ar-inte-over-3322344.aspx (Accessed October 30. 2014).

Sörberg, Anna-Maria. "Malcolm XL," June 7, *Aftonbladet* (Kultur), 2011. www.aftonbladet.se/kultur/article13130418.ab (September 30, 2014).

Spivak, Gayatri Chakravorty. "Can the subaltern speak?" in *Marxism and the Interpretation of Culture*, edited by C. Nelson and L. Grossberg. Urbana, IL: University of Illinois Press, 1998.

——— *A Critique of Postcolonial Reason. Toward a History of the Vanishing Present*. Cambridge, MA: Harvard University Press, 1999.

Street, John. *Politics and Popular Culture*. Philadelphia: Temple University Press, 1997.

Svensson, Patrik. "Patrik Svensson om Malcolm X" (Patrik Svensson about Malcolm X) *Sydsvenskan* (Kultur och Nöjen), April 24, 2005. www.sydsvenskan.se/kultur--nojen/patrik-svensson-om-malcolm-x/ (Accessed September 30, 2014).

Terry, Don. "W. Deen Mohammed: A leap of faith." *Hartford Courant*, October 20, 2002. www.courant.com/chi-021020-mohammedprofile-story.html#page=1 (Accessed October 29, 2014).

Trindvy, August. "Efter ockupationen av Husby Träff diskuteras Malcolm X av unga sossar," March 13, *Röda Järva* Socialdemokratisk nättidning för förortsungdomar, (Social-Democratic Web-Paper for Youth living in Public Housing, i.e. Projects), 2012. rodajarva.wordpress.com/2012/03/13/efter-ockupationen-av-husby-traff-diskuteras-malcolm-x-av-unga-sossar/ (Accessed September 30, 2014).

Turner, Richard B. "Malcolm X and youth culture." In *The Cambridge Companion to Malcolm X*, edited by Ronert E. Terril. Cambridge: Cambridge University Press, 2010.

Urla, Jacqueline. "We are all Malcolm X: Negu Gorriak, Hip Hop, and the Basque Political Imaginary." In *Global Noise: Rap and Hip Hop Outside the U.S.A.*, edited by Tony Mitchell. Middletown, CT: Wesleyan University Press, 2001.

Weitzer, Ronald and Steven A. Tuch. *Race and Policing in America: Conflict and Reform*, Cambridge: Cambridge University Press, 2006.

Weld, Theodore Dwight. *American Slavery As It Is: Testimony of a Thousand Witnesses*. Chapel Hill, NC: University of North Carolina Press, 2011.

West, Cornel. *Race Matters*. Boston: Beacon, 1994.

Wise, Amanda and Selvaraj Velayutham eds. *Everyday Multiculturalism*. New York: Palgrave Macmillan, 2009.

CHAPTER 11

From Malcolm X to Generation Y: The African American Muslim Community after 1965

Bethany Beyyette

Introduction

Until the second half of the twentieth century Islam was Black in America. Limits on immigration before 1965 restricted the ethnic diversity of Islamic practitioners, in contrast to the great diversity seen in the American Islamic community today. The first decades of the 20th century ushered in an explosion of African-American Islamic movements, and while these movements are attributed to larger Black Nationalist and Pan Africanist movements, and most have early ties to the Universal Negro Improvement Association and African Communities League (UNIA-ACL), their origins arguably far predate these efforts.

Malcolm X, one of the most predominant Civil Rights figures in American history, was responsible for bringing awareness to and about African American Muslim communities through media attention. After founding Muslim Mosque Incorporated (MMI), towards the end of his life, Malcolm explored Islam as the key to the ending racism in the United States. Despite his contributions to both civil liberties and the practice of Islam in America, there is a recent lapse in academic and historical memory of his and other African-American movements to Islam, contributing to the highly divided American Islamic mosaic seen today.

Some of these movements were well known to the Baby Boomer Generation and generations preceding them, yet many belonging to subsequent generations (Generations X, Y, and Z) have little knowledge or education on these important historical movements. While there are certainly many contributing factors to this recent lapse in historic memory, this paper will discuss the significance of several events during the year 1965, which began with the assassination of Malcolm X. These events altered not only the voice of the existing Islamic community (which was and still is predominantly African American), but the formation of future Islamic communities which today are far more racially divided than could have been predicted at the time of Malcolm X's passing. Structures of institutionalized racism affected historic memory of non-Muslims and mainstream society in the United States, which in turn shaped many Americans' expectations about who comprises the American Muslim community. The modern landscape of Islamic practitioners is highly divided in terms of every day interaction, socio-religious environments, and spheres of interaction. This chapter explores how the phenomena of Arab Whitening, black stereotyping and more recent mainstream biased stereotyping have affected African American Islamic communities since the passing of Malcolm X.

Background

African Americans who converted to Islam in the first half of the twentieth century viewed Islam, among many things, as a chance at both political self-determination and self-determination of group identity (Curtis, 2009). Islam was viewed as a mechanism to divert difference in identity away from racial differences, and refocus group identity on difference of religion. At the time it was perceived that if racial criteria were removed as the primary identifier for African Americans, inequalities could be effectively lessened if not removed by using Islam to shape public perception of the community. This was unsuccessful, however, because the response of white America was to demonize Black Islam. At first it was 'othered' as part of the orientalist tradition, but later this shifted to a discussion of whether black Muslims could call themselves Muslim at all. Race and racism are not and cannot be secularized in the Western discourse, as the very concept of race emerges out of 14th and 15th century religious exclusions dividing Christians, Jews, and African Moors (Rana, 2007). Winant (1994) suggests that racism derived from competing imperialist projects based precisely in religious ideology. Muslim identity in the West has always been constructed through a racial lens, and the early African American Islamic communities faced particular challenges as they were a constructed enemy already well known to white America. Muslims have historically been identified on visual cues, and the foe to the West has likewise been defined in relation to religion (specifically non-Christian identities) (Rana, 2007, 2011).

American Media coverage of Islam from the 1920's through the 1960's focused almost exclusively on the followers of the Nation of Islam. This accomplished two things. First, it diverted attention to the many other African American movements to Islam, which has resulted in an unfair and radical depiction of African American conversion to Islam. Secondly, it denied historic importance to these other movements, allowing them to go predominantly undocumented by scholars and unacknowledged or completely forgotten in the historical context of Afro-descended peoples of the Americas. While this community, the Nation of Islam (NOI), was especially rigorous in their attempts to subvert biological determinism in America with the concepts of religion and culture, the media cast these African American Muslims as racist, violent, and extremist. This functioned to maintain the racial status quo, and laid the groundwork for post-Jim Crow Era racism which focused less on biological attributes of minority populations and more on cultural differences. While 'Muslim' became a liberating term to many African Americans, the American public and media have continued to use it as a synonym for threat.

To this day the Nation of Islam is classified as a hate group by groups like the Southern Poverty Law Center, despite a long history of non-violence. The positive efforts and effects of this movement in terms of social reform are seldom acknowledged in the media, by non-Muslims, and even within the American Islamic community. It is important to emphasize the *American* Islamic community, as American Islamic leaders such as Shaykh Khalid Yasin among others have been arguably the most strongly critical of Minister Louis Farrakhan and his followers, specifically with regards to members of the NOI being allowed by Saudi Arabia to perform hajj, and attendance by international Islamic leaders at the annual Savior's Day Banquet hosted by the Nation. International leaders of Muslim communities are often far more accepting of the Nation of Islam than their American counterparts. The Nation of Islam has long standing positive relationships with Muslim communities, organizations, and leaders in both Africa and the Middle East. Members of the Nation of Islam are welcomed to perform hajj by the Hajj Court in Saudi Arabia (Curtis, 2007), and it would appear that the criticism of the NOI is far more prevalent within the United States than among the world's Islamic societies.

The Nation of Islam still receives a majority of the public attention so far as African American Muslims are concerned. Other predominantly African American Islamic communities, both national (such as the Moorish Science Temple and the Ahmadiyya) and local (regionally isolated African American mosques) have disappeared from public discussion, academic research, and go unacknowledged by a majority of American Muslims, most of whom immigrated after 1965. Shifts in ideological beliefs, waves of coming and exodus, reformation and the complex historic and power shifts within the Nation of Islam also go unacknowledged. The African American Islamic experience is diverse and complicated, yet simplistically homogenized into a singular and undeserving negative exploit. This reductionist approach to African American Islamic experiences both denies legitimacy and silences the complex history of African America.

The Islamic Racial Divide in America

The religious-racial divide facing African American Muslims is no longer only black or white. Since 1965 racial intricacies within American Islamic communities have become far more complicated. The year 1965 is of particular importance as it marks both the death of Malcolm X and the lifting of an important immigrant ban. Since that time, millions of Middle Eastern, North African, and South East Asian Muslims have immigrated to the United States and indigenous African American Islamic movements are now far less visible. Race and skin color continue to play a significant role in American Islamic experiences.

The silencing of the African American Muslim population is a key move in a battle to define who are rightful American Muslims and is indicative of the ways in which Afro-American communities are struggling to reclaim their place in both Islamic and American history. Following Leonard (2005) I divide and contrast the American Muslim community into two groups, the immigrant and the indigenous. By *immigrant* communities, I refer to a host of different ethnic and cultural peoples from the Middle East, Europe, South Asia and recent African immigrants. A majority of these communities immigrated to the United States after 1965 when the immigration ban was lifted, although I certainly acknowledge the presence of earlier immigrant communities in America from these same territories.

By *indigenous* I refer to largely to the African American Muslim community. A majority of the members of this community are descended from slaves and have returned to the Islamic faith espoused by a great deal of their West African ancestors following a historic break after their forced immigration to the Americas. To be clear, I am not referring only to members of the Nation of Islam, although they do comprise a rather large group, but to all African American Muslims, which include The Moorish Science Temple of America, the largely African American Ahmadiyya community in the United States, and countless Sunni, Shi'a and Sufi organizations. While classifying the Islamic community in America by only two designators far minimizes the complexity and diversity of Islamic expressions here in the United States, it fairly accounts for the largest divide.

I will not give a deep discussion of the history of indigenous Muslims in America, as far more detailed accounts than I could provide have been written elsewhere (Curtis, 2009; Diouf, 2009; GhaneaBassiri, 2010). Instead I focus this chapter on how the American Muslim community has formed and changed since the assassination of Malcolm X in 1965 and what factors contributed to the current climate of identity politics.

Immigrant Islamic Migration after 1965

Mass media coverage of black Muslims, albeit substantially negative press, exploded most notably between the 1930's and 1960's with the resurgence to Islam. African Americans were, at that time, the face of Islam in America. Few immigrant Muslim communities existed, and certainly did not often make their way into the public eye. While I don't mean to suggest that people of the time did not recognize that a majority of the American Muslim community were in fact African American converts, they were not denied authenticity as Muslims as many arguably are today. American people's primary experience and association with Islam was African American, but this was relatively short-lived.

In 1965 this changed. I attribute this primarily to two events: the first is the assassination of Malcolm X who, at the time of his passing, had turned to leading his community to more mainstream Sunni Islam. His death marks a critical point in the history of the African American community because he was a public icon that the media of the time bombarded. He was public, visible and outspoken; he was also elegant, articulate and unafraid to speak out against White Anglo-Saxon Protestant America in a manner very different from colleagues of his time. His passing left a media void that just weeks after his death was filled with ground breaking steps in the Civil Rights Movement, including the march in Selma, and the first American combat troops to arrive in Vietnam. The year 1966 ushered in yet another media focus; as the Black Panther Party was formed, and as the war grew in Vietnam, attention began to shift to a more international scope and away from the social problems that existed on American soil. This not only shifted attention away from the Muslim community, but away from the Civil Rights movement as a whole.

In October the *Immigration and Nationality Act of 1965* was passed. The law at that time excluded Latin Americans, Asians and Africans from immigrating to the United States and preferenced northern and western Europeans over southern and eastern immigrants. The American public strongly opposed the act, which permitted immigration from Asia and Africa, citing nativist fears that these immigrants would change the composition, culture, and way of life that people had grown accustomed to in the United States. President Lyndon B. Johnson reassured the country that the bill was not revolutionary and would not affect the lives of millions (Ludden, 2006). It was estimated that over the next five years only a few thousand Indian immigrants would come to the United States, and Senator Ted Kennedy assured the people that the demographic composition of the United States would not change. They were wrong. The demographic did change. Millions of immigrants, and an estimated 2.7 million Muslims, came to the United States (Curtis, 2009) and together now constitute over a third of the population growth. Arguably for the first time, American citizens were exposed to great numbers of Old World Muslims from southern Europe, the Middle East, South Asia, and North and West Africa. From that moment onwards both media and scholarly attention of the indigenous Muslim community in America was neglected.

These indigenous African American Muslims were soon refused Islamic recognition by both immigrant Muslims and non-Muslims alike. In an effort to bypass second class citizenship, which all peoples of color face in the United States, foreign and immigrant Muslims have often distanced themselves from African Americans. This division, which has not gone unnoticed (see Leonard, 2005), has been at the expense of co-religionist solidarity. After the mass migration of foreign Muslims post-1965, Muslims in the United States joined the mainstream press' criticism and negative portrayal of black leaders (Curtis, 2007). Criticism of black Muslims, and especially the Nation of Islam, became a public performance of Muslim identity, which expressed the growing cultural power of foreign and immigrant Muslims (Curtis, 2007: 693). While both communities have been the subject of surveillance, and as a result have been excluded from full cultural citizenship (Maira, 2009), a refocusing on religious solidarity which is not based on cultural principles seems pertinent. Schrag (2010) theorizes that contemporary waves of immigrants will not be whitened, positing the only solution to racial injustice as ending the American obsession with race and ethnicity. The absorption of white racial consciousness has divided the Muslim community and completely denied black Muslims' efforts to sidestep their position in the racial hierarchy through theological means (see also Curtis, 2007). African Americans are well versed in combating the racial hierarchy which many new immigrants struggle against, and have a deeper understanding of the potential political solutions for the liberation of peoples of color. African Americans are also better politically positioned to contest institutionalized inequalities, a point I will return to in the final segment of this chapter. If greater dialogue were open between these communities, the social condition of all Muslims in America could benefit greatly.

In the last fifty years, each group has struggled to define the American Islamic experience. This is visible in the continued separation of Islamic practice, religious space, social interaction, and political unity (Beyyette, 2015). For indigenous Muslims it also meant denied history of an Islamic experience. The number of mosques and Islamic centers grew rapidly after 1965 and continues at exponential rates. Muslim Student Associations, commonly referred to as MSA's, were also established in the 1960's as communities of immigrant Muslims, many of whom shared common cultures, language, and histories, sought an organization where ethnic and cultural differences could be transcended and people could come together to commune and debate the social and religious issues of the Islamic world, a world that principally excluded Black Muslim America.

The next two decades remained quiet in terms of media coverage of American Muslim populations, as Malcolm X himself had been the primary source of media and public interest. The passing of the Honorable Elijah Muhammad, leader of the Nation of Islam, drew only minor attention. News sources were focused on the escalating war in Vietnam, the Israeli-Palestinian conflict, the Iran Hostage Crisis, the Cold War, the wars in the Persian Gulf. During this time, Islam was further distanced from the American experience, and Islamic affairs fell strictly into the realm of international news with little bearing on American Muslim communities.

During this time a great number of these new Muslim immigrants, especially Arabs, assimilated into American society. Many became 'invisible' as they whitened themselves in terms of culture and appearance. Although still religious 'others,' many hid under the Caucasian racial label. First generation immigrants focused on 'how to be American' and many masked their identities by changing their names and building social relations with non-Arabs. Many Muslims went through a de-Islamification and took Christian names in an attempt to improve their social standing (Cainkar, 2002; GhaneaBassiri, 2010). This is not to say that all immigrant Muslims ceased to celebrate their cultural heritage, but many enjoyed the privileges and status of White America.

During this time there were many developments in the African American Muslim communities. Numbers within different African American Muslim communities continued to grow as new organizations formed and former organizations had been rebuilt. All of this happened out of the public eye until the late 1980's and early 1990's when media organizations once again turned their focus to the Nation of Islam. For over a decade Minister Louis Farrakhan had been diligently working to rebuild the Nation of Islam, following the passing of Elijah Muhammad. He was, for several years, bombarded and attacked with media coverage that, like that of the 1930's-1960's, held his efforts in strictly negative terms. By this point America no longer viewed African Americans as authentic Muslims. This reached its peak in 1994, as Minister Farrakhan geared up for the Million Man March in Washington D.C. A piece written for Time Magazine (Henry, 1994) begins with the bold statement that "Louis Farrakhan is a problem." Each sentence then begins with "He is a problem" for nearly everyone in the United States. It goes on to say, "He is a problem for the vast majority of Islamic Americans, who already suffer from having their religion equated with hostage taking and terrorism." It goes on to claim that the Nation of Islam has never been accepted as valid by the major branches

('Old World') of Islam, yet their acceptance by the Hajj Court in Saudi Arabia suggests otherwise. In this article, Mustafa Malik, director of research of the American Muslim Council stated, "There is nothing in common (presumably between immigrant Muslims and the Nation of Islam) except that we call ourselves Muslims and they call themselves Muslims" (Henry, 1994). Immigrant Muslims had become self-proclaimed authorities who actively challenged the authenticity of Black Muslims. The problem with media campaigns such as these is that they covertly label all Black Muslims as 'problems' as the American public never learns the true history of Islam in America or in the African American communities.

Over thirty years of exposure to a wide array of different ethnic and sectarian expressions of Islam had changed the way Americans viewed members of the Islamic community. Many Old World Muslims publicly and loudly denounced the many Black Muslims as not belonging to Islam at all (Curtis, 2007), and non-Muslim Americans have turned to immigrant Muslims as the authenticators of what was or was not Islam. The effects of this reached far beyond this single organization, the Nation of Islam, impacting the lives of most African American Muslims regardless of the organization to which they belonged. These effects of this mass immigration that occurred after the death of Malcolm X would certainly not have been predicted in 1965.

Malcolm X's perhaps overly optimistic aspirations for the welfare and collaboration of Muslims of America can be seen in his 1964 Letter from Mecca. He suggests that "America needs to understand Islam, because this is the one religion that erases from its society the race problem." This illustrates the centrality of the concept of race to his understanding of Islam. In his discussion of other Muslims with whom he interacted he states, "We were truly all the same (brothers) – because their belief in one God had removed the white from their minds, the white from their behavior, and the white from their attitude." His belief of supra-racial religious affiliations was not strongly grounded in accurate post-colonial histories of the Middle East and Africa. It is certain that Malcolm X would not have anticipated the great racial divides that entered Islam in America, as are evident today, which contrasted so sharply with his experiences abroad to both the Middle East and North Africa.

Members from many different African American Muslim communities report sharp racial and ethnic divides within the American Muslim community, and state that they are frequently questioned about their beliefs, practices, and sectarian following from Muslims and non-Muslims alike (Beyyette, 2015). African American and other Muslims that are not from recent immigrant families have effectively been silenced and the orientalist divide between the West and Islamic communities has filtered back into the Muslim community where clear hierarchical lines are drawn between ethnic and racially diverse communities of American Muslims. African American journalists, reporters, Imams, musicians, social and political activists are rarely the focus of media interviews. Leaders of African American Muslim communities seem to rarely, if ever, be asked to provide their opinions on relevant topics to American Muslim communities or provide experiences as Muslims in this country.

This division extends not only to interrelations between African Americans and Arabs, North African, and Asian Islamic communities, but also affects West African Muslim immigrant communities. I draw special attention to this community because while they are immigrant Muslims from the Old World, phenotypically many non-Black Americans may not differentiate them from African American Muslims. Most of the West African immigration occurred during the 1990's from the countries of Senegal, Ivory Coast, and Guinea (Abdullah, 2010). Zain Abdullah (2010) provides an excellent discussion of West African immigration into Harlem, a traditionally African American neighborhood with long standing roots with the Nation of Islam. He immediately highlights that these immigrants did not assimilate with African American communities. Harlem, historic home to both Malcolm X and Louis Farrakhan, and focal point for media coverage of Black expressions of Islam, has during the last twenty years had a large in-migration of West African Muslims. These Muslims wear traditional clothing and assert their African presence. They build ties with other Arab and South Asian Muslims and report disrespect for the history of the African American Islam, which still has a very strong presence in Harlem today.

Much like the Cape Verdean immigrants to Boston, Massachusetts African immigrants must struggle with processes of racial ascription and negotiate their own racial identities in an attempt to avoid the stigmatism and racism faced by many African Americans (Sanchez-Gibau, 2005). While Cape Verdeans struggled to be identified as a distinct black cultural group, different waves of immigrants expressed their identities in markedly different ways. Early immigrants labeled themselves as Portuguese in an attempt to distance themselves from established African American communities, but immigrants of the Civil Rights era (1960's–1970's) identified with the Black Power and African Liberation Movements. More recent immigrants negotiate their identities, identifying more with Latinos, while others adopt African American traits and styles and identify with but not as African American (Sanchez-Gibau, 2005). West African immigrants to Harlem often adopt one of two views of African American blacks; either that they are dangerous criminals, or a view of idealized fame accentuated by famous African Americans including movie stars, Malcolm X, Muhammad Ali, Dr. Martin Luther King, Jr., and famous Olympians (Abdullah, 2010). Like earlier waves of Cape Verdeans (Sanchez-Gibau,

2005), West African Muslims use traditional clothing as a means of asserting distinctly African presence, resisting ideologies of racial hierarchy and hegemony in the United States.

At times, Abdullah reports that there are tensions and even violence between Africans and African Americans in Harlem as African Americans are viewed as lazy, uneducated and ignorant of the continent of Africa, and Africans are viewed by African Americas as gentrified invaders (Abdullah, 2010). Africans are also drawn more toward American leaders like Dr. Martin Luther King, Jr. over Malcolm X, as the former sought full integration and a sharing of opportunities and resources and the latter gains less respect because of his early association with the Nation of Islam. This again suggests a separation from African American Muslim movements and organizations. Abdullah reports that there are sharp divisions between African Muslims and African American Muslims in Harlem, and this is visible in the mosques where language divides nationalities (Abdullah, 2010). Even among other Black Muslims, African American Muslims often find themselves isolated and perhaps excluded from full Islamic membership. This, I argue, is a process of whitening that is completely removed from phenotypic qualities, but rather focuses on the adoption of white American racial hierarchies and the continued implementation of them by many immigrant Muslim communities. It is important to note, however, that relationships between ethnically black Muslims is highly variable based on location and not always so marked as in these examples.

The last decade has brought even greater upheaval to the American Muslim mosaic. After September 11th, 2001, Arabs were no longer 'invisible' peoples of color, able to assimilate into what is left of WASP America. While I certainly do not mean to suggest that somehow all Muslim immigrants were free from Western stereotyping, discrimination and prejudice between 1965 and 2001, but many of these communities were afforded a lull, at least until the onset of the first Gulf War. 9/11 created a surge in hyper-orientialized views of Islam and millions of immigrant Muslims and their now American born children became highly visible outsiders.

But these negative stereotypes did not affect the African American Muslim communities in the same way. In fact, 9/11 almost entirely obliterated awareness of African American Muslims altogether (Abdo, 2007). These Muslims are not viewed by a majority of non-Muslim Americans as 'threats' to the nation or potential terrorists. They are rarely if ever interviewed in media broadcasts concerning Islamic rights, conflicts, and experience. Those seats have been reserved for the faces immigrant Muslims (Beyyette, 2014). Now the focus has begun to shift to Anglo-converts to Islam who predominantly marry immigrant Muslims and are often sympathizers with human rights violations both in the

United States and abroad, and who have drawn the attention of law enforcement as cultural defects, recruitments by extremist groups, or married to alleged terrorists.

Changes in Racial Ideology

This section examines the importance of post-Jim Crow Era racial ideologies in America and how it has affected the Black Muslim community. After the close of the 1960's and Jim Crow Era racism, the United States ushered in a new era of racist ideology, commonly referred to as 'Colorblind Racism.' In this era most whites claim that race is no longer relevant, in fact, since the inauguration of President Obama we are even said to be in a *post-racial* society. Bonilla-Silva traces this new era of racist thought to the 1960's (Bonilla-Silva, 2010: 2) and argues that unlike Jim Crow era racism which explained the social standing of African Americans as the result of their biological and moral inferiority, colorblind racism espouses the idea that low social standing is the result of 'natural' occurring phenomena and cultural limitations. New racist practices are subtle, institutional, and appear non-racial (Bonilla-Silva et al, 1999). Like Bonilla-Silva, here I explore the socially constructed effects of racial structure, the racialized social system that awards systemic privileges to dominant members of society. These social systems reinforce racial hierarchies, and studying them uncovers the mechanisms (whether they be social, economic, political, or ideological) that are responsible for the reproduction of racial privilege and prejudice in society. These structures remain in place because the dominant members of society receive benefits from the racial order and struggle to maintain their privilege in light of new anti-racist social thought.

In my own research among Muslim communities in St. Louis, Missouri, I examined patterns of interracial marriage among American Muslims and found that Caucasian Muslims aligned with immigrant Muslims, both in marriage, friendships, and cultural practice for the purpose of gaining authenticity as a member of the Muslim community (Beyyette, 2015). Attention and recognition from born Muslims, predominantly foreign-born, becomes a crucial source of power and validation for these converts. By aligning with born Muslims, or 'Muslim Muslims' as they are often called by converts, the perceived true and ideal bearers of Islamic practice, Caucasian converts promote sameness as a means of establishing themselves within the Muslim community. They seek acceptance from born Muslims, who hold the highest rank hierarchically within the community, based on the assumption that being born Muslim makes one 'more Muslim' because they have never been any other faith and have been raised in culturally Islamic societies where religious practices can potentially inundate every aspect of everyday life.

Here we begin to see an interesting conflation of social structural hierarchy. While within the Muslim community, the highest ranked are born Muslims (as perhaps evidenced in their disproportionate roles as Imams, and ranking positions on executive boards and boards of directors for mosques, community and cultural centers, and NGOs such as CAIR), in the broader context of American society in general, Caucasians are the hierarchical benefactors of privilege and others engage cultural imitation to seek approval from them. In this microcosm of Islamic interaction, which I expect is visible in various other contexts across the United States, born Muslims adopt the hierarchical racial structure of American society which is aided by close alliances, both socially and physically, with Caucasian Muslims. In effect, immigrant Muslims gain validation and begin to accrue white privilege through the almost exclusive interaction between Caucasian Muslims and non-black Muslims. Cultural capital is then transferred to symbolic capital, as we see a mirrored reflection of the racial hierarchy within American Islamic communities. Cultural capital plays a role in the creation of societal power relations since it "provides the means for a non-economic form of domination and hierarchy, as classes distinguish themselves through taste" (Gaventa, 2003: 6). According to Bourdieu, "social order is progressively inscribed in people's minds" through the use of "cultural products" which can include systems of education (private Islamic schools), language (both spoken and Qur'anic literacy), values (including sex segregation, which was present in all Caucasian contexts and not ever present in strictly African American contexts), methods of classification (which include naming practices), and activities of everyday life (including dress and diet) (Bourdieu, 1986: 471).

These contribute to what I would argue in this context may actually be conscious acceptance of social differences and hierarchies, and promote behaviors of self-exclusion as reflected from American racial traditions. Cultural capital, and the conformity to cultural practices, becomes a platform for the creation of power. Navarro states that "all forms of power require legitimacy and culture is the battleground where this conformity is disputed and eventually materializes amongst agents, thus creating social differences and unequal structures" (Navarro, 2006: 19). By not adhering to cultural practices of Islamic states, many African American Muslims find themselves socially and religiously distanced from other Islamic groups, and the recipient of unequal structures that mirror their host society. This is reflected at a much larger level, returning to the identity politics in institutionalized media (Beyyette, 2014), where African American Muslims are excluded as representatives of the Islamic faith in popular culture. The social hierarchy that results is not formed on the basis of religious doctrine, as many non-African American informants were terribly misinformed on the religious practices and beliefs of their black co-religionists, but rather on the basis of cultural difference. This is exactly what Bonilla-Silva (2010) refers to as *New Racism*, practices that are subtle, institutional, and apparently nonracial but which discriminate on the basis of different cultural practice, and which uphold existent racial ideologies and hierarchies. With such an effort put forth to illustrate the universality and non-racial nature of Islam, as often seen in Facebook memes, racism is rendered invisible within Islam and hierarchies are created on the basis of cultural conformity. This, I argue, has been acquired not only by many in the immigrant Muslim community, but through their affiliations with Caucasian converts to Islam who have essentially enacted a reverse enculturation, spreading American socio-racial hierarchy through diffusion within the national Muslim ethnoscape. While African American Muslims may be the numerical majority in the United States, they are collectively tasked with justifying claims to Islamic identity. Cowan et al. (2002) state that culture, tradition, and locality are often used to justify rights to culture through processes of strategic essentialism. While this is used by both Caucasian converts and immigrant Muslims alike to promote Asian ways of being Muslim, African American Muslims must fight for rights to historically Afro-American cultural traditions and expressions, while being denied recognition as Muslims both institutionally and individually by co-religionists.

This process of peferencing Asiatic ways of being Muslim deconstructs black Muslim communities, as African Americans are rendered inauthentic Muslims. It also creates a form of white privilege within Islam that is acquired from interactions with Caucasian Muslims and is reflected through the mirroring of the American racial hierarchy. The ability to grant and withhold legitimacy and authenticity is an instrument of white privilege, and continues the discourse of black inferiority (Martinot, 2003). With regards to the racialization of black Muslim society in America, we can examine a model discussed in Martinot (2003: 21–23). He discusses the 'purity condition,' sometimes referred to as the 1% rule that states that whiteness is based on a sliding scale of purity, which he categorizes as the 'politics of biologization.' Taking whiteness as the preferred and natural biological trait, it is believed that a white woman can give birth to a black child but a black woman can never give birth to a white child (Martinot, 2003: 1). This condition defines and conceptualized biological notions of race. Martinot argues that the purity condition was a response to a political problem of colonial administrations that depended on maintaining a boundary between colonizer and the colonized. This boundary, he argues, was invented and enforced through the prohibition of inter-racial marriage. He goes on to say that the purity condition "is self-superiorizing in the sense that its exercise of hierarchical power produces a stratification that inferiorizes" and that people are "excluded by definition" (2003: 2–23). In effect it politically produces a trait that colonizers provided to be noticed as of social importance. Historically in America, people are not necessarily born white, but rather people become white as a condition given by white society. For example, Irish have only recently been given white status in America, not based on the color of their skin which is often comparable to other white Euro-Americans, but on the basis of cultural assimilation and the granted legitimacy of American white society into the ranks of White America.

Likewise this model, which explores an instrument of white privilege, can be applied to the context of *Muslimness* in America. In this framework, one's rank and placement in Muslim society is evaluated on the basis of cultural phenomena, which is the produced trait to be noticed as being of social importance. This was visible in my dissertation research (Beyyette, 2015) when a Causacian female who was a convert to Sunni Islam discussed the Ahmadi, who she perceived to be only Pakistani and was unfamiliar with the strongly African American history in the United States. She stated that the differences between the Ahmadi and Sunni Islam were not great enough to question their Muslimness, unaware of the great persecution faced by international Ahmadi communities. She was also unaware that structurally, the Ahmadi are rather similar to the Nation of Islam in that both believe in the coming of a second prophet after Muhammad and both follow the teachings of their respective later prophets. Both also use the exact same translation of the Qur'an. Yet, this informant was unwilling to classify members of the Nation of Islam as Muslim, and had no reservations with designating Ahmadis as Muslim because she perceived them as being only Asian. Here an instrument which has historically defined white privilege is being used to recreate hierarchy in an American Islamic context. Certain groups are excluded by definition. While most Caucasian Muslims are not born Muslim at this time in America, but rather converts, the condition has been bestowed upon them through recognition by other Islamic institutions because of their high degree of assimilation with particular expressions of Islam in both religion and culture.

Arjun Appadurai (1991) suggested the use of an 'ethnoscape,' a term to describe landscapes of group identity in an era when people are no longer territorialized nor culturally homogenous. As in Appadurai's example, the Muslim community in the United States is diversely comprised of immigrants, refugees, exiles, native born converts and born Muslims, tourists, and other moving groups. Complicating this ethnoscape is the tendency to construct a hierarchy out of the members of this broad religious community on an evolutionary sectarian scale that begins with "people who call themselves Muslim but really are not" and ending with Sunni Islam, as though there existed a progression, unilaterally toward a single preferred expression of religious practice. This results in a basic essentializing of the Muslim community as a whole, which attributes essential characteristics to members of a religious community that is not culturally, nationally, ethnically, or religiously homogenous. The result is the promotion of over-generalized assertions and stereotypical and inaccurate representations to large, if not a majority, segments of the group (Carrier, 1992).

In the United States, this process of essentialization has promoted 'foreignness' as an essential characteristic for the category 'Muslim' (see Beyyette, 2014, for a discussion of this practice in U.S. media). The effect is that Americans who convert to Islam lose their social citizenship, meaning some experience second-class citizenship status and/or are no longer recognized as American citizens, but rather perceived as foreigners or immigrants. While legal citizenship is guaranteed regardless of religious following in the United States, many converts report feeling that they have their rights and authenticity challenged as a result of their religious conversion. Coutin (2003) defines whiteness as a historic and still existing prerequisite for citizenship in the United States, and whiteness itself becomes challenged for Caucasian converts who report having their ancestry challenged as a result of their new religious identity. Many Caucasian informants also report that their racial category seemed to change after their conversion to Islam (Beyyette, 2015).

The Influence of Malcolm X after 1965

It is certainly true that the legacy of Malcolm X still plays an active role in conversion to Islam in America, for both blacks and whites. He remains an icon and idealized role model for people of all different backgrounds. As a human rights leader Malcolm inspires American youth, especially African American, with his direct approach and well preserved eloquence in live interviews and in writing. Those with criminal records look to Malcolm as a model of transformation and those without adequate access to education find inspiration from his path of self-attained knowledge that was global in reach. Progressives also turn to his words for guidance with regards to political affairs and social consciousness. Yet despite all this, his descendants and others suggest he is being written out of American history.

Martinot discusses how white establishments in the United States have assumed the ability and power to grant recognition and legitimation to minority groups, and likewise prevent recognition of others (2003: 4). He uses the example of Dr. Martin Luther King Jr. who was granted legitimacy as a 'black leader' by various media outlets and people in positions of power. By linguistically defining him as a 'black leader,' a separation was made that white leaders need not undergo, relegating King as important only in relation to his own community but not to the dominant community at large. The assumption that recognition is something to be or not to be granted is an assumed part of white hegemony, a legitimacy that belongs to those who believe they have the power to grant it (Martinot, 2003).

One of the most important structures where this is visible is the institutionalization of Black History Month, in which leaders are taught about and others are intentionally ignored, as is the case with Malcolm X. Black History Month is constructed and taught to reflect a specific image of progress, recounting the stories of only select social reformers and political strategists, and simultaneously creating an intentional lapse of historic memory of leaders who many whites classified as racial nightmares. The result is that a majority of children who come up through the American public school system beginning with generation X – but now continuing to generations Y and Z – have grown up unable to talk about, write about, or otherwise learn the truth about Malcolm X. In February 2014, schools in Queens, New York, specifically barred children from talking about or writing book reports on Malcolm X despite the recent publication of a children's book about the childhood of Malcolm X by his daughter, Ilyasah Shabazz. His daughter confronted the school district and went to the schools to discuss their stance on her father, donating books about him to those institutions. Were it not for the Spike Lee production of Malcolm X's life, a greater number in recent generations would be completely oblivious to Malcolm X's contributions to society as a civil rights leader.

Mills (2003) discusses the significance of institutionalized racism such as this and its role in white supremacy as a sociopolitical system. He argues that white supremacy should be viewed as a theoretical concept that "enables us to pull together different phenomena and integrate these different levels: sociopolitical, economic, cultural, epistemological, somatic, metaphysical" (Mills, 2003: 48). Bartlett (2015) brought media attention to the issues of writing Malcolm X out of history. She discusses President Obama, who has publicly spoken on the influence Malcolm X had on him during his youth, yet installed a bust of Martin Luther King Jr. in the Oval Office. While Malcolm X is not left out of oral discourse, the efforts to memorialize him as icon, role model and leader have been virtually non-existent.

Historical silence has also negatively affected white anti-racist role models (O'Brien, 2003). The apparent lack of white anti-racist role models is socially constructed through both historical and modern silence. O'Brien argues that the effects of this silence, and I extend it to selective black silencing, are both political and personal, as the muting process impedes the development and maintenance of interpersonal relationships with other like-minded individuals. Socially prescribed preferencing of select anti-racist role models distorts the impact and volume of anti-racist research and literature, delegating it as insignificant, tangential, and falling strictly into the realm of 'black issues.' The distortion and marginalization of anti-racist theorizing and its diversity is significant both socially and within the academy, as negative portrayals of whiteness and in-depth discussion of white privilege at universities remains poorly received (see for example Planas, 2015 who discusses a recent media attack on an Arizona State University professor who implemented some well known publications on anti-racist theory in the classroom).

Deliberate character assassination has also affected the legacy of Malcolm X. Bartlett (2015) discusses negative memorialization by major media sources immediately following Malcolm X's assassination by corporations such as the New York Times and TIME magazine, both of whom demonized him. His early speeches became the center focus for discussion about his life and legacy with journalistic amnesia for his later works. His evolution as a man, leader, and activist were lost to time and the rewriting of his character in an ahistorical, decontextualized reconstruction of Malcolm X that completely the social and political ethnoscape that he inhabited during the Jim Crow Era.

Media demonization of Malcolm X extended far beyond his own being, impacting the understandings of black Muslims in general in the United States. The new era of post Jim Crow racism combined with the drastic change in cultural and ethnic composition of the American Muslim community has nearly written not only Malcolm X out of historic memory. It has also impacted the perceived value and recognition of Black Muslim communities across the country. Media coverage rarely presents African American faces to Islam, reducing Islam only to Arab experience (Beyyette, 2014). As Curtis (2009) notes, there is no recognition of African Americans by the media as speakers for Islam post-September 11th, and it has been argued that public perception of Islam is no longer even shaped by African American communities (Abdo, 2007). Suleiman (1999) refers to the, politics of "recognition" as a process of public affirmation of group identity that he claims is critical to cultural survival. This concept is essential to understanding the fabric of American Muslim relations both within the Islamic community and with the greater non-Islamic American public. There is an unofficial yet highly contested debate within the Islamic community over who should be allowed to represent and interpret Islam in America (Leonard, 2005) that hinges on the intersection between race, religion, history and belonging that still affects African American Muslims. It is problematic because a majority of African American Muslim communities are not being recognized as members of the Islamic faith by co-religionists. This, compounded with the absence of public media representation threatens numerous African American Muslim communities who are being pressured to assimilate into historically, culturally and socially different Islamic groups.

Increased strain between African American and immigrant Muslims peaked in the decade following September 11th, 2001. Some African American Muslims intentionally distanced themselves from immigrant run mosques and organizations. The formation of groups such as the Muslim Alliance of North America (MANA), highlight the very active struggle for equal representation among American Muslim populations. MANA specifically criticized immigrant organizations for their failure to reflect on the concerns of indigenous Muslims, their over focusing on overseas agendas, and their blatant efforts to become part of the dominant white mainstream culture (Leonard, 2005). Some have even called for versions of Islam tailored to race, class, and history within the nation (Leonard, 2005).

Conclusion

What lies ahead for the future of American Muslims? A majority of American converts to Islam in the United States continue to be African American. The Nation of Islam, although silenced in the media, remains active both on the ground in black inner-city communities and in the lecturing circuits at mosques, churches, colleges and universities. The Moorish Science Temple is dwindling in population, while the Ahmadiyya seems to be maintaining its numbers. The African American Muslim Mosaic is quite arguably more complex and diverse now than it has ever been. Sunni, Shi'a, and Sufi mosques continue to grow in number and ideological complexity, but still remain off the radar of both scholars and organizations that document the numbers and locations of mosques across the US. In fact, in St. Louis, I have documented more than a half dozen African American mosques, separate from ethnic African mosques, yet only one is listed on the numerous online directories. The impact of this denied existence is devastating, in that the regard of Islam in the African American community remains undocumented and unacknowledged. The experiences of a great, yet unknown, number of African Americans continues to be silenced. It is critical that future work be done to document the history of other African American mosques, their composition and their experiences while first and second generation members are still living to help record it. Without active participation in the continued education of American youth from previous generations and educators, we will continue to see the erasure of not only an accurate history but any knowledge of this important aspect of the deep history of African America. An immense about of basic ethnographic research needs to be completed, addressing everyday practice in American Muslim communities. This work is important to giving a voice to these communities, documenting a more complete history of Africans in the United States, and more broadly in allowing self-determination for countless communities who have been stripped of it by both the cultural majority, the racial majority and their fellow co-religionists.

More recently, since the August 9th shooting of Michael Brown in Ferguson, Missouri, a great deal of awareness has been brought to topics of racial discrimination, the value of black lives, and police brutality against minorities. Muslim leaders of many racial and ethnic backgrounds have become actively engaged in a civil rights movement. This is important, as non-black Muslims have been notoriously disengaged from civil rights violations on American soil, yet activists in this movement have put strong pressure on their religious leaders to involve their communities in this struggle. Iconic images and quotations attributed to Malcolm X have rejuvenated interested not only in him as a civil rights activist, but also as a Muslim and a political leader. This draws attention to whether black Muslims are finally being recognized by non-black Muslims as a substantial and important part of Muslim America. Black Muslim communities have united to fight racism in the modern era, and if joined by their immigrant co-religionists, could usher in a new era for the American Muslim community.

Bibliography

Abdo, Geneive. Mecca and Main Street: Muslim Life in America after 9/11. New York: Oxford University Press, 2007.

Abdullah, Zain. *Black Mecca: The African Muslims of Harlem*. New York: Oxford University Press, 2010.

Appadurai, Arjun. "Global Ethnoscapes: Notes and Queries for a Transnational Anthropology," In *Recapturing Anthropology Working in the Present*, 191–210. Santa Fe: School of American Research Press, 1991.

Bartlett, Karen. "Why Malcolm X Is Getting Written Out of History," *Newsweek*, February 20, 2015, http://www.newsweek.com/2015/02/27/i-worry-my-father-being-written-out-history- 307941.html.

Beyyette, Bethany. "Media as Social Action: How Non-Arab American Muslims Linguistically Challenge Negative Stereotyping." (113th annual meeting of the American Anthropological Association, Washington DC.), 2014.

——— Making Muslim Identities: Contested Meaning, Identities, and Racialization of Islam in Saint Louis, Missouri, 2015.

Bonilla-Silva, Eduard. *Racism Without Racists*, Lanham, MD: Rowman and Littlefield, 2010.

Bonilla-Silva, Eduardo and Lewis, Amanda E. "The New Racism: Racial Structure in the United States, 1960s–1990s," In *Race, Ethnicity, and Nationality in the United States: Toward the Twenty-First Century*, edited by Paul Wong. 55–101. Boulder, CO: Westview Press, 1999.

Bourdieu, Pierre. "The forms of capital," in *Handbook of Theory and Research for the Sociology of Education*, ed. J. Richardson, 241–258. Greenwood: New York, 1986.

Cainkar, Louise. "No Longer Invisible: Arab and Muslim Exclusion after September 11," *Middle East Report*, 224 (2002): 22–29.

Carrier, James G. "Occidentalism: The World Turned Upside-Down," *American Ethnologist* 19, no. 2 (1992): 195–221.

Coutin, Susan Bibler. "Cultural Logics of Belonging and Movement: Transnationalism, Naturalization, and U.S. Immigration Politics," *American Ethnologist* 30, no. 4 (2003): 508–526.

Cowan, Jane K., Marie-Bénédicte Dembour, and Richard A. Wilson. *Culture and Rights: Anthropological Perspectives.* New York: Cambridge University Press, 2002.

Curtis, Edward E. "Islamism and Its African American Muslim Critics: Black Muslims in the Era of the Arab Cold War," *American Quarterly* 59, no. 3 (2007): 683–709.

——— *Muslims in America: A Short History*. New York: Oxford University Press, 2009.

Diouf, Sylviane. *Servants of Allah: African Muslims Enslaved in the Americas.* New York: New York University Press, 1998.

Gaventa, Jonathan. *Power after Lukes: a review of the literature.* Brighton: Institute of Development Studies, 2003.

GhanneaBassiri, Kambiz. *The History of Islam in America*. New York: Cambridge University Press, 2010.

Henry III, William A. "Louis Farrakhan: Pride and Prejudice." *Time*, February 1994.

Leonard, Karen. "American Muslims and Authority: Competing Discourses in a non-Muslim State," *Journal of American Ethnic History* 25 (2005): 1.

Ludden, Jennifer. "1965 Immigration Law Changed Face of America," *NPR*, 2006, http://www.npr.org/templates/story/story.php?storyId=5391395 (accessed December 19, 2014).

Maira, Sunaina. *Missing: Youth, Citizenship and Empire after 9/11.* Durham, NC: Duke University Press, 2009.

Martinot, Steve. *The Rule of Racialization: Class, Identity, Governance*. Philadelphia: Temple University Press, 2003.

Mills, Charles W. "White Supremacy as Sociopolitical System: A Philosophical Perspective," In *White Out: The Continuing Significance of Racism*, edited by Ashley "Woody" Doane and Eduardo Bonilla-Silva. 35–48. New York: Routledge, 2003.

Navarro, Zander. "In Search of Cultural Interpretation of Power," *IDS Bulletin* 37(6) (2006):11–22.

O'Brien, Eileen. "The Political is Personal: The Influence of White Supremacy on White Antiracists' Personal Relationships," In *White Out: The Continuing Significance of Racism*, edited by Ashley "Woody" Doane and Eduardo Bonilla-Silva Eds. 253–267. New York: Routledge, 2003.

Planas, Roque. "Fox News Raises Alarm Over College Course About Race," *Huffington Post*, January 24, 2015, http://www.huffingtonpost.com/2015/01/24/fox-news-whiteness_n_6538986.html (accessed April 8, 2015).

Rana, Junaid "The Story of Islamophobia," *Souls: A Critical Journal of Black Politics, Culture, and Society* 9, no. 2 (2007): 148–161.

———. *Terrifying Muslims: Race and Labor in South Asian Diaspora*. Durham, NC: Duke University Press, 2011.

Sánchez Gibau, G. "Contested Identities: Narratives of Race and Ethnicity in the Cape Verdean Diaspora." *Identities: Global Studies in Culture and Power* 12 (2005): 405–438.

Schrag Peter. *Not Fit For Our Society: Immigration and Nativism in America*. Berkeley: University of California Press, 2010.

Suleiman, Michael W. ed. *Arabs in America: Building a New Future*. Philadelphia: Temple University Press, 1999.

Winant, Howard. *Racial Conditions: Politics, Theory, Comparisons*. Minneapolis: University of Minnesota Press: Minneapolis, 1994.

CHAPTER 12

From Hell to Heaven: The Malcolm X Narrative of Muslim Artists

The Meaning of his Life in Relation to the Doctrine of Predestination for British and American Performing Artists in the 21st Century

Yolanda van Tilborgh

Malcolm X and his call for revolution, self-determination and defense against racial oppression inspired politically charged poets and musicians to create the group *The Last Poets* in 1968. Considering themselves the final artists who would take up words instead of guns against social injustice, they represent several of the founding fathers of the style of socially 'conscious hip-hop' of socially committed (Black) MCs. In the late 1980's and early 90's, especially with the 1992 release of Spike Lee's film *Malcolm X*, based on his autobiography (Malcolm X, 2001), a remarkable resurgence of interest in Malcolm Little, a.k.a. *al-Hajj Malik al-Shabazz*, was expressed in popular culture. Rap bands like *Public Enemy* used him as a cultural and ideological icon in their work.

Now, in the 21st century, Malcolm's name and penetrating voice still emerge in lyrics of American Muslim rap artists who often use samples of his speeches. But, is Malcolm X also meaningful for the new generation of *Sunni* Islam-oriented artists in hip-hop, and for their colleagues with various ethnic and religious backgrounds in the transnational field of Muslim performing artists in music, spoken word, comedy and theatre in the United States and the United Kingdom? And if so, how is Malcolm X reflected in the practices and self-definition of contemporary Muslim artists who try to synthesize their artistic aspirations with their religious beliefs? This chapter explores the current signification of Muslim human rights activist al-Hajj Malik al-Shabazz to Muslim performing artists from the sociological perspectives of *the field of art* and the *doctrine of predestination* in relation with the social analysis of *narratives* as ways to convey meaning.

History in the Field of Muslim Artist in Relation to Malcolm X

As an adviser, theorist and polemicist, Malcolm X had a profound influence on the network of politically engaged African-American artists and art institutions (Marable, 2011: 481; Smethurst, 2010). Their collaborations matured into the *Black Arts Movement* or *Black Aesthetics Movement* (BAM), which involved thousands of poets, playwrights, dancers and other cultural producers (Marable, 2009, 2011; Smethurst, 2010). Starting in Harlem, BAM is considered the *aesthetic and spiritual sister* of the notorious political *Black Power* movement. Several parents of Muslim performing artists from the present study participated in this movement during the 1960's and 70's.

While Martin Luther King displayed middle-class oriented leadership, Malcolm X was a typical product of the modern ghetto, reacting to racism in an urban context (Marable, 2011: 7). Malcolm's engagement in the urban centers of the network inspired the activist producers of Black Arts, including Everett LeRoi Jones and Sonia Sanchez, to delve further into and even nurture their African-American and Black (ethic, aesthetic and spiritual) culture. Retrospectively, African-American novelist and visiting professor at California College of the Arts, Ishmael Scott Reed, praised the *Black Arts Movement*:

> Blacks [of BAM] gave the example that you don't have to assimilate. You could do your own thing – get into your own background, your own history, your own tradition and your own culture. I think the challenge is for cultural sovereignty, and Black Arts struck a blow for that.[1]

About forty years after BAM, during the backlash caused by the terrorist attacks of September 11th in the United States in 2001, Reed would prompt Pakistani-American Wajahat Ali to write a play about a modern Muslim Pakistani-American family, *The Domestic Crusaders*, under similar conditions of cultural authenticity.[2]

The *Black Arts Movement* is considered to have emerged from the Black community itself, causing African-American peoples to have a greater representation in the field of art, i.e. literature, poetry, speech and drama, which had been WASP-dominated (Smethurst, 2005). This changed the prevailing perception of 'popular culture' and 'high art.' However, BAM's belief that your ethics and aesthetics are one made it chiefly an ethical movement from the perspective of socially oppressed people (Neal, 1997). In this sense, the movement's

---

[1] Larry Neal. "...aesthetic and spiritual sister of the Black Power concept." aalbc.com. aalbc.com/authors/blackartsmovement.htm. And: Kaluma ya Salaam. "Historical Overviews of The Black Arts Movement." Modern American Poetry. *The Oxford Companion to Women's Writing in the United States*. New York: Oxford UP, 1995. www.english.illinois.edu/maps/blackarts/historical.htm (accessed August 24, 2015).

[2] Interview with the author, San Francisco Bay Area, CA, February 26, 2010.

main focus was not on (Black) aesthetics, but on achieving certain political goals (Taylor, 2004).

When LeRoi Jones a.k.a. *Amiri Baraka* – a name which carries the Islamic connotation of 'blessing' and 'wellbeing' (Shaw, 2013: 107) – claimed "We want poems that kill," his poem *Black Art* became a poetic manifesto for BAM in 1965. This militant expression coincided with Malcolm X's call for self-determination and the necessity for self-defense as a new way of thinking about possessing agency (Marable, 2011: 481; Terrill, 2010: 134). Rather than use poetry as an escapist mechanism, Baraka and the movement saw poetry as a weapon of action toward those responsible for an unjust society (Harris, 1985).

Similarly, the radical artists who formed *The Last Poets* were motivated by the Black Nationalist Islamic organization, the *Nation of Islam* (NOI).[3] They were especially attracted to the NOI's most prominent spokesman Malcolm X, approving of his militancy against racial oppression which was geared toward Black independence. Four years after Malcolm's break with the NOI and his assassination, whether by the NOI or by government agencies (Marable, 2011), various musicians and *The Last Poets* collaborated in an effort to get ahead of the younger generation that would probably deploy 'guns instead of words' to obtain their rights.[4] With "syncopated recitation verse over African-style drumming," the artists, of whom several had embraced Islam, earned the epithet 'Godfathers of rap' (Curtis IV, 2010: 331).

Based on Black oration and storytelling, hip-hop subculture developed as a vehicle for social political protest by African-American and African-Caribbean youth who resided on the margins of urban America during the 1970's (Alim, 2005; Euell and Alexander, 2009; Rose, 1994, 2008). Targeting racism and various social ills through cultural empowerment, a collective of MCs, graffiti artists and break-dancers were inspired by the unorthodox NOI and its breakaway sect the *Five Percent Nation* (FPN). While the Christian churches rejected secular, politically charged music that was not gospel, the NOI recognized the potential of the first (Black) hip-hop artists, seeing their performances as an act of preaching as well as an affective community restoration tool (Mohaiemen, 2008). The NOI's message of social justice, the importance of self-knowledge and community upliftment, as had been embodied in Malcolm X, profoundly impacted Black artists.[5] Along the way, many of the artists, in rap as well as

---

3 *The Last Poets* is named after a poem of South African poet activist Keorapetse W. Kgositsile.
4 Last Poets. *Encyclopedia of Muslim-American History.* www.fofweb.com/History/MainPrint Page.asp?iPin=EMAH0165andDataType=AFHCandWinType=Free (accessed August 24, 2015).
5 Suad Abdul-Khabeer. "Black and Blue: Remembering Islam and Hip-hop." The Islamic Monthly, June 17, 2012. www.theislamicmonthly.com/black-and-blue-remembering-islam -and-hip-hop/ (accessed August 24, 2015).

in comedy and acting, submitted to Islam through their engagement with the NOI. In the course of time, a lot of them adapted their views to the dominant branch of Islam, orthodox (*Sunni*) Islam.

Malcolm X appealed to potentially new Muslims because he delivered his compelling speeches in a "dizzying array of Black rhetorical styles" (Smethurst, 2010: 80). He could "artfully recount tales about his life that were partially fiction," but nevertheless resonated authentically to most Black Americans who had encountered racism (Marable, 2011: 10; Perry, 1991). By telling the truth in his profoundly personal way, it resonated as *the* truth. For this, Malcolm X was called the first master of the 'sound bite.'[6]

Especially in the late 1980's, combined with references to Islam, whether based on interpretations of the unorthodox *Five Percent Nation* or on orthodox *Sunni* Islam, hip-hop music became replete with samples of Malcolm's confrontational speeches. Groups like *Public Enemy* infused their rap with his ideology and by singing about 'the ills of our people,'[7] the artists gained considerable success with their socio-political contributions. Although *Public Enemy* was not the first rap group to artistically integrate the human rights advocate's rhetoric on hip-hop beat (that was Keith LeBlanc with *No Sell Out* in 1983), its massive popularity led other artists to follow the Malcolm X sampling style (Marable, 2009: 301–302). Following the popularization of Malcolm's work by the *Black Arts Movement* after the assassination, the phenomenon of al-Hajj Malik al-Shabazz became an explicit icon in hip-hop culture. Various genres of art, such as spoken word poetry, beat-boxing, graffiti and hip-hop theatre, seem to have developed a disposition for the Muslim social activist.

Malcolm X impacted audiences in the United Kingdom as well. In Europe, high profiled media figures like al-Hajj Malik al-Shabazz speaking on behalf of the majority of marginalized Muslims did not exist (Ahmed, 1993). As a result, hip-hop, Malcolm X and the religion of Islam gained the interest of many immigrant youth immersed in British popular culture (Reddie, 2009).

In the *Golden Age of hip-hop* between the late 1980's and early 90's, socially conscious MCs took Black self-determination, political empowerment, concerns of inner-city youth, and Islamic doctrines as their themes (Miyakawa, 2005), which they appropriated from the *Black Power* movement, *The Last Poets* and Malcolm X (Tobler, 1992). In time, conscious hip-hop extended the political style with religious topics, everyday life, love of humanity and the state

---

6　Peter Goldman's observation of Malcolm X. In Strickland and Greene (1994) *Malcolm X: Make it Plain*, p. 134. New York, NY: Viking. See also Byerman 2006: 15.

7　www.marxist.com/public-enemy-interview.htm (accessed August 24, 2015).

of hip-hop itself (Miyakawa, 2005; Rose, 2008: 241–247).[8] Nowadays, hip-hop has come to be dominated by 'gangsta rap,' which has eclipsed the Malcolm X-inspired socio-political rap. Although gangsta rap initially gained appreciation for putting tough social realities to the fore, in the perception of various audiences and critics now, the styles represent controversial *violence provoking* rap versus approved of *consciousness raising* rap. While its artists claim Malcolm X as well, gangsta rap, embodying the hallmark of drug dealing, sexual excess and violent Black masculinity, has gained a dominant position in the media, record and film industry (Marable, 2009: 302–303; Rose, 2008), a phenomenon that many of those involved consider to be result of the major American (media) corporations and institutions themselves.[9]

The smaller segment of 'conscious rap,' which tended to be practiced by *Sunni* Islam inspired artists, evolved from the militant political style, of *Public Enemy* to the more elevating style of Talib Kweli and Lupe Fiasco (Mohaiemen, 2008; Rose 2008: 244).[10] These trends in approach seem to be in line with another development on Muslim meta-level. Among Islamist revival movements, which once sought to battle discrimination against Muslim migrants in Europe, such as those from Morocco, Turkey and Algeria, the attitude of Islamist doctrine engendered the attitude of *post-Islamism* (Bayat, 2007, 2013; Boubekeur, 2007). Post-Islamism came to the fore when the justification of militant *jihad* gave precedence to the political over the religious in the name of Islam, which became increasingly questionable. It also derived from the endeavor to fuse Islam with tolerance, which opposed the rigidity of Islamist and *Salafi* doctrines (Roy, 2004: 3; Bayat, 2007: 6–15). This means that the militant Islamist approach is not replaced but complemented by a more flexible, tolerant approach (Bayat, 2005).

The Field of Muslim Performing Artists and Its Central Notions

In theory, artists are part of the field of cultural production in which participants *compete* for resources of cultural capital, e.g. cultural knowledge, and symbolic capital, i.e. recognition and legitimate authority (Bourdieu, 1996, 2004, 2009). Despite severe competition, the artists also act from certain central notions and *doxa*, which denotes unquestioned principles which helps to

---

8   rateyourmusic.com/genre/Conscious%20Hip%20Hop/2 (accessed August 24, 2015).
9   www.zulunation.nl/index.php/geschiedenis/the-founder/204-afrika-bambaataa-hip-hops-ambassador (accessed August 24, 2015).
10 rap.about.com/od/genresstyles/p/ConsciousRap.htm (accessed August 24, 2015).

determine a sense of one's place. At the same time, 'the field of cultural production' or 'field of art,' as Pierre Bourdieu conceptualized it, is distinctive from the concept of the 'art world' of Howard Becker, which was developed particularly by *shared conventions* and understandings through artistic collaborations and the practice of art (Becker, 1982).

Because current American and British Muslim performing artists prove to be committed to some particular central tendencies, I consider them participants of a transnational field of Muslim artists in the United States and the United Kingdom. This field can be understood as a 'subfield' of the field of cultural production. Through its cultural history, this subfield (from now on: *field* of Muslim performing artists) is importantly related to the legacy of Malcolm X, as described above.

One central tendency concerns the everlasting discourse on art and music in Islam. Similar to discussions in Christianity about whether art can serve in praise of God, for didactic purposes, and to motivate ethical action, or whether, on the contrary, it stirs immodest behavior and idolatry (Brown, 2000), Muslims hold an implicit as well as explicit debate on the (im)permissibility of (popular) art in Islam – about what is Islamically allowed, undecided, or disapproved of.[11] Disputes about dance are found in the *Hadith* compiled soon after the death of Prophet Muhammad (Abd-Allah, 2004); about musical instruments among theologians in the time after the Prophet (Shiloah, 1995: 31–35), and about hip-hop music, female voices and stage behavior in current times (*see also*, Abdul-Khabeer, 2007; Aidi, 2014: 44–70; Kubala, 2005; Mandaville, 2009). Generally, Islamic religious songs, *nasheeds*, are accepted when it concerns male voices in a cappella or just accompanied by the hand drum, the *daff*. Views on contested art concern not only the (im)permissible use of musical instruments but also touch upon moral themes, e.g. the effects of music on behavioral conventions between women and men. Knowing that the unorthodox NOI deployed musicians to express a social and political form of *da'wah* (invitation to the religion), Muslim performing artists often share a certain acceptance of the idea that (popular) art and Islam may exist next to each other. This notion characterizes the field by assessing one of its qualities.

It appears that the field of Muslim performing art is associated with the field of Islam, i.e. a subfield of the field of religion. This means that to various degrees, Muslim artists may communicate with Islamic teachers who hold divergent Islamic leanings and convictions regarding the perceived appropriate relation between art and Islam. The center of Islamic knowledge is considered

---

11 The author has benefitted from the advice of M.Sc. Pieter Coppens with regard to Islamic references.

to be in the Middle East, often represented by the traditional *Al-Azhar University* in Egypt. In the West, new indigenous Islamic institutions have emerged in the last decade, for example the American *Zaytuna College* of the respected teachers Imam Hamza Yusuf and Imam Zaid Shakir, who are to different degrees related to the American *Civil Rights* movement and the ideologies of Martin Luther King and especially the Muslim Malcolm X. In the Middle East, Islamic teachers who tolerate (popular) art, musical instruments and singing to certain extent, e.g. prominent *Al-Azhar* scholar Yusuf al-Qaradawi, display a moderate stance by stressing certain religious-artistic conditions to producing and consuming music (Baker, 2003: 53–64; Al-Qaradawi, 2001).[12] In the public discourse of Egypt, popular music and artistic performance are supposed to have a message or purpose: *all-fann al-hadif* (Zaman, 2004; Kubala, 2005; Tartoussieh, 2007; Otterbeck, 2008).

In the present study on American and British Muslim artists, the attitude of prominent Islamic teachers who do not oppose the new (hip-hop and comedy) productions in the field of Muslim performing arts in the West, have a similar moderate stance. Primarily to prevent people from digressing from faith, they tend to attach art to purposes that are considered socially and religiously relevant.

Next to the prevailing discourse on art in Islam, there are central (although not collective) notions regarding inspirational sources among contemporary American and British Muslim performers. In their field of art, inspirations may range from the 20th century Hindu Mahatma Gandhi, Indian politician of non-violent revolution for national independence, to African-American feminist author Alice Walker. However, the motivation and visions drawn from both the 20th century African-American Muslim activist and *Black Power* leader Malcolm X *and* the 13th century Persian poet, theologian and *Sufi* mystic Jalal al-din Rumi are shared among many performing artists. Malcolm X, who grew up in a time where White supremacist groups like Ku Klux Klan and its offshoot the Black Legion were still a powerful force in American society – the latter being widely hold responsible for his father's death – impresses these performers by his bold and uncompromising protest against social injustice through his promotion of Black (self-)consciousness. Rumi is appealing to the artists because of his expression of divine consciousness and spiritual love in a wide and tolerant sense. On the one hand, social action seems in contrast with spirituality as much as uncompromising boldness seems to be opposite of tolerant flexibility. Yet, in the ultimate phase of his life, Malcolm X turned to a more inclusive kind

---

12   Yusuf al-Qaradawi. "Yusuf al-Qaradawi on Music." The Revival, February 1, 2010. *Islam Online*. www.therevival.co.uk/article/yusuf-al-qaradawi-music (accessed August 24, 2015).

of spirituality, *Sunni Islam*. Rumi, although expressing an ecumenical attitude, can also be regarded as a conventional Muslim scholar. Both prominent figures combined rebelliousness with devotion. Moreover, they have gained international recognition from a social circle outside the African-American and Muslim circles in the West. In several ways, they importantly represent symbolic capital to Muslim performing artists in non-Muslim contexts.

In times of heated discourse and regulations on immigration and importation of the kind of Islam that is associated with terrorism, the symbol of Malcolm X as rooted in human rights activism may have reinforced a social political counter-discourse among many contemporary American and British Muslim artists, especially in hip-hop and spoken word. They define and legitimate their artistic expressions with the terms 'consciousness,' waking up and becoming 'aware' of social injustice, and the related understanding of 'conscientiousness,' having a clear sense of right and wrong. In their artistic practices, these Muslim performing artists strive for purposefulness, knowledgeability, truthfulness, and responsibility.

This shared understanding among many Muslim performing artists can be explained by various reasons. Firstly, added to the experience of being depicted as Islamic villains by the corporate film industry for decades (Shaheen, 2001), the mistreatment of Muslims after the attacks of September 11th, 2001, have triggered Muslim artists to improve the public image of Islam. The *self-consciousness* approach, once promoted by Malcolm X, may have contributed to the moral ideas and terminology used by Muslims in reaction to the tragic event. Secondly, contemporary Muslim performing artists, who grew up in the 'Golden Age' of hip-hop, generally object to advocating the lifestyle of gangsta rap artists with their excessive materialist and misogynic reputations. Expressing a different cultural taste might counter the pervasive pollution within the current image of (Black) Muslim rap. Lastly, the re-Islamization trend has brought many second generation Muslims of immigrant background to reassess and reformulate Islamic norms in terms of their moral values and ethics. They stress, for example, the importance of distinguishing themselves from what they regard as irresponsible behavior by embracing certain modern trends but principally through recasting traditional cultural customs and/or examining the fundamentals of Islam (Hamid, 2009; Roy, 2004: 5, 14; Van Tilborgh, 2009).

Malcolm X and His Trajectory in Narratives

Malcolm X passed through specific phases in his spiritual life. After being convicted for illegal activities as a "pimp, hustler, burglar, and drug dealer"

(Marable, 2009: 301) he spent much of his time developing himself by reading history and philosophy; subsequently, Malcolm joined the Black Muslims of the unorthodox *Nation of Islam* in prison (Marable 2011; Perry 1991). Later, in line with accomplishing the pilgrimage to Mecca, the *hajj*, where he experienced an epiphany that made him "recognize the Oneness of all Humanity," the human rights advocate embraced orthodox (*Sunni*) Islam (Marable, 2011: 311). Somewhere along the line, Malcolm realized that orthodox Islam and its claim to universalism, was at odds with the intolerance (regarding White people) of the NOI's racial doctrines (Marable, 2011: 12). In this sense, he abandoned the narrowness of Black Nationalism and embraced interracial and intercultural harmony. In other words, he went from expressing militant revolutionary views to spiritual *Sunni* Islamic views; and from representing *Black Power* to symbolizing Muslim pride (Ahmed, 1993). This was due to his expanding the struggle for *civil rights* to the broader aim of *human rights* (Smethurst, 2010: 84). In William D. Hart's representation, coinciding with Malcolm's journey from being raised in a Christian family to embracing the religion of Islam, Malcolm Little changed from a "social parasite to raceman" and from a "libertine to ascetic" (Hart, 2008: 24, 37, 90).[13] Malcolm progressed from being identified as a criminal, minister (of several NOI mosques), leader, and "ultimately an icon," phrases Marable (Marable, 2011: 479). This life long passage can be considered a journey of *jihad*, struggle in the path of Allah, from *jahiliyyah*, the pre-Islamic phase of ignorance, to performing the *hajj*, the religious duty of the Islamic pilgrimage to Mecca, which is a manifestation of solidarity between Muslims and a sign of their submission to God (Hart, 2008). Generally, the depiction of Malcolm's life in many representations displays a linear development with a clear sequenced structure. As we will see, Muslim performing artists are well aware of the different phases in Malcolm's life. Many of them relate to the sequenced structure of Malcolm's trajectory by way of personal narratives.

Narratives are perceived as sense-making tools among members of producers of culture (Polanyi, 1985). In the present case, these producers are Muslim performing artists. Narratives can become powerful because people utilize them to "determine, justify, and guide" their lives (Cunliffe, Luhman and Boje, 2004: 263). Prioritizing one interpretation of events over others, narrative constructions convey social meaning (Abolafia, 2010: 349–368; Riessman, 1993; White, 1980: 5–27), especially when the narrators integrate their ideologies in the depiction of sequences (McCloskey, 1990).[14]

---

13 www.uncg.edu/rel/faculty/hart.html (accessed August 24, 2015).
14 The author has benefitted from the work of M.Sc. Nataliya Komarova on contemporary art markets at the program group of Cultural Sociology of the University of Amsterdam (UvA).

In the following paragraphs, I intend to discuss the relationship of American and British Muslim performing artists in the field of art with the (representation of) Malcolm X, and particularly the meaning of their use of narratives concerning his and their lives and religious trajectories.

The Empirical Study of Muslim Performing Artists

The findings presented in this chapter are based on a broad ethnographic study of Muslim performing artists in the United States and the United Kingdom between 2009 and 2012 on how they synthesize their artistic aspirations with their religious beliefs.[15] These artists are, or have been, engaged in cultural production of Anglophone hip-hop and alternative music, spoken word and poetry, storytelling, theatre and acting, stand-up comedy, film performance and contemporary art on stage, often associated with the debate on Islam, art and music. These art forms are discussed through the concept of intersectionality, which focuses, among other things, on the significance of their ethnic and religious backgrounds. Apart from drawing on secondary literature from academic sources as well as traditional and digital media, semi-structured in-depth interviews on the relation between art and Islam are conducted among sixty-five female and male Muslim performing artists and eight stakeholders, including art managers and Islamic teachers in the United States and the United Kingdom.[16] In addition, twenty-three similar participants in art (artists and stakeholders) were studied through short interviews and/or secondary sources. The eventual focus group of *seventy* artists[17] includes a small category of artists with Muslim background.[18] Furthermore, I visited seventy cultural events,

---

15 This study *Singing or Sinning: Cultural Orientations among British and American Muslim Performing Artists* is partly funded by the *Netherlands Organization for Scientific Research* NWO, and has respectively taken place at Radboud University Nijmegen (Religious Studies) and University of Amsterdam (Cultural Sociology).
16 Using MQDA software for mixed qualitative and quantitative methods of analysing, the interviews are deconstructed along sensitizing sociological concepts deriving from process sociological theories, symbolic interactionist theories, and self-developed categories.
17 Information about the artists derives predominantly from (a) in-depth interviews, but also from combinations of (a), (b) short interviews, (c) content analysis of secondary sources and (d) content analysis of (biographical) performances and Q&A sessions. Information about Mutah Beale, Muslim Belal, Flesh-N-Bone, Zakariyya King and Aki Nawaz is drawn especially from combinations of (b), (c) and/or (d).
18 Studied for reasons of comparison, three artists do not self-identify as Muslim but tend to stand for Muslims after September 11th, 2001, or are affiliated with *Sufism*.

from seminars in the mosque to playhouse performances, to gather information about the orientation of Muslim artists and their cultural productions. This was done through participant observations.

Positioning toward the Style of Malcolm X

In the field of American and British Muslim performing arts, Malcolm's social activism has impressed many. Among these artists, I found two styles that carry on Malcolm X's fight for equality and self-determination of Black and Muslim people through the cultivation of self-awareness and self-consciousness. These styles seem to reflect the divergent properties of Malcolm X. In the narrative, trying to capture Malcolm X, these qualities tend to come to the fore as phases characterized by a kind of 'militant power' as well as a certain 'soft power.' Although much of the hip-hop population used to prefer to emphasize the militant elements of Malcolm's career (Marable, 2009: 303), contemporary artists who are in various ways related to the culture of hip-hop display more differentiated views.

The Style of 'Militant Power'

While Malcolm X and his followers tended to portray the Dr. Martin Luther King Jr. model as a strategy to *ask* for rights, the Malcolm X model is perceived as the strategy to *demand* rights (Marable, 2011).[19] The militant model signified that self-determination of communities meant that Black (Muslim) people had to do it for themselves, similar to the Black artists who rose to the forefront of the cultural arenas through the *Harlem Renaissance* in the 1920's and especially the *Black Arts Movement* in the 1960's. Therefore, the *Malcolm X model* stood for combining the intellectual, the political radical and the communicationally gifted artist at the same time (Smethurst, 2010: 88).

British-Pakistani Haq Nawaz Qureshi a.k.a. Aki Nawaz, leader of the controversial political punk-rock group *Fun-Da-Mental*, grew up in the racial volatility of Bradford, United Kingdom. Making music since the 1980's, Malcolm X still inspires Nawaz for fighting the system and "challenging the stereotypical

---

19   J. Hashmi. "Martin or Malcolm? MLK, Malcolm X, and Muslims." MuslimMatters.org. January 21, 2010. muslimmatters.org/2010/01/21/martin-or-malcolm-mlk-malcolm-x-and-muslims/ (accessed August 24, 2015).

thought process of Western intellectualism."[20] Similar to many American hip-hop bands, *Fun-Da-Mental* has sampled quotes from prominent protest leaders such as Malcolm X, the NOI's current leader Louis Farrakhan, and representatives of the formerly militant African-American *Black Panther Party* (Swedenburg, 2001). By mobilizing Islamic imagery in its lyrics, the group promotes the merits of militancy and self-defense as being essential to the anti-racism struggle, in congruence with the ideas of Malcolm X.

Being a Black man in the United States has politicized the work of African-American performance poet Amir Sulaiman. He drew on the radical *Black Art Movement* that was inspired by Malcolm's activist teachings.[21] Impressed by the late Amiri Baraka who declaimed "We want poems that kill" in 1965, forty years later in the HBO television series *Def Poetry*, Sulaiman presented his most famous poem *Danger*. *Danger* turned out to deeply shock the audience:

> I am not angry, I am anger
> I am not dangerous, I am danger
> I am abominable stress, illiotic relentless
> I am a breath of vengeance. I am a death sentence
> I am sick of repentance to the beast and its henchmen
> Armed forces and police men [...] I will slice his belly open and free
> the souls of the Navajo [...] the souls of great Black leaders
> the souls of Kandahar and Baghdad [...]
> Justice, is somewhere between reading sad poems
> And forty ounces of gasoline crashing through windows [...]
> Freedom is between a finger and a trigger [...] So I say down with Goliath
> [...] we must learn, know, write, read
> we must kick, bite, yell, scream
> we must pray, fast, live, dream
> fight, kill. And die free.[22]

In his lecture at the seminar *Contemporary Muslim Voices in the Arts* at *Harvard University*, Amir Sulaiman explains that he and his hip-hop colleagues embraced a particular kind of Islam from scratch.[23] This approach to Islam

---

20   www.opendemocracy.net/globalization-world/article_2138.jsp (accessed August 24, 2015).
21   www.facebook.com/pages/Amir-Sulaiman/260561480658178?id=260561480658178andsk =info (accessed August 24, 2015).
22   Part of the poem *Danger*. wewritethelyrics.blogspot.nl/2008/12/amir-sulaiman-danger .html (accessed August 24, 2015).
23   Seminar at *Harvard University, Contemporary Muslim Voices in the Arts and Literatures*, Cambridge MA, April 17/18, 2010.; interview with the author, Cambridge, MA, April 18, 2010.

expressed itself in striving for social justice. Their identification coincided with the *Malcolm X model* for social change, which the artists felt they had to reexamine in a new era. In the current times, the ongoing experiences of social injustice, economic inequality and political exploitation seem to warrant a resurrection of the Malcolm X model as a method of resistance against oppression.

American poet Safiyyah Fatimah Abdullah, who performs in a black burqa against modern-day slavery, distinguishes Malcolm X above Dr. Martin Luther King Jr. in his ambition to *get rid of the rotten pie and start over with a new pie* instead of simply aiming for integration the way King did.[24] Similar to many Black American artists and non-Black American artists who are sensitive about the Black American history, Safiyyah Abdullah, who has a mixed Native American, Norwegian and Dutch background, perceives that the justice system disproportionately targets racial minorities for imprisonment in the United States. In her view, which is expressed in the poem *Nemesis*, incarcerated African, native and Hispanic Americans are forced by *corporate America* to work for the industry of consumption. Their commercial mentality chains people to materialism like they once chained Black slaves.

In a sense, Native British stand-up poetry performer Lori Zakariyya King a.k.a. Zkthepoet,[25] draws as well from Malcolm X when giving the (British) Muslim community moral advice with his audio poem *Muslims are scared of revolution*.[26] He was inspired by the poem *Niggaz are scared of Revolution*, written by *The Last Poets*. The poem seems to carry the argument that Black people try to imitate Malcolm X but do not succeed in acting against their suppressor 'the White man,' caused by self-hatred.[27] At the time, Malcolm X distinguished between 'house negroes,' who obeyed their master, from 'field negroes,' who hated their suppressor and would rather sacrifice their lives than submit.[28] Zakariyya King is critical of what he observes as the similarities between the complacent attitude of African-Americans as described by the *Last Poets* and the attitude of contemporary Muslims in Muslim minority countries of the West. He wants to tell the Muslim community to act less like a submissive slave by talking the language of the ruling order. By emphasizing similarities between Malcolm X and the prophet Muhammad, King puts forward the Prophet

---

24 Interview with the author, Washington D.C., March 26, 2010.
25 *Breaking Down the Walls*, Herbert Art Gallery, Coventry, UK, November 19, 2010.
26 myspace.com/zkthepoet/music/songs (accessed August 24, 2015).
27 www.lyricsondemand.com/l/lastpoetslyrics/niggazarescaredofrevolutionlyrics.html (accessed August 24, 2015).
28 www.youtube.com/watch?v=znQe9nUKzvQ (accessed August 24, 2015).

who was a "soft and humble" man inside the house – mending his own clothes. However, "when he left the house – he was like a lion!"[29] Zkthepoet, who samples the voice of Pakistani born Islamic teacher Abu Hasnayn Murtaza Khan, who is considered to have a *Salafi* (conservative scripturist) anti-music stance similar to King, seems to advise Muslims to go along shrewdly to counter oppressive attitudes and at the same time stand up firm with self-confidence for their Islamic ideals the way Malcolm X and the Prophet did.

Among young Americans, the social activists Malcolm X and Dr. Martin Luther King Jr. are considered complementary because both aimed for Black freedom and equality (Marable, 2009: 299). Nevertheless, in the field of Muslim performing artists, some artists display clear preferences to the approach of the first leader. The uncompromising work of these artists can be regarded as social accusations to external as well as intra-group social developments. From an artistic point of view, their confrontational styles coincide with the characteristics of militant humanism of Malcolm X, which fits the attitude of Islamism and its reformative, politicized tendencies. Other artistic approaches can be understood as the style of soft or spiritual power.

The Style of 'Soft Power'

Rather than stressing his militant style, some Muslim performing artists seem to accommodate their way of remembering Malcolm X to the public's present cultural tastes, which appreciates a more flexible attitude towards Islam and Muslims and a less univocal kind of contemporary art.

In his song *Ghetto Messiah,* African-American *Sufi*-inspired rap artist Tyson Amir refers to the label that the Federal Government used for Malcolm X, the charismatic communicator of the NOI in the 1960's. The authorities, which deemed him subversive, feared Malcolm X as a security risk because of his ability to influence and politicize underprivileged people in the urban ghettos. Forty years after Malcolm's death, Tyson tries to transform the political understanding of the label *Ghetto Messiah* into a faith inspired explanation. The *Messiah*, Jesus, would equally influence people; the artist clarifies this messianic power as a 'gentle force' because people need 'spiritual change' when they are stuck in socially deprived circumstances. In Tyson's view, Malcolm X became a spiritual transformer who benefited people from the moment he finally and

---

29 Murtaza Khan in the audio poem *Muslims are scared of revolution.* myspace.com/zkthepoet/music/songs (accessed August 20, 2015).

completely chose Islam.[30] With his song, the artist tries to communicate an alternative: a softer representation of Malcolm X. At the same time, by explaining the word *Messiah* as 'being touched' gently, he tries to change the stereotypical image of hip-hop as being raw and uncivilized. Tyson hopes that his 'conscious art' style will encourage people to improve their treatment of other human beings.

African-American actress and director of the *Progress Theatre* Cristal Chanelle Truscott reveals the most important lesson she learned from Malcolm X. He criticized the *Civil Rights* movements and the United States by saying that even though it gave African-Americans full-scale civil rights, these institutions did not heal the wounds of slavery and structural racism: 'If you stick a knife in my back nine inches and pull it out six inches, there's no progress. If you pull it all the way out that's not progress. Progress is healing the wound that the blow made.'[31]

Truscott decided to contribute to this proposed healing process by legitimating her artistic work with Malcolm's plea. Her musical dance-performance *Peaches* on Nina Simone's song *Four Women* is based on Truscott's aim to "deconstruct the African-American female stereotype."[32] In the play, which creates a timeline from the epoch of slavery to the present, Truscott intends to discard the traditional representation of "the angry Black woman with the controlling attitude" and "the irresponsible single Black mother who is left by her irresponsible Black partner."[33] Regarding these biased images, Truscott depicts a (loving) relationship between a woman and a man who bear common, instead of particularistic, sorrows.

Malcolm X' style of soft power is also reflected in more recent works of *Sufi*-disposed performing poet Amir Sulaiman – taking Malcolm's model further into the new era. After having performed the *hajj*, as Malcolm X and many Muslims after him did, Sulaiman turns to the kind of art that he calls an 'inner journey,' in which he draws upon icons from the visual arts and popular culture. In the video *The Alchemist by Sulaiman's Temple* (from his work *The Meccan Openings*), he starts with the words "the alchemist turning lead to gold/a true

---

30   www.muslimhiphop.com/Stories/1._Tyson_Interview (accessed August 24, 2015). And: interview with the author, San Francisco, CA, February 16, 2010.
31   www.youtube.com/watch?v=cReCQE8B5nY (accessed August 24, 2015).
32   Asuzana Porter. "Progress Theatre: New voices Bridge Our Past to Our Future." *Black Masks*, 18(1) 2007. www.blackmasks.com/features_kkush.html (accessed August 24, 2015). And: interview with the author, Philadelphia, PA, March 21, 2010.
33   *Peaches, Lang Performing Arts Center, Swarthmore College*, Swarthmore PA.; interview with the author, March 21, 2010, Philadelphia PA.

alchemist is not lead by gold," which may refer to Renaissance alchemy as a spiritual discipline to achieve enlightenment.[34] Then Sulaiman depicts Denzel Washington, who played the title role in the documentary film *Malcolm X* by Spike Lee, with a gun pointed at his head. The video also shows Muslim pilgrims gathering around the *Kaaba* of Mecca in Saudi Arabia. His work has thus transformed from collective political consciousness to the political and spiritual consciousness of his private mind, which he perceives as an act of 'serving God.' Sulaiman explains the collage of images as a way of "coming to know oneself" – a condition to get closer in understanding Allah.[35] Developing as an artist from the *social political* to the multi-layered *avant-garde* style, Amir Sulaiman's artistic trajectory represents characteristics of the biography of Malcolm X that is understood to include both a militant and an activist spiritual phase.

While these Muslim performing artists take Malcolm's social activism further by stressing his aims in terms of soft power, such as 'touching,' 'healing' and spiritually 'coming to know yourself,' they simultaneously legitimate their own styles and aims. One of the artists' objectives is to present a more positive image of Muslims instead of furthering the image of the 'angry (young) Muslim.' Their less confrontational styles coincide with the attitude of post-Islamism, which is less politically militant compared to other expressions of Islamism.

Malcolm X and Islam Providing a Narrative

Conversion or reversion with regard to religion is generally considered as a process of going 'from darkness to light.' This process stresses an understanding that all sins committed before coming into the new religion are forgiven.[36] One of the founders of sociology, Max Weber, provided another view to enlightenment. Because it is impossible to know God's choice on who will be elected to receive salvation and go to Paradise, the puritan, ascetic lifestyle has emerged as a response to the doctrine of predestination (Collins, 1996: vii–xxxiii). This means, following Collins, that by turning one's work into a calling every moment of the day and "restricting any impulse to frivolous pleasure," one comes to experience a psychological state of mind that one can be a 'member of the Elect.'

---

34 amirsulaiman.wordpress.com/2009/03/07/the-alchemist-sulaiman-s-temple-from-the-meccan-openings/ (accessed August 24, 2015).

35 Interview with the author, Cambridge, MA, April 18, 2010.

36 www.muslimconverts.com/shahadah/sins_before_becoming_muslim.htm (accessed August 24, 2015).

In the YouTube video *How I Came to Islam From Darkness to Light*, Jamaican-born Islamic teacher Bilal Philips, who is understood to have a *Salafi* religious disposition, promotes conversion to Islam with the recommendation: "Spread peace! Earn Paradise! Bring the light of true faith to cease the darkness of ignorance!"[37] Philips, who once was a lead guitarist in a rock group, quit what he believed was ignorant by leaving the kind of music behind that is produced by "wind and strings" because musical instruments are *haram* (forbidden) and sinful.[38] This way, the trajectory 'from darkness to light' is explained as passing from the state of 'ignorance' and backwardness to the state of 'truth.' This passing suggests that by abstaining from musical pleasures a person can experience the state of mind that she or he may be a member of 'the Elect.' *In this perspective, enlightenment is equal to the anti-musical stance.*

Apart from Weber's view to the doctrine of predestination, there is the view to the doctrine of 'the Truth.' The eclectic movement of *Salafism* arouses among discontented, uprooted, discriminated people the potent kind of confidence of being part of the 'surviving group' (*al-firqa al-najiya*) that, by being elected, has immediate access to the Truth (Lohlker 2012: 95; Meijer 2009: 13).

Malcolm X particularly embodies the process 'from darkness to light.'[39] Not only did he progress in terms of symbolic capital from an unknown African-American man representing a deprived social group in the United States to a successful Black American cosmopolitan with an international reputation whose sayings were increasingly perceived as truths, he progressed by performing a double conversion process; first to the unorthodox, considered heretical *Nation of Islam*, and then to orthodox, widely accepted *Sunni* Islam.

To several Muslim artists who are inspired by the culture of hip-hop, their personal biographies seem to mirror the life trajectory of Malcolm X, as we will see in the next paragraph. His trajectory can be understood as a source of inspiration as it is used to reflect on their own lives. The biographies generate a kind of narrative, which I call the Malcolm X 'from darkness to light' or 'from hell to heaven' narrative.

Framing the Narrative

One artist who may experience, or aspire to, Malcolm's path of transformation – from the identity of criminal to that of respected Muslim – is Black American Stanley Vernell Howse a.k.a. *Flesh-N-Bone*. This member of the rap group *Bone*

---

37   www.youtube.com/watch?v=4Y8KakzkoZo (accessed August 24, 2015).
38   www.youtube.com/watch?v=buoX3yJYJYQ (accessed August 24, 2015).
39   www.whyislam.org/malcolm-x-from-darkness-to-light/# (accessed August 24, 2015).

Thugs-N-Harmony performed at Minnesota's *Malcolm X Memorial Day* in 2014. After being sentenced in 2001, *Flesh-N-Bone* exchanged his Christian faith for Islam. Still in prison in 2007, the former drug-addict, who was accused of violating violated family members,[40] says that as a Muslim he will continue to represent the street people in his music who are struggling to make it out of the ghettos, but now as a 'good person' and a 'better artist.'[41] So, *Flesh-N-Bone* describes a transformation 'from darkness to light' by (the intention of) going from performing sin to performing obvious virtue.

Another artist who went through an explicit passage is British Nabil Abdul Rashid, born in a Muslim Nigerian family.[42] After becoming convicted at a very young age for drug related street crimes, Nabil called his imprisonment a "wake-up call."[43] Having found stand-up comedy as a means to transform his past experiences creatively, he is eager to "give back to the community" e.g. by means of contributing to talent shows for (rootless) youngsters at risk of petty crime and more. As a 'born-again' Muslim, Nabil presents himself as a very proud Muslim on stage.[44] These transformations signify not just developments of becoming Muslim, or a better Muslim, but also a process of coming out of the gutter into the state of social enlightenment.

In the aforementioned lecture *Contemporary Muslim Voices in the Arts*, African-American poet Amir Sulaiman made an interesting observation; his statement indicates that the process of self-transformation of Malcolm X has become an example of shared framing among Muslim performing artists.

> The life of Malcolm X, although amazing, is almost a cliché to us. You were drunk, a little pimp, you would go to jail and you would find Islam. It is practically like a running joke.[45]

---

40 www.huffingtonpost.com/2010/03/30/bone-thugsnharmony-rapper_n_518321.html (accessed August 24, 2015).

41 Bilooh. "Flesh-N-Bone interview in prison." Xzbit Forums. July 27, 2007. web.archive.org/web/20110128163805/http://www.xzibitcentral.com/forums/showthread.php?t=2053 (accessed August 24, 2015). And: www.musicfanclubs.org/bonethugs/info/int/source_flesh.html (accessed August 24, 2015).

42 Interview with the author, London, UK, November 21, 2010.

43 Harry Miller. "Reformed criminal takes on talent show." Croydon Guardian. July 22, 2008. www.croydonguardian.co.uk/news/2406501.reformed_criminal_takes_on_talent_show/ (accessed August 24, 2015).

44 I use the identification of "born-again" Muslim for artists who, although born in a Muslim family, revalue the principles of Islam later in life by changing their ways of expressing religiosity and practicing faith.

45 Seminar at *Harvard University, Contemporary Muslim Voices in the Arts and Literatures*, Cambridge, MA, April 17/18, 2010.

Although the majority of the Muslim hip-hop artists cannot draw upon a 'savory' criminal past in a prison context like Nabil Abdulrashid, or especially *Flesh-N-Bone*, many of their life stories echo the kind of path Sulaiman is referring to. *Sufi*-oriented British-Nigerian rap artist Rakin Fetuga a.k.a. Rakin Niass of the band *Mecca2Medina*, who contributed to the *I am Malcolm X* tour via the cultural institution *Radical Middle Way* in 2009,[46] informs the visitors of the popular site *Muslimhiphop.com*:

> Before Islam, I was a street hoodlum involved with a lot of low-level crime. I lived a dark life that was surrounded by instant gratification. If I didn't become a Muslim, I could have ended up in prison or worst than that...dead. Islam has transformed my life completely. It gave me a thirst for knowledge, it gave me self-discipline, it gave me direction.[47]

In his autobiographical narrative, Niass depicts a process 'from darkness to light,' which resembles the life and religious trajectory of Malcolm X. This kind of narrative can be found among many artists who grew up in the culture of hip-hop that was partly inspired by Malcolm X.

Narrative as Group Activity

Converting to (another) religion establishes new boundaries (Rambo and Farhadian, 2014), but the transfer from one cultural group to another may be perceived as a lonely process. This consideration has lead e.g. to the founding of *Taleef Collective* for supporting Muslim converts and born-again Muslims in California. At formal spiritual gatherings, as well as in the context of educational or pop cultural settings – e.g. events of *Muslim Student Associations* at the campus – religious conversion can be perceived as a shared experience. Generally, positive experiences from interaction rituals may produce symbols of group membership (Collins, 2004). Particularly in hip-hop, which claims to have an inclusive spirit that makes no differences based on ethnicity, race or nationality in the fight against oppression, the flourishing of symbols and narratives is most likely, especially in relation to Malcolm X.

---

46 *Radical Middle Way* promotes a balanced understanding of Islam by trying to turn anger into "positive civic action" through performances and (Islamic) lectures for young people. www.radicalmiddleway.org/ (accessed July 22, 2009) and www.facebook.com/RadicalMiddleWay/info?tab=page_info (accessed August 24, 2015).

47 www.muslimhiphop.com/Stories/2._Mecca2Medina_Interview (accessed August 24, 2015).

Malcolm Little had become immersed in the world of hustlers, players, pimps, and gangsters, prior to his imprisonment and Islamic conversion (Marable, 2011; Perry, 1991). The state of feeling culturally endangered may sound familiar to many current American and British Muslim performing artists in the United States and United Kingdom in the present study. They often perceive themselves to be relegated to the lowest tastes of the glamorous and commercial entertainment industry that stereotypes Muslims as gangsters and has commodified gangsta rap. To artists in hip-hop, a threat of moral and ethical civilized behavior is particularly obvious when their life trajectories meet street gang culture, as in the words of Rakin Niass: "I lived a dark life that was surrounded by instant gratification."[48] Rap artists who experience danger from their socio-cultural environment may seek protection, similar to inmates in prison – converting to Islam could be perceived as a way out.

Describing the kind of pollution that is comparable to the first phase of Malcolm X's life trajectory seems part of the 'from darkness to light' narrative among Muslim artists in hip-hop, especially to those who practice the ideological style of socially 'conscious hip-hop.' In a session on 'gang culture' for a high school class that had experienced the North London riots in 2011, American conscious music collective *Remarkable Current*, founded by Muslim convert Anas Canon in 2001, explained the meaning of gangs, crime and rap music through the trajectory of Malcolm X.[49]

Conversion stories following the *shahada*, the Muslim profession to faith, can serve the purpose of justifying choices, edify past events, or to convince oneself and other people (Hermansen, 1999), similar to narratives. However, by using the terms 'cliché' and 'running joke,' African-American poet Amir Sulaiman suggests that Muslim (rap) artists, including his friends in the culture of hip-hop, have employed the Malcolm X trajectory as an example to structure their own lives. Indeed, narratives can be understood as 'actions' (Cunliffe and Coupland, 2012). All of this means in the present study that some conversion stories are refashioned based on the 'from hell to heaven' narrative but prior to their own factual transformation process.

The Traditional Growing Up Narrative

Generally, the life trajectory from sinful to moral behavior is a common report adults give when reflecting on their lives. Youthful sins may prove to be

---

48 www.muslimhiphop.com/Stories/2._Mecca2Medina_Interview (accessed August 24, 2015).
49 www.facebook.com/remarkablecurrent/posts/10151597454266335 (accessed August 24, 2015).

the hurdles grown-ups have faced in order to undertake the responsibility of adulthood. These sins usually comprise of going out, listening to extreme music genres, drinking alcohol or smoking hash (Ter Bogt, 2000). By using this common human narrative, rap artist Rakin Niass kindly plays down Malcolm's former engagement in criminal activities.

> He [Malcolm] went through a period when he was kind of partying... And then he converted to Islam. And then he became an intellectual. So, his whole experience is great.[50]

Although some of the 'hip-hop Malcolmologists' embraced Malcolm X as a notorious streetwise cultural rebel (Marable, 2009: 303), Niass' explanation of Malcolm's trajectory does not quite reflect a comparable glorification of Malcolm's early gangster career. Similarly, Niass does not seem to react to the presumption that Malcolm X exaggerated his criminal record in order to illustrate the destructive consequences of racism within the United States (Aidi and Marable, 2009: 11). But, as is usual in the particular construction of narratives (Riessman, 1993; White, 1980: 5–27), the quote displays a selective view. A narrative thus legitimates a specific attitude toward events in question (Cunliffe and Coupland, 2012: 66). By adapting the narrative to the development of a common life trajectory, Niass not only makes the phase of darkness part of Malcolm's final stage of enlightenment – "his whole experience is great" – he also reduces the distance between him and the famous Malcolm X. Plausibly, the 'from darkness to light' and 'from hell to heaven' narrative is a matter of identification with Malcolm X and his trajectory of gaining international admission by promoting "the unifying power of Islam."[51] Anyway, the watered down version by Niass of the dark phase of Malcolm's life makes recognizing oneself in the prominent Muslim social activist easier.

The Traditional Conversion Narrative

Many convert artists experience hurdles in the process of transferring from one culture to another culture which comprises a new religion and its different cultural environments (Hermansen, 1999; Wohlrab Sahr, 1999). These hurdles have to do with (lacking) opportunities of belonging, acceptance and identification. While recognizing the process of a similar brother in faith – who seems

---

50 Interview with the author, London, UK, October 20, 2010.
51 www.whyislam.org/malcolm-x-from-darkness-to-light/# (accessed August 24, 2015).

to stay forever young due to his early death – Muslim performing artists approve of the way Malcolm coped with the many problems in his life.

Black American-Jamaican female rap artist Aja Black admires Malcolm X for his "patient perseverance" to endure misery that was not even for the benefit of himself but for the support of other human beings. She considers him a role model in the sense of "not giving up when things are hard" in the course to improve the circumstances of people. To spoken word and former rap artist Spitz a.k.a. Yaqub Abdusalaam, who was born in an indigenous British family, Malcolm X proved more than anyone else that he "really struggled for the *Deen*" (religion) on his path to Islam.[52] After the NOI leader had defined White people as 'devils,' Spitz was enlightened to discover Malcolm's 'true stance' after having been to Mecca – apparently Malcolm was striving for the common good, not just for Black people but for Muslims in general. While Malcolm's path was thus set out to achieve the common good, he struggled so hard that he died for it. During his own trajectory, similar to Islamic teacher Bilal Philips, *Salafi*-oriented Abdusalaam quit using his favorite musical instruments in order to suffer and "get closer to God." While the media had often depicted Malcolm X as an irresponsible demagogue (Marable, 2011: 13), Abdusalaam considers Malcolm as a *shahid*, a martyr – a view shared by many Black Americans.

Muslim converts recognize themselves in Malcolm X's problematic path to belief. They are willing to identify with his trajectory because in their view Malcolm demonstrates that converting to Islam can be a matter of the utmost important, especially because of its humanistic values. Representing a symbol of shared meanings, Malcolm X seems to inspire artists who consider themselves socially 'conscious' artists to develop their autobiographical conversion narrative with a 'from darkness to light' structure.

The Narrative as a Condition to Success

In the general field of art in which artists compete for the right sources of cultural and symbolic capital, artists are dependent on "circles of recognition" (Bourdieu 1996; Bowness, 1989). These circles include but are not limited to *critical recognition, peer recognition* and *public acclaim*.[53]

When using the 'from darkness to light' narrative of artists, critics may enhance their public acclaim. Although *Salafi*-inspired British-Jamaican spoken

---

52 Interview with the author, London, UK, December 16, 2010.
53 The author has benefitted from the recommendations of Dr. Louis van Tilborgh and Prof. Anton Wessels and their work on art and religion in the case of Vincent van Gogh.

word artist and actor Ashley Chin a.k.a. "Muslim Belal," had not experienced prison himself, according to his autobiographical performance *From the Streets to Islam*,[54] he grew up participating in street gang culture, seeing his peers resort to a criminal lifestyle to make ends meet. *The Independent* describes his trajectory as "a journey that has scoured poverty, hardship and adversity" before gaining a successful break in his acting career as Muslim artist on the big screen.[55] The comment recognizes the artist's progression in an approvingly way.

The Malcolm X narrative may also be used to generate acclaim by the artist among her or his followers. In 2010, actor and spoken word artist Muslim Belal, who left music (except for occasionally singing *nasheeds*) for the same reason as Spitz Abdusalaam, twitters under the name Ashley Belal Chin, about his desired (future) status: "Malcolm X started as a hustler, ended as a inspirational Muslim. I Wanna go #Like Malcolm."[56]

The autobiographical story of former rap artist Mutah Wassin Shabazz Beale, a.k.a. Mutah Napoleon Beale, whose Puerto Rican and African-American mother and father – followers of Malcolm X and the NOI – were killed before his very eyes, is popular to various kinds of media. The *Salafi*- inclined artist, who quit using musical instruments similar to Spitz Abdusalaam and Muslim Belal, is eager to tell the audience how he as an orphan from deprived circumstances worked himself out of 'the hood' of dealers, drugs and a culture industry of gangsta rap.[57] After seeing the movie *Malcolm X*, Mutah Beale followed Malcolm X's example and went on *hajj*, to finally become an internationally invited Muslim motivational speaker.[58] By achieving critical recognition, the Malcolm X 'from darkness to light' narrative seems thus to support the artists on the rise to fame and in the creation of markets.

The Malcolm X narrative may also function as a legitimating force for similar artists to recognize a Muslim performing artist as a 'conscious artist.' In the field of Muslim artists, this recognition could mean distinction to those who are considered to glamorize possessions, women, forms of addiction and violence. Although any *one straight line* theory of progress is generally criticized

---

54 *Eid Celebration, University of Sussex*, Sussex, UK, December 12, 2010.
55 Hasnet Lais. "Faith and film: Actor Ashley Chin's balancing act." The Independent. October 10, 2012. blogs.independent.co.uk/2012/10/10/faith-and-film actor-ashley-chin's-balancing-act/ (accessed August 24, 2015).
56 twitter.com/ashleybelalchin/status/14302049164 (accessed August 24, 2015).
57 *4e Nationale Bekeerlingendag (4th National Converts Day)*, Den Haag, NL, January 8, 2011.
58 Khoulah Ibrahim. "From The Outlawz to Da'wah. A Rapper's Life." OnIslam, August 18, 2010. www.onislam.net/english/culture-and-entertainment/music/448878-rapperlife.html (accessed August 24, 2015).

nowadays, the Malcolm X narrative seems to be an exception by having become one of several central notions in the field of art by Muslims.

The Narrative and Recognition from the Field of Religion

The *one straight line* character of the Malcolm X narrative may be related to the idea of identifying 'Muslim' as the highest phase in the progression of being 'Black.' This kind of social elevation could be historically rooted in the distinct White American representation of slaves who were Muslim due to their considered qualities in literacy and learning (Aidi and Marable, 2009: 3). Social elevation or sublimation is also expressed by the 'primitivist view' that Malcolm X seemed to have accepted, which holds that Black people have a genius for religion similar to their purported genius for music, dance, and bodily expressivity (Hart, 2008: 195).[59] When this natural genius expressed itself poorly, Black people became Christians; when expressed well, they became Muslims.

At the seminar *Contemporary Muslim Voices in the Arts* in 2010, *Sufi*-oriented African-American poet Amir Sulaiman seems to relate the changing perspective on "Muslim as a higher state" in the recent cultural past of Black Muslims with the massive influx of (Middle Eastern and South Asian) Muslim immigrants after 1965 in the United States. Maybe more so, Sulaiman refers to the global *Islamic Revival* that brought forth stringent ideas about Islamic norms, values and culture since the 1990's (Lapidus, 2002: 823). While it used to be 'natural' to create and enjoy music for Black people in the United States, as hip-hop producer Anas Canon of mixed African American and White parentage explains, the influence from overseas became a pressure to change their cultural habits after 2001. Amir Sulaiman states,

> Earlier in the development of Islam in the Black community, Islam was not a foreign thing. It wasn't like you started dressing like a foreigner; you started talking like a foreigner. It was not something that separated one from their people. It was the highest station of Blackness. So if you were *super* Black, you were Muslim – Muslim was this super Black thing.[60]

---

59 According to Hart, *The Souls of Black Folks* of Du Bois provides the canonical formulation of this view (Hart, 2008: 195).

60 Seminar at *Harvard University, Contemporary Muslim Voices in the Arts and Literatures*, Cambridge MA, April 17/18, 2010.

As an indigenous Western Muslim, African American al-Hajj Malik al-Shabazz a.k.a. Malcolm X, who nearly always wore the Western style of dark suits and ties when he made his speeches, while showing discipline in following the behavioral rules of Islam, encouraged African American culture at the same time (Marable, 2011; Perry, 1991; Smethurst, 2010).

A certain conflation of race and religion seems familiar among several (convert) Islamic teachers in the field of the religion of Islam. These Islamic teachers are the kind of teachers who are related to many Muslim artists – particularly the artists who embraced Islam later in live.

Different from the field of art that is regarded as a quite autonomous field (Bourdieu, 1996), the field of Muslim performing artists, particularly with regard to converts and born-again Muslim artists, display a certain (temporary) dependency of the religious-artistic recognition from authoritative voices in the field of Islam (*see also*, Van Tilborgh, 2016). The artists have to deal with opponents and proponents in the discourse on the permissibility and conditions of the performing arts in Islam. Generally, particular performing artists feel, after having interacted with Islamic teachers or scholars, that their artistic work is Islamically legitimate or needs certain adaptation. They continue their artistic practices in a more informalized or formalized way.

A number of Muslim performing artists, such as British-Jamaican Sukina Abdul Noor and Muneera Rashida of the female band *Poetic Pilgrimage* and African-American Tyson Amir, feel supported by the interpretations of how art relates to Islam via certain significant Islamic teachers, or *sheikhs*, due to the moral sanction the 'interpreters' provide(d) them.[61] In the mystical Islamic tradition of *Sufism*, the relationship between beauty, art and remembrance of God has been a key element for centuries (Winegar, 2008). Contrarily to Bilal Philips, these sometimes *Sufi*-minded teachers from e.g. African or Caribbean-American descent inspire the stage performer to reconcile – up to a certain degree – the tradition of their art and culture with Islam – instead of disregarding their (Black) ethnic or national background concerning singing, dancing and playing musical instruments (Van Tilborgh, 2016). In this perspective, *Sufism* is not a quietist kind of spirituality; the authentic synthesis between *Sunni* Islam and *Sufism* has developed into a more scholarly, sophisticated and activist form in the United States to counter the success of literalist (British) *Salafi* trends (Hamid, 2008, 2009; Lapidus, 1997; Geaves, 2011).

In the initial days of hip-hop, many Muslim convert artists appreciated African-American Imam al-Hajj Talib Abdur-Rashid's advice about how they

---

61 Interviews with the author, London, UK, December 6, 2010, respectively: San Francisco, CA, February 16, 2010.

could perform in accordance with Islam.⁶² Abdur-Rashid works in the lineage of Malcolm X at the *Mosque of Islamic Brotherhood* in Harlem, which is a descendant of Malcolm's 1964 *Muslim Mosque*. The Imam defines Malcolm X as an enduring symbol of resistance against worldwide oppression, because the conditions that produced him still exist. From Malcolm's sense of social action and pride, 'hip-hop Imam Talib' inspires Muslim artists, women and men, to perform from a specific (Black) Muslim distinction – without repudiating their cultural background.

Talib Abdur-Rashid is not the only (Black) Imam who is actively transferring the values of Malcolm X into artistic-cultural environments. In the UK, Imam British-Sudanese Babikir Ahmed Babikir participated in the *I am Malcolm X* tour by *Radical Middle Way* in 2009. At this event, he introduced Malcolm X to the young audience as a man who 'has come from the darkness to the light.' That is, "by rejecting all that is evil to stand fair with what is right" he has become a "guide of goodness."⁶³ In between, Babikir connects the Malcolm X narrative with advocating art, i.e. poetry, music, dance and colorful dressing – albeit according to the limits of Islam. He identifies the opponents of expressive artistic behavior with their obviously non-African background, because, "In Africa, if you don't sing and dance, you're *not* human!" *In this perspective, enlightenment is equal to the pro-music stance.*

The life of al-Hajj Malik al-Shabazz does not only paradigmatically reflect the progression 'from darkness to light.' The Islamic teachers and converts – African-American Imam Zaid Shakir and *Sufi*-oriented American scholar Dr. Umar Faruq Abd-Allah, who relates Islam with the cosmopolitan, inclusive type of civilization (2004) – give an impassioned lecture on the life and legacy of Malcolm X in the video of film director Mustafa Davis *Passing the Baton* at *Taleef Collective* in 2013.⁶⁴ Malcolm X, who believed in "the threat of hell and the promise of Paradise," as argued by the teachers, stands for having "illuminated the darkness." He has "build new institutions" and transformed the *Civil Rights* movement with his continuing "struggle for the truth." They celebrate Malcolm X, who – despite or even because of having to deal with a world that "despised Black Muslims" – became father of the rebirth of "the civilization building religion of Islam" in the American (Western) world. Relying on the collective cultural memory of Black Americans regarding transatlantic slavery,

---

62   Interview with the author, New York, NY, May 1, 2010.
63   www.radicalmiddleway.org/media/i-am-malcolm-x/7 (accessed June 24, 2014). And: www.youtube.com/watch?v=1vL2wqYkP6A (accessed August 24, 2015).
64   web.archive.org/web/20131214185727/http://vimeo.com/81160189 (accessed August 24, 2015). And: taleefcollective.org/passing-the-baton-short-film/ (accessed August 24, 2015).

the emotionally involved teachers praise the human rights activist Malcolm X due to his engagement with African leaders and institutions.[65] This way, Malcolm had reconnected Islam with the "sound Islamic teaching of the ancestors" of African-Americans who had been forced to leave their original cultural heritage.

So, there seems to be an obvious connection between the admiration of several convert British and American Islamic teachers for al-Hajj Malik al-Shabazz, with his social activist kind of Islam, and Muslim performing artists who are inspired by him and use the Malcolm X 'from hell to heaven' narrative. Religious, artistic and cultural legitimation by authoritative voices of artists can be particularly relevant in the United States, where the differences between indigenous converts and immigrant Muslims, who are born into Islam, are often played out ideologically.

The Narrative and the Third Resurrection

The phases in the life of Malcolm X seem to symbolize the progression model of the three resurrections as discussed by Islamic scholar Sherman Jackson (2005). Sherman is well-known among the educated African-American performing artists. The "First Resurrection" indicated the turn of many African-Americans toward the NOI ideology in the time of its leader Elijah Muhammad; the "Second Resurrection" comprised their embracing of orthodox *Sunni* Islam. In the former century, African-Americans were susceptible to Islam on account of their spiritual protest against anti-Black racism, which reflects what Jackson calls "Black Religion" (*see also,* Jackson, 2009). In his view, Black American Muslims should take their religion to a "Third Resurrection" (Jackson, 2005: 3–21). Opposite to the dominant 'immigrant Islam' and 'the Muslim world,' they should keep their inborn kind of awareness and activist-indigenous American Islam alive to stay capable of resisting dominant culture – by finding their own voice in the tradition of historical (*Sunni*) Islam. If Malcolm X would have been alive today, Jackson supposes, he could have been able to shape this Third Resurrection which would be geared toward "producing Islam" instead of "consuming Islam." The human rights advocate would be able to demonstrate that his position as "champion of protest" is "consistent with the best tradition of *Sunni* Islam" as well as with full-heartedly being American (Jackson, 2005: 168).

---

65   Marable (2011) and Perry (1991).

Understanding Malcolm Little's 'progression' to Malcolm X as a similar process that much of the African-American community has experienced relates the Malcolm X 'from darkness to light' narrative to the present and future of Muslims in the West. African-American poet Dasham Brookins, a.k.a. Brother Dash, offers a platform with his audio and Internet blog to academic perspectives on race relations and Islam in the United States, e.g. Sherman Jackson and Cornel West, who propose alternatives as well (Houston, 2013).[66] In performance poetry, as if consciously contributing to this "Third Resurrection," Dasham Brookins displays his *Americanness* in combination with critical *Muslimness* by disseminating his poems with social critique, which are directed toward attitudes and behaviors both outside and within Islam.[67]

In the poem *Masjid Marauders* (mosque bandits), Brookins relays the complaints of a lot of his colleagues regarding the control of mosques by conservative, low educated immigrant Muslims in the West and how they persistently spread their conservative views on women and the performing arts.

> The house of prayer? A social club
> For men who share a foreign tongue…
> The first house was build on the dirt of slaves
> Not on the fringes of outer *Whitelandia*
> We beat our words on their inner ear *daffs*[68]
> But they turned away 'cause 'music is *haram*'
> Islam like a bomb, napalm for native dwellers "Sisters go pray in a cellar"
> They are the *masjid* marauders…[69]

Also producing discourse in Islam with their artistic expressions in rap, British-Jamaican Muneera Rashida and Sukina Abdul Noor, and British-Mozambican Mohammed Yahya, already criticized Middle Eastern leaders before the start of the 'Arab Spring.' In the graphic music video *Silence is consent,* these Malcolm X

---

66 brotherdash.com/embracing-the-goodbad-america-dr-west-dr-jackson/ (accessed August 24, 2015).
67 Interview with the author, New York, NY, April 27, 2010.
68 The hand drum, the *daff*, is used in the time of the Prophet Muhammad. Except according to extreme conservative views, it is a non-contested musical instrument in Islamic discourse.
69 Part of the poem *Masjid Marauders*. brotherdash.com/?p=399 (accessed August 24, 2015). Event: *Poetry with Brother Dash (Islam Awareness Week)*, Rutgers University, New Brunswick, NJ, April 13, 2010.

admirers morally accuse the dictators of exclusively serving themselves 'while people are *dying*'.[70]

Concrete social critique occurs in the artistic expressions of Muslim performers in the various genres of poetry, graffiti, comedy and music. They often condemn the foreign policies of the governments of the United States and the United Kingdom as it concerns Muslim countries; the unequal treatment of Muslim citizens by corporate America (both at the borders and in the prisons); the media hype which relates terror exclusively to Islam; Islamophobia; as well as the perceived vulgar tastes of the commercial culture industries. However, outspoken *internal* criticism and protest in Islam, as the examples of Brother Dash and *Poetic Pilgrimage* above, may be found sooner in the more activist genres of art, such as rap music and spoken word poetry, where the links with Malcolm X may still be the most strong.

The Narrative and Choices in Career Trajectories

The life of Malcolm X, as expressed in the 'from hell to heaven' narrative, is above all an expression of an active interpretation of Islam, which may be considered an 'inner-worldly' kind of religiosity by working toward a better, anti-racist and equal, world in the present. Max Weber distinguished between the 'inner-worldly' and the 'world-rejecting' kind of religiosity. The first draws from the world a duty to transform its reality in accordance with ascetic ideals as expressed in people's ethic of work and daily activities, and the latter is practiced from strict observance outside the center of mundane life, displaying a more ritualistic practicing of religion (Weber, 2007; Zaleski, 2010). As mentioned above about the doctrine of predestination, by restricting any impulse to light-minded pleasure one can generate a kind of sense of being a "member of the *Elect*" of God (Collins, 1996: vii–xxxiii). Without making any further comparison, it may be useful to keep the ways of practicing religiosity and the relation to predestination in mind when focusing on the following specific career trajectories of Muslim artists.

In the field of Muslim performing artists, convert and born-again Muslims go through different phases in their religious-artistic trajectories. These phases could be understood from the theories of Norbert Elias and Cas Wouters, which claim that the general drive of human beings for social mobility leads to the process whereby social and moral behavior is controlled by imitating

---

70 www.youtube.com/watch?v=z1orCqZg4SA (accessed August 24, 2015). Video produced by *Beat Thief*; filmed and directed by *Global Faction*.

higher social layers through external and internal regulation, leading to phases of behavioral "formalization," "informalization" and occasionally "reformalization" (Elias, 2000; Wouters, 2007).

The phase of (re)mastering the religion of Islam consists of many behavior constraining rituals, which can be regarded as a phase of formalization for convert and born-again Muslims (Zebiri, 2008: 60–70, 101–135). They may experience leaving a former state of darkness in order to gain cultural and religious enlightenment, but they feel they have not reached this superior position yet. Leon Moosavi explains the different phases that particularly convert Muslims go through as continuous overt adaptations to prove their "authentic Muslimness" toward suspicious Muslims who are born into Islam (Moosavi 2012).

In the case of Muslim artists, the seeking for the *right* kind of Islamic conduct tends to affect their artistic endeavors within (restrained) movements, the content of their art and the clothing in which they perform. For example, African American Anas Canon made a good living as a dancer and choreography teacher of *break* and *jazz dance* in California before he embraced Islam.[71] However, after his conversion, Canon decided to leave the world of dance and temptation of beautiful women to finally become an audio engineer, music producer and artistic director of *Remarkable Current*, the record label of a number of conscious (Muslim) musicians.

In the field of Muslim performing artists, the mastering of formalized conduct is often followed by two contrasting kinds of regimes regarding manners and emotions. Several artists enter a phase of 'informalization' regarding their religious-artistic conduct; they get more experienced in Islam and loosen up to some extent, while other artists enter a phase of 'intensified formalization' by consciously choosing to increase their religious-artistic restraint behavior (Van Tilborgh, 2016). From the perspective of the Malcolm X 'from darkness to light' narrative, I will focus especially on the last group.

The Narrative and Informalization

Initially convert Muslim performing artists, while still incorporating new Islamic habits and temporarily becoming 'strictly Islamic,' e.g. by traveling to the Middle East to gain knowledge that they perceive as authentic, may develop certain doubt about their way of producing art and music. The opponents of musical instruments or women on stage as well as their own considerations can make them feel slightly uncomfortable. They might even worry about

---

[71] Interview with the author, Los Angeles, CA, January 16, 2010.

being able to achieve the status of true Muslim and if not, they feel it could be wise to stick to the rules that respected Muslims scholars advocate. However, after being acknowledged by several renowned Islamic teachers in the West, the artists display certain informalized conduct.[72] They feel encouraged to keep some of their cultural (ethnic) habits alive, for example, working with female artists on stage, and decide to continue with their kind of artistic content and style when performing. They tend to act religiously and artistically more relaxed, although in a controlled way.

Coinciding, these often *Sufi*-inclined artists become specifically aware of the importance of spirituality in Islam. Modern-day Muslim storyteller May Alhassen, who was taught the 'mechanics of Islam' during her Syrian-American upbringing, translates Malcolm's process especially as a "spiritual struggle" that transformed him from a searching Muslim to a spiritual Islamic leader. Similar to British-Pakistani Canadian cultural manager Abdul-Rehman Malik, who calls Malcolm's autobiography one of the sacred texts after the Qur'an and *Hadith* that Muslims can rely on,[73] reading *Malcolm X* was one of the most transformative experiences of Alhassen's life. Suddenly, she became aware of the spiritual richness in Islam, "all the stuff that I loved in other Eastern traditions, like Buddhism, Taoism and the Hindu tradition appeared to be here in my religion, I just didn't know it!"[74]

In *Hijabi Monologues*, which depicts real-life stories of various Muslim women on stage, May Alhassen stresses the particularity of Muslim experiences among non-Muslims with regard to veiling and praying. She also displays the universal meaning of the struggles of Muslim women regarding matters of love and sex, which can be dubious from a religious point of view, but understandable from the humanist view.[75]

When performing the *hajj*, Malcolm is understood to have experienced an epiphany by meeting the kind of Islam that displayed respect for all believers of all racial backgrounds. After recognizing the similarities between (Muslim) Black and White people, he no longer embraced the segregationist ideas of the *Nation of Islam*. May Alhassen explains Malcolm's spirituality as "seeking unity for all peoples." Her aim to create unity herself suggests an active and tolerant kind of spirituality, which must be realized in the world of the present, the here and now.

---

72   This observation is based on fieldwork between 2009 and 2012, which may mean that the phases the artists are passing may have changed in the years after.
73   Interview with the author, London, UK, November 5, 2010.
74   Interview with the author, March 27, 2010, New York, NY.
75   *Hijabi Monologues*, New York University, New York, NY, March 26, 2010.

From the perspective on conversion as a hybrid, syncretic way (Szpiech, 2013: 224; Wohlrab Sahr, 1999), the performing artists in this category combine their 'old self' (and its world) with the 'new self' (and its social environment) after entering a phase of informalization and relaxation in their career and religious trajectories – in contrast to the next type of performing artists.

The Narrative and Intensified Formalization

Several rap artists seem to reflect on Malcolm's life by means of the 'from darkness to light' or 'from hell to heaven' narrative in a contrary way to the former artists by choosing to formalize their conduct more intensively. Similar to Malcolm X, their trajectories display a sequence of two kinds of conversions to Islam, of which I qualify the latter one as "intensified formalization" (Van Tilborgh, 2016). The hip-hop artists, Mutah Napoleon Beale and Muslim Belal, whom we have already met above, and Masikah Feesabillah a.k.a. Al Asadi a.k.a. Abu Siddiq, grew up in the environments of break dance, graffiti, rap music and its occasional references to Malcolm X and Islam.[76] At different moments in their lives, they have taken a strict, *Salafi*-oriented view that limits their artistic endeavors. This means they have abandoned the use of musical instruments in order to get nearer to Allah and intensify their relationship with the Creator.

Having encountered deprived social circumstances or a destabilized background, the artists experienced the hard-core street life of gangs and (petty) crime as some kind of 'jungle.' One of these former rap artists, Masikah Feesabillah, from a Saint Lucian-Jamaican family, whose brother was murdered by a youth gang, has been involved in drug dealing just like Malcolm Little.[77] Also, he converted to Islam in prison similar to Malcolm X. Thus, as a radical mode of identity transformation, Masikah had become Muslim and, at some point in the time after, acquired a strict religious orientation toward Islam by foregoing the production of music.[78] Since then, he has taught about his experiences in *Roadside2Islam*, a social *da'wah* project for vulnerable youth in the world of "gun and knife crimes." Expressing his identification with al-Hajj Malik al-Shabazz on stage, Masikah confesses that Malcolm X kind of "belongs to him"

---

76   Mutah Beale can be identified as convert as well as a born-again Muslim because his Christian grandmother brought him up by after his Muslim parents were murdered. The same counts for Masikah, whose mother was non-Muslim at the time of his youth.
77   muslimhiphop.com/Hip-Hop/Masikah (accessed August 24, 2015).
78   Interview with the author, London, UK, April 3, 2009.

because "The path that I came from 'till the path I am now is similar to the path of Malcolm X."[79]

The indigenous British rap artist, Jamie Spitz Renwick a.k.a. Yaqub Abdusalaam, differs in some respects to the former rap artists. Notwithstanding having "dabbled in the streets" and selling cannabis in his youth, he did not experience hard-core street life before his conversion. Nevertheless, he met the social ills of society, especially alcohol addiction, which killed his mother.[80] Having searched for a long time, and becoming convinced that Islam could cure society, he embraced Islam. In the first formalizing phase in adapting to his new religion, Spitz, whose passion was music, collected arguments to refute accusations that his practices in professional musical engineering were *haram*. The rap performer relied on the moderate stance of Islamic teachers, as expressed by prominent Yusuf al-Qaradawi, that art is conditionally permissible.

Seeking a more unambiguous, straight relation with Allah, Spitz routinely inspected himself on the matter of music: "Was I being sincere?" The statement of an anonymous Islamic teacher that music in its attractiveness is like "*Shaytan*'s Qur'an" impressed Spitz deeply. He changed his approach when a new theological anti-instruments interpretation dawned on him through *Islam Channel*. It may have been a similar kind of waking up as Malcolm X experienced when learning about orthodox *Sunni* Islam after having followed the *Nation of Islam* for so long. Entering the phase of 'intensified formalization,' Spitz took on the name Yaqub Abdusalaam. He abandoned his musical instruments, just like Masikah, Muslim Belal and Mutah Napoleon Beale and turned from practicing rap music to the genre of spoken word.

These Muslim rap artists believe that a majority of the classical scholars, stemming from the four *Sunni* schools within Islamic jurisprudence, judge musical instruments as impermissible – except for the *daff*, the hand drum. The performers are convinced they have to safeguard themselves and their religion from 'doubtful matters.' Regarding (popular) art and music, they demonstrate a 'world-rejecting' kind of asceticism that is practiced through strict observance to Islam. More than the former category, these performers are careful not to challenge the choice from Above at getting elected to be saved. Therefore, they have taken the attitude of certain intensified formalized behavior to sacrifice in the here and now.

The artists resemble the traditional representation of (Christian, Jewish or Islamic) conversion in which the convert has been "stripped of the old self with its practices" and has put on a new self (Szpiech, 2013: 224), as well as the kind

---

79   www.radicalmiddleway.org/media/i-am-malcolm-x/3 (accessed July 16, 2014).
80   Interview with the author, London, UK, December 16, 2010.

of Islamic conversion that is called "symbolic battle," on account of a radical break with their non-Muslim past (Wohlrab-Sahr, 1999). The feeling of being haunted by the threat of backsliding and apostasy of certain converts, as described by Szpiech, seems especially constitutive of this particular category of Muslim performers (Szpiech, 2013: 216–217). Regarding Malcolm X as an example, which can be explained from the common markers of socio-psychological experiences of street crime, drug dealing, and the world shaking loss (murder) of close family members, they perceive their own religious artistic trajectory as a process 'from darkness to light,' 'sin to virtue,' and 'hell to heaven.'[81] Because, when they return to their old communities after having initiated their 'intensified formalization' as a 'second conversion,' it is in the role of a Muslim motivational speaker as the chosen 'revealer' – almost like Malcolm X – who reveals what may happen in the afterlife if one gets stuck in the phase of darkness. In the video *I'm no longer a Victim*, former rap artist Muslim Belal states,

> Life is a test. This could be the last day. I believe in the life that goes on beyond the sky. I'm just trying to get there while I'm still alive. Die not or die in a state of submission – to get to Paradise is the mission. I am not a messenger – I am just a warner. Today can be your last morning – tonight we die. Like Malcolm, I'm a man on a mission.[82]

Giving this statement at the yearly conference of *Islamic Education and Research Academy: Changing the World through Da'wah* in 2011, Muslim Belal provides a clear illustration of how performers who choose the path of 'intensified formalization' explain the Malcolm X narrative via the idiom of predestination.

The Sequence of Light after Darkness

Clearly, the participants in the field of Muslim performing artists, including several Islamic teachers, stress the sequence of 'light' after 'darkness' and the quality of light in the dark periods of life as far as Malcolm X is concerned. They depict him as outstanding, a success. Still, it is also possible to see al-Hajj Malik al-Shabazz as a failure, considering the following list. Malcolm X could not quite harmonize the humanistic universalism of Islam with his particularistic belief in an essentialist Black identity, linking together all persons

---

81   twitter.com/AshleyBelalChin/status/14302049164 (accessed August 24, 2015).
82   www.yourepeat.com/watch/?v=BbYFyI8oeZw. And: www.youtube.com/watch?v=pXkut oosesA (accessed August 24, 2015).

of African descent into a common community (Curtis IV, 2002: 85). He did not change any law, nor did he establish a sustainable movement (Terrill, 2010: 125). Although setting out cultural projects, he did not constitute a cultural program for the *Black Arts Movement*, which was founded after his death, or for his *Organization of Afro-American Unity* (OAAU) after he left the NOI (Smethurst, 2010: 86). Both the OAAU and *Muslim Mosque Inc.* soon collapsed after his assassination (Marable, 2011: 462). To some, Malcolm's heritage just consists of his talks, speeches and rhetoric.

So, what exactly does the last sequence in the Malcolm X 'from darkness to light' and 'from hell to heaven' narrative mean to the performing artists? It is not just a matter of enjoying the symbolic capital which accompanies Malcolm's achievements, i.e. transnational respect, after his drawback from pursuing economic capital, i.e. profit from questionable activities. The sequence of 'light' after 'darkness' is related to the sense that gaining 'power' is within reach – to many Muslims and especially to Muslim performing artists.

Representing Achievable Power

British graffiti and multimedia artist Mohammed Aerosol Arabic Ali, from Bangladeshi descent, aims to "bring change on this planet."[83] He is encouraged by his faith in Islam and inspiration by people like Malcolm X to "fight for justice" and "bring back values."[84] Similar to many rap artists, Aerosol Arabic uses Malcolm's sayings in his art productions ranging from wall sprayings to sound events. In his eyes, the still outstanding Muslim human activist has been able to create a movement just by doing good. Malcolm's quote, "The future belongs to those who prepare for it today," teaches Aerosol Arabic that he could also initiate a global movement as a Muslim. By means of his art via principled mottos on international walls and graffiti workshops for the youth, he should be able to inspire young artists to change the world together.[85]

To British-Nigerian stand-up comedian Nabil Abdulrashid, Malcolm X developed his empowering speeches by standing up for what he believed in. Nabil was impressed when he realized that an average Muslim could develop

---

83 Interview with the author, Birmingham, November 26, 2010.
84 muslimobserver.com/interview-with-graffiti-artist-mohammed-ali/ (accessed August 24, 2015).
85 Tine Lavent. Aerosol Arabic: "Kalligraffiti geïnspireerd om te inspireren." Al.Arte.magazine. November 7, 2012. www.alartemag.be/art/aerosol-arabic-kalligraffiti-geinspireerd-om-te-inspireren/ (accessed August 20, 2015).

into an inspiring person who could lift the community out of its miserable condition and subsequently become a meaningful person to the whole world without knowing the Qur'an from beginning to end. He came to understand that the only condition for the 'power of speech' drawn from faith is that it must be informed by truthfulness.[86] In practicing comedy for hundreds of audience members at community centers and mainstream venues, Nabil feels confident he might achieve a similar power.

Likewise, Malcolm X provided Native British rap artist Spitz Abdusalaam, who exchanged his engagement in performing music for spoken word in order to live more thoroughly according to Islam, an important insight. In light of the speeches of al-Hajj Malik al-Shabazz, Spitz realized he did not need music; spoken word poetry might be just as compelling and influential for the improvement of society.[87]

At the time, poet Sonia Sanchez, an important contributor to the *Black Arts Movement*, experienced Malcolm's declaring "widely shared truths" in a variety of public venues as articulating what many Black people felt but would only discuss in private (Smethurst, 2010: 83). Malcolm X was even considered the *Black Power* generation's greatest prophet who spoke "uncomfortable truths" that no one else had the courage to utter in public (Marable, 2009: 300). At the same time, Marable put these truths into perspective. He argued in *Malcolm X, a Life of Reinvention* that, after having constructed multiple social masks as Malcolm Little, Malcolm X had acquired the "subtle tools to craft his language" that would fit the cultural contexts of his various audiences (Marable, 2011: 10).

Still, many contemporary American and British Muslim artists admire Malcolm's capacity for unconditioned powerful speech. They regard his speech as moral truth that is expressed by the virtue of honesty – he recognized his mistaken beliefs and shared his struggles in an open manner with different audiences. Sri Lankan-American M. Hasna Maznavi, at the time forthcoming film director, was in search of Muslim performers who maintained their Islamic values irrespective of the type of audience, which she thought to be exceptional. She observed that several Muslim performers tend to adapt the boldness of their jokes according to the Muslim or non-Muslim audience. It seems Maznavi finally found her role model in the late Malcolm X when she discovered him as a person of integrity who "truly lived by his words," not affected by the expectations and tastes of divergent audiences. Clearly feeling edified

---

86 Interview with the author, London, UK, November 21, 2010.
87 Interview with the author, London, UK, December 16, 2010.

by his representation, Maznavi qualifies Malcolm X as a "great American" and "great Muslim."⁸⁸

While the necessity to 'normalize' Muslims – not just by claiming to be a morally 'upright' but also normal human being with common human worries, desires and mistakes – is one of the central notions in the field of Muslim performing artists. Malcolm X seems to have been able to combine both in the eyes of several artists. They understand that fostering acceptance from other (non-Muslim) social groups through a certain 'normalizing' of behavior and expressions by daring to air dirty laundry is an achievable, alternative means to increase cultural power.

Altogether, the Malcolm X trajectory reflected by the 'from darkness to light' narrative represents to Muslim performers that power is accessible to artists, even though they are Muslim, by means of their artistic performances if emerging from honesty and faith.

Representing Western Islam

The sequence of 'light' after 'darkness' is also related to the sense of (global) identification. In different rankings, Malcolm X has been described as one of the most influential African-Americans in history (Asante, 2002; Marable, Frazier and McMillian, 2003). Muslim participants in the field of Muslim performing artists in the United States and the United Kingdom stress this assumption on three levels. British-Nigerian comedian Nabil Abdulrashid, for instance, asserts that "Malcolm X is probably one of the most influential modern day Muslims of all time."⁸⁹

Another perspective is provided by the British Canadian-Pakistani Abdul-Rehman Malik, the driving force behind *Radical Middle Way* (RMW) that organized concerts by Muslim musicians combined with lectures of modern-day Islamic scholars for the purpose of uplifting young Muslims. Identifying the gifted communicator from an East–West perspective, Malik is convinced that "Malcolm X is the quintessential Western Muslim."⁹⁰ Malcolm's trajectory, especially its ultimate phase, legitimates RMW's motto that "the power of faith can influence social action" and change the social environment for the better, which is directed toward unengaged, disgruntled identity-seeking Muslim adolescents, especially from South Asian background.

---

88   Interview with the author, March 13, 2010, Los Angeles CA.
89   Interview with the author, November 21, 2010, London UK.
90   Interview with the author, November 5, 2010, London UK.

Usama Canon, of mixed African-American and White descent, who was immersed in the hip-hop subculture during his youth, has become the spiritual advisor of the *Inner-City Muslim Action Network* (IMAN) after having co-founded the institution *Taleef Collective*, which aims to guide the conversion of non-Muslims to Islam in a way that is appropriate for Western societies, especially the United States. Furthering Maznavi's characterization above, he suggests a national identity; "Malcolm X means a popular representation of Islam in the American context – they don't really have that in England."[91] By issuing a postage stamp of Malcolm X in 1999, ironically, the same government that had once carried out surveillance against him formalized Malcolm's iconic meaning into a privileged degree of Americanization (Marable 2009: 303–304). By sponsoring the *I Am Malcolm X* tour of *Radical Middle Way*, the American and British governments even supported the moderate understanding of Malcolm X to counter radicalization among vulnerable youth (Aidi, 2014: 221–257).

Malcolm X is thus claimed to be a universal (cosmopolitan) kind of Muslim, a Western (instead of Middle Eastern) Muslim, and the ultimate *American* Muslim. In all cases, he is representing the modern Muslim. Considering the image of the non-modern, backward Muslim that is presented among non-Muslims especially after the terrorist attacks of September 11th, 2001, in the United States and July 7th in the United Kingdom, this claim firstly seems to suggest that the Malcolm X icon is foremost capable of negating this image (Mamdani, 2005; Morey and Yaqin, 2011). Secondly, the claim of representing modern Islam has to do with the fact that, although Malcolm's initial goal was to attack the structures of White power, in due of time, his critique demonstrated the possibility of liberation from the norms of the dominant culture (Terrill, 2010: 125). Taking the iconic meaning of Malcolm X further may refer to countering dominant social hierarchies (for instance, from 'the Muslim world') which curtail ideologies and views of indigenous and authentically American nature that do *not* repudiate the West. While the legacy of Malcolm X includes the politics of radical humanism (Marable, 2011: 487), the ultimate sequence of the Malcolm X narrative seems to express that he has brought an enlightened Islamic attitude to the forefront, being both human and critically active, which is considered by many Muslim performing artists, the users of the narrative, to fit their experience with the West, i.e. the United States and the United Kingdom.

---

91   Interview with the author, San Francisco Bay Area, March 9, 2010.

Representing New Social and Symbolic Boundaries

When the sequence of 'light' is related to the perception of (global) identification, it will affect the sense of social boundaries as well. Black performing artists may perceive Malcolm X as an international symbol for the fight against social injustice that arose from the African American community with its unique history of slavery and subculture. But, as the quotes of M. Hasna Maznavi and Abdul-Rehman Malik above demonstrate, several participants in the art field with immigrant background feel that al-Hajj Malik al-Shabazz is just as much *theirs* due to his Islamic faith.

Spike Lee's popular movie *Malcolm X* generated the effect of making the formerly controversial Black Nationalist leader socially legitimate to a broad kind of audience from 1992 onward – and thereby, presumably, to Muslims in general. Muslims from immigrant families, who were not accustomed to get praise regarding their Islamic identity in Muslim minority countries, may have met a changing approach due to the resurgence and celebration of Malcolm X. British-Pakistani actor Waleed Akhtar, who wore a Malcolm X t-shirt as an adolescent growing up in the hip-hop subculture of London in the 1990's, claims to have been touched by Malcolm's sense of Western *Muslimness*, successfulness and recognition that a connection with Malcolm X seemed worthwhile. "He [Malcolm] was so well regarded and being from the same background... It gives you a sense of *kudos*, you feel good about being Muslim."[92]

The sequence of enlightenment in the Malcolm X narrative is thus, among other meanings, related to certain social bonding, shared confidence and pride. While his legacy is considered to potentially have united certain institutions of African, Caribbean and Asian nations at an international level (Marable, 2009: 314), at the transnational level, the widespread identification with Malcolm X seems to have transcended some differences in ethnicity and race between African American Muslim performing artists and those of South Asian or Middle Eastern descent.

Finally, already before his death, Malcolm X reached out to Islamic sects that reflect widely divergent opinions and theological tenets, including African *Sufis* in Senegal and *Wahhabi* Muslims in Saudi Arabia (Marable, 2011: 486). As we have seen above, the different career options of artists can be understood as 'informalized' and 'intensified formalized' toward cultural manners, habits and tastes. Contemporary Muslim performing artists who are disposed toward *Sufism*, whereas others are inclined for *Salafism,* can both relate to the Malcolm X

---

92   Interview with the author, London, October 27, 2010.

'from light to darkness' and 'hell to heaven' narrative while still remaining faithful to their oppositional orientations drawn from a sense of predestination.

Conclusion

Above, I have discussed American and British Muslim performing artists in relation to al-Hajj Malik al-Shabazz a.k.a. Malcolm X. Representations of the life of Malcolm X have proven to be interwoven in several central notions within the field of Muslim artists in Anglophone hip-hop and alternative music, spoken word and poetry, storytelling, theatre and acting, stand-up comedy, film performance and contemporary art in the United States and the United Kingdom. As many contemporary Muslim artists strive for 'purposefulness,' 'knowledgeability,' 'truthfulness,' and 'responsibility' as important qualities of their artistic practices as Muslim performers, which indicates a certain synthesis between ethics and aesthetics similar to the *Black Arts Movement*, the field takes Malcolm X as one of its important inspirational sources. Aiming to counter a general adverse judgment regarding Muslim people after the terrorist attacks in the cities of the West in 2001, 2004 and 2005, Muslim performers seem to draw, among other means, on Malcolm's style and terminology regarding (self-)consciousness and universal humanism.

Conversion to a new religion can be perceived as a (lonely) individual struggle, but identification with the difficult yet successful self-transformation of the convert and 'born-again' al-Hajj Malik al-Shabazz makes conversion and reversion a shared experience that bears the promise of a similar progression. The involved artists perceive that his global example of strikingly truthful and uncompromising speech may enhance their own abilities to be 'conscious' artists in the oral performing arts.

The representations of the life and religious trajectory of al-Hajj Malik al-Shabazz by scholars as well as Muslim performing artists tend to emphasize his divergent qualities in an initial militant and a final activist spiritual phase. The field of contemporary Muslim artists can be understood as to echo this dual approach by displaying both the 'style of militant power' and the 'style of soft power.' This means that by taking Malcolm's social activism artistically further, the confrontational style of several artists – being e.g. concerned with (modern day) slavery and post-colonialism – seems to coincide with the militant social activist qualities of Malcolm X. The more tolerant activist style of other (and sometimes the same) artists seems to reflect the activist spiritual, humanist qualities of Malcolm X – artistically accommodating his disturbing content to the present cultural taste of art audiences. The latter style may fit the field's central goal of presenting a more positive image of challenging Muslims instead of continuing the already prevalent image of the 'angry Muslim.' On a meta-level, a more militant approach may reflect an Islamist trend and its political tendencies, while the style of soft or spiritual power fits more securely within post-Islamism and its inclusive qualities.

Because Malcolm's transformations have generated a certain shared framing among Muslim performing artists, I have focused on the significance of their narratives in order to better understand the relationship between the artists and the late human rights activist. In the present case, narratives do not just structure events but have performative effects as well. As discussed by the authors Bruce Perry and Manning Marable, Malcolm X reinvented himself throughout his life, which was continued by pop culture after his death. Still, not many contemporary artists put his 'one-straight-line' progress into perspective as expressed in his 'from darkness to light,' 'from sin to virtue' and 'from hell to heaven' narrative. While developing autobiographical conversion narratives is typical to new believers in any faith, Malcolm X, as a symbol of shared meanings, seems to inspire particular converts and born-again Muslim artists to continue to developing their own conversion narrative with a similar 'from darkness to light' structure, possibly even starting prior to the transformation process.

The use of narratives by the artists can be explained from various perspectives that concern the overall field of art as well as the particular field of Muslim performing artists. Generally, seeking sources of symbolic capital, artists are dependent of critical recognition, peer recognition and public acclaim. While culturally distinguishing themselves from the commodified (gangsta) genres of popular art, artists of the 'conscious' style benefit from presenting their religious-artistic trajectories within a 'from darkness to light' narrative that resembles the conversion narrative of Malcolm X. Yet, they follow the prevailing objectives of artists in general to gain fame and create markets.

Specific to the field of American and British Muslim performing artists is its relation to the field of the religion of Islam. Various Islamic teachers, especially in the West, reflect on the Malcolm X narrative with respect to the artists' concern for combining their artistic and religious aspirations. Teachers, preachers and scholars are able to influence the field of Muslim artists due to the fact that one of its most striking central notions concerns the discourse on how (popular) art and music should relate to Islam. Both *Salafi*-inclined teachers, who are eager to restrict specific artistic expressions of Muslims, as well as *Sufi*-inclined teachers, who conditionally encourage musical productions, may draw on Malcolm's 'from darkness to light' narrative in their attempts to establish the 'right' kind of Islam in the West. The latter aims to establish a 'relevant Western

Islam' that consists of civic engagement in the present society as well as the improvement of the entire world (*dunya*). Although stimulating social reform in the present as well, the first communicate warnings that artistic activities in music and popular culture may jeopardize the artists' position in the afterlife.

Seeking the 'true Islam,' American and British Muslim performing artists can be identified according to two different religious-artistic trajectories based on feeling recognized or warned by respected Islamic teachers as well as by different interpretations of the Malcolm X 'from darkness to light' sequence. In the lives of these converts and born-again Muslims, Malcolm's conversion narrative is to some level regarded as a justification of the trajectory of the artist's own career.

While most of these performing artists pass a formalizing phase by incorporating new Islamic habits and manners, many artists subsequently enter a phase of 'informalization' in their religious-artistic trajectory. They resolve any doubt in combining art and music in Islam because, realizing that all Muslims can be differently cultured, they are able to harmonize old and new cultural habits. The state of becoming more relaxed in being a Muslim performing artist emerges through religious-cultural recognition of Islamic authoritative voices and inclusive ideas on spirituality in the here and now.

Other Muslim performing artists, especially in rap and spoken word, pass through the formalizing phase into an 'intensified formalization' phase in their religious-artistic trajectories. These converts with *Salafi* tendencies have chosen to be born-again at a certain point in their careers. Although these artists know they cannot influence what God has determined and achieve personal salvation, this way of mirroring the Malcolm X 'from darkness to light' narrative may at least reduce the human fear of damnation. These hip-hop artists cannot synthesize old and new habits as the other artists because their former life consisted of street and gang culture, (petty) crime and disturbing sociopsychological experiences. Reinforced by the *Salafi* kind of confidence of being a distinguished people, their plural conversions and musical sacrifices may have brought them a strong sense of the possibility of being a member of 'the Elect.' Although their specific abandonment of particular forms of entertainment can be considered 'world-rejecting' acts, some of these performing artists are as much involved in (economic, cultural and symbolic) capital producing, inner-worldly kind of spiritual activities as the previous artists. Being more obviously focused on Hell and Heaven, their symbolic battle results in becoming 'revealers' to their former community about the appropriate relation between art, music and Islam, inspired by the Malcolm X 'from hell to heaven' narrative.

Altogether, the Malcolm X narrative is a performative, sense making, and bonding tool in the field of Muslim performing artists in the United States and the United Kingdom. Taken for granted, like *doxa*, it turns out to be co-constitutive of this particular field. Considering a certain consensus after the terrorist attacks of 2001, the 'from darkness to light' sequence is regarded as a salient means to the objectives of many participants in the field to present a non-violent, socially active and enlightened Islam that fits the West. At the time, the need for the survival of the Muslim community in Muslim minority environments seems to have instigated a (light) third resurgence of the iconic status of Malcolm X after Malcolm's biography, his documentary, and the terrorist attacks in New York and London. It would be valuable to study his significance again during the latest radical Islamist developments.

The empowering narrative of Malcolm X promises the potential of an achievable power for Muslims in general and particularly in the oral performing arts regardless their different ethnic backgrounds or religious orientations. Despite its socially bonding quality, the sequence with its one-straight-line progress turns out to be of use to *opposing* interpretations and ideologies of Muslim performing artists and teachers concerning the expression of Islam in the West. By providing a scope for severe differentiation on achieving religious-artistic enlightenment, the Malcolm X narrative has ultimately contributed in preventing the field of Muslim performing artists from evolving into a particularistic kind of 'Muslim art world' that is characterized by unanimously agreed upon religious-artistic conventions and views.

Bibliography

Abd-Allah, Umar F. *Islam and the Cultural Imperative*. Burr Ridge, IL: Nawawi Foundation, 2004.

Abdul-Khabeer, Suad. "Rap that Islam: The Rhyme and Reason of American Hip-Hop." *The Muslim World* 97, no. 1 (2007): 125–141.

Abolafia, Mitchel Y. "Narrative Construction as Sensemaking: How a Central Bank Thinks." *Organization Studies* 31, no. 3 (2010): 349–367.

Ahmed, Akbar S. *Living Islam: From Samarkand to Stornoway*. London, UK: BBC Books Limited, 1993.

Aidi, Hisham. D. *Rebel Music: Race, Empire, and the New Muslim Youth Culture*. New York: Pantheon Books, 2014.

Aidi, Hisham D. and Marable, Manning. "The Early Muslim Presence and Its Significance." In *Black Routes to Islam*, edited by Manning Marable and Hisham D. Aidi, 1–14. New York, NY: Palgrave Macmillan, 2009.

Al-Qaradawi. *The Lawful and the Prohibited in Islam (Al-Halal Wal Haram Fil Islam)*. Cairo, EG: Al Falah Foundation, 2001.

Alim, H. Samy. "A New Research Agenda: Exploring the Transglobal Hip Hop Umma." *Muslim Networks: From Hajj to Hip Hop,* edited by Miriam Cook and Bruce B. Lawrence, 264–274. Chapel Hill, NC: The University of North Carolina Press, 2005.

Asante, Molefi Kete. *100 Greatest African Americans: A Biographical Encyclopedia.* Amhert, NY: Prometheus Books, 2002.

Baker, Raymond W. *Islam Without Fear: Egypt and the New Islamists.* Cambridge, MA: Harvard University Press, 2003.

Bayat, Asef. "What is Post Islamism?" *ISIM Review* 16 autumn (2005): 5.

——— *Making Islam Democratic. Social Movements and the Post-Islamist Turn.* Stanford, CA: Stanford University Press, 2007.

——— Ed. *Post Islamism: The Changing Faces of Political Islam.* New York, NY: University Press, 2013.

Becker, Howard S. *Art Worlds.* Ewing, NJ: University of California Press, 1982.

Boubekeur, Amel. "Post-Islamist Culture: A New Form of Mobilization?" *History of Religions* 74, no. 1 (2007): 75–94.

Bourdieu, Pierre. *The Rules of Art: Genesis and Structure of the Literary Field.* Translated by Susan Emanuel. Cambridge, UK: Polity Press, 1996.

——— *Distinction. A Social Critique of the Judgement of Taste.* Translated by Richard Nice. London, UK: Routledge and Kegan Paul Ltd., 2004.

——— *The Field of Cultural Production. Essays on Art and Literature.* Edited by Randal Johnson. Cambridge, UK: Polity Press, 2009.

Bowness, Alan. *The Conditions of Success: How the Modern Artist Rises to Fame.* London, UK: Thames and Hudson, 1989.

Brown, Frank B. *Good Taste, Bad Taste, and Christian Taste: Aesthetics in Religious Life.* New York: Oxford University Press, 2000.

Byerman, Keith. *Remembering the Past in Contemporary African American Fiction.* Chapel Hill, NC: University of North Carolina Press, 2006.

Collins, Randall. "Introduction." In *The Protestant Ethic and the Spirit of Capitalism.* Translated by Talcott Parsons. Los Angeles, CA: Roxbury Publishing Company, 1996.

——— *Interaction Ritual Chains.* Princeton, NJ: Princeton University Press, 2004.

Cunliffe, Ann and Chris Coupland. "From Hero to Villain to Hero: Making Experience Sensible Through Embodied Narrative Sensemaking." *Human Relations* 65, no. 1 (2012): 63–88.

Cunliffe, Ann L., John T. Luhman and David M. Boje. "Narrative Temporality: Implications for Organizational Research." *Organization Studies* 25, no. 2 (2004): 261–286.

Curtis IV, Edward E. *Islam in Black America. Identity, Liberation, and Difference in African-American Islamic Thought.* New York: State University of New York Press, 2002.

——— ed. *Encyclopedia of Muslim-American History.* New York: Infobase Publishing, 2010.

Elias, Norbert. *The Civilizing Process. Sociogenetic and Psychogenetic Investigations.* Translated by Edmund Jephcott. Dublin: University College Dublin Press, 2000.

Euell, Kim and Robert Alexander, eds. *Plays from the Boom Box Galaxy. Theater from the Hip-Hop Generation.* New York: Theatre Communications Group, 2009.

Geaves, Ron. "Book Review: Sufism and the 'Modern' in Islam." Eds. Van Bruinessen, Martin and Julia Day Howell, 2007. *Fieldwork in Religion* 5, no. 2 (2011): 254–256.

Hamid, Sadek. "The Development of British Salafism." *ISIM Review* 21, spring (2008): 10–11.

———. "The Attraction of 'Authentic Islam:' Salafism and British Muslim Youth." *Global Salafism: Islam's New Religious Movement.* Edited by Roel Meijer, 352–371. New York: Oxford University Press, 2009.

Harris, William J. *The Poetry and Poetics of Amiri Baraka: The Jazz Aesthetic.* Columbia, MO: University of Missouri Press, 1985.

Hart, William D. *Black Religion. Malcolm X, Julius Lester, and Jan Willis.* New York: Palgrave Macmillan, 2008.

Hermansen, Marcia. "Roads to Mecca: Conversion Narratives of European and Euro-American Muslims." In *The Muslim World* 89, no. 1 (1999): 56–89.

Houston, Sam. "Sherman A. Jackson and the Possibility of a 'Blackamerican Muslim' Prophetic Pragmatism." In *Journal of Africana Religions* 1, no. 4 (2013): 488–512.

Jackson, Sherman A. *Islam and the Blackamerican. Looking Toward the Third Resurrection.* Oxford: Oxford University Press, 2005.

———. "Black Orientalism. Its Genesis, Aims, and Significance for American Islam." In *Black Routes to Islam*, edited by Manning Marable and Hisham D. Aidi, 33–47. New York, NY: Palgrave Macmillan, 2009.

Kubala, Patricia. "The Other Face of the Video Clip: Sami Yusuf and the Call for al-Fann al-Hadif." *Transnational Broadcasting Studies* 14, no. 2 (2005): 38–47. tbsjournal.arabmediasociety.com/Archives/Spring05/kubala.html (accessed August 27, 2015).

Lapidus, Ira M. "Islamic Revival and Modernity: The Contemporary Movements and the Historical Paradigms." *Journal of the Economic and Social History of the Orient* 40, no. 4 (1997): 444–460.

———. *A History of Islamic Societies*, Cambridge, UK: Cambridge University Press, 2002.

Lohlker, Rüdiger. *New Approaches to the Analysis of Jihadism.* Göttingen, GE: VandR Unipress, 2012.

Malcolm X as told to Alex Haley. *The Autobiography of Malcolm X.* London, UK: Penguin Books, 2001.

Mamdani, Mahmood. *Good Muslim, Bad Muslim: America, the Cold War, and the Roots of Terror.* New York: Random House LLC, 2005.

Mandaville, Peter. "Hip-hop, Nasheeds, and 'Cool' Sheikhs. Popular Culture and Muslim Youth in the United Kingdom." In *In-Between Spaces: Christian and Muslim*

Minorities in Transition in Europe and the Middle East, edited by Christiane Timmerman, et al. Leuven, 149–168. BE: Peter Lang, 2009.

Marable, Manning. "Rediscovering Malcolm's Life: A Historian's Adventures in Living History." In *Black Routes to Islam,* edited by Manning Marable and Hisham D. Aidi. 299–315. New York: Palgrave Macmillan, 2009.

Marable, Manning. *Malcolm X. A Life of Reinvention.* London, UK: Allen Lane, 2011.

Marable, Manning, Nishani Frazier and John McMillian, eds. *Freedom on My Mind: The Columbia Documentary History of the African American Experience.* New York: Columbia University Press, 2003.

McCloskey, Deirdre N. *If You're So Smart: The Narrative of Economic Expertise.* Chicago: University of Chicago Press, 1990.

Meijer, Roel, ed. "Introduction." In *Global Salafism: Islam's New Religious Movement,* 1–29. New York: Oxford University Press, 2009.

Miyakawa, Felicia M. *Five Percenter Rap. God Hop's Music, Message, and Black Muslim Mission.* Indianapolis: Indiana University Press, 2005.

Mohaiemen, Naeem. "Fear of a Muslim Planet: The Islamic Roots of Hip-Hop." In *Sound Unbound: Sampling Digital Music and Culture,* edited by DJ Spooky. 303–325. Cambridge, MA: MIT Press, 2008.

Moosavi, Leon. "British Muslim Converts Performing 'Authentic Muslimness'." *Performing Islam* 1, no. 1 (2012): 103–128.

Morey, Peter and Amina Yaqin. *Framing Muslims. Stereotyping and Representation after 9/11.* Cambridge, MA: Harvard University Press, 2011.

Neal, Larry. "The Black Arts Movement." In *The Norton Anthology of African American Literature,* edited by Henry L. Gates and Nellie Y. McKay. 1960–1972. New York: W.W. Norton and Company, 1997.

Otterbeck, Jonas. "Battling over the Public Sphere: Islamic Reactions to the Music of Today." *Contemporary Islam* (Online) 2, no. 3 (2008): 211–228.

Perry, Bruce. *Malcolm: The Life of a Man Who Changed Black America.* Barrytown, NY: Station Hill, 1991.

Polanyi, Livia. *Telling the American Story: A Structural and Cultural Analysis of Conversation.* Norwood, MA: Ablex, 1985.

Rambo, Lewis R. and Charles E. Farhadian, eds. *The Oxford Handbook of Religious Conversion.* Oxford, UK: Oxford University Press, 2014.

Reddie, Richard S. *Black Muslims in Britain.* Oxford, UK: Lion Hudson plc, 2009.

Riessman, Catherine Kohler. *Narrative Analysis* (Qualitative Research Methods Series 30). Thousand Oaks, CA: Sage Publications, 1993.

Rose, Tricia. *Black Noise. Rap Music and Black Culture in Contemporary America.* Lebanon, NH: University Press of New England, 1994.

——— *The Hip Hop Wars. What We Talk About When We Talk About Hip Hop – and Why It Matters.* New York: Basic Books, 2008.

Roy, Olivier. *Globalized Islam. The Search for a New Ummah.* London, UK: Colombia University Press, 2004.

Shaheen, Jack G. *Reel Bad Arabs: How Hollywood Vilifies a People.* New York: Olive Branch Press, 2001.

Shaw, Lytle. *Fieldworks: From Place to Site in Postwar Poetics.* Tuscaloosa, AL: University of Alabama Press, 2013.

Shiloah, Amnon. *Music in the World of Islam. A Socio-Cultural Study.* Aldershot, UK: Scolar Press, 1995.

Smethurst, James E. *The Black Arts Movement: Literary Nationalism in the 1960s and 1970s.* (The John Hope Franklin Series in African American History and Culture). Chapel Hill, NC: The University of North Carolina Press, 2005.

——— "Malcolm X and the Black Arts Movement." In *The Cambridge Companion to Malcolm X*, edited by Robert E. Terrill. 78–98. New York: Cambridge University Press, 2010.

Swedenburg, Ted. "Islamic Hip-hop versus Islamophobia: Aki Nawaz, Natcha Atlas, Akhenaton." In *Global Noise: Rap and Hip-hop Outside the USA*, edited by Tony Mitchell. 57–85. Middletown, CT: Wesleyan University Press, 2001.

Szpiech, Ryan. *Conversion and Narrative. Reading and Religious Authority in Medieval Polemic.* Philadelphia: University of Pennsylvania Press, 2013.

Tartoussieh, Karim. "Pious Stardom: Cinema and the Islamic Revival in Egypt." *The Arab Studies Journal* 17, no. 1 (2007): 30–44.

Taylor, Jeneal M. *Differences between the Harlem Renaissance and the Black Arts Movement.* Major Dissertation. Charlotte, NC: Johnson C. Smith University, 2004.

Ter Bogt, Tom. *Wilde jaren, een eeuw jeugdcultuur.* Amsterdam, NL: Uitgeverij Boom, 2000.

Terrill, Robert E. "Judgment and Critique in the Rhetoric of Malcolm X." In *The Cambridge Companion to Malcolm X*, edited by Robert E. Terrill. 78–98. New York: Cambridge University Press, 2010.

Tobler, John. *NME Rock 'n' Roll Years* (1st ed.). London, UK: Reed International Books Ltd, 1992.

Van Tilborgh, Yolanda. "Het islamdebat en de strategische emoties van moslima's." In *Jaarboek KennisSamenleving: Gevoel voor kennis*, edited by Bertien Broekhans, et al. 98–120. Amsterdam: Uitgeverij Aksant, 2009.

——— "Career Trajectories and (In)Formalization among Muslim Performing Artists in the UK and the US: Accommodationism or Fundamentalism?" *Journal of Contemporary Religion*, 2016 (forthcoming).

Weber, Max. *The Protestant Ethic and the Spirit of Capitalism.* London, UK: Routledge, 2007.

White, Hayden "The Value of Narrativity in the Representation of Reality." *Critical Inquiry* 7, no. 1 (1980): 5–27.

Winegar, Jessica. "Purposeful Art: Between Television Preachers and the State." *ISIM Review* 22, autumn (2008): 28–29.

Wohlrab-Sahr, Monika. "Conversion to Islam between Syncretism and Symbolic Battle." *Social Compass* 46, no. 3 (1999): 351–362.

Wouters, Cas. "The Spiral Process of Informalization: Phases of Informalization and Reformalization." In *Informalization: Manners and Emotions Since 1890*, edited by Cas Wouters. 167–197. London, UK: SAGE Publications Ltd, 2007.

Zaleski, Pawel S. "Ideal Types in Max Weber's Sociology of Religion: Some Theoretical Inspirations for a Study of the Religious Field." *Polish Sociological Review* 3, no. 171 (2010): 319–325.

Zaman, Muhammad Q. "The Ulama of Contemporary Islam and their Conceptions of the Common Good." In *Public Islam and the Common Good*, edited by Amando Salvatore. 129–155. Leiden, NL: Brill, 2004.

Zebiri, Kate. *British Muslim Converts: Choosing Alternative Lives.* Oxford, UK: Oneworld, 2008.

CHAPTER 13

Rationalization of Malcolm X's Religious Understandings, Political Perspectives and Organizational Objectives

Nuri Tinaz

There is no doubt that Malcolm X was one of the most prominent charismatic leaders in both the history of American Muslims in particular and African-Americans in general. He became the most controversial figure in terms of his political rhetoric and objectives, his religious and spiritual quest, and his journey from Black Nationalism to mainstream Islam. He eventually became an icon for justice and the struggle against racism, discrimination, and oppression. His life, struggle, and transformations have remained contentious yet still appeal to many. They give hope to various people in all walks of life, in particularly the Black Diaspora in the United States, Muslims, as well as oppressed people throughout the world. Multiple aspects of Malcolm X's legacy have been claimed by diverse interest groups, namely, the Civil Rights movement, Black Nationalist organizations, socialist and revolutionary groups, as well as several indigenous African-American and immigrant Muslim communities. Within the scope of this chapter, I will explain the rationalization of Malcolm X's religious understandings, political perspectives and organizational objectives. Organizational and political-economic causes, power struggles and personal conflicts, interactions with other circles and manipulative elements within the U.S. government have all played important roles in the polarization and eventual schism between Malcolm X and the Nation of Islam (NOI), popularly known the Black Muslim movement, in which he had become a charismatic leader. These elements and factors have been discussed from a sociological perspective at length elsewhere (Tinaz, 2001). This paper will first examine and explore the social and political circumstances and environment in the late 1950's and the early 1960's in order to get better understanding of his transition from a particularistic stance to a pluralistic and universalistic perspective. Then it will analyze in detail the impacts of various interactions and relations that played significant roles in his religious understanding, his political perspectives, and his organizational objectives. It will also examine how these aspects evolved and were subject to fundamental and considerable transformations and rationalizations.

Before moving onto that, I will give a brief background of the social and political environment in the late 1950's and the early 1960's where Malcolm became a nationally as well as internationally renowned political figure. It seems to be impossible to fully comprehend the transformation of Malcolm X and the schism that occurred between him, Elijah Muhammad and the ruling stratum of the NOI, without considering the social and political developments in the early 1960's, as that period had a tremendous influence on the movement's political teachings, objectives and organizational policies. It was in the early 1960's that the movement reached its peak in terms of organizational structure, economic achievement, and membership.

Social and Political Developments in the Late 1950's and the early 1960's

Historians agree that Malcolm X was behind the nationwide achievement and popularity of the NOI, as he had become its focal point. Malcolm Little converted to the NOI while he was serving time in prison and was later released on parole in 1952. Having been renamed 'Malcolm X' by Elijah Muhammad, the organizational founder and leader of the movement; he later became an assistant minister of the NOI's Temple No. 1 in Detroit in 1953. He rose rapidly in the ranks of the ministerial hierarchy and in a short period of time surpassed senior ministers and officials of the NOI. Malcolm was commissioned with a special mission to establish Temples in Boston (No. 11), Philadelphia (No. 12) and New York City, Harlem's Temple No. 7 (Marsh, 1984). Upon realizing Malcolm's exceptional abilities, Elijah Muhammad gave him more responsibilities and liberties than other ministers. Malcolm, with his charisma, organizational talents and oratory skills, expanded his leader's teachings throughout country and set up more than one hundred mosques in many major cities in the United States (Malcolm X, 1968).

Despite the Nation of Islam's organizational expansion and accomplishment, the movement was confined to the Black ghettoes as it was still relatively unknown in mainstream society. In the summer of 1959, American society for the first time was shaken by the sudden and extensive TV documentary called *The Hate That Hate Produced* by Mike Wallace and Louis E. Lomax. This documentary highlighted the NOI's alarming and controversial nationalist and religious teachings as well as its political objectives and organizational developments (Lincoln, 1973; Malcolm X, 1968; Evanzz, 1992). Although the Black ghettoes were already familiar with the NOI through the Black press, after the airing of the documentary the white controlled media gave greater coverage to the NOI.[1] *Life, Look, Newsweek, Reader's Digest, Time, New York Times* all published articles about the organization and its charismatic leader (Lincoln, 1973: 190; Essein-Udom, 1970). Most of the coverage of the NOI, as Lincoln indicates, was negative as they often described Elijah Muhammad as a 'purveyor of cold black hatred' (Lincoln, 1973: 113; DeCaro, 1994: 409). Around the same time, the publications of two scholarly works on the movement, C. Eric Lincoln's *The Black Muslims in America* and E.U. Essien-Udom's *Black Nationalism: A Search for an Identity in America,* increased an academic interest in the NOI among universities and colleges. Consequently, through those channels, the NOI's contentious ethnic, nationalist, political teachings and objectives as well as religious beliefs, were no longer confined to the Black ghettoes. Now professional circles and the American society at large were exposed to their teachings.

Through the young and energetic ministers and officials within the NOI of the early 1960's, the movement launched massive rallies in order to reach out to African-Americans and recruit more members in urban neighborhoods where Blacks were densely populated. These publicity campaigns helped attract those disaffected black masses to join the movement, most of who had been disappointed and frustrated with the official American policies towards Black people. At the public rallies, demonstrations and marches, organized in the Black neighborhoods, the messenger Elijah Muhammad was often the keynote speaker along with his prominent ministers and 'laborers.'[2] Elijah Muhammad had to often cancel some of his public engagement and administration duties because of his health problems; he suffered with bronchial asthmatic disorder. He frequently rested in Phoenix, Arizona, where the dry climate had been recommended by his doctors. Elijah Muhammad was unable "to work the daily long hours he had previously worked in Chicago" and to regulate "the heavy decision-making and administration duties" of the NOI (Malcolm X, 1968: 370; Marsh, 1984). Because of this, a select few of his loyal ministers began to represent him at rallies, public speaking events and radio and television shows. Soon, Malcolm X was designated his preferred and favorite representative.

No one ever doubted Malcolm's loyal and devoted to Elijah Muhammad's teachings and programs during his ministerial post (1953–1964) in the NOI.

---

[1] Major Black newspapers initially gave generous coverage of the NOI and its activities. They helped to introduce the NOI's organization, members, activities and rallies in black ghettos to larger audiences. Those newspapers, namely, are the *Chicago Defender, Los Angeles Herald Dispatch, New York Amsterdam News, Pittsburgh Courier* and etc. (Lincoln, 1973: 149–153).

[2] The term 'Laborer' has been used in the past and is still used in the NOI of Minister Farrakhan for high-rank members who occupy an official duty in the administration structure of the NOI.

From separatist political and nationalist perspectives, Malcolm championed the economics, political and identity philosophies of the NOI (Munir, 1994). He absolutely believed that Muhammad's ethno-nationalistic and religious teachings made Blacks proud of their ethnic identity, as it gave them a sense of belonging, history and race (Karim, 1971: 23–66). Malcolm made these teachings more appealing to the Black masses by maintaining that "no one will know who we are until we know who we are! We never will be able to go anywhere until we know where we are! The Honorable Elijah Muhammad is giving us a true identity...," that is "you are not a Negro," but you are "members of the Asiatic nation, from the tribe of Shabazz" (Malcolm X, 1968: 356–357; Muhammad, 1957: 15).

Unlike the conventional patterns of Black Nationalism, which assumes a sharing of political power between whites and blacks in the U.S., the NOI inserted a new understanding of politics with a more powerful and appealing tone. The movement advocated a complete separation from and disengagement with the American political system while simultaneously claiming that the U.S. system had always been unequal and unjust and had not done anything to change the socio-economic destiny of the Black masses over the years. Therefore, the NOI refused cooperation with the civil rights movements that supported integrationist policies. As a talented orator and representative of Elijah Muhammad, Malcolm harshly criticize d and ridiculed the conventional Civil Rights teachings, objectives and programs in matters of race relation, and maintained the idea that integration policies had not resolved the problems of the Black masses (Munir, 1994). Instead, he proposed a permanent and long-lasting solution: the 'complete separation from the white man' (Malcolm X, 1968: 348). Consequently, Malcolm clarified the NOI's political objectives:

> We reject segregation even more militantly...We want separation... The Honorable Elijah Muhammad teaches us that segregation is when your life and liberty are controlled, regulated, by someone else. To segregate means to control. Segregation is that which is forced upon inferiors by superiors. But separation is that which is done voluntarily, by two equals – for the good of both!.
>
> MALCOLM X, 1968: 348

Having been inspired by this separatist political ideology, the NOI totally restrained itself from actively participating in American politics and asked its members to focus on 'economic self-improvement' and to develop and elevate the social and 'moral' status of 'the black lower class' (Essien-Udom, 1970). There was a certain ambiguity and no clear direction in the NOI's political objectives. The NOI officials sometimes advocated a territorial separation in the United States in order to form an independent black state, and if this would not seem possible, they eventually proposed a nostalgic and Garveyite 'return to our native/own land,' i.e. Africa (Muhammad, 1965:38). That would be the final solution in their attempts to overcome racism, discrimination and segregation that Blacks had been subjected to for centuries. Yet, the NOI ruling stratum had never attempted to clearly define and/or actualize those goals. However, these separatist teachings provided a psychological departure from the mainline American society (Essien-Udom, 1970; Munir, 1993).

Because his long term illness and ailment, Elijah Muhammad appointed Malcolm X in 1963 as the National Spokesman/Representative in charge of the NOI's affairs. With his trust and confidence in Malcolm, Muhammad gave him more power and freedom to represent the Messenger and the NOI at national and even international platforms.[3] Because of his recognized status and credibility, Elijah Muhammad endorsed Malcolm X with two important statements: "Brother Malcolm, I want you to become well known... Because if you are well known, it will make *me* better known" (Malcolm X, 1968: 370). But the Messenger, from the very outset, cautioned him about the envy that would arise among the high-ranking lieutenants and officials in the NOI. The second endorsement came in 1963, at the NOI's public rally in Philadelphia, where Muhammad embraced Malcolm before the huge crowd and told them that "this is my most faithful, hardworking minister. He will follow me until he dies" (Malcolm X, 1968: 402; Perry, 1992).[4]

Having been officially and spiritually endorsed by the Messenger, Malcolm, with his new prominent status and administrative duties, began representing the Honorable Elijah Muhammad and the NOI on television, radio and university campuses (Malcolm X, 1968). As the NOI grew, Malcolm "was not only intricately involved with every temple" and institutionally associated with the

---

3   With the Messenger's confidence and trust in Malcolm, Muhammad appointed him in 1959 as his and the NOI's ambassador to Muslim Countries in the Middle East and Africa (Lincoln, 1973). The other example of Elijah Muhammad's trust in Malcolm was when he left Malcolm X in charge of the NOI's affairs when he and two of his sons made *Ummrah* (small pilgrimage or hajj that is fulfilled outside the hajj season) to the holy city of Mecca in early 1960 (Essien-Udom, 1970; Lincoln, 1973, Malcolm X, 1968; Tinaz, 1993).

4   The messenger, similarly, praised his favorite lieutenant declaring that "Minister Malcolm is a much better speaker than I am, and I am blessed to have such an assistant" (Worthy, 1962: 35). The Honorable Elijah Muhammad reiterated his praise of Malcolm in the NOI's 1962 Annual Saviour Day saying that "...He [Malcolm] is one of the most faithful ministers that I have. He will go everywhere – North, South, East or West, to China if I say go to China, he will go there. So I thank Allah for my Brother Malcolm" (Essien-Udom, 1970: 177: De Caro, 1994).

movement, "but he became virtually an extension of Elijah Muhammad himself" (DeCaro, 1994: 329). Consequently, Malcolm, with his organizational and oratory talents, began to reshape and design the social structure and rhetoric of NOI in a more militant, radical and revolutionary way.

It is certain that Malcolm X's political thinking and perspectives were inspired by the NOI's Black Nationalist teachings. Yet his more militant, radical and revolutionary tone went beyond the boundaries of the NOI nationalist thought. As George Breitman pointed out, Malcolm "stretched the bounds of Muhammad's doctrine to the limit, and sometimes beyond. He introduced new elements into the movement, not only of style but of ideology" (Breitman, 1967: 9). That point was also confirmed by the NOI's New York ministers, James 3X and Henry X, who replaced Malcolm as head of Harlem Mosque No. 7 after the schism. They said that "it was Malcolm who injected the political concept of Black Nationalism into the Black Muslim movement which…was essentially religious in nature" when Malcolm joint. (Breitman, 1967: 9; Handler, 1964h). After reviewing the objectives and consequences of major revolutions in the 20th century, Malcolm severely criticize d the passive Black struggle, saying that,

> brothers and sisters, to show you that you don't have a peaceful revolution. You don't have a turn-the-other-cheek revolution. There is no such thing as a non-violent revolution. The only kind of revolution that is non-violent is the Negro revolution. The only revolution in which the goal is loving your enemy is the Negro revolution.[5]
> BREITMAN, 1967: 9

Malcolm was seeking to apply more active, radical and revolutionary policies in order to gain concrete results. In the context of NOI's policy and demand for a separate territory to establish a Black state, or to send African-Americans back to Africa with satisfactory reparation, Malcolm formed his revolutionary political ideology. He said,

> Revolution is based on land. Land is the basis of independence. Land is the basis of freedom, justice and equality… Revolution is bloody, hostile, knows no compromise. Overturns and destroys everything that gets in its way… A revolutionary wants land so he can set up his own nation,

---

5   Mainly these are the Russian, Chinese, Algerian and Cuban revolutions in the late 1950's and the early 1960's (Breitman, ed, 1966, pp. 7–11).

an independent nation...When you want a nation, that's called nationalism... A revolutionary is a black nationalist. He wants a nation.
BREITMAN, 1965: 9–10

Admitting his role in and contribution to the radicalization of the NOI's political teachings and objectives, which made them more laudable, Malcolm pointed out that,

> I had helped Mr. Muhammad and his other ministers to revolutionize the American black man's thinking, opening his eyes until he would never again look in the same fearful, worshipful way at the white man. I had participated in spreading the truths that had done so much help the American black man rid himself of the mirage that the white race was made up of 'superior' beings.
> MALCOLM X, 1968: 397

What were the incentives and factors that compelled Malcolm X to take a more active role in the Black struggle along with other African-American organizations whose politics were in stark contrast to the NOI's non-engagement and abstentionist policies? To understand Malcolm's motives, it has to be taken into consideration the important developments in the United States of America in the 1950's and 1960's, as well as the context abroad, particularly in Africa and the Muslim World. In the latter, political radicalism and independence struggles were raging. The liberation struggles in Africa and the Muslim World against Colonial Powers were influential on the Black leaders in the United States (Muhammad, 1984; Marsh, 1984; Tinaz, 1993, 2001, 2009). Around the same periods, when the countries in the Muslim World and Africa, one by one, gained their independences from colonial and mandate systems, Black Nationalist leaders in the United States where inspired by their struggle against racism, segregation and discrimination. Bridging the artificial divide, these same Black Nationalists were often supported by their political and religious counterparts in Africa and the East in their own struggles against the United States (Marsh, 1984; Breitman, 1967).[6] The rise of political awareness and militant radicalism against colonial power and colonization in Africa and the Muslim world had excited the NOI members; they believed that their prophetic beliefs and teachings were materializing and that the Devil's rule was ending in the Original Man's territories (Muhammad, 1984).

---

[6] Namely the independence of Egypt, Pakistan, Algeria, and Ghana had affected the mood of the NOI (Muhammad, A., 1984: 206–7).

Black Nationalism has reached its momentum in the United States. In various cities, Black civil rights groups were organizing protests, demonstrations and marches to raise awareness of African-Americans' political and civil rights as well as their basic human rights. On several occasions, they approached the NOI officials in hopes of forming a coalition, and urged them to participate in their protests as to form a unified force which could pressure the government to pass a comprehensive Civil Rights Bill. These requests were categorically rejected by the NOI because the Hon. Elijah Muhammad advocated and sanctioned that his followers should refrain from the 'white man's politics.' He was also reluctant to allow his ministers to engage in political activities and programs organized by African American Civil Right leaders and professionals. He thought that the white political system was doomed for destruction and that the blacks who declined to separate from whites would be destroyed with it on the Day of Judgment (Perry, 1992: 210). While a Black Nationalist mood was sweeping across Black America, the NOI's passive and non-engagement policies resulted in two negative effects; first, the NOI was subjected to harsh criticism by civil rights leaders and organizations. Second, the NOI's policies and critics paved the way for dissatisfaction and embarrassment among the young members of the movement. Although the civil rights organizations appreciated the NOI's contribution to the improvement of Black social status – getting respect for Black identity – they remained critical of the movement's apolitical tendencies. "They [Muslims] clean people up, don't drink, don't smoke...but they don't *do* anything. Don't even *vote*" (Goldman, 1979: 93; Perry, 1992); "they Muslims *talk* tough, but they never *do* anything, unless somebody bothers Muslims" (Malcolm X, 1968: 397). Breitman points out this dichotomy between the NOI's rhetoric and its practices. Although Elijah Muhammad consistently advocated for Black unity, in practice he and his followers stayed on the side-line watching the action of others from afar. In terms of the political struggles, the NOI remained isolated from the rest of the Black community (Breitman, 1967: 14). Yet pressure and criticism began to emerge from within the organization. The young, radical and revolutionary inclined members were frustrated and would later compel the community towards a more active political engagement within the Black struggle.[7] The NOI could

---

7 In 1963, along with the members of the CORE (Congress on Racial Equality), Louis Lomax and James Farmer staged a demonstration to protest the employment of only white workers on the construction of a new hospital in Harlem. Malcolm and members of the NOI could not participate in the demonstration because of Elijah Muhammad's order and sanction that he imposed on them. Muslims stayed on the sideline watching the protesters. Lomax and others challenged Malcolm and the Muslims, "quit talking and put your life on the line with

not escape from the pressure (Breitman, 1967: 14). Having, sharing, and feeling the same impetus with younger members of the NOI, Malcolm kept insisting that Mr. Muhammad relax the movement's strict non-engagement policies. He hardly secured the Messenger's permission to boycott Harlem stores that refused to hire or promote black employees (Perry, 1992: 211). In February of 1959, when Malcolm organized a protest demonstration in nearby Newark, New Jersey, the Messenger made him apologize publicly for his insistence.[8] Mr. Muhammad furthermore inhibited Malcolm from taking part and assisting other Black organizations in their struggles (Perry, 1992). The competing attitudes towards political activism generated a strained condition; this polarization or divergence in the ideals and policies was at the core of the NOI. As Wilson points out, "a condition of strain is a necessary factor in occurrence of schism" but it is not adequate one. To become more effective, that strain must be associated with other resident factors (Wilson, 1970: 9). For the case of the NOI, the determining strain which produced the growing cleavage and schism between Malcolm X and the NOI was Malcolm's active political involvement in the Black Struggle and/or Civil Rights movement.

The political dichotomy was the result of the rising tensions between the 'ruling stratum,' or 'Chicago Muslims Officials,' and the young East Coast Muslims represented by Malcolm X by the early 1960's.[9] Along with the political and economic differences among the elites of the NOI, the internal leadership struggles, personal conflicts on the periphery of the movement, and the U.S. government's constant monitoring of the movement's affairs and internal matters, all furthered the already tense polarization. Apart from these factors,

---

us." As a leader of New York City Muslims, Malcolm was frustrated and apparently hurt in front of a very crowded protest because of the NOI's non-activist and non-engagement policies (Lomax, 1968: 98–99).

8 Similarly, in May of 1963, Malcolm had to write Mr. Muhammad in order to apologize for his political eagerness. But the following month, Malcolm launched a voter registration campaign in New York City without first getting full support from the Messenger. Although the campaign had vaguely been announced in *Muhammad Speaks*, the official newspaper of the NOI, Mr. Muhammad and the administration body in Chicago were reluctant "to initiate a nation-wide voter registration drive." Malcolm, however, went further and in August 1963 advocated a "united black front" with other black organizations such as CORE, SCLC (Southern Christian Leadership Conference), the NAACP. (Perry, 1992: 210–212, 235–38).

9 The Ruling stratum or the Chicago Muslim officials were composed of Elijah Muhammad's family members and close relatives, namely, Herbert Muhammad, the Messenger's son and editor of Muhammad Speaks; Raymond Sherriff, the Messenger's son-in law and supreme Captain of the Fruit of Islam (FOI) and John Ali, the National Secretary of the NOI (Malcolm X, 1968).

there were other significant reasons for this polarization which have been overlooked by scholars, especially the polarizations produced by the antagonism between particularity and universality. These were caused by the NOI's relations and interactions, at organizational and individual levels, with mainstream Muslim individuals, professionals, organizations, countries, and other leading black actors, leaders and organizations, both in the U.S. and in Africa (Tinaz, 1993, 2001, 2009, 2005; DeCaro, 1994).

Organizational and Political Economic Causes for Polarization

To understand the polarization between the ruling stratum of the NOI and the younger members of the movement, one has to consider the Nation's organizational developments and economic achievements as well as their influences on the movement's political objectives, transcendental ideals, teachings as well as their transformations. As demonstrated earlier, the NOI reached its peak organizationally, economically as well as in number of membership in the early 1960's. The question is how the organizational and economic accomplishments have influenced the direction and transformation of the political and ideal objectives of the NOI? The movement's principle political objective was a demand for land for the purpose of complete separation from white society and the implementation autonomous economic principle: "do for yourself" (Muhammad, 1965).

There is a consensus among social scientists that all types of movements, social, political, and religious, undergo processes of change and transformation, both organizationally and ideologically over the course of their histories (Weber, 1978; Michels, 1958; Zald, and Ash, 1966). No movement, in its very inception, comes into existence with a comprehensive ideology, a set of policies and an established organizational structure; those elements take a long time to become firmly established.

The transformations of social and religious organizations have been analyzed mostly from an institutionalization model. According to this model, when social and religious groups attain substantial levels of economic and political influence, as well as high membership, they tend to modify their organizational structures, ideologies and agendas, which will eventually lead to institutionalization. Being inspired by Weber and Michels' theoretical framework, Zald and Ash attempt to formalize the model in the following way:

> As an MO [movement organization] attains an economic and social base in society, as the original charismatic leadership is replaced, a

bureaucratic structure emerges and a general accommodation to the society occurs. The participants in this structure have a stake in preserving the organization, regardless of its ability to attain goals. Analytically there are three types of changes involved in these progress; empirically they are often fused [these are] goal transformation, a shift to organizational maintenance, and oligarchization.
ZALD AND ASH, 1966: 327

As far as the NOI is concerned, these three kinds of transformations appeared in organizational patterns of the movement in the early 1960's. The movement's transcendental goals and political ideology had transformed from being militant, radicalized and became revolutionary, to being conservative and overly concerned with material interests. Secondly, after attaining organizational and economic institutionalization, the NOI tended to modify its goals and policies in a direction closely aligned with dominant societal norms. Thirdly, the movement formed a centralized official hierarchy consisting of, in Zald and Ash's terms, a "minority of the organization's members" (1966: 327), that is, Elijah Muhammad's family and 'ruling stratum' in Chicago.

Borrowing Weber's analysis of culture, Michael Parenti argues that "certain beliefs of a cultural system can set in motion social practices and social organization which, in turn, eventually negate the very end values of that cultural system" (Parenti, 1964: 182). Weber points out this kind of differentiation, i.e. the space between ideals and transcendental values with relation to charismatic leadership. He contends that charismatic leaders enthusiastically initiate ideal moral teachings and ask for their followers' absolute devotion. But eventually in the course of time, "enthusiasm dies away...the pure faith is materialized, encrusted with conceptions that are...dislocated, and distorted, till its first features have almost disappeared" (Gerth and Mills, 1970: 53). Behind the departure from ideal objectives, Weber indicates that the causes are the results of structural and doctrinal rationalizations as well as the reutilization of the charismatic movement. He argues that "the original doctrines are democratized, intellectually adjusted to the needs of that stratum which becomes the primary carrier of the leader's message" (Gerth and Mills, 1970: 54). He finally concludes that:

A charismatic movement may be routinised into traditionalism or into bureaucratisation...upon the institutional framework of the movement, and especially upon the economic order. The routinisation of charisma, in quite essential respects, is identical with adjustment to the conditions of the economy, that is, to the continuously effective routines of workday life.
GERTH AND MILLS, 1970: 54

For the members of the NOI, Elijah Muhammad's divine status as the Messenger of Allah was unquestionable and there was no doubt he was guided by Allah. His stances were the primary sources of everything in the religious realm, including worldly practices, group social cohesion and even the utopian ideals of the community. He was, in short, a charismatic leader. Predicting the destiny of the charismatic leader and his followers in relation to the material world, Weber argues that continuity and stability of charisma depend upon

> the holders of charisma, the master as well as his disciples and followers, [who] must stand outside the ties of this world, outside of routine occupations...the fate of charisma, whenever it comes into the permanent institutions of a community, to give away to powers of tradition or of rational socialization.
>
> GERTH AND MILLS, 1970: 248, 253

The status of Elijah Muhammad as a charismatic leader and his movement's sacred mission for the Black people became determined by material and mundane affairs; the movement's agenda and policies gradually diversified from its original teachings, ideals and aspirations and eventually went through the institutionalization and rationalization processes. Consequently, the movement reached to the levels of economic and organizational saturation. This relative improvement in material comfort caused 'goal transformation' among the officials of the NOI who adjusted and moderated the movements extreme and uncompromising 'pure beliefs' and 'original policies' which they had previously advocated. For the case of the NOI, Parenti has observed that these worldly interests and material conditions adulterated and undermined the transcendental values of the community (Parenti, 1964). Essien-Udom also argues that "members of the Nation appear to be economically more secure than many Negroes" as a result their observance of the moral codes and economic principles of the Messenger. He concludes that "an improved economic status tends to moderate the militancy of the members. In fact, this interest in the acquisition of wealth appears to be one of the important internal constraints on the possibility of the movement becoming politically significant or revolutionary" (Essein-Udom, 1970: 170).

Upon his disaffiliation with the NOI, Malcolm clearly indicated the turning point in the goal transformation of the movement. He recounted that until the early 1960's,

> there was not a better organization among Black people in this country than the Muslim movement [NOI]. It was militant. It made the whole

struggle of the Black man in this country pick up momentum because of the unity, the militancy, the tendency to be uncompromising... But after 1960, after Elijah Muhammad went over there [Muslim countries] in December of '59 and came back in January of '60 – when he came back, the whole trend or direction that had formerly been taken began to change.[10] And in that change there's a whole lot of other things that had come into the picture. But he began to be more mercenary. More interested in money...in wealth....

MALCOLM X, 1992: 118; Perry, 1989

Unlike the ruling stratum of the movement, Malcolm always stuck to the NOI's idealistic political teachings and policies, not engrossing himself in materialistic concerns. As cited in Karenga's article, Malcolm devoted nearly his entire adult life to spreading the NOI's programs and Mr. Muhammad's teachings. He made a firm commitment not to own anything because he thought that material possessions would lessen his dedication and estrange him from the NOI's austere programs and the aspirations of the Black masses (Karenga, 1982; Malcolm X, 1968; Goldman, 1979).

A structural condition of a social movement is one of many important causes of division as well as transformation. A number of studies have showed that organizational structure, power sharing and institutional roles are possible determinants for schism (Wilson, 1961; Wilson, 1971; Gamson, 1975). When in the 1960's the Honorable Elijah Muhammad appointed his family and close relatives to the NOI's administration structure and hierarchy, those nepotistic policies created internal problems. Malcolm later commented on the negative impact of nepotism. He says that "the movement itself began to deteriorate only after Elijah Muhammad put members of his own family in positions of authority, which weakened the structure and caused internal bickering and division and eventually the movement just petered out" (Malcolm X, 1992: 189).

Goal displacement in a social movement may take several forms in order to maintain a broad range of targets according to the Weber-Michels' institutionalization model, but it always moves in the direction of greater conservatism (Zald and Ash, 1966). From the political perspective, the NOI's positions seemed to have mutated from being militant, radical and revolutionary, to one

---

10   Between March 8 and April 13, 1964, he made several conciliatory statements to credit the teachings and programs of the NOI and criticized other aspects of it. (See further information about Malcolm's remarks; Malcolm, 1965; 1970; Handler, 1964c; Spellman, 1964; Breitman, 1967; Evanzz, 1992, interview with the late Imam W.D. Mohamed, 5 July 1995a; 25 December 1995b.).

that embodied conservative traits. In the early 1960's, the ambiguous and complex political position of the NOI was begetting two distinctive consequences as the result of its organizational maturity, economic gains, as well as the external and internal pressures on its members. The first was identified by Lomax, who observed that critics of the NOI highlighted their conservative tendencies. He noticed that the Black masses were beginning to blame the NOI for their non-action policy, complaining that "the Black Muslims are flirting with the same doom that overtook Christianity" i.e., institutionalized conservatism (Lomax, 1963). Unity among Black organizations has never been achieved due to their distinctive approaches towards the endemic problems of the Black masses. While most civil rights organizations put forward moderate integrationist policies, the NOI advocated radical separatist solutions (Samuels, 1963). The formula that the NOI asserted for the Black struggle, Malcolm perceived, was more practical than the civil rights organizations. He considered the NOI as a religio-political movement that was "best suited [to achieve] freedom, justice, and equality for blacks" (Samuels, 1963).

Second, the 'Muslim officials' or 'ruling stratum' of the NOI received resistance from inside of the NOI. Younger and more politically motivated Muslims desired to engage in a proactive role in politics, joining together with civil rights organizations. However, all their demands to relax the normative political restrictions of the NOI were refused by the leading officials. These kinds of conflicting norms and values inevitably created feelings of frustration, anomie and anger due to the NOI's structural strain (Wilson, 1971). Malcolm tried to convince Mr. Muhammad that the NOI should be involved in a nation-wide campaign to launch a voter registration campaign in the summer of 1962, but that political activity was cancelled by the officials without advance notice or an explanation (Breitman, 1967). In that context, Wallis and Bruce speculate about the consequences of internal constraints within religious movements. They argue that

> Undermining institutional structure and patterns not only constitutes change and eliminates constraints upon further change, it also creates ambiguities and conflicts of policy and practice which leave the members without any clear guidelines to action. Only by constantly watching the leader, subordinating themselves totally to his inspiration of the moment and being willing to humble themselves for their failure to follow that inspiration closely enough, can they remain among the favoured (1986: 124).

The ambiguous policies and political uncertainties of the NOI's positions had created a polarized atmosphere between the elders and youngsters within the movement. While the elders were constantly watching for divine inspiration and guidance from Elijah Muhammad, the young Muslims wanted to get involved in action. Therefore, the recalcitrant policies of the NOI caused, mostly among younger Muslims, frustration and dissatisfaction. Consequently, the apolitical posture of the NOI led the rank and file Muslims to perceive that the growing political differences were primarily between the Chicago officials and Malcolm X. When the differences between him and The Messenger were made public by the *New York Amsterdam News*,[11] Malcolm vehemently denied the newspaper's allegations. Later, Malcolm was interviewed by Lomax on these alleged rumors. He said that the "'minor' difference between Mr. Muhammad and me is a lie. There is no such thing as a minor difference with the Messenger" (Lomax, 1968: 104). While refusing these allegations and expressing his continued loyalty to the Messenger, Malcolm eventually revealed this annoyance to Lomax that younger Muslims had been dissatisfied with the NOI's official non-engagement policy:

> The Messenger has seen God. He was with Allah and was given divine patience with the devil. He is willing to wait for Allah to deal with this devil...the rest of us Black Muslims have not seen God, we don't have this gift of divine patience with the devil. The younger Black Muslims want to see some action.
> LOMAX, 1963: 179

After his disaffiliation with the NOI, Malcolm talked over his personal constraints and disappointments with the official policy and its possible consequences, saying that,

> privately I was convinced that our Nation of Islam could be an even greater force in the American black man's overall struggle if we engaged in more *action*. By that, I mean I thought privately that we should have amended, or relaxed, our general non-engagement policy... I felt the very real potentiality that, considering the mercurial moods of the black masses, this labeling of Muslims as "talk only" could see us, powerful as we were, one day suddenly separated from the Negroes' front-line struggle.
> MALCOLM X, 1968: 397–398

---

11 New York Amsterdam News reported two times the differences between Malcolm and the NOI Officials on July 6 and July 20, 1963 issues (Perry, 1991: 456).

These disagreements over policies inside the NOI had been noticed by the leading scholars on the movement such as C. Eric Lincoln (1973), Louis Lomax (1963) and Michael Parenti (1964). In his classic work on the movement, Lincoln, for example, predicted the consequences of the economic and political achievements of the NOI:

> As the movement [NOI] gained vested interests – real estate and commercial enterprises, as well as economic and political weight in the black and white communities – one block of the Muslim leadership has become increasingly conservative. It will urge the case for maintaining a stable status quo, rather than risk the loss of so much that will have been so arduously gained. This block will very quickly realize that the Muslim gains can be protected only while there is a fairly stable white society in America.
> LINCOLN, 1973: 218; 1961

Zald and Ash also asserted three types of changes in the institutionalization process. Goal transformation in organizational maintenance is when "the primary activity of [the] organization becomes the maintenance of membership, funds, and other requirements of organizational existence" (1966: 327). To bring about this kind of substantial modification within the movements' policies and beliefs, they should be brought into closer alignment with the mainstream society's dominant norms and values "in order to avoid conflicts that could threaten the organization's viability" (Zald and Ash, 1966: 327). In the case of the NOI, Lincoln attributes a similar moderation in the NOI's officials' thought and stance. Realizing the social forces against the Muslims, they asked their ministers to tone down their anti-white rhetoric as not "to antagonize the opposition so that the movement will be destroyed" (Karenga, 1982:194).

On the contrary, Lincoln described the tendency of younger Muslims as being "scornful of mere material and negotiable gains" (Lincoln, 1973: 218, 1961). He argues that the younger generation of Muslims clung "to the spirit of the original revelation and [held] it capable of continual renewal in each generation" and that they thought "it will demand a restless war on the detested status quo, with its entrenched white domination" (Lincoln, 1973: 218). As many scholars have written, Malcolm was more concerned with social doctrines and politics of the NOI through which he attempted to translate the aspirations of the Black masses, despite the continuing confrontation with the established political system (Perry, 1992; Evanzz, 1992; Lomax, 1963; Goldman, 1979). Consequently, Malcolm's inability and/or reluctance to moderate his revolutionary and militant rhetoric against the status quo of the movement created animosity and hostility among the Chicago officials (Karenga, 1982). Under the close scrutiny of the NOI's cautious and jealous observations of Malcolm's independent behavior and regional authority, Malcolm gradually modified his administration of Muhammad's Mosque No. 7 and its branches in New York City. He initiated Arabic class for Muslims and built up a close political and diplomatic relationship with Muslim and African countries' representatives in the UN (Muhammad, 1995). Having learned of Mr. Muhammad's immoral conduct with his secretaries in 1963, Malcolm gave more emphasis on social doctrine, politics and programs of the NOI than religion, and morality (Malcolm, 1968; Muhammad, 1995). Furthermore, according to Professor Akbar Muhammad of Binghamton University, SUNY, son of Elijah Muhammad who had undergraduate degree at Al-Azhar University in Egypt and then graduate degrees at Edinburgh University in Islamic studies in Britain, Malcolm put less emphasis on the NOI's teaching about the white man's demonic nature after the disclosure of Elijah Muhammad's relations with his secretaries.

Parenti also observed that in the early 1960's there were further signs of changes in organizational and political patterns in the movement. He realized and followed several accommodationist tendencies within both the NOI's official literature and among its leadership. Among these were the following; the changed attitude towards integration; putting less emphasis on the separatist objectives of the movement; the emergence of a more conventional interest in political life; a tacit acceptance of the feasibility for improvement within the existing political system; and a moderation of their traditional anti-White rhetoric. (Parenti, 1964: 187–190).

Malcolm was suspended for three months from his official duties on Elijah Muhammad's order when he made an unauthorized remark about the US President John F. Kennedy's assassination in November of 1963. Calling it a case of the 'chicken coming home to roost,' Malcolm was silenced for ninety days. Despite the suspension period being over, he was not reinstated and the disciplinary action became permanent. With the combination of other factors discussed above, on March 8, 1964, Malcolm announced at a press conference that he was leaving the NOI and organizing a new movement called the Muslim Mosque Inc. (MMI) (Handler, 1964c; Samuels, 1964).

Despite his political divorce from the NOI, Malcolm still regarded Elijah Muhammad as his spiritual father. As Akbar Muhammad points out, "Malcolm's public confrontation with Muhammad was not essentially doctrinal." During the suspension period and immediately after, Malcolm constantly confessed that Elijah Muhammad was still "his spiritual leader and he asserted that their differences were primarily political and moral" (Muhammad, 1995: 39). There was no complete separation between Malcolm and the NOI until his trip to

Mecca and various African countries in April of 1964. Once abroad, Malcolm made several public statements via interviews and press conferences that revealed his ambivalence towards the NOI. On the one hand, he still spoke in favor of his affiliation with the NOI stating that,

> I am and always will be a Muslim. My religion is Islam. I still believe that Mr. Muhammad's analysis of the problem is the most realistic, and that his solution is the best one. This means that I too believe the best solution is complete separation...' (Malcolm X, 1965: 20) I am a follower of the Honorable Elijah Muhammad.[12] I believe in the Honorable Elijah Muhammad. The only reason I am in the Muslim Mosque, Inc., is because I feel I can better expedite his program by being free of the restraint and the other obstacles that I encountered in the Nation.
> MALCOLM X, 1970: 5; SPELLMAN, 1964; EVANZZ, 1992

Malcolm continued, "I have reached the conclusion...that I can best spread Mr. Muhammad's message by staying out of the NOI and continuing to work on my own among America's 22 million non-Muslim Negroes" (Handler, 1964c).

On the other hand, Malcolm publicly stated his political and emotional dissatisfaction with the NOI by asserting that "the movement had 'gone as far as it can' because it was too narrowly sectarian and too inhibited" (Handler, 1964c). On March 8, 1964, he announced his own political objectives and willingness to work with other leading Black civil right leaders and organizations. He declared, "I am prepared...to cooperate in local civil rights actions in the South and elsewhere and shall do so because every campaign for specific objectives can only heighten the political consciousness of the Negroes and intensify their identification against white society" (Handler, 1964c; Samuels, 1964). While he was in the NOI, to defend the Messenger's separatist teachings, Malcolm had ridiculed other civil rights groups and leaders both for their methods of passive resistance and their ill-conceived desire for integration. Explaining his previous absence from the civil rights struggle, he said that the Messenger had not allowed him to take part in politics, particularly in civil rights struggles even though he had many calls from several civil rights leaders to get involved for the sake of unity. However, Malcolm indicated a change in his political direction saying that "it is going to be different now... I am going to

---

12   In a telegram Malcolm had sent to Elijah Muhammad, he made similar compliments saying that...You are still my leader and teacher, even though those around you won't let me be one of your followers and helpers... (Evanzz, 1992: 217; Interview with the late Imam W.D. Mohamed, July 5, 1995a; Conversation with Imam Darnel Karim, June 25, 1995).

join in the fight whenever Negroes ask for my help, and I suspect my activities will be on a greater and more intensive scale than in the past" (Handler, 1964c). Consequently, Malcolm announced at his press conference on March 12, 1964, that he was organizing a new religious movement called *The Muslim Mosque, Inc.* He drew the outline of objectives of his newly founded organization. In the realm of religion, Malcolm assumed that the Muslim Mosque, Inc. "gives us a religious base and the spiritual force necessary to rid our people of the vices that destroy the moral fiber of our community" (Malcolm, 1965: 21).

On the other hand, Malcolm drafted the political goals for his new organization declaring that "our political philosophy...economic and social philosophy will be Black Nationalism. Our cultural emphasis will be Black Nationalism" (Malcolm, 1965: 21). He further clarified his objectives of Black Nationalist policies saying that it no longer meant black separation, but rather the potential for 22 million African-Americans to autonomously determine their politics, economics, social and educational lives (Breitman, 1967; Perry, 1992). To find out remedies and solutions for the socio-political-economic problems of the Black masses, Malcolm was ready to collaborate with others, even if they were Christians, atheists, socialists, etc. (Handler, 1964a; Breitman, 1967).

From his physical divorce from the NOI, through his religious and political visits to the Muslim World and Africa, Malcolm kept his mind open to new perspectives, teachings and policies. Upon his later extended stay in the Muslim World and Africa, as well as his discussion with political leaders and professionals in the Black diasporas in Europe and Africa, Malcolm's political views and policies as well as religious beliefs had to be subjected to transformations, adjustments and improvements, or in one word, *rationalization*.

The Impact of Malcolm X's Interaction and Relations with Others Circles: Rationalization of Religious Understanding, Political Perspectives and Organizational Objectives

Zald and Ash argue that interaction among organized movements may lead to co-operation, coalition and merger (1966). However, they put a greater emphasis on the importance of coalition and merger over interaction. They argue that these two "may lead to new organizational identities, changes in the membership base, and changes in goals." They further maintain, in general, that these two factors "require ideological compatibility" (Zald and Ash, 1966: 335).

When Malcolm left the NOI, there was no clear distinction between his religious and political teachings and the movement's. He was ambivalent about his defection and held conflicting notions and objectives in his mind. On the one hand, he was still preaching the blackness of God and the demonic nature of whites and still regarded Elijah Muhammad as his spiritual leader and teacher. More importantly, he still believed the analysis and solutions proposed by Elijah Muhammad were the best and most realistic for the conditions of blacks. At that time, he had not abandoned Elijah Muhammad's insistence on complete separation from white society. On the other hand, criticizing the NOI's confined and shallow political teachings, Malcolm desired to cooperate with other Black organizations by broadening the content of Black Nationalism. The attitude Malcolm displayed after he left the NOI was similar to attitudes of ex-members of other religious movements. As an ex-member of the NOI, Malcolm's position constitutes the same findings of Beckford about ex-members of the Unification Church (UC). Beckford has discovered that ex-members of the UC still felt love and admiration towards the practicing members and, more interestingly, they did not have a "clear or well-grounded" picture of the religious movement that sometimes they used to belong to. Furthermore, this is, he suggests, a result of "a high degree of confusion and ambivalence among ex-members...about the precise nature of their feelings towards the cult" (Beckford, 1985:153; Beckford, 1978). In the case of Malcolm's defection, it is conceivable to see his ambivalence and confusion in both his public and private statements concerning Elijah Muhammad and the NOI's programs. While he was in favor of some aspects of the movement, he was still critical of other features of it, particularly on its political and organizational positions.

Nevertheless, the clouds of confusion had dissipated when Malcolm began interacting with other religious and political circles in the United States, the Muslim World, as well as in other African countries. The importance of this interaction has been overlooked or given less emphasis by scholars. Louis A. DeCaro rightly highlights this point. Although most scholarly studies and works of the NOI accommodate the role of Malcolm in the evolution of the movement, there is "considerably less appreciation for the religious elements of Malcolm's impact on the NOI" (DeCaro, 1994: 429).

Malcolm had probably more interactions both at the individual and organizational levels than any other member and/or official within the NOI, including both Black and Muslim leaders and organizations at home and abroad. Because of that his thinking gradually modified. This did not happen suddenly. Interaction is a process which does not occur abruptly. Observing the signs of its impact requires a long time. Furthermore, influence does not only go one-way, rather it is mutual and reciprocal. Interaction contributes to the finding of common ground and comradeship among identical organizations and is likely to lead to an alliance in order to make common purpose and cooperation. In the case of Malcolm X, interaction broadened his horizons, both in religious and political realms. He attempted and sought to build emotional and organizational ties with identical racial and political figures as well as co-religionists following his defection. Therefore, the interaction factor further accelerated Malcolm's alienation, disaffiliation and differentiation from the NOI's beliefs, organizational programs and political objectives.

Encountering co-religionists and political figures in Africa and the Muslim World during his two intensive trips in 1964 had an enormous impact on Malcolm's political and religious thinking. Consequently, upon his close interaction, Malcolm had to reconsider and reason not only his religious beliefs, but also to tailor his political teachings (Tinaz; 1993, 2001, 2009; DeCaro, 1994; Munir, 1994; Perry, 1992). In other words, Malcolm abandoned the particularistic beliefs and teachings of NOI and embraced pluralistic and universalistic understandings of religion and objectives of politics.

Rationalization of Religious Understandings

Religious transformations are not immediate. They are a process. Brinkerhoff and Burke, for example, argue that "religious disaffiliation is a gradual, cumulative process in which negative labeling may act as a catalyst accelerating the journey to apostasy while giving it form and direction" (1982: 52). Similarly, Malcolm's disaffection from the NOI's religious beliefs had gradually developed over years, through interaction and sometimes interpersonal negotiations with other mainstream Muslim individuals and institutions in the United States and abroad. As briefly argued above, Malcolm did not suddenly and entirely modify and left his old religious and racial understandings when he encountered Muslims from different ethnic, racial and cultural origins in the US. Prior to *the Hajj* (Pilgrimage) in 1964, while he was still an influential figure in the NOI, Malcolm had met on several occasions with mainstream Muslims on both personal and organizational levels (Essein-Udom, 1970; DeCaro, 1994).[13] Nonetheless, after his defection and newly gained intellectual and political independence, Malcolm's intensive interaction and acquaintance with the multi-ethnic and multi-cultural international Muslim community while on Hajj was a turning point which culminated in his more confessional religious understandings as well as his new outlook on racial issues.

Through extensive media coverage in the late 1950's and the early 1960's, the NOI became familiar to American society mostly through derogatory and damning media exposure. The movement and its leaders began to receive

---

13   Dr. Alauddin Shabazz, interview, August 21, 1995.

harsh criticism from mainstream Muslim individuals and organizations in the United States because of its exclusivist, heterodox and unconventional beliefs and practices. But, at the same time, the NOI and its leaders enjoyed warm receptions and cordial relations with some Muslim personalities and dignitaries from Muslim countries (Essein-Udom, 1970; Lincoln, 1973; Tinaz, 1993, 2001, 2009; DeCaro, 1994).[14] To answer the critics and defend the teachings of the NOI and Elijah Muhammad, Malcolm served as the lead apologist.

It is interesting to note the gradual changes in Malcolm's rhetoric and attitudes upon his intensive interaction with mainstream Muslims. Malcolm's tour of the Middle East in 1959 as Mr. Muhammad's emissary first introduced him into some basic features and realities of Islam and Muslims. He confessed to the *Pittsburg Courier* and *New York Amsterdam News* that he encountered Muslims with a variety of racial appearances. In the *Pittsburg Courier* on August 15, 1959, Malcolm wrote:

> The people of Arabia are just like our people in America in facial appearance. They are of many different shades, ranging from regal black to rich brown. It is a safe postulation to say that 99 per cent of them would be Jim-crowed in the USA ... But none are white.
> DECARO, 1994: 379, quoting from Pittsburg Courier, 15 August, 1959

Malcolm, more remarkably, noticed the racial tolerance stating that, "there is no color prejudice among Moslems, for Islam teaches that all mortals are equal

---

14 These Muslim critics and cordial relations of the NOI are well documented in the works of Essien-Udom (1970), DeCaro (1994), and Lincoln (1973). Some Muslim individuals and groups such as Talib A. Dawud, the leader of the Moslem Brotherhood of America Inc., the representatives of the Ahmadiyya Movement or Nur Al-Islam Adib Nuriddin and Abdul Ghafoor Soofi the Federation of Islamic Associations in the US and Canada, were outspoken opponents and critics of the NOI and its leaders (Essien-Udom, 1970: 310–319; Lincoln, 1973: 182–86; DeCaro, 1994: 385–410). On the other hand, for various reasons, the NOI and its officials enjoyed mutual relations with Muslim personals such as Abdul Basit Naeem, M.Y. Shawarbi and the heads of Muslim and African countries such as President Gamal Abdel Nasser of Egypt, President William V.S. Tubman of Liberia and the President of Ghana. Consequently, these mutually beneficial and cordial relations bore fruit in the late 1950's and early 1960's when the NOI, for the first time, interacted with the Muslim World to congratulate the hosts and participants of the Afro-Asian Solidarity Conference in Cairo. Following that event, in 1959, Malcolm visited the Muslim and African countries as "Mr. Muhammad's emissary" and in early 1960 Elijah himself toured the Muslim World. The main purpose of their visits was to seek legitimacy and recognition from the Muslim World but not to adjust controversial religious differences (Lincoln, 1973; Essien-Udom, 1970; DeCaro, 1994; Tinaz, 1993, 2009).

and brothers. Whereas the White Christians in the Western world teach this same thing without practicing it" (DeCaro, 1994: 379).

Although his impressions and observations left him ambivalent how to evaluate the Messenger's teachings concerning the mythological nature of white people, upon his return from the visit to the Middle East, Malcolm apparently still continued to assert that all Whites were devil and Blacks were divine and Muslim by nature. While he was representing Elijah Muhammad and the NOI in public appearances in the media and at college campuses in the early 1960's, he fervently discredited the criticism of mainstream Muslim individuals and groups in the United States. Going even further, he ridiculed individual Muslims (DeCaro, 1994: 410–417). But on various college campuses, Malcolm encountered students from the Muslim World. Malcolm regarded these students to be "highly intelligent" and "amazingly open-minded and objective in their reception of the raw, naked truths" (Malcolm, 1968: 392). According to Benjamin Karim, who accompanied Malcolm to many appearances on various campuses, Malcolm regarded students to be generally impartial and "always alive and searching." Karim recalled the attitude of the students, he said,

> most students, black and white, received his [Malcolm's] massage openly, and after a lecture would crowd around him, asking all kinds of questions. I always had the feeling that the students were not only impressed by him, but that they really liked him.
> KARIM, 1971: 18–20

On several occasions, Malcolm encountered Muslim students from various parts of the Muslim World. He and many of those students had heated arguments about the NOI's controversial and heretical and unconventional beliefs and practices as well as their doctrine of hatred of Whites. Malcolm took their criticism seriously and could not ignore what they had to say. There is further evidence in support of the claim that Malcolm's break with NOI was neither abrupt nor complete. In fact, his thinking gradually evolved as he was influenced by the ideas from whom he came in contact with. For example, DeCaro (1994) citing Louis Lomax (1968) relates an episode which occurred between Malcolm and Muslim students at UCLA. When the students disputed Malcolm's 'white devil' utterances and accused him of preaching false beliefs, he apologetically replied by saying that it was crucial for him to follow "the white devil" method in order to "wake up the deaf, dumb and blind American Negroes" (DeCaro, 1994: 420–21; Perry, 1989). That kind of reasoning and explanation, however, did not satisfy the Muslims students. Not all of Malcolm's interpersonal relations ended up in polemical exchanges. Some of them, undoubtedly, contributed to Malcolm's proper understanding of religious beliefs of Islam. As he indicated in *The Autobiography*, Malcolm informally interacted with several friendly and sincere Muslims from Islamic countries after his speaking engagements on campuses. Apart from his White hatred statements, they treated Malcolm kindly and strongly urged him to explore "true Islam... understand it, and embrace it" (DeCaro, 1994: 421). With those heartfelt suggestions, while he was still a follower and a representative of Elijah Muhammad, Malcolm was 'bridled.' In this respect, DeCaro, for example, narrated Malcolm's close friendship with a Sudanese Muslim student named Ahmed Osman, from Dartmouth College, who visited the Mosque No. 7 in 1962. After listening to Malcolm's speech delivered at a Sunday service, he wanted to make some comments about the content of his preaching. Osman told Malcolm that,

> many of this statements and the beliefs of the Black Muslims are contrary to the teachings of Islam, particularly the claim of Elijah Muhammad that he is the Messenger of God and the interpretation of the race problem.
> DECARO, 1994: 504

Despite of the Fruit of Islam's (the NOI's paramilitary security unit) and the congregation's opposition, Malcolm allowed him to make his points. But their point-counterpoint discussion did not reach any conclusion. Later, Osman kept in touch with Malcolm by sending letters and providing literature on Islamic beliefs and practices. Eventually Malcolm replied to Osman's letters and asked him to send more Islamic literature and consulted him on various religious issues. Through this cordial exchange, there developed a genuine and honest friendship between Malcolm and Osman.

After frequent interactions with mainstream Muslims, Malcolm began questioning his own beliefs, saying that "if one was sincere in professing a religion, why should he balk at broadening his knowledge of that religion" (Malcolm, 1968: 430). This kind of religious search was encouraged by Wallace Muhammad (the late Imam W.D. Mohammed), Elijah Muhammad's son, whom Malcolm had always respected and consulted on religious issues. During my interview with Imam W.D. Muhammad, he confirmed his influence on Malcolm by saying that "he [Malcolm] was curious but he was not as informed in religion that I was, so he would depend on me to answer certain questions for him."[15] Highlighting the impact of these types of interactions upon Malcolm's

---

15   Imam W.D. Muhammad also maintains that Elijah Muhammad encouraged Malcolm to work closely with his son. (Interview with Imam, W.D. Muhammad, 5 July 1995a; 25 December 1995b).

religious dissatisfaction, Imam W.D. Mohammad personally admitted the influence of Muslim *individuals* such Jamil Diab as well as other members of the Muslim students associations that he associated with.[16] They undoubtedly contributed his Islamic religious understandings and knowledge. As a result of these interactions in the early 1960's, even before his defection, Malcolm began to moderate his statements regarding religion and race issues. At the end of March 1963, for instance, Malcolm appeared on *The Ben Hunter Show* in Los Angeles and made significant points about the basic tenets of Islam without referring to The Messenger's theology. He pronounced that,

> One becomes a Muslim only by accepting the religion of Islam, which means belief in one God, Allah. Christians call him Christ, Jews call him Jehovah. Many people have different names but he is the Creator of the Universe.
> DECARO, 1994: 418; quoting from FBI file

According to DeCaro, Malcolm further listed Islamic principles by saying that becoming a Muslim requires "submitting to God and practicing prayer, charity, fasting, brotherhood, respect to for authority and respect for other people" (DeCaro, 1994: 418).

The above statement indicates the important components of the religious pillars of Islam. After two months, in May 1963, in an interview in Washington D.C., Malcolm uttered more humanistic and religiously reconciliatory remarks that seemed to indicate his gradual transition to mainstream Islam. He declared that,

> When you are a Muslim, you don't look at the color of a man's skin [,] whether he is black red white or green or something like that; when you are a Muslim, you look at the man and judge him according to his conscious behavior.
> DECARO, 1994: 424-25, quoting from FBI file

Of course, Malcolm's interpersonal acquaintance and interactions with sympathetic White liberals and social democrats, along with other Muslims, began slowly influencing his thought and rhetoric. For example, in the early 1960's, Malcolm appeared to change his perception of White people. He said that "unless we call one white man, by name, a 'devil,' we are not speaking of any

---

16   Jamil Diab was Palestinian teacher when he was employed by Elijah Muhammad at the University of Islam, elementary and high schools, in which he taught Arabic.

individual white man. We are speaking of the *collective* white man's historical record" (Malcolm X, 1968: 371).

Furthermore, in 1963, Malcolm clarified his understanding of the White race. He admitted that 'white devil' is just an epithet. As DeCaro points out, Malcolm's judgement of White people had shifted, "strictly on the basis of ethical, not biological terms" (DeCaro, 1994: 424). At two media appearances in 1963, one being in Washington D.C. on May 13 and the other in Chicago on March 3, 1963, on the television show *At Random*, Malcolm made objective and balanced charges against White people. He said in the radio interview,

> many people in this country think we are against the white man because he is white. No, as a Muslim we don't look at the color of a man's skin; we are against the white man because of what he has done to the black man.
> DECARO, 1994: 425; quoting from FBI file

More importantly, his perception of a 'devil' seemed to have undergone fundamental modifications. On a television show, Malcolm gave a clear definition of a devil, referring not to Elijah Muhammad's beliefs but rather to normative sources of Islam: the Qur'an and the teachings and practices of Prophet Muhammad. He argued that the Prophet said "you judge a man by his conscious behavior or by his intentions...which means that anyone who intentionally or consciously carries into practice the attributes or characteristics of the devil is a devil" (DeCaro, 1994: 425).

As clearly displayed above cases, it is certain that long before his *Hajj*, Malcolm was already experiencing a process of detachment from the beliefs of the NOI. DeCaro describes this gradual transition of Malcolm's from the confines of NOI to the preliminary understanding of Islam as "foreshadowing Mecca" (DeCaro, 1994: 425). In disengagement terms, even before his split, Malcolm underwent a 'cognitive transition' and 'cognitive linkage' (Rockford, 1989) between his religious beliefs and the religious teachings of the NOI. In this transition or internal conversion to mainstream Islam, there is no doubt that interaction with mainstream and conventional Muslims at various levels played a significant role. Beckford does not want to give this factor great importance, although he does accept it as contributing factor to religious defection (Beckford, 1978). He argues that a "cognitive dissonance may not always be an important outcome of interpersonal negotiations and that the entry of other factors" have to be considered (Beckford, 1985:141). For example, in Malcolm's disengagement and detachment from the NOI, besides interpersonal interactions with Muslim individuals and groups, some other factors must have also contributed to his cognitive transition or diversion. Elijah Muhammad's moral teachings and political constraints should also be considered as important factors.

Before his defection from the NOI, Malcolm, of course, did not only moderate his religious understandings but he also appeared to veer away from the movement's conservative and abstentionist political perspectives and policies as an outcome of interaction with other circles. His initiatives further intensified his escape from the straitjacket policies of the NOI. Prior to his pilgrimage to Mecca and tour of Muslim and African states, Malcolm attempted to form an pluralistic organization in order to offer his cooperation with Muslims, Christians and non-religious Blacks, nationalists and leftists. He said that "the organization... I hoped to build would differ from the Nation of Islam in that it would embrace all faiths of black men, and it would carry into practice what the Nation of Islam had only preached" (Malcolm X, 1968: 427; Handler, 1964d). These objectives were attained as the results of his long process of interaction and interpersonal negotiations with other circles. While Malcolm's new organization, the Muslim Mosque Incorporated (MMI), delineated the attributes of a 'pluralistically legitimate' movement, the NOI preserved the aspects of its 'uniquely legitimate' status (Wallis, 1979:182–3). All of these preliminary religious, organizational and political changes happened to Malcolm in the 'Pre-Meccan period.'[17] His various initiatives and thoughts on politics and religion were further modified and broadened with his experience with the multiethnic nature of Islam, its rituals, especially the Hajj, as well as with his two long diplomatic tours to Muslim and African countries.

Weeks after his defection from the NOI, Malcolm's primary concern was to escape from his Black Muslim racist image and to further build religious and political ties with the Muslim World and African countries (Muhammad, 1995; Essien-Udom, 1991). To correct his image, Malcolm was also advised and urged to make the Hajj by sympathetic Muslim professionals and organizations that he often interacted with. When he decided to make the Hajj, he encountered two obstacles; the first was financial, but that was solved with the help of his sister Ella, who would finance his trip (Malcolm X, 1968).[18] Second and the most crucial one was that legitimacy and recognition issue as a 'bona fide'

---

17 In analyzing the changes that the Nation of Islam underwent, Munir properly divides these two periods as 'Pre-Meccan' and 'Post-Meccan' periods referring to Malcolm's pilgrimage (Munir, 1994).

18 Malcolm's sister Ella was a sporadic member of the Nation of Islam's Boston Mosque No. 11. Once she was expelled because of her obstinacy, and then come back. Later, Ella voluntarily left the NOI, even before Malcolm, when she learned and studied Islam through her interactions with orthodox Muslims in Boston (Malcolm, 1968; Perry, 1991).

Muslim, which he would have to prove in order to enter 'the Holy Land,' i.e. Mecca. For approval of his status as 'an authentic Muslim' and subsequently to receive a visa for the Hajj, those Muslims professionals whom he met and the Saudi Consulate officials asked Malcolm to contact to Dr. Mahmoud Y. Shawarbi, who was an Egyptian academic and the director of *the Federation of Islamic Associations in the United States and Canada* (Malcolm X, 1968; Goldman, 1979). Malcolm was already acquainted with Dr. Shawarbi as he encountered him on a number of occasions while he was still in the NOI. Although some Muslims remained suspicious of the sincerity of the NOI members in general, and Malcolm in particular, because of their racist and unconventional and heterodox beliefs, Dr. Shawarbi was very patient with and consistently showed a moderate posture towards the movement (Lewis, 1964; Goldman, 1979).[19] However, the relationship between the NOI and mainstream Muslim individuals and organizations did not develop friendly relations because of Elijah Muhammad's reluctance "to move closer to Sunni Islam" (DeCaro, 1994: 506; Tinaz, 2001, 2009). According to Dr. Shawarbi, following his defection from the NOI, Malcolm came to him both to learn proper Islam and to get his endorsement letter for the visa application to make the Hajj (Lewis, 1964; Malcolm X, 1968). When Malcolm came to the Shawarbi's office, he stated that he was already Muslim and believed in Allah and what he needed was to broaden his understanding of pure Islamic beliefs and practices (Lewis, 1964; Goldman, 1979). After being fully convinced of his sincerity, Dr. Shawarbi did not only provide the requisite letter, during the six weeks preceding Malcolm's trip to Mecca, he also gave him several introductory courses regarding the basic

---

19   Dr. Shawarbi appeared on a number of occasions in the Nation of Islam's social and religious events. For example, he accompanied Malcolm X to the Afro-Asian Bazaar in New York's Rockland Palace that was sponsored by the NOI's Harlem Mosque No. 7, which aimed to bring together African and Asian merchants and people. When the New York Amsterdam News, on October 22, 1960, published a story that alleged that two top representatives of the Islamic Federation, referring to Maulana M.F. Ansari and Dr. Shawarbi, were critical of the NOI Muslims for distorting Islamic beliefs, on November 5, 1960, he refuted those allegations and told the crowd that "I have never denounced anyone... We are Muslims and Muslims do not denounce each other... All Muslims are Brothers." On the contrary, Dr. Shawarbi praised the NOI's mission and its "unique position" among African-Americans. Referring to the radio show called "Mr. Muhammad Speaks," he said that "I thank God that once a week the teaching of our faith can be heard on the air in this area." Consequently, expressing his gladness over Elijah Muhammad's lesser pilgrimage (*umrrah*) to Mecca, his trip to the Muslim World, as well as Malcolm's travels, he encouraged all Muslims in the NOI to make the Hajj. (Evanzz, 1992; *New Crusader*, Nov, 12, 1960; DeCaro, 1994).

Islamic tenets and the requirements for the Hajj (Lewis, 1964; Perry, 1992).[20] In addition to these, Shawarbi also supplied him with Islamic literature and some contact names of Muslim dignitaries like Abd al-Rahman Azzam, his son Dr. Omar Azzam and others in case he needed any help while on hajj.[21]

Through the contacts provided for him by Dr. Shawarbi, Malcolm was treated as a State Guest and received warmly from various Muslims as well as Saudi officials. He also was impressed by the sympathetic and friendly conduct of both the distinguished and ordinary Muslims from all over the Muslim World, who were from various racial, ethnic and national origins.[22] During on Hajj, Malcolm relished the privileges he received (Handler, 1964e). Furthermore, he internalized his 'reconversion' or 'internalization of conversion' to mainline Islam as a result of observing the experiential and practical dimension of Islamic beliefs, practices, true brotherhood, equality and unity – regardless of color, race, ethnicity, and social status – while simultaneously broadening his understanding of Islam by reading the literature provided. In Lofland and Skonovd's terms, Malcolm was experiencing 'intellectual' and 'experimental' conversion motifs (1981). The most important feature of Malcolm's transformation had happened as a result of the intensive interaction between him and other Muslims on the Hajj. As Snow and Phillips allege, that intensive interaction is "the key to understanding [his] conversion" (Snow and Phillips, 1980: 444). There is no doubt that the Hajj was a significant event for Malcolm's religious transition. The Hajj is the largest collective and multicultural communal ritual in the world and "one of the most potent unifying factors in the world of

---

20   It was certainly understood that Malcolm became very conversant with Islamic terminology in general, and rituals of the Hajj in particular, as a result of orientation course he took and from his interactions with Dr. Shawarbi. That influence could be seen when one observes the Islamic concepts Malcolm used in the last three chapters of *The Autobiography*. Regarding that issue, Malcolm later publicly admitted that Dr. Shawarbi was "instrumental in helping me to understand true Islam, a religion that teaches brotherhood and tolerance between peoples of all colors and national origins" (Lewis, 1964).

21   Dr. Shawarbi gave Malcolm a copy of the book *The Eternal Message of Muhammad* especially sent by its author, Abd ar-Rahman Azzam. Later Malcolm also received two more books on Islam given to him by The Hajj Committee Court Judge Sheikh Muhammad Harkon, who recognized and approved his status as a authentic Muslim before he could embark on the Hajj from Jeddah, Saudi Arabia (Malcolm, 1968).

22   On the Hajj, Malcolm encountered a number of important Muslim personages, whose sincere, courteous and amiable treatments made an impact on him, namely, Prince Faisal of Saudi Arabia, Abdul Aziz Maged, the Deputy Chief of Protocol for Prince Faisal, Hussein Amini, Grand Mufti of Jerusalem, Kasem Gulek of the Turkish Parliament, Sheikh Abdullah Eraif, the Mayor of Mecca, and two Dr. Azzams (Malcolm, 1968).

Islam" (Lewis, 1976: 27). Thus, it generates a "suitable network of communications" among all kinds of Muslims from various ethnic and racial backgrounds (Lewis, 1976: 27). It is generally believed that the Hajj provides Muslim peoples with social, cultural, economic and religious interactions. More importantly, it certainly engenders "a sense of belonging to a single, vast whole," *the Ummah* (Lewis, 1976: 27).

Through his observations and personal experiences, Malcolm underwent a drastic change in his conversion, which led to him radically reorganizing his "identity, meaning and life" (Travisano, 1970: 600). In letters he sent back home, the US and to the press, he reflected on his fundamental changes and experiences that he was undergoing during the Hajj which affected his thoughts on religion and matters of race (Handler, 1964e; Booker, 1964). He publicly expressed his observations by stating that,

> During the past seven days of this holy pilgrimage, while undergoing the rituals of the Hajj [pilgrimage], I have eaten from the same plate, drank from the same glass, slept on the same bed or rug, while praying to the same God not only with some of this earth's most powerful kings, cabinet members, potentates and other forms of political and religious rulers – but also with fellow Muslims whose skin was the whitest of white, whose eyes were the bluest of blue, and whose hair was the blondest of blond – it was the first time in my life that I didn't see them as 'white' men...[they] didn't regard themselves as 'white.'
> HANDLER, 1964e

Malcolm continued his evaluation of people he encountered with,

> their belief in the Oneness of God (Allah) had actually removed the 'white' from their minds, which automatically changed their attitude and behavior toward people of other color's.
> HANDLER, 1964e

Comparing Muslims from different racial and ethnic backgrounds on the Hajj with American whites, Malcolm said,

> their belief in the Oneness of God has actually made them so different from American whites, their outer physical characteristics played no part at all in my mind during all my close associations with them.
> HANDLER, 1964e

He further reflected on the racial tolerance he witnessed and experienced, stating that,

> their [pilgrims'] true acceptance of all non-white as equals makes the so-called 'whites' also acceptable as equals into the brotherhood of Islam with the 'non-whites.' Color ceases to be a determining factor of a man's worth or value once he becomes a Muslim...
> HANDLER, 1964e

More importantly, the racial tolerance and sincerity he observed and received forced Malcolm to revise and modify his previous understanding of racial issues. He confessed that,

> The *color-blindness* of the Muslim world's religious society and *color-blindness* of the Muslim world's human society: these two influences had each day been making a greater impact, and an increasing persuasion against my previous way of thinking.
> MALCOLM, 1968: 453

At the end of pilgrimage, upon his own reflections, Malcolm faced the fundamental and structural transformations of his formerly held understanding of religion, race and color issues, and came to the following conclusion:

> You may be shocked by these words coming from me. But on this pilgrimage, what I have seen, and experienced, has forced me to *re-arrange* much of my thought-patterns previously held, and to *toss aside* some of my previous conclusions.
> MALCOLM X, 1968: 454; HANDLER, 1964e

The Hajj environments, therefore, provided for Malcolm, in Berger and Luckmann's terms, 'plausibility structures' (1966: 154) wherein he found and experienced sincerity, racial tolerance, racial and color harmonies, and above all the same faith and beliefs observed in accordance with the sacred text, the Qur'an and the deeds and practices of the Prophet Muhammad. As it has already been indicated, Wright argues that a defector's adoption a 'new plausibility structure' helps to legitimize his leaving from a movement that he used to be a member (Wright, 1987: 75). Moreover, he maintains that the new plausibility structure "provides a contrasting set of ideas and beliefs from which to discredit the old plausibility structure..." (Wright, 1987: 75). Similarly, after the Hajj, Malcolm began to question the exclusive nature and practices of the religious and racial teachings of the NOI.

After performing the duties of Hajj, Malcolm extended his tour visiting African countries which provided him with new political perspectives. The impact of these visits will be examined in the next section. On his return to the United States, Malcolm openly admitted the Hajj had a massive impact on his thinking, which he elaborated on during various interviews and speaking engagements. For example, at *The Barry Gray Show*, Station WMCM, New York, July 8, 1964, he said that

> I think that the pilgrimage to Mecca broadened my scope probably more in twelve days than my previous experience during my thirty-nine years on this earth... And many of things that I experienced, that I witnessed, and many of the people that I conversed with, I don't know whether or not they *changed* my mind, but I must say they did *broadened* my mind... my scope...my outlook.
> GOLDMAN, 1979: 166

In the summer of 1964, Malcolm made his second long and intensive trip to Africa and the Middle East aiming to strengthen his political and religious connections. Besides his political interests, during this long tour (July through November 1964), Malcolm particularly sought authentic religious legitimacy as a Muslim leader. He was also in search of financial support from various Islamic authorities and organizations in the Muslim World. He spent several months closely working and studying with Muslim scholars and the Muslim World League in Saudi Arabia "to prepare himself for his new role as a Muslim evangelist in the United States" (Handler, 1964f, g). Malcolm, through these intensive interactions, broadened his Islamic knowledge and internalized his new religious understandings. It eventually paved the way for Malcolm to adjust his 'ideological compatibility' (Zald and Ash, 1966) with Islamic World. Accordingly, he modified his theological doctrines as well as the organizational policies of the MMI. In Egypt, having convinced the Islamic authorities of his *bona fides*, he got his Islamic credentials; the rector of *Al-Azhar*, the famous Islamic University in Cairo, Sheikh Hassan Ma'moun, formally recognized Malcolm's Islamic Mission, accrediting him a "duty to propagate Islam and offer every available assistance and facilities to those who wish conversion to Islam" (Handler, 1964g; Goldman, 1979). In addition to that, Malcolm secured twenty scholarships from *the Supreme Council on Islamic Affairs in Cairo* and fifteen from Saudi Arabia for Muslims of the MMI to study at Al-Azhar and Islamic University in Medina respectively. As a result of his close association with Islamic scholars and organizations, his mission bore tangible fruit. For example, Sheikh Muhammad Surur Al-Sabba, the Secretary General of the World Muslim League (WML) appointed Malcolm as an official representative of the organization in the United States with the authority to open a Muslim Centre in New York.[23] He also arranged for Malcolm to have a religious teacher, Sheikh Ahmed Hassoun (of Sudanese origin) to teach Islam and Arabic at Malcolm's Muslim Mosque Inc. (MMI) (Handler, 1964g; Perry, 1992; Goldman, 1979). Hassoun's main task was to help Malcolm "correct the distorted image that the religion of Islam has been given by the hate groups" in the United States (DeCaro, 1994: 584–85).

Those relationships between Malcolm and various Islamic authorities and organizations, of course, did not only bring about a *religious* co-operation, but they were also *organizational*; there was a, in Zald and Ash's terms, "merger or coalition" that contributed to a "search for a common denominator to which both parties can agree" (1966: 335). There was likely a similar result for Malcolm's religious organization, the Muslim Mosque Inc. that also aimed at a closer association with the Muslim World.

Referring to his pilgrimage and trips to Africa and Muslim countries, Malcolm said "I hope that once and for all my Hajj to the Holy City of Mecca has established our Muslim Mosque's authentic religious affiliation with the 750 million Muslim of the orthodox Islamic World" (Malcolm X, 1968: 478). Malcolm stated that this coalition "gave us direct ties with our brothers and sisters in Asia and Africa who are Muslims..." (Malcolm X, 1992: 123).

Having being granted religious credentials by the leading Islamic authorities, Malcolm, while he was still abroad, launched his boldest attacks on Elijah Muhammad through letters sent to M.S. Handler, a *New York Times* journalist. He denounced the Messenger and exposed him as a "religious faker." His harsh attacks of the Messenger were evidence that the final cord had been broken in his defection. He wrote that,

> For 12 long years I lived within the narrow-minded confines of the 'straitjacket world' created by my strong belief that Elijah Muhammad was a

---

23 The World Muslim League – WML (Rabita-ul Islamiyya) is an umbrella organization that co-ordinates all other Muslim organizations and develops greater co-operation and unity in the Muslim World, mostly Muslims in the West. It is dedicated to the propagation of Islam and supports various causes financially, such as construction Islamic Centres and mosques and salaries and expenses of Muslim clerics, imams and preachers. The organization was founded in Mecca, May 18, 1962 and was governed by a constituent council of 23 grand imams in the Muslim World at the time of early 1960's (Handler 1964g; Perry, 1992).

> messenger direct from God himself, and my faith in what I now see to be a pseudo religious philosophy that he preaches.
> HANDLER, 1964f

Having clarified his religious posture regarding the NOI, Malcolm continued,

> I declare emphatically that I am not in Elijah Muhammad's 'strait jacket'... I am a Muslim in the most orthodox sense; my religion is Islam as it is believed in and practiced by Muslims here in the Holy City of Mecca.
> HANDLER, 1964f

This internalized conversion and understanding of Islam propelled Malcolm to renounce the NOI's racist philosophy and to embrace an inclusive, embracing universal religious and Islamic humanism. He declared that

> The religion [Islam] recognizes all men as brothers. It accepts all human beings as equals before God, and as equal members in the Human Family of Mankind. I totally reject Elijah Muhammad's racist philosophy, which he has labelled 'Islam' only to fool and misuse gullible people, as he fooled and misused me.
> HANDLER, 1964f

With Malcolm's rejection of racism, his scope of friendship was broadened and eventually contained all kinds of people regardless of their "religious, political, economic, psychological and racial ingredients" (Handler, 1964f).

However, he was determined to fight the cancer of racism. He defiantly stated that "I shall never rest until I have undone the harm..." (Handler, 1964f). On his return to the US in the early days of November 1964, Malcolm renewed his campaign against Elijah Muhammad by talking about his domestic life on TV and radio programs, in which he portrayed the Messenger as an 'immoral man' (Malcolm X, 1992: 123; Perry, 1989). The NOI responded to these critics with violent acts against Malcolm and other members of the MMI. By the time Elijah's former secretaries filed the paternity suits against him, the personal and morally problematic life styles of Elijah Muhammad had already become public. In criticizing the moral lapses of the Messenger and his teachings, Malcolm was not alone. Many in Elijah's immediate family, including two of his sons, Wallace D. Muhammad (the late Imam W. D. Mohammed) who had already been excommunicated before Malcolm, Akbar Muhammad (now Professor of history at Binghamton University, SUNY) and his grandson Hasan Sharrieff, all defected from the NOI due to religious and moral reasons (Evanzz, 1992: 245–46; Perry,

1992: 289, 308).[24] At least two of his sons left as a result of their father's moral and controversial personal practices. The late Imam Mohammed admitted that his own understanding of Islam developed through his search and interactions with mainstream Muslim individuals. Since Akbar Muhammad, the Messenger's youngest son, was student at Al-Azhar University in Cairo at that time, he became very familiar with mainstream Islamic beliefs and practices. Both repudiated their father, accusing him of being guilty of immorality and religious deception (*New York Times*, August 18, 1964). Akbar especially denounced his father's teachings stating that "my father's concocted religious teachings... are far from and in most cases diametrically opposed to Islam" (Smith, 1965). He expressed his support of Malcolm and his brother Wallace's attempts to establish an orthodox Muslim movement among African-Americans.[25]

Behind the arguments that led to the fragmentation and defections in the NOI, were the problem of 'cognitive linkage' (Rochford, 1989), and other times its 'liturgical disputes' (Greenslade, 1953). Additionally, 'doctrinal purity' induced "questioning the basis of organizational authority and behavior of leadership" (Zald and Ash, 1966: 337). In light of this, there is often a gradual process of *falling from the faith* (Bromley, 1986). Therefore, it seems possible to make a compelling case for Malcolm's gradual transformation; it was a process-detachment from the NOI as the partial result of his interactions and relationships with Muslim personages and organizations.

Rationalization of Political and Organizational Programs and Objectives

As it has already been discussed at length, in the early 1960's the NOI underwent two distinctive political tendencies: one was the conservative and abstentionist policies represented by the ruling stratum; the other was the political activism

---

24   Following Malcolm's defection, when the Messenger's moral failings became public, a considerable number of Muslims left the NOI for religious and political reasons. Munir predicts the number of defectors were 10% (1993). Akbar Muhammad estimated that 300 members had left out of 7,000 (Smith, 1965). Wallace augmented this amount and assumed that the NOI had lost almost half of its members (Perry, 1992). But it is impossible to accurately determine the number of defectors since some members joined and left the movement voluntarily when they were dissatisfied.

25   During the Hajj, Malcolm recalled Wallace's similar objection to the NOI. He said Wallace once expressed his conviction that "the only possible salvation for the Nation of Islam would be its accepting and projecting a better understanding of orthodox Islam" (Malcolm X, 1968: 453).

and revolutionary tendency adopted by Malcolm and some younger members of the NOI. The polarization was presumably, as far as Malcolm's part was concerned, a consequence of a long process of interactions with other Black leaders and organizations (Breitman, 1967; Perry, 1992). In the realm of politics and practical policies, there is no doubt that Malcolm was far ahead of the NOI's official leadership. The polarization and later schism in the NOI was an inevitable precondition for his ideological and political transformation as it would eventually liberate him from the confines of Elijah Muhammad's religio-racial teachings. Once he was no longer affiliated with the NOI, he wished to co-operate with other civil rights organizations upon his defection from the movement (Handler, 1964c). Previously, Malcolm advocated that *separation* was the only solution, but on the day he declared his independence from the movement, he said "separation back to Africa is still a long-range program" (Malcolm, 1965: 20). Before his trips abroad, which represents his period of gradual transition, separatist political thinking and Black Nationalist views had been modified and improved (Spellman, 1964). Malcolm gradually abandoned his advocacy of a separate state and began to consider that blacks should stay in the United States and "fight for recognition as human beings...the right to live as free humans in this society" (Malcolm X, 1965: 51; Breitman, 1967; Breitman et. al., 1992).

Through the Hajj and his long trips and visits to African and Muslim World in 1964, Malcolm's political perspectives and objectives were subjected to fundamental modifications and rationalizations just as his religious and racial understandings had been. At the press conference on May 21, when he was asked whether he still advocated separatism and a return to Africa or not, he answered that,

> after speaking to African leaders, he was convinced that "if black men become involved in a philosophical, cultural and psychological migration back to Africa, they will benefit greatly in this country."
>
> BREITMAN, 1967: 63

Calling upon the Jewish experience in the United States, Malcolm said that "we can learn much from the strategy used by the American Jews. They have never migrated physically to Israel, yet their cultural philosophical and psychological ties to Israel has enhanced their political, economic and social position right there in America" (Booker, 1964).

Along with his gradual abandonment of separatism, Malcolm's understanding of Black Nationalism had also periodically been revised and redefined.[26]

---

26 For the chronological changes and modifications of Malcolm's understanding of separatism and Black Nationalism, see Breitman, 1967, and Goldman, 1979.

Prior to his defection from the NOI, he used to advocate the establishment of a separate Black nation. But right after his defection from the NOI, Malcolm modified his conception of Black Nationalism to mean that African-Americans need to control their own politics, economics, as well as their own social and educational institutions (Malcolm X, 1965; Perry, 1992). However, his particularistic and exclusivist political philosophy had shifted from Black Nationalism to internationalism and Pan-Africanism when Malcolm interacted with political leaders and revolutionaries in Africa and the Muslim World, especially during his visit to Ghana where he was compelled to rethink and review his political philosophy. There, Malcolm had one remarkable conversation with the Algerian Ambassador to Ghana, Taher Kaid, who promptly dominated his political discourse. According to the story, Kaid inquired him, "Brother Malcolm, what are your plans? What are you going to do?" Malcolm responded evasively with a long explanation about Black Nationalism. Smiling gently, Kaid said, "Brother Malcolm, that sort of leaves me out, doesn't it?" "What do you mean?" Malcolm reacted. "Well, said Kaid, I'm a Muslim brother and a revolutionary. But I'm not Black – I'm Caucasian" (Perry, 1992: 273). As a result of that exchange of ideas and conversation, Malcolm began to realize that the politics of blackness might isolate him from potential sources of support and solidarity from Africa, the Middle East and other Third World nations that fought for their independence against the colonial powers at that time (Malcolm, 1965; Goldman, 1979). Consequently, Malcolm's conversation with Kaid in particular and other influential political and revolutionary figures and statesmen in general, had broadened his political objectives and views. Thereafter, Black Nationalism became less appealing to him and he gradually abandoned it. More importantly, Malcolm's experiences abroad enabled him to perceive that the fundamental problem facing Third World people and other peoples of color was not race but the system of exploitation and disadvantageous capitalist economic system. With a new synthesis of insights, accordingly, he appeared to comprehend that the African-American problem is only a part of that system, both domestic and international (Ruby et al., 1991; Goldman, 1979).

After his interactions with various political figures, Malcolm publicly admitted that the heads of states and other political leaders whom he encountered with had influenced his thought.[27] He said that "the understanding that I got from conversations with these men...broadened my scope so much that I felt I could see the problems confronting Black people in America and the Western Hemisphere with much greater clarity" (Malcolm X, 1992: 111; Perry,

---

27 Those heads of states and political figures Malcolm had intensive interactions and conversation were, President J. Nyerere of Tanzania, President J. Kenyatta of Kenya, President of Azikiwe of Nigeria, President of Nkrumah of Ghana, President of Toure of Guinea, and Prime Minister M. Obote of Uganda (Malcolm X, 1992: 111; Perry, 1989).

1989). Especially when the race issue was concerned, Malcolm acknowledged their impacts saying "listening to leaders like Nasser, Ben Bella and Nkrumah awakened me to the dangers of racism. I realized racism isn't just a Black and White problem" (Parks, 1965:15).

Malcolm's diplomatic visits and political encounters did not only affect his political outlook, it also made a huge impact on his organizational programs and strategies. After having broadened his perspectives, he noticed and felt that the scope of his organization, the *Muslim Mosque Incorporated*, was limited and confined to only African-American Muslims in the United States. When he established the MMI, Malcolm initially assumed that it would embrace the active participation of all Negroes, but the very name of the organization was an obstacle for as such collective solidarity and collaboration. Because it was too narrowly defined and drew its framework and perspectives from Islam, it was a hindrance to non-Muslims who might sympathize and wish to partake in Malcolm's cause (Goldman, 1979; Breitman, 1967). Having realized the MMI's organizational and strategic restrictions and narrow perspectives, Malcolm established a new organization as soon as he returned from abroad by the end of May, 1964. He wanted to draw a distinction between his religious and political objectives. In an exclusive interview he gave to *New York Amsterdam News,* May 30, 1964, Malcolm said that he would launch a new national organization "to work in the political economic, and social areas" (Malcolm, 1964b:52). Asserting that most Black organizations' leaders see the African-American race problem "in the scope of their own organizations," he believed that was "a very narrow approach," and he desired that his new organization "will be open for the participation of all Negroes, and we will be willing to accept the support of people of all races" (Malcolm, 1964b:52). On June 24, 1964, Malcolm publicly announced the establishment of a new organization called the *Organization of Afro-American Unity (OAAU)*, inspired by the *Organization of African Unity (OAU)* which was founded in Addis Ababa, Ethiopia, in May of 1963 (Essein-Udom, 1991; Breitman, 1967). The new organization's primary objective was "to unite Afro-Americans and their organizations around a non-religious and non-sectarian constructive purpose for human rights" (Breitman, 1967: 77). Being a more secular-political oriented organization, he expected to draw the widest possible spectrum of African-Americans in forming *one solid front* as well as a bridge between African-Americans and people in Africa (Sales, 1999).

Almost a month later, on June 28, Malcolm formally declared the basic aims and objectives of the OAAU.[28] The first and foremost objective of the newly

---

28 To see the full text of statement of basic aims and objectives of the OAAU, see Breitman, 1967, Appendix A, and Clark, 1991: 335–42.

established organization, he asserted, would be to "add a new dimension to the black struggle and then elevate it from civil rights level to human right level" (Breitman, 1967: 77). This political objective, Malcolm believed "could be achieved by internationalizing" the American race problem and bringing it before the United Nation in the same way that South African apartheid was elevated to an international level (Handler, 1964i). For the recognition and announcement of his new organization, Malcolm launched his second trip to African and the Middle East in July of 1964, both to attend the OAU conference in Cairo as an official observer and representative of the OAAU and to search for political support. Despite the sympathetic and friendly audience he received from delegates, Malcolm was not permitted to address at the Summit. However, he was allowed to circulate a memorandum urging the African leaders to bring the American race problem before the United Nations. Malcolm persistently lobbied delegates in an attempt to explain the situation of Afro-Americans. He emphatically conveyed the deteriorating conditions of Blacks stating that "we are...your long-lost brothers and sisters" in America and we've "spent over three hundred years...suffering the most inhuman forms of physical and psychological tortures imaginable" (Clarke, 1991:289).[29]

Malcolm furthermore clarified his main intention and goal maintaining that "our problem is your problem. It is not a Negro problem, nor even an American problem but a world problem. It is beyond civil rights, but it is human rights problem. So it had to be resolved by the international community" (Clarke, 1991:290; Barnes & Waters, 2008). Consequently, Malcolm pleaded and sought the leaders of African states' support the destiny and cause of the Afro-Americans by bringing the race problem before the UN "on the grounds that the United States Government is morally incapable of protecting the lives and the property of 22 million African-Americans" (Malcolm X, 1964d:292; Handler, 1964a).

Although Malcolm's efforts and attempts received enormous moral and psychological support, it resulted in no official posture and declaration taken against the United States' racial politics, because some African leaders were reluctant to endorse Malcolm's memorandum because of what they perceived as its anti-Americanism. Their hesitations and anxieties seemed to be grounded in two factors. First was that "they have enough problems" in African continent "without adding the Afro-American Problem" (Handler, 1964i). Second was, more concrete one, most of Africa's newly independent states were still economically and financially dependent on American foreign aid. In other

---

29 John H. Clarke argued that Malcolm would had delivered a speech at the summit, but in reality, he just circulated an eight-page petition among the OAU delegates. See the text of the memorandum, Clarke, 1991: 288–295.

words, their national survival takes precedence over international race issues. Having sensed that, Malcolm stated that "we pray that our African brothers have not freed themselves of European colonialism only to be overcome and held in check by American dollarisim" (Malcolm X, 1964d:293; Handler, 1964i; Goldman 1979 and Perry, 1992). Nevertheless, his tireless lobbying efforts were eventually rewarded by the passing of a resolution at the OAU conference. Instead of condemning the racism in the United States, they instead praised the government's *Civil Rights Act of 1964* which was enacted to protect the civil rights of American Blacks. However, the OAU delegates still expressed their concerns about the racial discrimination and oppression against African-American people of the United States. In their conclusion, they wished the American authorities would take tougher actions to eliminate "all forms of discrimination based on race, color or ethnic origin" (Malcolm, 1965: 92; Goldman, 1979; Perry, 1992). In fact, the resolution that passed simply paraphrased and reaffirmed the old one that was passed at the first OAU summit held in Addis Ababa in 1963, which was devised without Malcolm's lobbying efforts (Goldman, 1979; Perry, 1992). The outcome of the summit was disappointing for Malcolm's end, because he could not secure a tangible backing from the African leaders for his political objectives.

Consequently, Malcolm's diplomatic tour overall resulted in neither failure nor success. He learned to come to terms which political objectives and realities are more rational, reasonable and logical. Yet Malcolm learned an important lesson and experience from the summit in international politics; when he could not attain his desired backings, he began to perceive domestic and international problems not from the perspective of race, but rather from the perspective of international relations and political power structures. Eventually, upon his return to home, Malcolm began talking "in more general terms about internationalizing the struggle and less about the particulars of bringing America formally to book before the UN" (Goldman, 1979: 218).

Although Malcolm never abandoned the OAAU's fundamental views and goals, he gradually put less emphasis and priority on his political program and rhetoric. His political perspectives and organizational objectives had been subjected to a process of rationalization. Nonetheless, the positive outcomes of Malcolm's participation in the OAU conference gave an opportunity, at the organizational level, to revive the lost, interrupted and broken historical, ethnic, cultural and emotional ties between people in Africa and African-Americans in the United States, as well as to open a new chapter in that history. Moreover, as far as Malcolm's political organization, the OAAU, is concerned, those newly established relations led to 'co-operation and coalition' (Zald and Ash, 1966) with Black leaders and organizations in Africa and at home with Civil

Rights leaders (Malcolm X, 1992; Handler, 1965). More interestingly, on his return, Malcolm began to ridicule the political perspectives and objectives of the NOI which were abstentionist, passive, or simply unrealistic. Therefore, his political transformations from Black Nationalism to more mainstream political perspectives and objectives happened through his interaction and relations with like-minded Black leaders and revolutionaries in both Africa, the Muslim World as well as in the US.

Conclusion

Malcolm X's tragic assassination on February 21, 1965, when he was beginning to deliver his speech at the Audubon Ballroom in Harlem, cut his mission short and left it unfinished. His two organizations, the Muslim Mosque Incorporated (MMI) and the Organization of Afro-American Unity (OAAU) did not survive because of his long absences and lack of authority as well as personal conflicts among their members. However, the multifaceted legacy of Malcolm X has been maintained and kept alive by a variety of religious and political groups and organizations. As Adib Rashad has written, "Malcolm means many things to many people" (Rashad, 1991: 118; Dyson, 1996). After his death, Malcolm's comrades and followers in both organizations began quarrelling among themselves. It caused a level of polarization that resulted in two camps; the religiously inclined old Muslims assembled around Benjamin Goodman (renamed as Benjamin Karim) and the more secular members gathered around James 67X (Goldman, 1979).

On the other hand, various aspects of Malcolm's legacy have been claimed by many diverse interest groups. For example, various socialist groups claim that Malcolm made an overture to socialism when he criticized the oppression and evil of capitalism (Breitman, 1967; Barnes & Waters, 2008; Barnes, 2010); many civil rights and Black Nationalist organizations such as the Urban League, the *National Association for the Advancement of Colored People* (NAACP), the *Congress of Racial Equality* (CORE), the *Student Non-violent Coordinating Committee* (SNCC), and others seized upon some of Malcolm's emotional and rational political teachings and objectives, and revolutionary ideas (Van Deburg, 1992; Wainstock, 2008); many immigrant and indigenous Muslim groups, notably the late Imam W.D. Mohammed's community (who inherited the NOI's organization after the death of Elijah Muhammad in 1975) the Muslim American Society and the Mosque Cares, and the Darul Islam Movement, the Islamic Party of North America, the Mosque of Islamic Brotherhood and other smaller mainstream Muslim groups embraced Malcolm X's religious, spiritual and moral legacy and mission and actively promoted his Islamic image (Nyang, 1993; McCloud, 1994a, 1995).

Finally, Spike Lee's internationally acclaimed film *Malcolm X* (1992) revitalized ethnic and racial consciousness and interest in Islam among young African-Americans as well as racial and ethnic issues (Wilkerson, 1992; Crumm, 1993; Clark, 2002). Malcolm X still appeals to young African Americans in order to reinvent their life as he still gives them a sense of pride in their identity and race (Marable, 2011).

Despite the long years that have passed since the *Civil Rights of Act of 1964*, Malcolm X is still one of the most important figures in the history of African-Americans capturing with revelatory clarity a man who constantly strove, in the great American tradition, to remake himself anew (Marable, 2011). However, racial prejudice and discrimination in America have not been changed substantially since then. Recent racially motivated social conflicts that have spread throughout the country upon the killings of civilians and the stop and search by the security forces show that these epidemic social illnesses are still on the agenda of social policies of the US (Anderson, 2013; Smith, 2014). These events and occurrences still invokes the political teachings, programs and formula of Black Nationalists and Civil Rights leaders, who once again call for a struggle against institutionalized racism, just as Dr. Martin Luther King Jr. and Malcolm X had done. These developments caused to mobilize Black masses to stage demonstrations and marches throughout the country. The criminal justice system's unfair and hostile treatments of Black Americans, coupled by the "frustration over blocked opportunities and the denial of equal access to descent jobs, high-quality education, health care and other sources" (Smith, 2014), further legitimize and validate the Civil Rights Movement's and Black Nationalists' cause and agenda. It is impossible to disregard the continuing relevance of Malcolm X's political rhetoric and teachings as they are still valid today. His legacy continues to appeal to African-Americans in their hopes of forming a united stance against any form of racial prejudice, discrimination and oppression. Malcolm X's quest for unity is echoed in their attempts to mobilize and empower Black people to work together for a common cause and interest.

Bibliography

Anderson, Elijah. "Emmett and Trayvon: How racial prejudice in America has changed in the last sixty years." *Washington Monthly*, January/February, 2013.

Barnes, Jack. *Malcolm X, Black Liberation, and the Road to Workers Power*. Atlanta, GA: Pathfinder Press, 2010.

Barnes, Jack and Mary-Alice Waters. *Revolution, Internationalism and Socialism: The Last Year of Malcolm X.* New York, NY: New International, 2008.

Beckford, James A. "Through the looking-glass and out the other side: withdrawal from Reverend Moon's Unification Church." *Archives de Sciences Sociales des Religions* 45, no. 1 (1978): 95–116.

——— *Cult Controversies: The Societal response to the New Religious Movements.* London: Tavistock Publications, 1985.

Berger, Peter and Thomas Luckmann. *The Social Construction of Reality.* New York: Doubleday, 1966.

Booker, James. "Is Mecca trip changing Malcolm?" *New York Amsterdam News*, May 23, 1964, p. 14.

Breitman, George. *The Last Year of Malcolm X.* New York: Pathfinder Press, 1967.

Breitman, George, Herman Porter, and Baxter Smith. *The Assassination of Malcolm X.* New York: Pathfinder Press, 1992.

Bromley, David G., and Anson Shupe. "Affiliation and disaffiliation: a role theory interpretation of joining and leaving new religious movements" *Thought* 61 (1986): 192–211.

Clark, Steve. *Malcolm X Talks to Young People: Speeches in the United States, Britain and Africa.* Atlanta, GA: Pathfinder Press, 2002.

Clarke, John Henrik ed. *Malcolm X: The Man and His Times.* Trenton, New Jersey: Africa World Press Inc, 1991.

Cone, James H. *Martin & Malcolm & America: A Dream or A Nightmare.* Maryknoll, NY: Orbis Books, 1991.

Crumm, D. "Malcolm X interest draws many to Islam, leader says" *Detroit Free Press*, January 21, 1993.

DeCaro, Louis A. Jr. "Malcolm X and the Nation of Islam: two moments in his religious sojourn (Sunni Islam)" Unpublished Ph.D. Dissertation, New York University, 1994.

Dyson, Michael Eric (1996) *Making Malcolm: The Myth and Meaning of Malcolm X.* New York: Oxford University Press, 1996.

Essien-Udom, E.U.. *Black Nationalism: A search for an Identity in America.* Chicago: The University of Chicago Press, 1970.

Essein-Udom, E.U., and M. Ruby. "Malcolm X: an international man" In *Man and His Times*, edited by John Henrik Clarke. Trenton, New Jersey: Africa World Press Inc, 1991.

Evanzz, K. *The Judas Factor: The Plot to Kill Malcolm X.* New York: Thunder's Mouth Press, 1992.

Gamson, William A. *The Strategy of Social Protest.* Homewood, IL: Dorsey Press, 1975.

Gerth, H.H., and C. Wright Mills. eds. *From Max Weber: Essays in Sociology.* London: R.K.P., 1970.

Goldman, Peter. *The Death and Life of Malcolm X.* Chicago: University of Illinois Press, 1979.

Greenslade, Stanely L. *Schism in the Early Church*. New York: Harper and Row Publishers Inc, 1953.

Handler, M.S. "Malcolm X's role dividing Muslims." *New York Times*, February 26, 1964a, p. 39.

——— "Malcolm X splits with Muhammad." *New York Times*, March 9, 1964b.

——— "Malcolm X sees rise in violence." *New York Times*, March 13, 1964c, p. 20

——— "Malcolm X pleased by whites' attitude on trip to Mecca." *New York Times*, May 8, 1964d, p.38.

——— "Malcolm rejects racist doctrine." *New York Times*, October 4, 1964e.

——— "Malcolm X reports he now represents world Muslim unit." *New York Times*, October 11, 1964f.

——— "Malcolm's plans irk Muslims." *New York Times*, November 8, 1964g.

——— "Malcolm X seeks UN Negro debate." *New York Times*, August 13, 1964h.

——— "Malcolm X cites role in UN fight." *New York Times*, January 2, 1965.

Karenga, Maulana. "Malcolm X, Muhammad and the Nation of Islam: political analysis vs. psychological assumptions." *The Western Journal of Black Studies* 6, no. 3 (1982): 193–201.

Karim, Benjamin. ed. *The End of White World Supremacy Four Speeches by Malcolm X*. New York: Seaver Books, Arcade Publishing Inc, 1971.

Lewis, Bernard. ed. *Islam and the Arab World*. New York: A. Knopf, 1976.

Lewis, J.W. "The man 'tamed' Malcolm is hopeful." *Washington Post*, May 18, 1964, p. 3.

Lincoln, C. Eric. *The Black Muslims in America*. Boston: Beacon Press, 1973.

Lofland, J., Skonovd, L.N. "Conversion motifs." *Journal for the Scientific Study of Religion* 20, no. 4 (1981): 373–85.

Lomax, Louis. *When the World is Given*. Cleveland: World Publishing Co, 1963.

——— *To Kill A Black Man*. Los Angeles: Holloway House, 1968.

Malcolm X. "Malcolm says he is backed abroad." *New York Times*, May 22, 1964.

——— "'My next move-' Malcolm X an exclusive interview." *New York Amsterdam News*, May 30, 1964, p. 1, 52.

——— "Speech to African summit conference." In *Malcolm X: The Man and His Times*, edited by John Henrik Clarke Trenton, NJ: Africa World Press, 1964.

——— *Malcolm X Speaks: Selected Speeches and Statements*. Edited by George Breitman. New York: Grove Press, 1965.

——— *The Autobiography of Malcolm X as Told to Alex Haley*. England: Penguin Books, 1968.

——— *By Any Means Necessary*. Atlanta, GA: Pathfinder Press, 1992.

——— *February 1965: The Final Speeches*. Edited by Steve Clark. New York: Pathfinder Press, 1992.

Marable, Manning. *Malcolm X: A Life of Reinvention*. New York: Viking, 2011.

Marsh, Clifton E. *From Black Muslims to Muslims: The Transition from Separatism to Islam, 1930–1980*. Lanham, MD: Scarecrow Press, 1984.

McCloud, Aminah. "Epilogue." In *The Black Muslims in America*, by C. Eric Lincoln Grand Rapids, MI: William B Eerdmans Publishing Company, 1994a.

——— "Racism in the Ummah." In *Islam: A contemporary Perspectives*, edited by A.M. Siddiqi, 73–80. Chicago: NAAMPS, 1994b.

——— *African-American Islam*. New York: Routledge, 1995.

Michels, Robert. *Political Parties*. Glencoe: Free Press, 1958.

Muhammad, Jabril. *A Special Spokesman*. Phoenix: Arizona Truth Publication, 1984.

Muhammad, A. "Malcolm X." In *Oxford Encyclopedia of the Modern Islamic World*, edited by John Esposito. New York: Oxford University Press, 1995a.

Muhammad, Elijah. *The Supreme Wisdom: Solution to the So-called Negroes' Problem*. Chicago: The National Newport News and Commentator (vol. I), 1957.

——— *Message to the Blackman in America*. Virginia: United Brothers Communications Systems, 1965.

Muhammad, Imam Warith Deen, personal interviews with author. July 5, 1995a; December 25, 1995b.

Munir, Fareed. "Islam in America: an African-American pilgrimage toward coherence" Unpublished Ph.D. Dissertation, Temple University, 1994.

Nyang, Sulayman S. "Islam and the Black experience in the USA." In *Islam in Africa*, edited by N. Alkali and *et al*. Lagos: Spectrum Books Ltd, 1993.

Parenti, Michael. "The black Muslims: from revolution to institution" *Social Research* 31 (1964): 175–194.

Parks, G. "Violent end of a man called Malcolm X." *Life*, March 5, 1965.

Perry, Bruce. ed. *Malcolm X: The Last Speeches*. New York: Pathfinder Press, 1989.

——— *Malcolm: The Life of a Man Who Changed Black America*. New York: Station Hill, 1992.

Rashad, A. *History of Islam and Black Nationalism in America*. Beltsville, MD: Writer's Inc, 1991.

Rochford, E.B. "Factionalism, group defection, and schism in the Hare Krishna movement." *Journal for the Scientific Study of Religion* 28, no. 2(1989): 162–79.

Ruby, M. and E.U. Essein-Udom, "Malcolm X: an international man." In *Malcolm X: The Man and His Times*, edited by John Henrik Clarke Trenton, NJ: Africa World Press Inc., 1991.

Sales, William. W. *From Civil Rights to Black Liberation: Malcom X and the Organization of Afro-America Unity*. New York: South End Press, 1999.

Samuels, G. "Two ways: black Muslims and NAACP." *New York Times Magazine*, May 12, 1963.

——— "Freud within the Black Muslims." *New York Times Magazine*, March 22, 1964, p. 17, 104–107.

Smith, Darron T. "The Historical Context of the Ferguson Riots." *The Huffington Post*, December 3, 2014.

Smith, H. "Elijah's son quits as Black Muslim." *New York Times*, January 15, 1965.

Snow, David. A. and Cynthia L. Phillips. "The Lofland-Stark conversion model: a critical reassessment" *Social Problems* 27, no. 4 (1980): 430–47.

Spellman, A.B. "Interview with Malcolm X." *Monthly Review*, May, 1964.

Tinaz, Nuri. "The Black Muslims and Their Relations with the Orthodox Muslims and Muslim World in Political, Economic and Religious Perspectives." Eurames Annual Conference, University of Warwick: Coventry, UK, 1993.

—— *Conversion of African-Americans to Islam: A Sociological Analysis of the Nation of Islam Associated Groups.* Unpublished Ph.D. Dissertation, University of Warwick, 2001.

—— From the Periphery to the Centre: A Sociological Analysis of the Transformation of African-American Muslims with Specific Reference to the Imam W.D. Mohammed and Minister Louis Farrakhan Communities. *İslam Araştırmaları Dergisi (Turkish Journal of Islamic Studies)* 14, (2005): 57–86.

—— The Transition from the Particularistic Black Nationalist Stance to a Universalistic Mainstream Religion: The Role of Relations and Interactions between the Nation of Islam, Muslim Organizations in the USA and Muslim Countries (1950–1990). *İslam Araştırmaları Dergisi (Turkish Journal of Islamic Studies)* 21, (2009): 89–112.

Travisano, R.V. "Alternation and conversion as qualitatively different transformations" In *Social Psychology Through Symbolic Interaction*, edited by G.P. Stone and H.A. Faberman Toronto: Xerog College Publication, 1970.

Van Deburg, William L. *New Day in Babylon.* Chicago: The University of Chicago Press, 1992.

Wallis, Roy. *Salvation and Protest.* London: Frances Pinter Ltd, 1979.

Wallis, Roy and S Bruce. *Sociological Theory, Religion and Collective Action.* Belfast: The Queen's University, 1986.

Wainstock, Dennis. D. *Malcolm X: African American Revolutionary.* Jefferson, NC: McFarland, 2008.

Weber, Max. *Economy and Society.* Edited by G. Roth and C Wittich. Berkeley: University of California Press, 1978.

Wilkerson, I. "Young believe Malcolm X is still speaking to them." *New York Times*, November 18, 1992.

Wilson, Bryan R. *Sects and Society.* Kingswood, Surrey: The Windmill Press Ltd, 1961.

—— *Religious Sects.* New York: McGraw-Hill, 1970.

Wilson, J. "The sociology of schism." In *A Sociological Yearbook of Religion in Britain*, edited by M. Hill. London: SCM Press Ltd, 1971.

Wright, Stuart A. *Leaving Cults: The Dynamics of Defection.* Washington D.C.: Society for Scientific Study of religion, 1987.

Zald, M. and R. Ash. "Social movement organizations: growth, decay, and change" *Social Forces* 44 (1966): 327–41.

Index

Abd-Allah, Umar Faruq 298
Abdal-Rashid, Talib 297–298
Abdulrashid, Nabil 290–291, 307–309
Abdusalaam, Yaqub (Spitz) 294, 305
Adorno, Theodor W. 92, 144, 165, 170, 173
Afghani, Seyyed Jamaluddin 203
African Communities Legue (ACL) 252
Akhtar, Waleed 311
Algeria 108, 222, 277, 327(n6)
Ahmad, Jalal Ale 136
Ahmadiyya 14, 252–255, 269, 342(n14)
Alhassan, May 303
Al-Muslimoon 18
Alatas, Syed Hussein 132, 195(n1)–196, 199–205, 208
Ali, Muhammad 260
Ali, Mohammed Aerosol Arabic 307
Ali, Noble Drew 13–14, 30–31(n)
Ali, Sayyidina 204
Ali, Wajahat 274
Amini, Hussein (Grand Mufti of Jerusalem) 171, 349(n22)
Amir, Tyson 286–287, 297
Anti-Capitalism (see Capitalism)
Anti-Imperialism (see Imperialism)
Árbenz, Jacobo 108
'Asabiyya 119–121(n16)
Asadabadi, Seyyed Jamal al-Deen 133
Audubon Ballroom 32, 133, 361
Auschwitz 142
Autobiography of Malcolm X 1, 5, 12, 12, 15, 20, 22, 24–25, 31, 59–60, 93, 95(n), 109(n), 111, 119, 159, 168, 182, 185–188, 190, 208, 239, 273, 303, 344, 349(n)
Azhar (al-) 109, 279, 337, 352, 355
Azzam, Abd al-Rahman 349
Azzam, Omar 349

Babu, Abdul Rahman Muhammad 84
The Ballot or the Bullet 38, 76, 78, 101(n10)
Babikir, Babikir Ahmed 298
Barnett, Ross 47
Beale, Mutah Wassin Shabazz (Mutah Napoleon Beale) 282(n17), 295, 304–305

Ben Bella, Ahmed 108–110, 358
Benjamin, Walter 92, 172, 146
Berrigan Brothers 145
Berton, Pierre 221
Bible 27, 125(n21), 161
Black, Aja 294
Black Arts Movement 274, 276, 203, 307–308, 312
Black Aesthetics Movement 274
Black Bourgeoisie 57, 158
Black Imperialism 29
Black Liberation 50, 62, 72, 81, 181, 183–184, 188, 221, 242
Black Messiah 28
Black Power 159, 244, 260, 274, 276, 279, 281, 308
Bloch, Ernst 146
Bolsheviks 114
Bourdieu, Pierre 168, 263, 278, 297
Breitman, George 56, 80(n68), 83, 180, 183, 326, 328
Brothers Cardinal 145
Brown, John 179–193, 219
Breton, Pierre 17
Brookins, Dasham (Brother Dash) 300
Brown, H. Rap 173
Brown, Michael 153, 270
Burkett, Randall 27–30

Canon, Anas 292, 296, 302
Capitalism 107
Carter, Shawn 'Jay-Z' 40
Castro, Fidel 81–82, 161, 196
Catholicism (Roman Catholics) 28
Chande, Abdin 229
Chenault, Kenneth I. 40
Cherry, F.S. 30
Chevannes, Barry 26
Chicago Eight 173
Chicken Wing, Right Reverend Bishop T. 22
Chin, Ashley (Muslim Belal) 295
Christianity 2, 7–10, 20–22, 33, 62, 66, 91–129
Civil Rights Act of 1964 360
Civil Rights Act of 1968 172–173

INDEX

Civil Rights Movement   151–152, 179, 181, 187, 192, 227, 256, 270, 179, 298, 321, 329
Clegg, Claude   30(n12), 75, 94
Colonialism   77, 79, 83, 109, 174, 201, 204, 232, 312, 360
Communism (see Marxism)   57, 81–82, 107, 110, 168
Congress on Racial Equality (CORE)   328
Constantine (Emperor)   100
Critical Theory   92, 96, 195–196, 205, 236
Crummell, Alexander   75, 77
Curtis, Edward   19, 21, 243

Davis, Angela   170
Davis, Ossie   2, 128
Dawkins, Richard   163
DeCaro, Louis   229, 340, 344–346
Delany, Martin R.   69–70, 77, 236
Democracy   38, 40, 44–45, 101(n), 110, 118, 137, 158, 164, 203, 207
Detroit Red   25, 225
Dialectical Materialism (see Marxism)
Dollarism (see Capitalism)
Drake, St. Clair   28
DuBois, W. E. B.   19, 187, 189
Durkheim, Emile   163

Egypt   31, 73, 75–76, 84, 96, 109, 214–215, 220, 222, 240, 279, 327, 337, 342, 352
El, John Givens   14
Engels, Friedrich   206
Epton, Bill   48, 82
Erlich, Leonard   191–192
Evanzz, Karl   13, 30(n12), 82
Evers, Medgar   155, 161

Fanon, Franz   4, 131, 137–138, 196
Fard, (Master) Wallace. D.   13–17, 31, 67, 76, 94, 214, 220, 222
Farrakhan, Louis   153, 225, 254, 258, 260, 284, 323(n2)
Feesabillah, Al Asadi (Abu Siddiq)   304
Fetuga, Rakin (Rakin Niass)   291
Feuerbach, Ludwig   65, 102
Fiasco, Lupe   277
Field Negro (slave)   134
Five Percent Nation   275–276
Ford, Rabbi Arnold   30
Francis, Pope (Jorge Bergoglio)   3, 149

Frankfurt School (see Critical Theory)   92, 96, 107, 170, 236
Fromm, Erich   140, 170, 173

Gandhi, Mahatmal   104–105, 143, 145–147, 149–151, 196, 204, 279
Garvey, Marcus   13–14, 26–33, 75, 77, 92–93, 145, 185, 236
Ghana   85, 121(n18), 145, 213, 220, 342, 357
Ghazzali (al-), Muhammad   204
Giddens, Anthony   9–10
Gilbert, Michele   49
Global Policy Solutions   40
Goldman, Peter   183, 188
Gramsci, Antonio   165
Guevara, Ernesto 'Che'   85, 108, 110

Hadith   204, 278, 303
Hadid (al-), Amiri   228
Haley, Alex   9, 21, 23, 25, 159, 187, 215
Hajj   12, 32, 109, 117, 169, 182, 211–212, 215–217, 323, 524, 259, 281, 287, 295, 303, 341, 346–356
Handler, M. S.   182–183, 218, 353
Harding, Vincent   185
Harper's Ferry   179, 181, 184, 187, 198
Harris, Sam   163
Hassoun, Sheik Ahmed   71, 240, 353
Hayden, Tom (see Chicago Eight)
Hedges, Chris   143–144, 156
Hegel, Georg W. F.   99–100, 146–147, 149, 165, 168
Herberg, Will   9
Hijabi Monologues   303
Hijra   133–134
Historical Materialism (see Marxism)
Hitler, Adolf   143, 171–172
Hoekema, Anthony A.   9
Holder, Eric   153
Horkheimer, Max   92, 96, 98, 100–101, 112–114, 118–119, 127, 165, 170
House Negro (slave)   24, 43, 57, 105, 134, 200–201
Howse, Stanley Vernell   289
Hurricane Katrina   42, 65(n43–44)

Imitatio Christi (see Jesus of Nazareth)   122
Imperialism   55, 58, 72–75, 80–84, 92, 107–108, 110, 115, 128, 201

INDEX

Inner-City Muslim Action Network (IMAN) 310
Invandrare (immigrants) 230, 233–234, 245
Iqbal, Muhammad 133, 204
Iraq 2, 85, 144, 146, 152–153, 220
Islam
    Sunni 5, 9, 12, 14, 17–18, 20–24, 32–34, 70–72, 91, 109, 197, 211, 220, 224, 227–228, 236–243, 255–256, 265–266, 269, 273, 276–277, 280–281, 290, 297, 299, 305, 348
    Shi'a (Shi'ite) 11, 255
Islamic Internationalism 131–133
Islamophobia 3, 242, 301
ISIS (Islamic State in Iraq and Syria) 144, 146

Jackson, Sherman (Abdul-Hakim) 299–300
Jahaliyyah 96, 122
Jarvis, Malcolm "Shorty" 213, 214
Jaures, Jean 143
Jesus of Nazareth
    Sermon on the Mount 147
Jihad 121, 124, 246, 277, 281
Jim Crow 29, 31, 99, 106, 113, 128, 246, 254, 262, 268
Johann Wolfgang Goethe Universität 170
Johnson, Lyndon B. 44, 47, 256
Jones, LeRoi (Amiri Baraka) 274–275
Jones, Mack H. 46
Jones, William R. 64–65
Judaism 21, 30, 98, 128, 147, 163, 171–172
Jus Talionis (see Lex Talionis)

Kaid, Taher 220, 357
Kane, Gregory P. 44–45
Karim, Benjamin 61, 343, 361
Kaunda, Kenneth 81
Keil, Charles 191
Kemble, Frances "Fanny" 186
Kennedy, John F. 142–443, 157, 154–155, 158–161
Kennedy, Robert 47, 142, 149, 152, 154, 159, 173
Kenyatta, Charles Morris 357
Khaldun, Ibn 204
Khrushchev, Nikita 82
King, Lori Zakariyya (Zkthepoet) 285–286
King Jr., Martin Luther 2, 95, 110, 150–152, 160, 174–175, 181, 188, 196, 200, 208, 260–261, 267, 283, 285–286, 362

Kristall Nacht 169
Ku Klux Klan 61, 133, 279
Kweli, Talib 277

Lansing, Michigan 31, 122, 141, 174, 208
Last Poets (The) 273, 275–276, 285
Lee, Spike 267, 288
Lenin, Vladimir 97, 165
Lex Talionis 103, 125, 145, 147, 171
Liberation Theology 244
Liebknecht, Karl 143
Lincoln, C. Eric 32, 323, 336
Little, Earl 7, 103, 122, 145
Little, Louise 31, 122
Little (X), Philbert (Abdul Aziz Omar) 5, 60–61, 82, 196, 349 (n22)
Little (X), Reginald 16, 196
Little (X), Wilfred 7–8, 196
Little-Collins, Ella 169, 347
Lomax, Louis 14, 109, 116, 322, 328, 333–336, 343
Louis, John 155
L'Ouverture, Toussaint 115, 181
Lumumba, Patrice 81, 108, 161
Luxemburg, Rosa 143

Mahdi 14, 99, 127
Majied, Eugene 190
Malik, Abdul-Rehman 309, 311
Marable, Manning 25, 31, 50(n15), 188, 308, 313
Marcuse, Herbert 107, 170, 173
Marsh, Charles 13
Marx, Karl 102–103, 113–114, 125, 136, 149, 165, 168, 207
Marxism 22, 203–205
Masjid Marauders 300
Mau Mau 81, 181
Mauritania 82, 220
Maznavi, M. Hasna 308–311
McGovern, George 142
Mecca 13, 29, 31, 67, 71–72, 80(n68)–82, 93, 95, 110, 114, 117, 121, 123, 134–139, 147, 150, 168–170, 182, 187–188, 211–225, 242, 259, 281, 287–288, 294, 346–349(n22), 325–353, 388
Meccan Epistle 133, 135–136, 139
Mercieca, Charles 143–144
Meredith, James 47

Message to the Black Man 56, 63
Message to the Grass Roots 97
Messiah 13, 98–99, 101, 114, 128, 175–176, 286–287
Messianic Judaism (see Messiah)
Michigan State University 105
Miller, James 150
Mimesis 128
Mississippi 41, 47–48, 155, 160, 198, 231, 245
Mohammed, Warith Deen 237–242
Moorish Science Temple of America (MSTA) 13–14, 30–31, 254–255, 269
Morocco 85, 220, 277
Moses 96, 162, 192
Moses, Wilson Jeremiah 26, 29–30, 77
Muhammad (Prophet) 3, 119, 122, 124, 127, 133, 149, 204, 215, 222, 237, 278, 285, 300(n67), 346, 351
    Final Sermon 215
Muhammad, Akbar 337, 354–355
Muhammad, Wali Farad 239
Müntzer, Thomas 102, 145
Muslim Alliance of North America (MANA) 269
Muslim Mosque Incorporated (MMI) 55, 71, 123, 167, 240–241, 252, 307, 337–339, 347, 358, 361
Muslim Student Association 257, 291

Narayan, Jayaprakash 204
Nasser, Gamal 81, 109–110, 342
National Urban League 39, 41
Necrophilia 122, 152, 158
Nelson, Truman 191
New Black Panther Party 153
New York Amsterdam News 191, 323(n1), 335, 342, 348(n19), 358
Nietzsche, Friedrich 27, 100, 119
Nixon, Jay 80, 153, 173
Nkrumah, Kwame 74–75, 81, 357(n27)–358
Noah 70
Non-Violence 95–96, 103–104, 125(n21)–126, 150, 152, 174, 254
Noor, Sukina Abdul 297, 300
Nyerere, Julius 84, 357

Obama, Barack 1–2, 40, 44(n5), 48, 153, 166, 230, 262, 267
Olmstead, Frederick law 186

Organization of African Unity (OAU) 358
Organization of Afro-American Unity (OAAU) 17, 32, 55, 84, 180, 307, 358, 361
Orientalism 131
Original Man 16, 31, 69–70, 196, 327
Osman, Ahmed 344
Oxfam 39
Oxford Union 221, 223, 226

Pan-Africanism 31, 56, 72, 207, 357
Parenti, Michael 331–332, 336–337
Parkhurst, Lewis 186–187
Parks, Gordon 20, 223
Parousia Delay 101, 227
Paul (Apostle) 17
Pentecostalism 7, 20–21, 34
Philips, Bilal 289, 294, 297
Pilate, Pontius 14
Plimpton, George 182
Post-Islamism 277, 288, 313
Public Enemy 273, 276–277

Qaradawi (al-), Yusuf 279, 305
Quadragesimo Anno 143
Quarles, Benjamin 179, 184
Quietism (political) 59–60, 62
Qur'an (Koran) 18, 24, 91, 103, 119–124, 133, 204, 215–216, 222, 263, 265, 303, 305, 308, 346, 351
Qureshi, Haq Nawaz (Aki Nawaz) 283

Rabaka, Reiland 195
Ramadan, Said 19
Randolph, A. Philipp 158
Rashid, Nabil Abdul 290–291, 307, 309
Rashida, Muneera 297, 300
Rastafarianism 26
Rathenau, Walther 143
Redpath, James 187
Reed, Ishmael Scott 274
Religion
    Positive 91, 96, 115
    Negative 96, 102
Ricoeur, Paul 17
Riefenstahl, Leni 171
Robinson, Dean E. 54
Roosevelt, Franklin D. 143, 164–165
Rowan, Carl T. 224
Rumi, Jalal al-din 279–280

Sackey, Alex Quaison 81
Said, Edward 196, 199
Sanchez, Sonia 274, 308
Sankofa 17
Satan 21, 225
Segregation 44, 47, 65, 116, 151, 208, 219, 222–223, 230, 263, 303, 324–325, 327
Seventh day Adventism 6–7, 9, 20
Shabazz, Betty 135, 225
Shabazz, Ilyasah 1, 267
Sanborn, Franklin B. 187
Shariati, Ali 4, 131, 133–134, 196
Shawarbi, Mahmoud Youssef 169, 342(n14), 348–149
Sheldon, Charles 192
Simba Movement 108
Skinner, B. F. 150
Smalls, James 184–185
Smith, Will 44
Socialism 57, 80(n68), 83, 107, 168, 203–207, 361
Soviet Union 82, 109, 133
Spellman, A. B. 17
Stevenson, Adlai 155
Stokes, Ronald 160–161
Stowe, Harriet Beecher 186
Student Non-Violent Coordinating Committee (SNCC) 155, 361
Sulaiman, Amir 284, 287–288, 290–292, 296
Sunnah 119, 122, 246
Sweden 136, 229–230, 233–235, 237, 244, 245
The Supreme Wisdom 63, 67

Tawhid 119, 170
Tibawi, L. 196
Tillich, Paul 27, 151
Tjokroaminoto, Haji Omar Said 203
Tolstoy, Leo 204

Totally Other 96, 99, 128
Touré, Sékou 81, 357
Treblinka 142
Tricknology 16, 94
Turner, Henry McNeal 75
Turner, Nat 105, 115, 181, 186–187
Tutu, Desmond 196

Ummah 119–120, 211, 350
Uncle Tom 22, 24, 97, 103, 156, 186, 200
Universal Negro Improvement Association (UNIA) 7, 28, 31, 185, 252

Vesey, Denmark 181
Vietnam War 110, 141, 149–150, 152, 173–174, 256, 258

Wagner, Richard 171
Wahhaj, Imam Siraj 239
Walker, Alice 279
Washington, Booker T. 78, 187
Washington, Denzel 133, 288
Weber, Max 136, 288–289, 301, 330–333
West, Cornel 156, 300
Western Michigan University 142, 150–152
White Devil 16, 27, 188, 343, 346
White Supremacy 3, 12, 19, 22, 25, 29, 94–96, 103–106, 110, 112, 115, 125(n21)–126, 182, 184, 192, 205, 267
Wilson, Darren 153–154
Wilson, Jamie J. 12
Wright, Richard 22–23

Yacub/Yakub (Dr.) 16, 66, 94–95, 98, 242
Yahya, Mohammed 300
Yasin, Shaykh Khalid 254

Zionism 29–30
Žižek, Slavoj 2

CPSIA information can be obtained
at www.ICGtesting.com
Printed in the USA
LVOW10s0727170118
562930LV00007B/13/P